The Making of the
Second Reform Bill

The Making of the
Second Reform Bill

F. B. SMITH

Lecturer in History
University of Melbourne

CAMBRIDGE
AT THE UNIVERSITY PRESS
1966

PUBLISHED BY
THE SYNDICS OF THE CAMBRIDGE UNIVERSITY PRESS
Bentley House, 200 Euston Road, London, N.W.1
American Branch: 32 East 57th Street, New York, N.Y. 10022

Published in Australia and New Zealand by
MELBOURNE UNIVERSITY PRESS

Dewey Decimal Classification Number 942.081
Library of Congress Catalogue Card Number 66-16531

Printed in Australia at The Griffin Press, Adelaide, S.A.

ACKNOWLEDGMENTS

I am grateful to many people for their help. At Cambridge and later, during his visit to Melbourne, Dr G. S. R. Kitson Clark gave me great encouragement and wise advice: I owe an immense debt to him. Professor H. J. Hanham saved me from a number of serious errors, and Dr Geoffrey Best made many enlightening suggestions and cheered me with his enthusiasm. Mr J. M. Main, Professor J. A. La Nauze, Dr A. M. McBriar and Dr Allan Martin, all read parts of the book and improved it by their criticisms. For many kindnesses and help in preparing my manuscript I thank Mrs G. E. Moore and Mrs Barbara Bell of Cambridge, and Mrs M. Beever and Miss Gwenyth Williams of Melbourne. I am deeply grateful to my wife, who cheerfully endured the Second Reform Bill and put aside her own interests to help me complete the book.

For access to private collections of manuscripts and permission to publish extracts from them, I thank: the Marquess of Salisbury; Viscount Hampden; Commander the Lord Hampton; and the directors of the National Trust. Dr J. F. A. Mason gave generously of his time in helping me find my way through the Salisbury Papers. Unpublished Crown-copyright material in the Public Record Office has been reproduced by permission of the Controller of H. M. Stationery Office.

This work was begun with the aid of a British Council Scholarship and its completion was aided by the Research Fund of the University of Melbourne. I am beholden to them both.

F. B. SMITH

CONTENTS

INTRODUCTION

The Second Reform Act is the 'Serbonian Bog' of British constitutional history in the nineteenth century. It has never received the minute and lucid investigation that has been devoted to its predecessor of 1832 and it lacks the elegant conclusiveness which is attributed to the Act of 1884. Instead, it lies sprawling between them, avoided, or hastily reconnoitred by the armies of historians who have traversed the region. Only two full-scale studies of the Second Reform Act have been published: the acute and detailed political narrative of Homersham Cox[1] in 1868 and Dr J. H. Park's dissertation[2] of 1920 on the philosophical background to the Act. I have endeavoured to reinterpret the background and the politics of 1866-7 upon the basis of material which has become available since 1920 or which has not hitherto been closely studied.

The Reform Bills of the sixties were founded upon a morass of rating, tenancy and franchise law and a profusion of doubtful statistics. It is treacherous ground which aptly deserves Disraeli's use of the Miltonic metaphor,[3] and the great bill-makers, Russell, Bright, Gladstone, Derby and Disraeli, all occasionally found themselves lost in it. The Reform struggles also exhibit a tangle of tricky manoeuvres, of apparently senseless wrangles and misdirected votes, of discrepancies between declared intention and action. It is only by tracing the pressures behind the scenes, as reflected in such private papers of the protagonists as are available, that the historian can begin to explain what happened. The leading participants were frequently unaware of their actions, and their ignorance of their material led them to rely—more than in most political battles—upon hopeful assertions, stubborn denials and intricate deceits. After the Bill was passed they made their self-justifications in the same spirit and succeeded in making confusion worse confounded.

1

Restrictive, incomplete and fumbling as the Second Reform Act was, it increased the electorate of the United Kingdom from 1,430,000 to 2,470,000, or almost half the adult male occupiers of the nation. And most of the new electors belonged to the urban lower orders. This large scale enfranchisement of workingmen made the Act the decisive moment in the transformation of the electorate from the exclusive, propertied constituency of 1850 to the unselective, inclusive, mass constituency of 1900.

This enfranchisement of the workingmen overturned the principle, embodied in the First Reform Act, that property was the sole indicator of fitness to vote, and that the demonstrable fitness of the chosen voters sufficiently compensated for the loss of variety and popular enthusiasm in the constitution. The rule of the educated élite, which Lowe, Bagehot and Earl Grey so much approved in the mid-sixties, was believed to be sustained by these chosen voters. Furthermore, the élite was able to rule efficiently, its defenders argued, precisely because it was insulated from popular enthusiasms and the pressures of the masses. It might be too closely allied with the stupid landed interest, but to place the élite at the mercy of the populace or the provincial 'commercial men' whom they would reinforce, would be to destroy it. But, against this view, Russell, Gladstone, and the contributors to *Essays on Reform*[4] asserted that good government was no longer dependent upon the insulation of the élite, but rather that the élite needed the backing, and perhaps even the pressure, of a wider section of the country if it was to legislate for greater self-government among the people and economy in national finance. The promotion of self-discipline by ennabling legislation was essentially a moral enterprise and it would be best furthered by the participation of representatives of the class which was most affected. Moreover, the recent conduct of the workingmen, their reverence for a hierarchical social order, their recognition of the inviolability of private property and the benefits of the free market, guaranteed that if they shared in elections they would increase the amount of righteousness and altruism in public affairs. Ultimately, Gladstone and the Reformers believed, there was a wisdom in the 'right feelings' of a harmonious nation which was superior to the calculations of an isolated élite, however well-disposed. The inclusion of respectable individuals from the working class would also widen the range of classes represented in the constituency and so refine that balance of classes which it was the purpose of government to maintain. Thus, Gladstone hoped, the enfranchisement of the artisans would reduce the coercive role of government and promote that growth of sympathy between classes which reconciled the progress of the nation with the stability of its institutions.

This optimistic view clashed with Lowe's and Cranborne's conviction of the depravity of the masses and the need to preserve the strength of the executive in order to protect property, public order and 'the polity of discussion'. By contrast with Gladstone and Bright, Lowe and his supporters were certain that the dominance of the workingmen in the constituency would lead government to interfere in private economic and social contracts, to the injury of property and personal liberty. In Lowe's case there is probably an element of intellectual gamesmanship, but the Reform debates and the passing of the Bill of 1867 do mark a division of the ways. Lowe, Bagehot, Stubbs, J. F. Stephen and Sir Henry Maine were to begin a desperate search for precedents for coercive authority, while Gladstone and the younger Reformers were gradually to acknowledge the claims of democracy.

In this context the Second Reform Act is the culminating move in that sequence of measures after 1820 which levelled the religious and political barriers inherited from the later seventeenth century, and which incorporated minorities and new classes into the political nation. But while earlier Acts had freed Roman Catholics of disabilities, permitted trades unions to operate or opened the way for working-class people to invest in government annuities, the Second Reform Act was a piece of incorporation which directly affected the distribution of power in the State: it is the crucial Act in that process by which Britain, alone among large European nations, peacefully adjusted her institutions to meet the emergence of a powerful working class.

The Liberal leaders' eloquent reiteration of the incorporation theme finally bore fruit in 1867 when Derby and Disraeli and the country gentlemen of both sides had recourse to it to justify their support of such a sweeping extension of the franchise. The members' subscription to this faith enabled them to evade the democratic implications of the Bill. They abjured any theory of rights when supporting it, but the measure they passed created a situation in which claims for universal suffrage based on assertion of rights could become irresistible. The Bill made virtually nominal the tests for 'independence' in the potential borough voter, while its unselective enfranchisement of the occupiers fatally weakened the concept of the vote as a 'trust'. Though the country gentlemen abhorred the idea, they had opened the way to the enfranchisement of their labourers in the counties. The gross extension of the franchise made the disparities among the sizes of borough electorates more blatant than ever and thereby strengthened the demand that votes should have equal value, irrespective of the voter's interest, locality or standing as a citizen.

Indeed, considering the aims of the men who introduced the Bill and the social and political assumptions of those who accepted it, the Second Reform Act was a paradoxical measure. Ultimately it was shaped by chance. Like its predecessors, the Bill was first drafted to perpetuate the control of the propertied classes and rule by the educated. Derby and Disraeli set out to enfranchise a small number of workingmen, sufficient to recognize their improvement and to quiet agitation, and to render their votes nugatory. But partly by Gladstone's intransigence, partly by Disraeli's devious stratagems to keep the Bill and the minority Ministry afloat, and partly because of the intractability of the occupancy and rating law involved in the Bill, the Conservatives lost control of the franchise clauses and were forced to accept Hodgkinson's amendment with its threat of 'borough democracy'. This amendment, which quadrupled the Ministry's intended enfranchisement, passed into law after virtually no debate and without a division, although it was agreed that its implications were almost unknown. The resignation with which members accepted a measure which promised only to raise electoral costs and add to the difficulties of borough management showed their fear of popular unrest and their bewilderment at the network of laws which entangled the franchise. As one Liberal member confessed: 'Events had been too strong for men.'[5]

1866-7 also saw the first great combat between those heroes of the Victorian parliamentary arena, Gladstone and Disraeli. Their brilliance and their contrasting attitudes in the House directly influenced the fate of the Reform legislation. Gladstone's role is simple enough to understand. He had clear principles, he sought to implement them, and in so doing he acted too inflexibly to hold his supporters. His apparently naïve faith in the artisans, coupled with his overbearing attitude, lost him votes in 1866, while his intemperate onslaughts on the Conservatives' Bill only made Disraeli's task easier in 1867. Disraeli, too, had his principles. Throughout the Second Reform period he fought to preserve the landed interest, the interest which gave stability and independence to British government and thereby under-pinned British liberty. But he was quite indifferent to the other element in the Reform puzzle, the enfranchisement of the artisans. He was prepared to denounce their enfranchisement so long as the Tories were prejudiced against it, but after his party had carried the Bill, he admitted to as much faith in the deference of the artisan voters as Gladstone himself. His defence of the landed interest secured him support from country gentlemen on both sides of the House, while his pliancy on the borough franchise won him the esteem of men who wanted a settlement. His success enabled him to consolidate his place at the head of the Tory party.

The parliamentary struggle and the great speeches of 1866 and 1867 typify the glories and defects of the exclusive parliamentary system. The oratory of Bright, Lowe, Gladstone, Disraeli and Cranborne and the contributions from Mill, Fawcett, Hughes, Laing, Cairns and Beresford Hope gave the debates an eloquence and intellectual force which is unrivalled in the history of the House of Commons. However, the speeches which thrilled contemporaries and now delight and instruct the historian were sadly ineffectual in the final shaping of the Bill. Lowe's magnificent onslaught in 1866 played a leading part in destroying Russell's Bill, but when Derby resolved to carry a Bill in 1867 Lowe found himself unable to influence its form. Parliamentary eloquence in this age of champions served to exacerbate the want of discipline in the parties, and helped delude members that they knew more about the potential electorate than they actually did. Both the elaborate speech-making and the independence of members required an exclusive electorate, but at the moment of trial these virtues stultified attempts to preserve the character of that electorate. Nevertheless, Gladstone's and Bright's great performances did teach the Parliament and the country that there had been a major social change in the kingdom and that workingmen could no longer be excluded from the political nation.

The effects of the Act were diverse and far-reaching. The mass entry of the workingmen quickly realized the members' fears about electoral costs and constituency management. Many found themselves having to cope with huge numbers of possible voters whose political allegiance was probably non-existent and was certainly not explicit. Most members were compelled to give extra support to local agents and registration bodies, who now had the task of enrolling a poor and often apathetic multitude and then mobilizing them to vote correctly at the hustings. The new electorate widened the scope for sectional groups like the Liberation Society and the National Education League to arrange registrations and bring pressure to bear on candidates. It enhanced the role of central party organization, which grew to assist candidates in priming their constituencies and paying for their contests, and thereby increased the members' subjection to the Whips and a uniform party line.

The Act also hastened the development of the boroughs into preserves of the commercial interest and tipped the balance of representation in the Commons to the towns. In this way the Act broke the age-old rural bias of Parliament and brought the representative system into conformity with the realities of the nineteenth century. The elections of 1868, 1874 and 1880 all added to the number of ambitious 'commercial men' in the House, at the expense of the country gentlemen. Thus the fears of the more prescient members of the Lords that the Act would smash the congruity of interest between the Houses were soon fulfilled. The Lords' acquiescence in Reform, in the clear knowledge that it would isolate them as defenders of the landed interest and the Church, was the last positive act of co-operation between representatives of that interest in both Houses.

That the 'commercial men' should profit by the enfranchisement of the lower orders is again something of a paradox. Bright and his fellow Reformers had prophesied that the workingmen would reinforce their campaign for economy, humanitarian reforms and the abolition of religious disabilities, and so it proved. The spokesmen for the workingmen accepted incorporation on these terms and refused to press for the extension of the reform programme to include their own class interests. Apart from this ideological barrier, there were practical deficiencies in the Act which prevented the workingmen from capitalizing on their votes. The Commons' rejection of the proposal to have electoral costs defrayed from the rates and the opposition to payment of members blocked for a generation attempts by workingmen to enter Parliament on behalf of their own class on a scale proportionate to their share of the constituency. The postponement of this result has obscured the part played by the Second Reform Act in opening the way to modern British politics.

The reader may find the detail in this book as tedious as the members found it in 1866-7; although, unlike them, he may if he wishes skip to the final passing of the Bill. But if the reader wants to see how the morass of occupancy and franchise law defeated the politicians and how it helped to shape the Act he will have to persevere with the main body of the book. Apart from its intrinsic interest as a difficult feat of legislation in a brilliant Parliament, the Second Reform Act's vital consequences make a traverse of the 'Serbonian Bog' worthwhile.

THE EMERGENCE OF THE LABOUR ARISTOCRACY

In 1861 Henry Parkes, a prominent member of the legislature of New South Wales, revisited his homeland for the first time in twenty-two years. He observed many changes, but that which struck him most forcibly was 'the large amount of self-directed effort on the part of the working-classes to improve their own condition . . . in the temperance societies, in free-hold land societies, in penny banks, in co-operative shops, in workmen's libraries'.[1] Though his remarks have a tinge of patronizing exaggeration, Parkes reported what many of his English contemporaries had already noticed, and like them he saw this improvement as the most important social development of the age. The exemplars of the change were the skilled tradesmen, the working-class élite.

Their emergence in the years after 1851 was both encouraging and embarrassing to those concerned with the theory or practice of politics. They were the great hope, the living proof that, while the improvident masses might be irredeemably dangerous and depraved, the artisan class was capable of aspiring to middle-class standards of Christian observance, sobriety, thrift, orderliness and cleanliness. Yet they were unenfranchised. How could the exclusive electorate be widened sufficiently to include them while still preserving the balance of classes and the rule of the educated? The solution to the puzzle was not found until 1867; and then it was arrived at largely by default.

The working-class élite had developed with the tremendous expansion of those basic industries which employed a high proportion of skilled men: iron and steel, engineering, shipbuilding, railways and building. The figures are well known, but some are especially striking. Between 1851 and 1871 the number of 'engine makers' in the census returns more than doubled, the number of 'shipwrights' almost doubled, while the 'puddlers, forgers and moulders' engaged in the iron industries rose from 80,000 to 180,000. The 29,000 'railway servants', exclusive of labourers, became 84,000 in an industry which offered comparatively secure and regular employment. In these years, as E. S. Beesley noticed, the title 'artisan' and 'workingman' took on the specific meaning of 'skilled, respectable workingman' to differentiate its holder from the more casually employed, unskilled 'labourer'. The number of respectable tradesmen was also swelled by the increase in those occupations which ministered to a prosperous consumer society: 'plumbers, painters and glaziers' increased from 62,805 to 103,382, while 'cabinet makers and upholsterers' and 'printers' both nearly doubled.[2]

In 1867, Dudley Baxter, the brilliant political statistician, calculated from the taxation returns that 28s. per week was the wage level which demarcated the tradesmen: shipwrights, engineers, puddlers, forgers and moulders, engine drivers, cabinet makers and upholsterers, painters, carpenters, bricklayers, bakers and butchers, among others, engaged in 'higher skilled labour and manufacture'. He estimated them to be 831,000 out of the 5,300,000 adult males of England and Wales.[3]

The artisan's wage, according to Baxter, was almost twice that of a regularly employed unskilled labourer and this, together with the trade skills and rules he strove to protect, helped to deepen his sense of calling and separateness. His working day remained agonizingly long, his nutrition was poor, his prosperity hazardous, and his expectation of life short, but the artisan and his wife saw their prospects in the age of free trade as more allied to those of his managers and employers than to the lesser hopes of the labourers and the hopelessness of the poor. He lived in a cleaner cottage, in a different street from the labourer; he joined a different Friendly Society and frequented a different public house. He and his wife often joined a chapel, or went to church; they sent their children to school, and many seem to have employed a charwoman. The freehold land societies which they utilized tended to seal them off in their new housing estates. At Sheffield, for example, respectable tradesmen lived at Walkley, 'the Working-man's West End'. They felt no affinity of status with a ragged labourer for, as the 'Journeyman Engineer' explained, 'there [was] a certain understood dignity and exclusiveness of caste pertaining to the artisan class which every individual in it is compelled to respect and support. A mechanic when out of employment can scarcely take work as a labourer, even if it is offered to him'.[4] Nevertheless, the gulf was always open, and one could fall by economic misfortune, illness or drunkenness; the maintenance of respectability required unceasing effort.

The growth of the élite was accompanied by a gradual softening of manners and the spread of primary education and literacy. Ludlow and Jones claimed to have observed a widespread improvement in public decency in the fifties, and street brutality became less common. 'Footings' in factories were said to have largely disappeared and in Barnsley, for example, the men abandoned 'Saint Monday' after 1856 and the local pastime of dog-fighting was being transformed into whippet racing. Contemporaries agreed that the artisans of the sixties were better informed and more intellectually independent than any previous generations of workingmen.[5] They formed the market for the burgeoning penny press, which opened to them a new world of manners, fashions, religious intelligence and political information from their local corporation, London and the world.

> The daily penny press . . . that finds its way into the house of the working man . . . keeps him well-informed without the least disparagement to other classes, upon public affairs . . . making him feel that he has become in a new sense a citizen of his country, that his country owns in a new manner his title to a share in public affairs. He feels it; his bosom enlarges with the sense of it; and in that bosom so enlarged, there spring up a continual growth and increase of love and attachment to the Queen, and to the institutions of the country.[6]

The reality is obscured by the exhortation, but, as far as the future course of politics was concerned, the important thing was that Gladstone and his audience believed it.

The artisans invested part of their income in new savings institutions which had arisen to cater for small-scale depositors. The friendly societies, housing associations and co-operative groups revivified the ideas of self-help and mutual improvement that were part of the old Co-operative-Chartist endeavour, but they left dormant those political claims which tended towards equality: 'The present co-operative movement does not seek to level the social inequalities which exist . . . as regards wealth', the *Co-operator* announced in 1860.[7] If the members of the societies reflected at all upon the long term impact of their activities, they hoped that their efforts might succeed in elevating the status of their own class rather than diminishing the natural distance and distinction between themselves and the poor.

The freehold land and housing associations, like the co-operative and friendly societies, were concentrated where the élite was strongest, in the Northern industrial counties and London: by 1859 there were twenty-eight in Lancashire, twenty-seven in County Durham, twenty in Yorkshire and fourteen in Middlesex, while East Anglia and the West Country, by contrast, had only nineteen between them.[8] Samuel Smiles, the evangelist of self-help and social improvement, believed that the land societies had wrought an immense peaceful advance, for

> the accumulation of property has the effect which it always has upon thrifty men: it makes them steady, sober and diligent. It weans them from revolutionary notions, and makes them conservative. When workmen, by their industry and frugality, have secured their own independence, they will cease to regard the sight of others' well-being as a wrong inflicted on themselves: and it will no longer be possible to make political capital out of their imaginary woes.[9]

The upper classes, for their part, welcomed these developments as proof of the worthy aspirations and new contentment among the working class, while the more high-minded among them worked to foster these developments. Gladstone's Industrial Classes' Annuities Act of 1864 allowed smaller payments at shorter intervals, and the £30 annuities were taken up at the rate of over 13,000 a year, reflecting a working-class trust in government that had barely existed a generation earlier.[10] Immediately before he made his extraordinary 'pale of the constitution' declaration in 1864, Gladstone had welcomed a trade union deputation which sought permission to deposit union funds in the Post Office Savings Banks.

The volunteer movement did most perhaps to spread the ideal of a bond between the classes. It offered a new field for the gentry to exercise leadership and public duty, and gave the working-class members a sense of incorporation and standing in society. The gentry's real concern to extend class harmony is reflected in the numbers of them who were active officers in the Corps: among them, W. E. Forster, Lord Ripon, Sir Henry Edwards, Lord Robert Grosvenor, A. J. Mundella, Thomas Hughes, Lord Elcho, all were prominent politicians in the sixties

and all led working-class companies. The movement was re-
organized in 1859 and made a rapid advance, its membership
rising from 162,681 in 1862 to 199,194 in 1868. The volunteers,
proudly arrayed in their heavily brocaded uniforms, became the
model of class mutuality and co-operation, the symbol of English
freedom and patriotism against the despotism of France. In 1862,
in a new preface to *Alton Locke*, Charles Kingsley described the
movement as:

> one absolute proof of the changed relation between the upper
> and the lower classes. . . . The late twenty years of increasing
> right-mindedness in the gentry, who have now their reward in
> finding that the privates in the great majority of corps prefer
> being officered by men of a rank socially superior to their own.
> And . . . so this volunteer movement, made possible by the
> goodwill between classes will help in its turn to increase that
> goodwill. Already, by the performance of a common duty, and
> the experience of a common Christianity, these Volunteer Corps
> are become centres of cordiality between class and class; and
> gentlemen, tradesmen and workmen, the more they see of
> each other, learn to like, to trust and to befriend each other.[11]

As Tom Hughes recalled before a meeting of his non-elector
supporters at Kennington in 1865:

> Only seventeen years ago, upon the neighbouring common,
> which is now a park, stood a body of men who were deter-
> mined by main force to compel Parliament to pass a measure
> of Reform. The very class of men who then filled the ranks of
> the Chartists were now Volunteers, armed by the Government
> for the defence of the Kingdom. Could there be any better
> proof that there was no reason to fear the people of this
> country.[12]

Hughes' audience broke into cheers.

By comparison with the total number of the lower classes, and
even with the numbers of the unskilled, the élite was small but,
by its influence on its aspirants and the image of the working man
that it projected to the upper classes, it had a social and historical
influence out of all proportion to its size. Its members imbued
themselves with the ideal of respectability almost as an end in
itself, yet by contrast with the crudity of life around them their
aspiration formed a major step in the amelioration of life. Respectability entailed thrift and self-reliance, deference to one's betters,
self-improvement in education and personal propriety. It was the

yeoman ideal transformed: the 'John Bull' figure in the *Punch* cartoons of the sixties was frequently a working man. Edmond Beales, the radical barrister, was repeating a common belief in 1865 when he ascribed to the workingmen a 'shrewd, sound and clear common-sense . . . warmth of heart, a self-reliant, sturdy and incorruptible independence of spirit, a deep sympathy with the wrongs and a sensitive regard for the rights of others, combined with a generous, hearty, self-denying love of freedom and hatred of oppression'.[13] The artisan class had come to enshrine the liberal virtues. They had accepted the belief in social order, the advantages of free trade, the necessity for economy in public business and the keeping down of rates, all of which had proved their utility since 1848. The working-class attack on the new Poor Law had died to a murmur. Only the wages fund theory remained to divide them from their betters, and some of the trade union leaders, by their espousal of arbitration and works co-operation, seem to have accepted even that.

The publicity given to the fine behaviour of the Lancashire mechanics during the cotton famine helped to crown the image of the respectable, altruistic working man. Despite great privation, the operatives held firm for the North. There was very little disorder and only one food riot, that in Stalybridge in 1863. Their quietism made a deep impression on the upper classes and prompted them to considerable generosity to alleviate distress. Lord Derby headed the Relief Association, and the dignity of the operatives greatly affected Gladstone:

> Self-command, self-control, respect for order, patience under suffering, confidence in the law, regard for superiors . . . were all these great qualities exhibited in a manner more signal . . . more illustrious, than under the profound affliction of the winter of 1862?[14]

Yet these deserving persons were commonly believed to possess, as Gladstone put it, only an 'infinitesimal' portion of the constituency. The moral earnestness and self-help attributed to them made them appear sufficiently independent to exercise a 'deliberative' vote, and deferential enough to use that vote to uphold the existing social order. The difficulty was to discover the exact cottage rating level above which the occupant could be assumed to possess these virtues. The corollary was the continued exclusion of 'the residuum' of improvident, uninstructed, brutal and venal labourers and paupers. And even if the rating and residence qualifications could be nicely determined, the sheer numbers of worthy artisans presented a further difficulty—which the advocates of Reform recognized as fully as their opponents among the country gentlemen.

Those artisans who were politically conscious gradually came to regard the bestowal of the franchise as the formal public recognition of their improvement and the proof that they had become politically responsible. They saw the franchise as a passport of approval, rather than as an instrument of political power. The growth of class co-operation seemed to make the granting of the passport an easy process; all that the artisans had to do was to show their worth and the ruling classes would perform their reciprocal duty by bestowing the vote. The artisans remained quiescent about Reform, partly because their conditions were improving without it, and partly because it seemed ultimately inevitable. It was not until their acceptance into the political community was rudely and decisively rejected that they began to exert force to enter the pale. Robert Lowe's vivid attack on their morality and political trustworthiness, their qualifications for the passport, became the fuel for the engine of emotional pressure that the Reform question had hitherto lacked. London, Birmingham, Sheffield, Manchester, Leeds and Glasgow, the cities which nurtured the élite, were to become the centres of the largest and yet most peaceable working-class demonstrations of the century.

2

THE SYSTEM OF REPRESENTATION

The Parliament that governed the British Isles a generation after the Great Reform Act was still predominantly aristocratic. Despite the tremendous social and economic changes in the country and despite, or perhaps more accurately because of the Act itself, the House of Lords remained a citadel of hereditary privilege and membership of the House of Commons was still largely the perquisite of the old ruling caste. In the Commons that assembled after the General Election of 1865 there were 37 peers or elder sons of peers, 64 younger sons and 15 grandsons, making a total of 116 members. There were also 71 baronets, 11 elder sons, 19 younger sons and 8 grandsons, giving the baronetage 109, and the peerage and baronetage together, 225 members. In addition, there were 100 commoners in the House who were connected with the peerage by marriage or descent. Thus the aristocratic element in the Commons amounted to at least 326 members, or half the House. They divided fairly equally between the parties, 175 being Conservatives and 150 Liberals. At least one member had 30 other sitting members related to him by birth or marriage. In the 1859 House, 31 families had supplied 110 members, a representation equal to that of Ireland, double that of Scotland and five times that of London. 'Talk of trade unions!' exclaimed Bernal Osborne, 'why, is not this House a trades union? . . . [for] there are no less than 1,500 members of great families who constitute the whole of the Upper Chamber and one-third of this House'.[1]

The aristocracy's function at Westminster remained substantive as well as decorative. In Palmerston's second Administration, eleven of the fifteen Cabinet posts were held by members of great families, and in Russell's 1865 Cabinet the number was only one less. Derby's 1866 Cabinet, except for Disraeli, Chelmsford and Gathorne-Hardy, was drawn exclusively from the traditional ruling families.

The reasons for the continued supremacy of the gentry were partly social, and partly the result of the fact that the electoral machinery helped to maintain their influence. The distribution of seats, with four exceptions, remained as it had been settled by the Reform Act which had largely conserved the old pattern of electoral power.[2] In the midst of a greatly changing distribution of population and local wealth, the map of representation remained much as it had been in Stuart England. The South and West were grossly over-represented by comparison with the Midlands and the North: England and Wales were over-represented as compared with Scotland and Ireland. And the disparity was growing worse: Wiltshire, Radnor, Montgomery, Norfolk, Suffolk and Cambridgeshire all showed an absolute decline in population between 1841 and 1861, yet they continued to send, together with the rest of rural England and Wales, many more representatives in proportion to population and rateable value than did London, Birmingham, Swansea and other expanding cities.

The population decrease in the West Country and East Anglia was reflected in the decrease in numbers in the eleven smaller boroughs. Wells, Totnes, Thetford, Dartmouth, Northallerton, Marlborough, Ashburton, Lyme Regis, Evesham, Honiton and Arundel had a combined population in 1864 of only 44,000, with 3,247 electors among them, yet they returned 17 members. The 9 largest boroughs, from Tower Hamlets with 647,845 people, Liverpool with 443,934 and Marylebone, Finsbury, Manchester, Birmingham, Lambeth, Westminster and Leeds, each over 200,000, contained a total population of 3.3 millions and had but 18 members to represent them. This kind of inequality pervaded the system: there were 67 boroughs under 10,000 in population, with 106 members; 145 boroughs between 10,000 and 20,000, with 215; while 26 boroughs between 50,000 and 200,000 returned 52. In 1866, 250,291 electors in the small boroughs of England and Wales, one-fifth of the electorate, were able to return 328 members, or half the House of Commons. A slightly greater number in the fifteen largest boroughs could return only 32, or one-twentieth of the House.[3]

This distribution formed the basis of the power of the old governing classes. The nobility were still firmly established in their traditional localities. They were drawing high profits from farming and mining, and their investments in railways and real property were increasing in value. Secure in their local influence

and economic position, the heads of the old families were still
confident of their birthright as an exclusive order of service in
the State. Given the strength of representation of the rural communities, where traditional deference was still almost unbroken,
it is not surprising that the membership of the House of Commons was predominantly representative of the landed interest.

Many of the smaller towns were still the pocket boroughs of
territorial magnates or the local squire. The rest, with a few
apparent exceptions, were controlled by cabals of wealthy election managers. Dod, after the General Election of 1865, named
forty-five boroughs in the United Kingdom as being subject to
the influence of a single family and six where two families divided
the control. The Grosvenor family, for example, had 'great
influence' in Chester; the Marquess of Exeter 'possess'd most of
the £10 houses in the borough' of Stamford; Peterborough was 'a
borough of Lord Fitzwilliam's' and he also 'had considerable
influence' in Malton. All the pocket boroughs had fewer than
1,000 electors.[4] Newcastle-under-Lyme, the Duke of Sutherland's
borough, had 975 among a population of 13,000, while Arundel
had 174, and Portarlington, where Lord Portarlington was 'sole
proprietor', had 106. Even in large, comparatively fluid urban
electorates, voters usually returned nominees of the family
traditionally associated with the borough, particularly if the
family were landlords in the constituency, as were the Grosvenor
clan in Lambeth and Westminster, the Stanleys in Liverpool and
the Butes in Cardiff.

In 1867 Bernard Cracroft estimated that of the 396 borough
members, 246 were primarily associated with land, and of the
remaining 150, only 31 appeared to have been connected
primarily with manufactures.[5] To this we must add the 262
county members who were, with perhaps a dozen exceptions, all
aristocrats or country gentlemen. Thus, so far as membership
of the Commons was concerned, the traditional ruling class had
withstood the challenge from the commercial and industrial
interest.

Only the large new industrial boroughs and the more notorious
of the 'open' boroughs were relatively free of aristocratic influence. In the industrial boroughs there was room for dissident
factions and interlopers to angle for the somewhat less predeter-
mined votes of the electors and this brought into play the skills
of the local registration agents and solicitors, and the cliques of

Churchmen and Dissenters, the members of the Corporation, the partisan shopkeepers and publicans, as they arranged the registration of the citizens, fostered their party loyalty and shepherded them to the poll. Smaller boroughs with large proportions of freemen electors, like Great Yarmouth, Lancaster and Reigate, were traditionally corrupt and open to the highest bidder.[6]

The selection of those entitled to register in these various constituencies depended to a remarkable degree upon chance. Under the suffrage qualifications contained in the Reform Act, males over twenty-one were entitled to enrol to vote for parliamentary representatives in the boroughs of Great Britain if they had not been in receipt of poor relief in the preceding twelve months, paid the poor rate and assessed taxes, or in Scotland, the assessed taxes only, for at least the past twelve months, and occupied premises for twelve months at a net estimated minimum rating of £10 a year, and resided for six months from the beginning of the calendar year within the parliamentary borough, or within seven miles of its limits. Those who had been created freemen of the borough before 1832 were also permitted to register by virtue of their ancient right franchises, which the Reform Act retained to them for their lifetimes. Peers, lunatics, criminals and certain government officers such as police magistrates, excise and customs officers and post office men, were excluded.

Tenants of £10 occupancies who compounded with their landlords for their rates possessed a legal right to be enrolled, but effectively they were disfranchised. The compounders paid their rates and assessed taxes with their rent to their landlord, who paid the collector. The arrangement suited the tenant because it spread his rates into an 'invisible' charge, it suited the corporation because it made for ease and certainty of collection and it benefited the landlord because the corporation allowed him a rebate on his rates. By law and general custom only the name of the payer of the rate was entered against the dwelling for which the rate was paid, and so the name of the compounding tenant did not normally appear in the rate-book. Yet the rate-book was usually the only source from which the electoral rolls were compiled. Under section XXX of the Reform Act, tenants were permitted to claim to be rated and upon their paying the 'full' rate, to have their names entered in the rate-books, and so become eligible for the electoral rolls. But the clause remained almost completely inoperative: the compounding system was so

convenient that few tenants were willing, and few landlords were
ready to allow their tenants to 'de-compound' in order to attain
the vote. (The landlord remained ultimately liable for the rate.)
The electoral courts raised a further difficulty when they interpreted the clause and the Rating Amendment Act[7] to mean that
the intending voter had to renew his claim upon the payment of
each rate, which could involve the expense of as many as six
separate claims a year. An attempt, not altogether successful, had
been made to remedy this with Clay's Act of 1851.[8] This allowed
the compounder to make a single claim and have his name kept
on the roll during such time as he continued to pay his rate; some
courts interpreted the third, ambiguous clause of this Act to
allow him to become eligible after paying only the 'compounded'
amount of the rate, instead of the 'full' rate. Still, the efficacy of
Clay's Act depended upon the diligence of the local agents. Its
patchy results can be gauged from the returns for two metropolitan boroughs: in 2 of the 3 parishes of Lambeth, 10,000 of 15,400
£10 compounders were on the rolls in 1865-6, while in the third,
Camberwell, there were only 5 out of 4,900. Of the parishes of
Southwark, Rotherhithe had only 6 registered out of 1,426; St
Olave's 2 out of 202; St George the Martyr 2,000 out of 4,200;
while Bermondsey had 4,000 enrolled out of 4,383.[9]

In the counties of England and Wales men over 21 qualified
for the registers if they held a 40s. freehold, or a £10 copyhold,
or a 60-year leasehold at £10 or a 20-year leasehold at £50 a year.
In Scotland the tenancy qualifications were set at slightly lower
levels in accordance with the lower valuations in the North, but
even so, there were only half as many voters in proportion to the
county population as there were in England. In Ireland, under
the provisions of the Reform Acts of 1832 and 1850, the borough
qualification was set at £8 annual value[10] and the county franchise
at £12 with additional qualifications for lessees and copyholders.
In addition, freeholders in the boroughs of the United Kingdom
could register in the county in which their borough was situated
if their borough freehold was tenanted and the tenant exercised
the franchise pertaining to it.

As even this outline shows, the voting qualifications were a
complicated web of legal technicalities. The exercise of the franchise really depended upon the registration of the occupier, and
the comprehensiveness of registration depended upon the varying
degrees of care and assiduity shown by the local collectors,

guardians and partisans. Apart from the many who remained uninterested and unrecorded, others refused to enrol because they disliked the possible ordeal of the registration courts where their qualifications and applications might be canvassed, while many others, often a third to a half in a large urban constituency, failed to vote because they could not afford to leave their employment or because they feared the clamour and possible danger of the hustings.

The system was too complicated and the registration machinery too rudimentary to allow of an exact enumeration of those qualified, or even registered, to vote. The Poor Law Board calculated from the 1866 electoral returns that there were about 1,432,000 men enrolled in the counties and boroughs of the United Kingdom in 1865: 1,260,000 of them were in England and Wales, 105,000 in Scotland and 203,000 in Ireland.[11] Baines' return of 1864-5 showed that there were at least 120,000 adult male £10 occupiers in the boroughs who had less than twelve months' occupation, while a further 60,000 had not paid their current rates.[12] In 1867 only 70 per cent of the known £10 male occupiers were enrolled.[13]

The radicals commonly asserted that the high borough qualification and haphazard registration procedure effectively disfranchised the workingmen. Edward Baines, for example, declared in 1864 that only one man in five in the United Kingdom had the vote and reiterated the common belief that the workingmen were almost completely excluded. He argued that the £10 level was beyond the means of the artisans, excepting a few in London, and that in the North where rents were lower, it uniformly debarred them. He added that the gradual expiry of the freeman suffrages had also served to diminish the working classes' share of the constituency.[14] In fact these confident assertions were largely guesswork, for no one really knew how the structure of the electorate was related to the various classes in the country.

There was no reasonably comprehensive and accurate analysis of the electorate until the returns were made in 1866. These showed that the £10 householders registered in England and Wales had increased from 174,179 in 1832 to 463,548, and that the ratio of £10 electors to population had risen from 3·34 per cent to 4·96 per cent in 1865.[15] Gladstone disparaged this increase by arguing that it had not kept pace with the rate of growth of the population, but if we take into account the decrease of freemen and other ancient right voters, from 108,219 to 50,478, we find that the true rate had outstripped the population increase.[16] The prosperity of the period had clearly brought an increase in the number of occupancies at £10 and above.

The returns also showed that of the 490,000 registered voters in the parliamentary boroughs of England and Wales, 129,000, or 26 per cent, were workingmen as technically defined. In eight boroughs—Coventry, Stafford, Maldon, Newcastle-under-Lyme, Pembroke, Beverley, Greenwich and St Ives—they even constituted the majority of the electorate. In Coventry, they were 70 per cent of the total. The workmen's voting strength was disguised because it was not organized to support any specific working-class programme or candidate. Maldon was a nomination borough, and in Pembroke, Beverley and St Ives, the lower-class elector's interest in his vote extended only as far as its market value. The fourteen members returned from the eight boroughs in 1865 were in no way distinctive from their colleagues.[17] The astute Bernard Cracroft pointed the moral for the future: the working class would have to learn to utilize its potential voting power to further its proper interests, and a generation was to pass before it began effectively to do so.[18]

The composition of the House showed that it was not only the working-class vote that was submerged. The industrial and commercial middle class also split its vote between Conservative manufacturers like Eaton and Liberal gentlemen like Allan, and the mal-distribution of seats ensured that the reserve of radical free-trade voting strength was confined to a few enormous industrial electorates like Birmingham and Sheffield.

There is no greater fallacy than this—that the middle classes are in possession of power [declared Bright in 1866]. The real state of the case . . . [is] that the working men are almost universally excluded . . . from political power, and the middle class, while they have the semblance of it, are defrauded of the reality. . . . The middle class have votes but those votes are rendered harmless . . . by the unfair distribution of them, and . . . the voter . . . can neither fight for further freedom, nor defend that which his ancestors have gained.[19]

Thus, the agitation to amend the constitution was led by the radicals, who saw in a redistribution of seats to the industrial towns the hope of fulfilling the promise of the Reform Act and the Repeal of the Corn Laws. The radical Reformers, John Bright,

Edward Baines, 'Corn Law' Smith, Duncan McLaren, and their allies, knew redistribution must eventuate if the anomalies of the representative system were rendered more blatant by an extension of the franchise. Of course, redistribution and the franchise had to be taken together, for as Bright warned, 'it would be easy to double the number of electors, and at the same time to increase the aristocratic influence in Parliament'.[20] They believed, too, that a large-scale enfranchisement of the respectable workingmen would reinforce the radical middle classes in their efforts to break the Parliamentary and social ascendancy of the landed interest. Extension of the franchise was the first step in their campaign to provide a degree of power for the commercial and manufacturing interests commensurate, as they saw it, with their contribution to the nation.

The unjust predominance of the landed interest, the radicals insisted, was reflected in its selfish, inefficient government. John Bright, in a typical onslaught, declared that it maintained a system of taxation that bore unfairly on industry, it had proved itself bellicose and incompetent in the Crimean War, it arrogantly upheld the Game Laws, it defended the Established Church and the exclusive universities, and its engrossing of power and isolation from the enterprising classes served only to divide the nation.[21] Behind him were ranged the various groups of Financial Reformers and activist Dissenters, who regarded the existing Commons as the main obstacle to commercial enterprise and religious equality. The *Financial Reformer* demanded that 'the House of Commons must become what it is most erroneously supposed to be—viz., a real representation of the wants, rights, interests and feelings of the people of the country, instead of the mere tool of the ruling, receiving, and spending upper ten thousand'.[22] 'Help forward the suffrage wherever you can', Miall urged in 1852, 'help forward the separation of Church and State . . . but if you cannot do both, help forward the suffrage, and the other will be secured.'[23]

The basic unity of interest that existed in the nation could be furthered when a fair balance of the representation of interests was achieved. Thus the way to social harmony lay through Reform:

It is only when Governments are oligarchical or class that there are separate interests. In fair and equal Governments the common interests of all citizens are . . . the same, from the duke down to the man who breaks stones.[24]

Edmond Beales, the president of the Reform League, explained that the extension of the franchise to the workingmen would 'put an end to animosities . . . amongst the different classes . . . and . . . weld all classes together by unity of interest into one harmonious whole'.[25]

The Reformers sought to demonstrate that the workingmen had developed a stake in the country through the self-help organizations they had created. They might not own extensive lands, but by their building societies, co-operatives, savings banks and their participation in the Volunteer Movement, they had come to emulate the possessing classes and to join with them in helping to forward enterprise and husband property. Their increasing prosperity had caused the artisans to shed any bonds that once might have linked them with the improvident who possessed nothing but their labour, and it had instead enabled them to acquire an interest congruent with that of their employers. The Northern railway magnate, George Leeman, asserted that the individual livelihoods of the artisans were bound up with the success or failure of their masters in the competitive economic system: sharing an interest in 'prosperity', they, as rational beings, would direct their votes to the reform of the taxation system and the removal of restrictions on trade.[26]

The Reformers also sought to counter the argument that these workingmen still largely lacked possessions and social status by claiming that they had aspirations to defend, and as these were akin to those of the enterprising classes, their votes could only operate to purify elections and diminish the influence of the landed magnates. Duncan McLaren, the draper and railway investor, and M.P. in 1865, told a Reform meeting in Edinburgh that those who opposed the admission of the workingmen did so, not 'because . . . the working classes have not enough intelligence, but because . . . they have too much . . . and they would vote for the best man, not caring a fig whether the candidates were sent down by the Carlton or some other club in London'.[27]

So, without selfish interests to further, working-class voters could only have altruistic objectives and would automatically serve as reinforcements to the middle-class improvers. Tom Hughes claimed that the existing Parliament was lethargic, and that a sense of 'the duty of social progress' could only awake

there if the members of that class which most desired a 'better
future' were given a hearing. While the status and education of
upper-class persons were usually assured, the prosperity and
social advancement of the workingmen was still too much 'a
matter of chance and accident'. And because the prospects of the
upper classes were assured, they were too little ready to press
their representatives to undertake difficult ventures to help the
workingmen, such as the reform of a taxation system which fell
too oppressively on industry and too lightly on land, the provision
of wider elementary education, industrial arbitration, and the
strenthening of the regulations concerning dangerous trades and
the adulteration of foodstuffs.[28]

John Stuart Mill went further in arguing that the House of
Commons stood at the opening of a new era of legislation in
State education, reform of the criminal law and industrial relations. In the discussion of such matters it was essential for the
House to have the views of the class most affected, for no upper-
class representatives, however sympathetic, could properly
express the attitudes of the workingmen to such questions as
strikes and the regulation of apprenticeship. The contribution
from the working-class members would widen the area of debate,
and remind members of 'their own fallibility'.[29] This view, as well
as presupposing that workingmen would actually enter the
House of Commons, envisaged an interventionalist, regulating
function for Parliament beyond its role as a forum for the airing
of grievances and the discussion of public business. Mill's immediate concern was to widen participation in debate as a means
to the elucidation of problems; his argument implied a transformation in the relation between Parliament and the community
which was anathema to the Whigs. Earl Grey, for example,
admitted the need to recognize the improvement of the artisans
and to enlarge their share in the constituency, but he was utterly
opposed to any extension which 'would render the House of
Commons a mere instrument of expressing . . . the wishes of the
numerical majority of the population'. For this would destroy the
function of the House as 'a deliberative Assembly, in which the
opinions and wishes of all classes are heard, but which habitually
acts under the guidance of those best able to judge what is really
most for the common good'.[30]

The radical manufacturing employers were concerned to extend
the functions of the House because they were agreed that if the

workingmen were kept outside the electorate, they would come to believe that they held an interest independent of their masters, and would resort to strikes and coercion to gain higher wages and shorter hours. Sir Francis Crossley, the carpet manufacturer from Halifax, declared that 'by passing . . . a Bill . . . and by taking men into the citizenship their attention would be diverted from strikes and combinations to that of interesting themselves in the welfare of the country'.[31]

The radicals desperately wanted to revitalize the medieval bond of sympathy between classes, expressed through patronage by the upper, and deference from the lower, ranks. John Bright, for instance, believed that the various classes had shared a happy unity of social intent in medieval Britain, but that the Tudors had weakened it and that it had been all but destroyed when the Stuarts and the Established Church had persecuted the Puritans. 'Our great object is this,' he declared at a Reform soirée in 1866, 'to restore the British constitution in all its freedom to the British people.'[32] Every move to extend the suffrage among ratepayers, every move towards the restoration of the ancient constitution, would help to create industrial harmony. 'I, living amongst a very dense population, believe, and I think every employer of labour in this House will believe, that every interest in this country will be safer, more comfortable, and more happy in every particular if some 200,000, 300,000 or 400,000 persons were added to those who now possess the franchise.'[33]

But even at 400,000, this left over four million adult males without votes. The radicals were completely opposed to any indiscriminate enfranchisement of the lower orders—of the men who were unable to pay considerable rates and taxes and thereby revealed that they were improvident and had no standing as citizens. They possessed neither enterprise nor self-discipline and they offered no prospect of using their votes for the best interests of the community. Their improvidence gave them an envy of the classes which supported them and, if they were given the vote, they would use it only to attack the property of the upper classes. Moreover, by their numbers, they would overwhelm the exclusive electorate and destroy that balance of classes which the radicals were working to create.

Furthermore, the ancient constitution, according to its students, had not been democratic. The old 40s., scot and lot and burgage franchises had been privileges received reciprocally with the payment of taxes and performance of civic duties, upon the grounds that those who paid rates and had public responsibilities were best fitted to participate in decisions about the levying and spending of their taxes and the arrangement of their tasks.[34] Thus the ancient constitution, in the Reformers' estimation, authorized their claims for the re-enfranchisement of the worthy and justified the continued exclusion of the rest.

The Reformers' advocacy of a selective enfranchisement on the grounds of social utility necessarily involved the rejection of any claim that the franchise was a natural right; at most, extreme radicals of the middle class, like Beales, claimed it was a utilitarian right, but it was more usually spoken of at the time, and it is best thought of, as a 'trust'. The franchise remained the property of the political nation and was only to be extended to the prospective voter after he had shown by his financial standing, established residence, and contribution to the economic burdens of the community, that he was likely to use his vote rationally and independently to elect representatives who would uphold the good order and best interests of the State. Even the Reform League, which stood for 'manhood suffrage', specifically demanded a residence qualification, and excluded as 'half-adult', men such as criminals and paupers, whose condition proved that they would not exercise their vote independently and rationally.[35]

The improvident were already 'virtually' represented, in that their wants were considered by their betters when the latter were taking decisions about the policing of their liberty and the relief of their distress.[36] And their enormous numbers constituted an insuperable difficulty. Even among the enfranchised, the relative powers of votes had to be selectively distributed in order to preserve the representation of the widest possible range of small interests. Reformers like John Stuart Mill and Henry Fawcett advocated schemes of proportional representation and minority voting expressly to maximize the number of interests that could find representation and to avert the danger of collapse into a uniform constituency dominated by a simple majority, especially a majority composed of the least educated.

As the vote was a 'trust', it was distinct from the rights of property and liberty of the individual. The proof of this distinction, according to the radical Reformers, lay in the fact that no voter had the right to sell his vote. The eminent radical, Sir

Francis Crossley, demonstrated the logical absurdity of the argument from natural right by remarking that if it were so, the vote would have to be given to women.[37]

These abstract arguments about the balance of the representation and the isolation of the ruling caste failed to arouse enthusiasm in the country. Some argument of right was necessary in order to assert the prerogative of the workingmen to enjoy the franchise, and Gladstone hit upon the formula in an inspired moment in 1864. In the course of a rambling apology for a future instalment of Reform he

> venture[d] to say that every man who is not presumably incapacitated by some consideration of personal unfitness or of political danger is morally entitled to come within the pale of the Constitution, [provided that this did not lead to] sudden or violent, or excessive, or intoxicating change.[38]

Apart from signalling his conversion to a reduction of the franchise qualification, these few sentences gave the Reformers an argument of even greater potential popular appeal than any assertion of natural right, for the words were charged with the aspirations of the age. The radicals quickly translated the moral right to mean 'the opportunity to further aims consecrated by public conscience', such as the reform of the army and abolition of public hanging. Gladstone's argument also placed the opponents of Reform in the position of having to deny the moral fitness of the working man, and denial was disastrous, as Robert Lowe was to learn. But most important, Gladstone had produced a claim which made exact calculations irrelevant, and this flexibility, with its moral aura, helped the nation to acquiesce in an amendment of the constitution sufficient to accommodate a vast movement in society.

3

THE SECOND REFORM PERIOD, 1851-1865

The overture to the Second Reform Act played on for sixteen years. The inconclusive politics and the long series of ineffectual bills introduce the main themes of the tragi-comedy which followed.

The years between 1850 and 1866, the great years of Victorian prosperity and confidence, were also a time of political stalemate. The Tory smash in 1846 devitalized the struggle between the two traditional gentry parties, leaving the Whig-Peelite coalition with an almost permanent majority and a near monopoly of office, however much they mismanaged affairs and squabbled among themselves. Outside the House, the Chartist débâcle of 1848 wrecked the main channel of working-class opposition to the régime. In the absence of a real party conflict and pressure from the country, the development of policy and the formation of ministries, more than at any other period in the century, became the outcome of factional struggle and short-term expediency in Parliament itself. Cabinets aimed at little beyond producing policies which might stabilize a majority, and avoiding legislation which might alienate the uncommitted. Parliamentary politics, as played in the London clubs and the great houses, really became the irresponsible game it is often thought to be: it was the golden age of the independent member.

The Tory side consisted of a ragged, discordant phalanx which was reluctantly coming to accept Free Trade and its own seemingly ineluctable minority status. Through the fifties it acted as a reinforcement to the Whigs whenever they needed help to overcome the radicals, and it acquiesced in this minor role when the system congealed into a party truce for the remaining third of the period.

The great majority of the followers of Palmerston and Russell on the Liberal side were the heirs of the men who had governed Britain through generations. They were akin to their Tory opponents in that they were normally landowners and adherents of the Established Church. They approved the general tendency of Gladstone's budgets to reduce indirect taxation on consumer goods, but they were determined to maintain the tax advantages enjoyed by the landed interest. They readily supported government spending on the Services, the Volunteers, and the Court, and usually approved British belligerence, if not intervention, abroad. They were lukewarm about social reform, but usually could be persuaded to vote for permissive municipal improvements, extension of protective legislation in factories and enabling legislation for working-class self-help schemes, provided these measures did not promise to increase public taxation. Parliamentary Reform they liked least of all. They knew that one day it must come, but throughout the fifties they seized every opportunity to thwart it.

The bills for reform and social improvement were usually brought forward in the party by the small band of radicals, or 'advanced Liberals' as they often called themselves. They rarely counted more than seventy in the House, and much less than that between 1857 and 1859, but they wielded an influence out of all proportion to their numbers. Russell always turned to them when he wanted backing in his contests with Palmerston, and they in return could bargain for his support for their projects. His successive Reform Bills, 1852, 1854, 1860 and 1866, were the outcome of this relationship.[1]

The 'advanced Liberal' wing had its roots in the Anti-Corn Law League; John Bright was their spokesman and Richard Cobden their tactician, and through Milner-Gibson and C. P. Villiers they had links with the Whig ruling caste. The group was composed of two kinds of members. The stronger, numerically and in ability, was drawn from men associated with manufacturing and commercial enterprise in the Midlands and the North. They were mostly second-generation magnates, eager to play a role in national politics and society commensurate with the eminence they had attained in their industries and towns, but whose kinship connections with the national élite were tenuous at best, and more often, non-existent. In addition to Bright and Cobden, they included William Scholefield, the son of a banker and merchant, the first mayor, and member for Birmingham; James Stansfeld, the friend of Mazzini, the son of a Halifax solicitor, a Nonconformist brewer and member for Halifax; Michael Thomas Bass, also a brewer, (Derby); and William Ewart, the son of a Liverpool merchant, the advocate of free libraries and the abolition of capital punishment, (Dumfries). During the fifties they were joined by Francis Crossley, the son of a Halifax carpet manufacturer, (Halifax); Edward Baines, the Nonconformist son of the proprietor of the *Leeds Mercury*; James Clay, the son of a London merchant, (Hull); J. B. 'Corn Law' Smith, the son of a Manchester cotton merchant, (Stockport); Llewellyn Dillwyn, the son of the Quaker ironmaster of Swansea; John Locke, the legal reformer, son of a London merchant, (Southwark); E. A. Leatham, the son of a Quaker banker of Wakefield, (Huddersfield); and Edward Miall, the Independent preacher, and prophet of Disestablishment, (Rochdale).

The other part of the radical wing was formed by a small number of country gentlemen. They were difficult, idiosyncratic men, secure in their constituencies, and intrepid in the House. They represented, in their generation, that tiny but continuous stream of gentry radicalism which has so greatly influenced English constitutional development. In addition to Gibson and Villiers, there was Peter Locke King, one of the members for East Surrey, the second son of the seventh baron King, educated at Harrow and Trinity; and Francis Henry Berkeley, member for Bristol, the untiring advocate of the ballot, born the illegitimate son of the fifth Earl of Berkeley, and educated at Christ Church; Sir Wilfrid Lawson, the temperance reformer, one of the members for Carlisle, and Robert Duncombe Shafto, a member for North Durham, both heirs of old North Country families, while the radical M.P. for Westminster, Sir John Villiers Shelley, was also a scion of the gentry. Together with their commercial allies, they formed an earnest, able, hardworking fraternity which, despite its numerical weakness and informal organization, decisively influenced the course of social and political change in the mid-nineteenth century.

They made their first breakthrough, as a pressure group for Parliamentary Reform, in 1851. While Russell's Government was was riven over the budget and the Ecclesiastical Titles Bill, Locke King introduced a motion to assimilate the county qualification to the borough level and carried it against the Ministers.[2] The effect of the Bill would have been to extend the vote to £10 occupiers living in unrepresented towns in the counties. Locke King and his allies intended that this urban element should counter the deference vote commanded by the landed interest in the villages, and as such it was an outright attack on the electoral strongholds of the landed gentry. The £10 qualification would also have confirmed Locke King's position in East Surrey, which had many suburban householders who occupied £10 houses.

Lord John Russell admitted that the men whom Locke King proposed to enfranchise would use their votes 'with intelligence and integrity', but he opposed the motion because its effect would be to change the historical basis of the representation.[3] Traditionally, the county vote represented those whose interests were founded in real property, and the borough vote those whose interests derived from personalty. The county vote represented the permanent wealth of the community, the borough vote the movable, and the two elements combined to give stability and vivacity to government. Locke King's motion would 'diminish the just influence of . . . [the] freeholders', and abridge the variety of interests represented in the constituency. And a uniform constituency, in which a few interests predominated, was unlikely to be zealous for the widest public good.

Russell's speech was the forerunner of many similar ones. They are profound and earnest disquisitions on a subject which fascinated him and of which he had considerable historical knowledge, yet at the same time they often read like humbug, and frequently issued in very dubious manoeuvres. They mirror Russell's own febrile, ambitious personality. On this occasion he was attempting to parry the motion by giving a vague promise of a bill for the following year.[4] He made the promise without any consultation with the Cabinet and it dismayed Russell's Whig and Peelite colleagues. But Locke King pressed his motion in the thin House and carried it by 100 votes to 52, the minority consisting of Ministers and Tories.[5] Later in the year Berkeley also carried his ballot motion for the first time against the Government.[6]

In April, Locke King renewed his motion and Fox Maule, on behalf of the Ministry, hastened to make Russell's promise more definite.[7] This headed off a few of the less truculent radicals, althought the motion still received 83 votes. But the real balance of forces in the House is shown by the combination of 299 Whig, Peelite and Conservative votes against it:[8] the gentry were quick to forget their party differences when they saw their interest threatened. And the radicals explicitly presented their motions as

assaults on the power of 'the Landocracy'. Locke King declared
that the extension of the county franchise would smash their
dominance in the countryside. Berkeley argued that the ballot
would free the tenant from the intimidation exercised by his
'political bully' of a landlord, while Joseph Hume carried the
attack to the next stage by praising the ballot as an instrument
which would help to transform the composition of 'that House as
a means of lessening taxation and checking extravagance in the
public expenditure'.[9]

The Ministerial promise was definite only to the extent that
there would be an official bill in the following year. Bright
taunted the Prime Minister to reveal the kind of measure he
envisaged, but Russell refused to commit himself beyond the
announcement that it would recognize 'the improvement and
intelligence of the people and the general spread of information
since 1832'.[10] Nevertheless, Russell had budged from that position
of 'finality' to which he had adhered since 1837.

Towards the end of the session Russell began to draw up an
elaborate scheme to refurbish the 1832 Act. He proposed the disfranchisement of up to forty of the smallest boroughs and the
allocation of their seats in equal shares to the most populous
counties and town. He planned to reduce the county franchise to
£20 and the borough franchise to £5 rateable value. To obviate
the possible numerical preponderance of the new voters, he proposed that the various trades and professions in each borough
should form themselves into electoral colleges and that each
college should choose two or three electors to vote in the parliamentary election in the borough. The Cabinet found the
scheme fantastic and threw it out.[11] Its main interest is that it
shows how far Russell was prepared to go to avert the numerical
predominance of the lower orders. In a period which was rife
with all kinds of extraordinary constitutional proposals, Russell's
schemes were by far the most creative, and potentially revolutionary in their impact on the Constitution. In the event, all but
one of them proved abortive, and his minority voting system did
not work out as planned.[12]

It was the disfranchisement proposal, at once more feasible and
therefore more dangerous, which raised the fiercest objections.
Sir Charles Wood, Palmerston, who was concerned for Tiverton,
and Lord Lansdowne, the proprietor of Calne, wanted it deleted,
and the last threatened to resign.[13] Russell gave way, and the Bill

was thus shorn of its disfranchisement clauses even before it entered the House.

When Parliament reassembled in February 1852, Reform was not mentioned in the Queen's Speech. The Government had entered a new crisis with Palmerston's enforced resignation from the Foreign Office, and Russell was trying to hold the remnants together by avoiding contentious policies. The omission provoked an angry response from the radicals, and on 9 February Russell foreshadowed another Reform Bill in a statement to the House. The speech was a diffident apologia rather than a confident appeal for Reform, for he was more concerned to placate the Whigs and Peelites than to satisfy the radicals.[14]

The projected Reform Bill followed the same lines as the 1851 memorandum, with a £5 borough qualification and a £20 county level. The former would bring in a 'safe and intelligent' class and the latter would equate the county franchise with the jury qualification. In addition Russell proposed to create a new franchise in both counties and boroughs for men who paid 40s. a year in direct taxes. This was to cater for the 'well-educated men who [were] . . . not occupiers', that is, the young doctors, lawyers, curates and schoolmasters, who were usually lodgers. It was the first official, rudimentary fancy franchise, and the forerunner of the lodger qualification of 1867. Russell also proposed to reword the Parliamentary Oath to make it less obnoxious to Roman Catholics and Jews.

For the redistribution, he proposed to group English and Welsh boroughs containing less than five hundred electors with neighbouring unrepresented towns. With Palmerston once more out of the Cabinet, he could afford to stand by his earlier scheme. The plan involved sixty-seven boroughs, nearly all in the south-west. Russell tried to soften the blow for his Whig and Tory hearers by assuring them that there would be no disfranchisement and no re-allocation of seats to the industrial towns. That would 'depress the agricultural interest', and that was 'not what we are prepared to do'.[15] The Bill was far from being a sweeping Reform: it offered instead a minimal extension of the franchise and a reactionary strengthening of the small boroughs. Russell aptly defined the Bill as: 'A supplement to the Reform Bill, and not . . . a substitute for it'.[16]

The sketch of the Bill did not satisfy the radicals. Joseph Hume declared that he could find 'no intelligible principle' in it, for it made no provision for the ballot and triennial parliaments and it would still leave two or three million workingmen unenfranchised. Sir Joshua Walmsley and Bright demanded the actual disfranchisement of the small boroughs and the allotment of their seats to the great towns.[17]

The House had begun to empty even as Russell was making his introductory statement. The members received the proposals with 'frigid indifference', and the Tories contented themselves with objections to the amendment of the Oath, 'the Jew portion of the Bill', and with denouncing the Government for truckling to 'the Manchester party'. Neither Tories nor Whigs were greatly worried, for they already knew that the Bill was doomed.[18] A week later, with defeat looming on the Militia Bill, Russell withdrew his promised Reform Bills. He showed more relief than regret, and the radicals were angry. Tom Duncombe protested that Russell had broken his word and deceived them. They had 'kicked out Locke King's Bill' on the understanding that the Government would bring in a Bill, and now Russell had abandoned them and the Bill.[19] 'He is in this fix', Greville recorded, 'that he cannot do much without offending the Whigs, nor little without alienating the Radicals.'[20]

The articulate portions of the country were preoccupied with the sectarian and financial controversies of the session and they ignored the failure of the projected Reform Bill, while the inarticulate remained so. 'There was no doubt that there was considerable apathy . . . among the unenfranchised themselves', Hume admitted, 'and when people were fed and fully employed, they did not think much of troubling Parliament.'[21] Bright, who had toured the English and Scottish industrial towns attempting to arouse support for Reform, confessed to Villiers that he did not 'think the time [had] come yet for great changes'.[22]

At the opening of the session in 1853 Russell promised to revive the Bill of the previous year. In November he convened another committee of Cabinet to draft a new bill and laid before it the heads of a plan which became the Bill of 1854. The plan included the reduction of the county and borough qualifications, the total disfranchisement of all boroughs with less than three hundred voters and the withdrawal of one member from double boroughs with less than five hundred, and the redistribution of the sixty-six seats thus obtained among the larger counties and towns. Russell also proposed to ensure the representation of minorities

in the big constituencies by giving them a third member and
allowing each elector only two votes.[23]

Palmerston quickly voiced his complete opposition to the introduction of another Bill. As before, he objected primarily to the
redistribution clauses. He argued that the move towards reform
derived from Russell's rash offer in the House and not from any
favourable decision in the Cabinet or urgent demand in the
country.[24]

Russell defended himself by arguing that the progress of the
country had made a further adjustment of the representation
inevitable. 'The necessity for Reform now exists not in any declarations of mine, but in the existence of abuses and defects which
it becomes our duty to remedy . . . I need not remind you of what
Mr. Burke says of early reformations. The capitulations made
with the Catholic Association and the Anti-Corn Law League are
not to me inviting examples to follow.' He concluded by claiming
that the Bill would fulfil the spirit of the Reform Act, by taking

> power from individuals or classes who are weak and odious,
> and giv[ing] . . . it to large bodies of the same class who are
> strong and popular. Thus Wilton, Harwich, Honiton, etc., lose
> their power, but it is transferred to Kent, Devonshire, Lincoln-
> shire, etc., agricultural counties rich and populous, where the
> privilege once placed can be maintained. . . . In giving more
> members to Manchester and Leeds, we should not give mem-
> bers of the same class. The Conservative minority of these
> towns would for the first time have representatives.[25]

This was Russell's Reform credo throughout his career. From his
first Reform efforts in 1819 he had aimed at preserving the power
of the landed interest, whilst gradually extending the responsibility for choosing representatives among a more numerous and
stable electorate. The greater the share that rival interests had in
the Constitution, the less cause they would have to challenge it.
The theory was rent with the contradiction between the extension
of the suffrage and the determination to nullify the power of the
new voters, and was unreal in that it ignored the trends of the
age and sought to fob off the growing industrial urban interest
while maintaining the power of a pre-industrial élite: but it
influenced the making of every Reform Bill of the period.

He failed to convince Palmerston, who resigned a fortnight
later, with Lansdowne likely to follow suit. But before the session
opened Pam was back in the Cabinet and it was commonly

accepted that the abandonment of the Bill had been the price of his return. The country was absorbed with the coming war and uninterested in reform, while the fragile coalition was not prepared to try the House by threatening to dissolve on the question. On 10 February, three days before Russell was due to introduce the Bill, Viscount Jocelyn, Palmerston's brother-in-law, adumbrated under the guise of a question a strong Whig opposition to the Bill and virtually demanded that it be dropped. Disraeli was quick to reinforce the threat from his side and offered a pledge of 'uncompromising opposition . . . [to] a measure the object of which is to reduce the interest which the land already possesses in the representation of this House'.[26] He insinuated that the Bill had been shaped according to the demands of the radicals, while Lord John Manners somewhat ambiguously dismissed it as ' a delusive bait to a section of the people with whom the noble Lord . . . wished to curry favour'.[27]

Russell persevered to the extent of introducing his Bill. In the counties he proposed to extend the vote to £10 occupiers, with the proviso that they should inhabit a house rated at over £1 to the poor rate, or if the occupancy consisted of a building and land, that the structure should be valued at £5 a year. These petty details are important, for they represent the first official endeavour to stop the creation of faggot votes, by requiring the occupancy claim to be based upon a substantial building rather than a shed. In the boroughs Russell planned to reduce the qualification to £6 annual rateable value, coupled with the municipal residence requirement of two and a half years within the same borough, which meant, given the delays of registration, effectively three years. This latter refinement, he explained, would eliminate all but 'those who are most remarkable for steadiness of conduct'.[28] Finally, he announced four new fancy franchises, to complement the 40s. direct tax qualification, revived from 1852. Firstly, men who received a minimum yearly salary of £100 paid at least quarterly, so as to exclude workingmen, were to become eligible to register; secondly, men who possessed £10 a year income from the Funds, Bank Stock or East India Company shares; thirdly, graduates of any university in the United Kingdom; and fourthly, any man who had £50 deposited for at least three consecutive years in a Savings Bank in the borough in which he resided. Only the last qualification related primarily to the workingmen, though Russell was doubtless completely justified in believing that any

working man who could salt down £50 for three years was 'a
person who had given such a proof of prudence . . . as will justify
his being entrusted with the . . . franchise'.[29] It would hardly have
been an artisan franchise at all, for the only large group of regular savers among the lower classes were the domestic servants.[30]

However, the fancy franchises were meant to have a nobler
function than the mere counter-weighting of the working-class
enfranchisement. Russell believed that they would be assays to
test for that Whig ideal, 'the independent voter'. This was the
man who would exercise his vote rationally and free of unworthy
influence to further his own interests and so ultimately the interests of the State. In this way the fancy franchise would enlarge
'the deliberate voice of the country', so-called by Russell's great
exemplar, Charles James Fox.[31]

The redistribution section also contained an important innovation, for it introduced the principle of the triangular constituency
with the two-member vote which became law in 1867. Russell
proposed that the counties should have forty-six additional representatives as third members, together with the nine provincial
boroughs over 100,000. The county scheme was a party dodge,
because it would have enabled Whig voters to return most of the
minority members, but above its effect on party, Russell espoused the minority principle because it seemed to ensure an
effective vote to the widest possible section of the political nation.
His clause preceded J. S. Mill's first published advocacy of the
principle by five years.[32]

The radicals were far from satisfied with the Bill. They attacked
its high residence qualifications as excluding too many artisans
and denounced the redistribution as cheating the manufacturing
towns.[33] At the beginning of March Russell postponed the Bill,
ostensibly because of the approaching war, but Sir John Shelley
declared that Russell was using the war as a pretext, and that
really he was afraid of a revolt in his party if he proceeded with
the redistribution.[34] Five weeks later, Russell withdrew the Bill.
In recollection of Shelley's attack he began to vindicate his integrity as a Reformer and he was finally moved to tears. The
House recognized his sincerity and supported him with its
cheers.[35] Russell had a deep emotional regard for the Constitution,
and he never forgot that he was descended from one of the
families that had made it, but he was also an opportunist politician. In the course of his apology he remarked wearily that

Reform 'attacks many interests, wounds many prejudices, and loses many friends'.[36]

The Bill of 1854 is much more important than its course would indicate. It became the model for the succeeding official Bills of the period. It outlined the first complete set of fancy franchises and the first system of minority representation, and it was the first Bill which sought both to lower the franchise and to create electoral machinery to defeat the lower-class numerical pressure resulting from the extension. It is the most elaborate and interesting of the attempts to preserve the exclusive electorate.

The Bill also marked the end of the advanced Liberals' first thrust. They lost their point of pressure in the Cabinet when Russell withdrew in 1855, and their attention was diverted by the war and Palmerston's aggressive foreign policy. They paid heavily for their peace programme in the 'Chinese' elections of 1857, when Cobden, Bright, Gibson, Miall and Fox were all unseated, and Bright suffered a mental breakdown. Apart from a county franchise motion from Locke King in February 1857, which had the usual effect of embarrassing the Whig Ministers, Reform lapsed for three years.[37]

In April 1857, in response to Palmerston's election victory, Disraeli took up reform as a possible means of restoring the fortunes of the Conservative Party. 'I suggest to you', he wrote to Derby, 'whether a juster apportionment of M.P.s may not be the question on which a powerful and enduring party may be established', and proposed raising the issue in the House. Disraeli hoped to strengthen the county representation at the expense of the 'small boroughs, which are ruled by cliques of Dissenters'. As the distribution stood, the small boroughs held the balance of power in the House.

> If fifty members were added to the counties, by reducing the small borough to one member, and every ten-pound householder in the county population were annexed to a borough constituency, you would add much to the constituency of the boroughs, and greatly increase the Conservative power at the same time. . . . Our party is now a corpse, but . . . in the present perplexed state of affairs, *a Conservative public pledged to Parliamentary Reform* . . . might . . . put us on our legs.

Derby remained unconvinced, and forbade mention of the scheme in the House unless reform were raised in the Queen's Speech.[38] He had refused to introduce a Reform bill in 1852 and had opposed the Whig measures of 1852 and 1854. He was now decided that the safest course for the Conservatives was tacitly to support Palmerston against Russell and the radicals. Nevertheless, Disraeli had mapped the path for the Conservatives. Their bills of 1859 and 1867 were to be planned to strengthen the counties at the expense of the Whig boroughs, while they were to reject the bills of 1860 and 1866 because they promised to have the opposite effect.

Lord Derby probably changed his mind about a Conservative bill in June 1858. When he had come to office with minority support earlier in the year, he had tried to fend off reform motions from the Opposition by making a vague promise of a bill in the next session.[39] But the promise failed to quiet the radicals and Locke King once more moved for a reduction of the county franchise, this time to £10 clear annual value, as in the Bill of 1854. Palmerston and Russell availed themselves of the opportunity to embarrass the shaky Ministry by voting for the motion, and the Government was defeated by fifty-eight votes.[40] This defeat seems finally to have persuaded Derby that he would have to rearrange the electoral structure and settle the question if ever his party was to enjoy security in office. The Tories had everything to gain by a carefully managed reform: their difficulty, as a minority, was to keep control of the details.

In the autumn Disraeli and Stanley drafted a bill. It adopted the principle of identity of suffrage which Locke King had previously carried. The redistribution clauses outlined a disfranchisement of between sixty and ninety small boroughs, and the addition of fifty-two seats to the counties. There was a further provision that all existing qualifications deriving from borough freeholds should be transferred from the counties and exercised exclusively in the boroughs.[41] This scheme became the basis of the Bill of 1859.

Meanwhile, Bright, Clay, Miall, McLaren and Roebuck set out to organize a fresh agitation for Reform on the lines of the Anti-Corn Law League.[42] Bright was deputed to draw up a bill and go on a speaking tour through the great towns. In the light of the Act of 1867 his Bill is remarkable for its moderation, and it shows very clearly that the middle-class radicals were preoccupied more with redistribution than with extending the franchise widely among the lower classes. Bright provided for a £6 rental qualification in the boroughs, which he assumed would have doubled the

existing constituency of the United Kingdom by including commercial clerks and the higher ranks of the artisans in London and
the greater towns. The redistribution would have swept away the
eighty-six smallest boroughs, and semi-disfranchised sixty-nine
more; only twenty-five of their seats were to be allocated to the
counties, while the rest were to go to the industrial towns.[43]

Bright's tour aroused considerable enthusiasm in Birmingham,
Manchester and Glasgow, but not enough to disturb the House of
Commons. In 1859 Cobden admitted to a group of Northern Dis-
senting clergymen that the Reform campaign had failed:

> What is wanting is some multitudinous demonstrations by the
> unenfranchised in favour of Parliamentary Reform—something
> as earnest as in the days of Hunt, but without the disorder of
> that time. But I am afraid you are too prosperous, and the
> people too well fed, to warrant the hope that Lancashire will
> come to the rescue.[44]

The radicals' campaign led Disraeli to institute a secret enquiry
among the Conservative agents to assess the probable results of
Bright's scheme if it became law. By an irony of which Bright
apparently remained unaware, the information they supplied
about his Bill moulded the 'Tory dodge' of 1859. The agents were
uniformly against the £6 rental because it would enfranchise too
many men whom they believed would vote Liberal. Also, the
poorer the electors, the greater became the difficulties of registration and the costs of 'nursing' the borough. Some hesitantly
accepted a £6 rating, which meant effectively as much as a £9
rental, but the endless variations in rating rebates and local
political jobbery made every forecast provisional. But the sum of
the information was clear in confirming the Tory leaders in their
belief that they had nothing to gain by a reduction of the borough
franchise. As the Yarmouth agent advised, Bright's plan would
'double the most corrupt class of voters [and] . . . make it too
expensive for any but [the] lowest Radicals to contest', while the
Cambridge man declared that the Conservatives were 'gone
coons' if the Bill went through.[45]

The agents were generally more sanguine of a reduction to £10
in the counties. F. W. Barlow thought it would be very favourable
to the Conservative interest in Cambridgeshire:

> The £10 occupiers in Villages are Tradesmen all under the
> thumb of the Agriculturalists in Parishes who are mostly Con-
> servatives. The £20 Occupier in a *County Village* is an *indepen-*

dent man not to be biassed, and caring not for the Farmer, the Squire or my Lord . . . the Conservatives would gain more from £10 than £20.

The county agents were agreed that if a £10 level were adopted in the counties it was desirable, indeed vital, that the counties be relieved of the growing numbers of voters in the unrepresented towns; while those from Yorkshire, Lancashire and Warwickshire pressed strongly for the re-division of their counties to seal off the urban industrial parts from the agricultural areas.

On the basis of their returns, Disraeli and Philip Rose prepared a memorandum on Reform. They declared that the Conservatives' object should be to present 'a fair impartial contrasting scheme to Bright's' that would enable them to appeal to the country if necessary. It should also promise finality: 'This can only be attained by removing anomalies in the elective franchise and so defining it as to embrace the influence of property, station and intelligence without regard solely to population.'[46] However, a prescription which promised finality whilst ignoring redistribution could only be delusory and 1867 was to prove it so.

The corollary to permanence was party advantage and Disraeli and Rose suggested that, 'if the Boros & Counties had . . . identical qualifications & were so separated from each other that the votes . . . arising in Boros were confined to Boro[s] . . . the disturbing element of the Town Voters interfering in and controlling the County Elections . . . would be destroyed'. But the level of the borough qualification had to be maintained, otherwise the Conservatives in market town boroughs would be swamped and the costs of contests would become exorbitant. Disraeli still believed that the future of the Conservative party lay in tacking against the increasing urbanization of the age. Together with his contemporaries, he thought of the electors in stereotypes in which 'urban, commercial, industrial, Dissenting' equated with 'Liberal', and 'rural, agricultural, Church' equalled 'Tory'.[47] Not perhaps until Reform became an actuality in 1867 did he come to realize that the Conservatives would have to set their course in the unfathomed waters of the suburbs.

The Conservative Bill of 1859 followed the principles in the memorandum. It left the borough qualification unaltered, but sought to enlarge the borough constituency by transferring the borough freehold voters from the counties, while the county qualification was reduced to £10. It appeared to offer a generous enfranchisement, by adding 200,000 voters to the existing county electorate of 400,000. But 90,000 of these were voters 'infected with the radicalism of the larger Boroughs in which they dwell', who were to be made to vote in those boroughs; 70,000 were rated at £20 and over and these were 'likely to add strength to the Conservative party'. This left 40,000 'questionable votes', but Disraeli emphasized that the agents in rural boroughs like Shoreham, Cricklade, Bassetlaw and Aylesbury were agreed that the local proprietors were 'in control' and that the ten-pounders voted Conservative. Here too, his opinion was still strongly traditional, in that he believed that the Conservatives would have to continue to depend upon a deferential rural electorate managed by the local proprietors. Although his Conservative colleagues already had experience of successfully managing Liverpool, Disraeli persisted in regarding the problem of attracting and mobilizing the votes of a relatively independent constituency in a large town as belonging peculiarly to the radicals and Liberals.

The Bill also contained a set of fancy franchises copied from the Bill of 1854, and proposed three other innovations which are important in the context of the Tories' intentions. First, they proposed to make the county registration similar to the borough system, by requiring the parish overseers to compile lists of owners and occupiers, as the sources for a separate county register. Under the existing law, the prospective voter had to appear before the revising barristers as each new roll was compiled, and as this was onerous and costly, the county constituency was always a decaying one. Disraeli hoped that his streamlining of the registration would stabilize the enrolment where the Conservatives were strongest. The second and third proposals, to increase the number of county polling places and pay for them out of county rates, and to introduce 'voting papers' for absentees, were also conceived as devices to lower election costs and enlarge the rural proportion of the poll.[48]

The redistribution was a shunken vestige of the scheme envisaged in the memorandum, for instead of transferring about ninety seats, it dealt only with fifteen. The larger plan had no hope of surviving the members who were threatened by it, and the Cabinet rejected it as potentially too disruptive. Disraeli followed the agents' advice in disposing of the fifteen seats: eight were to go to the counties and the other seven were to be allotted to new parliamentary boroughs excised from them.[49]

Disraeli defended the Bill as offering a safe 'lateral' extension of the franchise among electors whose merits would be proven by the fancy franchises and the worth of their occupancies. The redistribution would cause a minimum of disturbance, yet satisfy the demands of the growing towns. The country gentlemen of both sides disliked the Bill, but they also saw that it offered a settlement and the opportunity to buttress the landed interest against the encroachments of the towns and the 'improvers'. Disraeli's evident determination to stand by his Bill deepened their dilemma, and produced the first prolonged and serious debate on Reform in the decade. Members from both sides were apprehensive of the increase in costs that an enlargement of the constituency would bring, but while some of them wanted voting papers, others feared them as a fresh source of corruption and as the harbinger of the ballot.[50] Some members applauded the fancy franchises as means of strengthening the righteous portion of the electorate, while others derided them as new-fangled impositions on the British tradition of simple qualifications based on property. The men from the small boroughs railed against the redistribution, while several of their county colleagues declared that it did not go far enough.[51] The Whigs distrusted the proposal to disfranchise an estimated 95,000 county freeholder voters residing in boroughs, and denounced it as abridging the suffrage and tending towards a dangerous uniformity of representation.

Henley and Walpole also objected to the increased uniformity in the county constituency, but they believed that the suffrage level had been lowered too far. They finally resigned from the Cabinet after they had persuaded themselves that the introduction of a common level of franchise between the counties and boroughs would make the county franchise vulnerable when the borough qualification came under attack. They both wanted the borough level reduced to £8 or £6 rating to make a settlement.[52] Their lonely resignations reflected their failure to persuade their Cabinet colleagues and their Conservative fellows: the latter did not like the Bill, but they liked the prospect of losing office even less.

The advanced Liberals liked the Bill least of all. It sought to dislodge the Liberals in the counties, its redistribution plan neglected the claims of the towns and it failed to extend the vote to enough deserving artisans. According to W. J. Fox, 'the Bill did not recognize Improvement', while James Wilson, the free-trade economist, protested that its 'whole tendency . . . was to give influence to land . . . [and] to take away influence from trade and commerce, and from all the progressive pursuits of the country'.[53]

Lord John Russell, who was itching to turn the Ministry out, followed in the wake of the radicals with a resolution aimed at capitalizing on the general antipathy to the Bill. He moved that:

> this House is of opinion, that it is neither just nor politic to interfere, in the manner proposed in this Bill, with the Freehold Franchise as hitherto exercised in the Counties of England and Wales; that no re-adjustment of the Franchise will satisfy this House or the Country, which does not provide for a greater extension of the Suffrage in Cities and Boroughs than is contemplated in the present Measure.[54]

It was a clever motion which neither questioned the general object of the Bill nor challenged confidence in the Ministry, and it was not an overt motion against the second reading, for it called for more Reform, not less, though it offered no specifications. The resolution was designed to attract both radicals who wanted more Reform and Palmerstonians who did not want any. It was too mild to cause the Government to dissolve if they were defeated on it, yet it was strong enough to make them resign. The thrust succeeded, and Derby never forgave Russell. When Derby again became head of a minority Government in 1866, one of his strongest resolves was to avoid having to submit to a similar humiliation.

A small but significant group of those who sat behind Russell had refused to be netted by his resolution. They argued that Reform was too important a question to be stifled by a party manoeuvre. There was still time for the House to make a moderate and secure settlement, but if that settlement was again to be postponed by factious spite they would find themselves eventually coerced from outside into making a Reform that would be 'democratic' instead of safe and limited. The dissident Whigs and Liberals numbered about thirty. Their spokesmen were Edward Horsman, Lord Elcho and W. B. Beaumont, three of the leading Adullamites of 1866, and they included other future Caveites in Lord Charles Bruce, Townshend Mainwaring, Sir George Bowyer and W. H. Gregory.[55]

There was a further cluster of independents and radicals who voted for the resolution with great reluctance. Roebuck, for

instance, though he disliked the Bill, asserted that Russell's resolution was a party dodge which would only turn out the Ministry
and so postpone Reform for another year. He demanded a fresh
resolution which would outline the principles of a bill and allow
the Liberal majority to coerce the Tories into carrying an
effective Reform.

Two other radicals, Cox and Crossley, declared that they had
too often been gulled by the Whigs on reform and that the resolution offered no guarantee that the Whigs would back a satisfactory bill if they were restored to power.[56] They finally voted for
the resolution, more, apparently, from party loyalty and distrust
of Disraeli than from any great hope that they could wring a
worthwhile bill from Russell and Palmerston. But just as the
proto-Adullamites were to play out their roles in 1866-7, so Roebuck, Clay, A. F. Kinnaird, Crossley, T. E. Headlam, and Locke
were to be among the leaders of the tea-room movement and the
Liberal freebooters in 1867. The revolts and collusions that were
to mark the climax of the period were the expression of opinions
and forces which had been gaining in definition throughout the
fifties, and had become fixed seven years before the final contests
began.

The Reform venture of 1859 also influenced the course of its
successors by establishing the necessity for preliminary research.
It inaugurated that mountainous collection of electoral statistics
which was to overwhelm the members in 1866-7. Russell's Bills of
1860 and 1866 were both contrived upon a basis of 'exact calcula-
tion' from the returns. Disraeli depended upon statistical information too, but unlike Russell and Gladstone, he had learnt to
employ auxiliaries to filter it. The 'Enquiry' of 1858, the 'Reform
Memorandum' and the researches of Philip Rose, were developed
in 1866-7 into the network of agents and secretaries who supplied
Disraeli with an immense amount of psephological information
and legal advice. His flexibility and coolness in 1867 owed a
great deal to his intelligence service.

After the Whigs returned to office, the Cabinet began to collect
electoral statistics, in order to carry out the bargain implied in
Russell's resolution. The figures strengthened Palmerston in his
opposition to any reform.

> The returns we have got show an awful increase in voters in
> all the large towns, whatever standard of franchise we may
> adopt. . . . Then as to our county franchise we seem to be

taking a leap in the dark. We have no returns . . . that give
us the least notion what numbers the ten-pound franchise . . .
would add to the present county voters, nor what effect that
addition would be likely to produce.[57]

However, the Ministry had a majority of only about forty and
was as usual dependent upon the votes of the radicals. Despite
Palmerston's apprehensions, the Queen's speech duly announced
that measures would be introduced to place the representation
'upon a broader and firmer basis'.[58] On 1 March 1860 Russell
brought down his Bill. As compared with its predecessors it was
a simple measure, allowing for a £6 rental qualification in the
boroughs and £10 in the counties.[59] He explained that he had
been forced to adopt a rental basis after studying the returns,
which showed that rating levels varied by as much as 30 per cent
between adjoining parishes and could not provide a uniform
qualification. He added that he had calculated the influx of
workingmen exactly, and that their very small numbers made it
unnecessary to create fancy franchises for educated voters. All this
was mere assertion, for until 1866 no one knew the precise social
composition of the potential, or even existing, electorate; when
the number of working-class voters was roughly established
Russell was as surprised as everyone else.

The Bill was introduced 'amidst profound indifference in the
House and in the country'.[60] The radicals were lukewarm about it
because it did not go far enough, the Palmerstonians denounced
it as superfluous, and the Tories objected to it because it would
'greatly reduce . . . the just and salutary influence of the land'.[61]
The debate maundered on for several weeks, although the members knew that the Bill was doomed. Their compulsion to have
their say sprang from their bewildered disquiet. They knew that
they would ultimately have to make a settlement, yet few of the
gentlemen wished to disturb the arrangements by which they
enjoyed their places in the House, least of all those members
whose seats would vanish in a redistribution. It seemed impossible, and finally it proved so, both to extend the franchise to the
workingmen and yet nullify the weight of their votes in the constituencies. It appeared certain that any extension would increase
violence at the polls, swell corruption and raise election costs.
And it was hopeless to try to make a redistribution that would
both maintain the representation of the landed interest and
satisfy the 'Manchester men'. As long as the country remained

quiet it seemed easier to the Whigs and Tories to force Ministers
to drop Reform; the members duly compelled Russell to abandon
his Bill in 1860 and the public received its demise as apathetically
as it had accepted its introduction.[62]

There was no mention of Reform in the Queen's Speech for
1861 and both Russell and Derby rose to approve the omission.[63]
Reform was impossible, Russell explained, without 'a great tide
of public opinion' to carry it through Parliament. Under Pam's
genial leadership the gentry's truce against Reform gradually
hardened into an almost formal arrangement that continued until
1865. In effect, it had existed since 1846, for the Whig, Peelite
and Tory parties had continually been dependent upon each
other in divisions against the radicals' Reform motions.[64] But the
truce had not been viable in the fifties because of the personal
animosities resulting from the collapse of 1846, while the even
balance of the parties and the unsettled nature of the factions
made it easy for ambitious individuals to wreck the successive
coalition and minority Ministers. By contrast, the 1859 Parliament
was the longest and the Cabinet the most stable for half a
century. Pam was firmly in control of policy, the Tories were
restrained by their leaders and Russell's retirement to the Lords
cramped him as the main disrupter of the landed interest's
common front.

Palmerston's Indian summer was also the Indian summer of
the closed, gentry politics and the exclusive electorate which had
flourished after the Reform Act. There were no more Government
Reform bills while he lived, and even Locke King, Berkeley and
Baines grew tired, for during 1862 and 1863 there were no franchise or ballot motions. The advanced Liberals and artisan reformers turned their attention to causes which appeared to be more
immediately rewarding: they thronged the Volunteer brigades,
and organized support for the Polish, Hungarian, Greek, Circas-
sian, Italian and various other liberal movements, and for the
Northern States in the Civil War.

The advanced Liberals disinterred the Reform question in 1864,
with the intention of making it a leading issue in the approaching
general election. They knew that they had no hope of carrying it,
but they also knew that Palmerston could not live for ever. As it
happened, Baines' motion transformed the question, for it evoked
Gladstone's declaration of the argument from moral right. They
gained thereby not only an immensely strong ideological weapon,

but a brilliant, committed, passionate captain at the centre of power.

The early sixties saw his emergence as 'the People's William',[65] and his changing views on Reform are a crucial part of this development. The declaration of 1864, though unpremeditated, was the culminating expression of a trend in his thought which is discernible in 1860. Though his views on the mechanism of Reform remained almost static, his sense of moral duty to the working classes came to possess him, and he gradually convinced himself that he had to bring the most upright among them into the political nation. In 1859 he had ignored the claims of the artisans and instead had defended nomination boroughs and the need for a restrictive settlement, and had gone on to vote for Disraeli's lateral extension of the suffrage and against the ballot.[66] In 1860, while supporting the Government Bill, he remarked that:

> the best course . . . is—avoiding excess and extreme change— at the time when you think it your duty to consider the admission of a portion of the labouring class to take care that the portion you do admit is not too small, but such as will increase the confidence of the working men in general in the laws by which they are governed. . . . The quality of that body of our working men is good enough to entitle them to a share in the privileges of Parliamentary representation.[67]

His belief in a limited extension and a firm settlement remained the same, but the final sentence, solicitous rather than imperative, passed unnoticed

In October 1862 he had made a tour of Tyneside, organized by the local radicals, and found himself treated for the first time as a popular idol. Two years later he toured Bolton, Liverpool and Manchester and at the end of this 'exhausting, flattering' and, Gladstone hoped 'not intoxicating circuit', he reflected in his diary: 'God knows I have not courted them. I hope I do not rest on them. I pray I may turn them to account for good. It is, however, impossible not to love the people from whom such manifestations come.'[68]

These years mark a turning point in Gladstone's career. His social sympathy was intensified and he emerged as the prophet of ordered social unity:

> It has been given to us of this generation to witness . . . the most blessed of all social processes; I mean the process which unites together not the interests only but the feelings of all

the several classes of the community, and throws back into the
shadows of oblivion those discords by which they were kept
apart from one another. I know of nothing which can contribute, in any degree comparable to that union, to the welfare of
the commonwealth . . . than that hearts should be bound
together by a reasonable extension, at fitting times, and among
selected portions of the people, of every benefit and every
privilege that can justly be conferred upon them.[69]

His argument carried the franchise claim far beyond the limit
that was consonant with the preservation of the exclusive electorate. It led him directly to his confused and inflexible handling
of the Bill of 1866.

Baines' motion came up again in 1865, and it provoked a debate
which finally disposed the forces for the coming struggle. For the
first time in the period Disraeli led the Tories to oppose Reform
outright, and he made the first of his attacks on 'democracy'. Lord
Elcho, the Whig heir to the Earl of Wemyss, a vain busybody
who patronized the artisans he commanded in the Volunteers,
announced his opposition to their becoming a force in the electorate. Similarly, Robert Lowe, who had been recently forced
from office, declared his utter resistance to Reform. He sought to
refute the 'moral right' argument and straightway was trapped
into denying that the workingmen were morally and intellectually
fit to exercise the franchise.[70] He and twenty-four other followers
of Palmerston voted with the Tories to defeat the second reading.[71] The future Adullamites had won their first battle.

4

THE REFORM BILL OF 1866

I *The Origins of the Bill of 1866*

The general election of 1865 offered little indication that the
ensuing Parliament was to have its energies absorbed by Reform.
The dissolution came quietly and Baines' Franchise Bill seemed
forgotten. Palmerston did not mention Reform in his nomination
address and a majority of candidates of both parties ignored it.[1]
He conducted the election as a vote of confidence, calling for
support for his premiership as a guarantee of continued unity
among the political nation. Gentry candidates of all persuasions
echoed him in assuming the extension of his leadership and the
prolongation of the gentry truce, and declared their support for
the old Canningite as the safest and most popular opponent of
radical innovation; forty-two men described themselves simply as
'supporters of Lord Palmerston', while several others who sat on
the Tory side dubbed themselves 'Liberal-Conservatives'.

The Tory, Lord Robert Montagu, remarked that the political
landscape was as level as the Fens, but nevertheless it is possible
to distinguish a gradient of policy between the Tory and radical
candidates. Reform was a side issue, but together with church
rates, the malt tax, and fiscal policy, it formed the substance of
difference between the alliances. At one end of the gradient were
Tories like Montagu, the Hon. Algernon Egerton and Lord
Eustace Cecil, who were against any attack on 'our ancient and
well-beloved Church', who viewed the malt tax with the 'strongest
disfavour', and were all but completely opposed to any attempt
at Reform because they could see no way of safely controlling
the extension. They were unusual among Tory and Whig candidates, not in fearing a Reform Bill, but in making their objections
explicit.[2]

Several Conservatives, like Sir Lawrence Palk, Colonel Fane,
Sir J. R. Bailey and S. T. Kekewich, while pledged to defend

church rates, were prepared to support a vague prescription for
Reform that would, in Kekewich's words, 'let in intelligence and
preserve the balance of classes'.[3] Those Whigs who did mention Reform usually indicated, like Sir George Grey, that they
would support 'some safe measure', but like him again, generally
went on to say that neither the House of Commons nor the
country was ready to support it.[4]

At the other extreme there were radicals like Thomas Bayley
Potter, standing for Rochdale, who wanted

> united action on the part of the advanced Liberals in the House,
> to compel the Government to bring forward a satisfactory
> Reform Bill, greatly to reduce the national expenditure, to
> persevere in the application of the great principles of com-
> mercial freedom, and fully to recognize in every department of
> Church and State civil and religious liberty.[5]

These declarations would, of course, have more meaning if we
knew more about the particular electorates to which the candidates were appealing and the nature of the contests they were
facing. But if the constituencies did influence the content of
speeches at all in 1865, clearly the candidates believed that the
electors were more interested in economy in governmental
expenditure, a dominant foreign policy, church rates and the
malt tax, than in Parliamentary Reform. Even Gladstone avoided
speaking of it directly. He told the electors of Liverpool that he
would work for the improvement of society, free trade, lower
taxes, education—'the uplift of the masses, mentally, materially
and morally'—and presented himself as 'a young, a late, a feeble
labourer in this happy . . . this holy cause'. But he advocated
Reform only by implication:

> I have never swerved from what I conceived to be those truly
> conservative objects and desires with which I entered life. . . .
> But experience has brought with it lessons. I have learnt that
> there is wisdom in a policy of trust, and folly in a policy of
> mistrust. [Cheers] . . . I have not refused to receive the signs
> of the times.[6]

The gradient of promises on Reform was not very steep. All
the candidates saw the problem as one of contriving a safe,
limited, tranquillizing extension. They differed as to where the
limits should be set, but none stood for 'democracy' or for manhood suffrage, or equal electoral districts. Even thoroughgoing
radicals like Baines and Lusk repudiated the theory that the

vote was a natural right and emphasized that they stood for a selective, limited extension.[7]

Contemporaries regarded the election as an unusually peaceful one; party feeling was low and there was no threat of nation-wide disorder. Yet gross drunkenness, brutality and violence were widespread. The accounts of the riots make it easy to under-stand why the radicals were so determined to eliminate treating, why the Temperance Alliance so abhorred drunkenness, and why most men of good will approved their aims, if not their pertinacity and methods. The violence at the hustings also helps to explain why many men of good will, radicals included, feared manhood suffrage. At the Derby nomination Bass was pelted with dead cats and rabbits because he had voted for the Night Poaching Bill.[8] At Lewes the 'gentlemen of the borough' threw handfuls of a mixture of rotten eggs, flour, soot and red brick dust, and gradually beslubbered the crowd near the hustings with a 'nauseous paste'. 'Several thousands . . . were present' at the Montgomery nomination, and 'a large proportion being under the influence of drink, the proceedings were of a turbulent and eventually of . . . a riotous character'.[9]

Yet these were minor affrays beside the battles at Rotherham and Nottingham. Rotherham was in the hands of the mob for several hours, during which time they wrecked most of the shops of the town. The 15th Hussars had finally to drive them off by striking with the flats of their sabres.[10] At Nottingham a battle between the Dissenting, teetotal forces of Samuel Morley and the drunken navvies imported by the Tory, Sir Robert Clifton, lasted for two days. Shops were wrecked and pillaged, and Morley's committee rooms were burned. By the time the Riot Act was read and the soldiers went into action, an estimated 30,000 people were milling and scuffling in the market place. Morley and Clifton were both later unseated for bribery, though Morley was probably blameless.[11] These communities were still isolated and poorly-policed, with a long tradition of election sprees and brawls.[12] The proletariat eagerly awaited a contest, as a holiday replete with free beer, blankets, colours and the chance to jeer their betters. The inchoate, fickle preferences of the working classes and the poor reflects a condition which might be described as 'pre-political', and indicates some of the dif-ficulties which were to be experienced in organizing them when they eventually received the vote.

Contemporaries also regarded the election as the most expensive for years. More money seems to have been spent, not because there was significantly more bribery and beer, but because the prosperous sixties allowed many more men to try for a seat and there were many more contests. A place in the House of Commons conferred unrivalled social esteem and it gave access to vital select committees controlling railway, shipping and commercial contracts. The period of Palmerston's ascendancy marked the heyday of the member who was responsible to no one but himself and the traditional party allegiance of his family or his patron. Party organization was weak, and the Whips had no means of effectively disciplining members: men chose to follow a leader by their own volition and because it was customary, rather than because it was a necessary prerequisite for nomination and electoral support. Members thought of themselves as independent gentlemen who had joined the best club in the land to forward their particular interests and to support or oppose the Ministers who settled the affairs of the nation. The big issues—British trade and overseas power, financial reform, institutional improvement, Parliamentary Reform, the Irish Question and the prerogatives of the Established Church—all seemed to be in the process of agreed settlement or, as with Reform, so much in futurity that they could be easily ignored. Parliament existed to permit the discussion of grievances and necessary measures, not to supply an excessive flow of legislation. Politics had become a pastime, marked by oratorical combats and divisions, of which the outcome did not matter very much. Many students of politics believed that the parties would eventually coalesce, for want of difference between them.[13] It was the golden age of politics as a system of personal rivalries and adjustments of interests among the members of a secure and confident ruling class; the system which Trollope portrays in the early 'Palliser' novels.

The election returned the Liberals with a majority commonly accepted as about 70, Palmerston having about 360 followers and Derby 290. The radicals increased their numbers at the expense of the Whigs by about eight seats.[14] But this pattern of stability masks several important changes. The first was in personnel, with more than 150 members taking their seats in the Commons for the first time.[15] Their ignorance of procedure and determination to cling to their new, expensively won pre-eminence were to become leading elements in the muddles and scrapes of the seventh Parliament.

The second development was the entry of the Victorian intelligentsia into the parliamentary sphere. They were nearly all radicals, and they made the radical advance much more important than its numbers would indicate. In John Stuart Mill, Thomas Hughes, Henry Fawcett, G. O. Trevelyan, Laurence Oliphant, Duncan McLaren and J. D. Coleridge, the cause gained a striking accession of intelligence, political capacity and public influence. Rarely can such a brilliant group of new members have entered the Commons at one election. They had all put Reform at the head of their programmes and they were to play a crucial part in 1866 and 1867 by demonstrating that Reform could be intellectually respectable.

The third important change was the emergence of Gladstone as a figurehead for the radicals. Defeated at Oxford University, he was returned 'unmuzzled' by South Lancashire. The Reformers had hitherto lacked a leader whom they could trust in the Cabinet, a man with the devoted energy and ability to force through their objectives. Now they had a political genius in a position of power who seemed ready to pledge his career to their support. They were soon to find that Gladstone was more prophet than leader, but his topping the poll in the Liverpool and Salford Divisions appeared to complete that commitment to Reform which he had first disclosed in 1864.

Contemporaries found these developments intriguing, but they regarded them as peripheral to the main result of the election, which was the return of the Palmerston Government and the endorsement of its mode of unspectacular improvement in domestic affairs. Derby expected to resume his subordinate role in the new Parliament. 'Our game must be purely defensive', he wrote to Disraeli, 'and we must be ready to support the moderate portion of the Cabinet, and watch for every opportunity of widening the breach between them and the [Rads?]'[16]

But, more important than the radicals, the sheer weight of Palmerston's majority threatened the policy of quiescence. Even the stolid Brand attempted to persuade his chief that the country would expect the Government to utilize its majority to make a settlement. Palmerston remained unpersuaded:

Much might be said against meeting a new Parliament with a Proposal to make great Changes in the Constituency. . . .

Bright I know says that on every Hustings Reform was the main Topic, but verily the Truth is not in him, and indeed never has been.[17]

He quelled Brand easily enough, but a much stronger man also saw his opportunity. Gladstone was canvassing support for a venture into Reform and Argyll agreed that the 'majority [was] too big by half for "resting and being thankful".'[18]

Thus influential opinion was beginning to quicken when three months after the election, on 18 October, Palmerston died. As one elderly Whig remarked, coming away from the funeral: 'Our quiet days are over; no more peace for us.'[19]

Throughout the Second Reform period Palmerston had captained the territorial interest as they fought their rearguard action against the radicals. His belligerent foreign policy and bluff good humour, in a time of domestic prosperity and confidence, had enabled him to maintain his popularity and power long after his rivals had hoped for his retirement. The truce of parties ended with his passing. It began the disintegration of the Whig party and their gradual removal, through the next generation, to the Conservative ranks. The great check to the radical forces was gone and Gladstone had come forth as their leader. The Conservatives, so long divided and bereft of office, were now confronted with the necessity to counter Russell and Gladstone: in rallying to oppose them the Tory party was preparing itself to take office once more as a viable alternative Government, and this preparation was to find fulfilment in 1874.

Gladstone informed Russell, as soon as he heard the news, that 'any Government now to be formed' could not 'be wholly a continuation [but] . . . must be . . . a new commencement'.[20] He was now not only unmuzzled, but unleashed. Russell, volatile as ever at seventy-three, relished the prospect of power unshadowed by his late rival and briskly agreed with Gladstone.[21] Disraeli viewed the future with foreboding, though not without a certain zest for the resumption of the fray. He wrote to Lord Lonsdale, also on the 20th: 'If Johnny is the man, there will be a Reform Bill—very distasteful to the country. The truce of parties is over. I foresee tempestuous times, and great vicissitudes in public life.'[22]

Johnny was the man. On 19 October the Queen wrote to her 'old and tried friend' asking him to become Prime Minister and Russell accepted by return telegram. He set about choosing his ministers with the aid of numerous memos to himself containing diverse permutations of names and offices. In the Cabinet itself Russell made only one immediate change: before he had even received the Queen's letter he had invited the Earl of Clarendon to succeed him as Foreign Secretary.[23] The Cabinet remained the predominantly aristocratic group it had been under Palmerston. In February 1866 it contained two dukes, and the brother and the son of two more, five peers or sons of peers, and only five men without titles.

Russell's views on Reform were less forward than Disraeli assumed. He was less securely in control than Palmerston and more open to advice from Argyll and Gladstone, but his activities upon becoming Prime Minister show that he intended to move charily. His immediate task was to consolidate his leadership by winning the Palmerstonians and forestalling the radicals. To win the Palmerstonians, he had to give an earnest of his intentions on Reform to those men who had voted against Baines' Bill. So he contemplated offering Horsman a place in the Cabinet,[24] and he sounded Gladstone as to whether he would stand aside to allow Sir George Grey to lead in the Commons.[25] He offered W. H. Gregory, the important Irish Palmerstonian, a Lordship in the Admiralty, which Gregory refused, ostensibly because of his mother's ill health.[26] Lowe posed a bigger problem. He had already shown himself to be a very damaging debater and he had to be silenced if the Government was to move on Reform. Granville and Sir Charles Wood pressed for his inclusion in the Cabinet, both to quiet him and to propitiate his influential sponsor, Lord Lansdowne.[27] But Russell loathed him and Lowe had so committed himself against Reform that his entry into the Cabinet could only alienate the radicals and those moderate Liberals who wanted a settlement. The best course was to try to remove him altogether and Russell offered him, as Lowe boasted, everything 'short of the Governor General of India, out of England'.[28] But Lowe knew that his deepest beliefs were about to be placed in hazard and he stayed to fight.

Russell even sought to continue the party truce by renewing Palmerston's invitation to the Conservative, Lord Stanley, to join the Cabinet. Stanley was disposed to accept, for his participation in the Ministry, as he explained to Disraeli, would help 'to strengthen the hands of the moderate as opposed to the thorough-going reformers'.[29] But Disraeli warned him against committing himself to Russell, especially on Reform. This was a reversal of opinion on Disraeli's part and it bewildered Stanley:

> Three weeks ago, you and I both thought that a very small bill, passed by Conservative support, would be the best solution of the difficulty; now you are against any bill. No doubt you have reasons for this altered view: but I don't know them, and can only take it on trust that they are good.[30]

Stanley, still pliant in Disraeli's hands, refused the offer. 'You understand tactics better than I do,' he wistfully concluded.[31]

Good reasons indeed would have been necessary to justify the rejection of this opportunity to continue the party truce and co-operate to settle Reform with a conservative bill. Yet Disraeli did not confide his thoughts to Stanley and, like him, we can only guess at them. Perhaps one of the reasons is adumbrated in Disraeli's letter to Ralph Earle, discussing the rumour that that Stanley was to form a coalition Ministry. Disraeli scorned the idea, arguing that as usual, the Whigs rapacity for office would hold them together and lead them to break any coalition they might enter.[32] He also believed that Russell would quickly be forced to give way to Gladstone, and that then the real battle for the landed interest and the Church would begin.[33] But if Russell annexed Stanley the attacks would be less easily repulsed. Disraeli saw the approach of the opportunity to engage with his rival, and given the balance of forces on Baines' motion, of destroying him. His vindictive envy of Gladstone was a prime determinant of his course in 1866-7.

Russell turned to the radicals only after he had been rebuffed by the conservative wing of his party. By 11 November he had decided to offer Goschen, Forster and W. E. Baxter immediate appointments outside the Cabinet and later, to promote Stansfeld.[34] Still, as his conversations with Forster show, Russell was still hoping to keep the peace by shunting the question off to a Commission, as demanded by Elcho and the Adullamites. The defeat of his Bill in 1860 had convinced him that no new measure should be attempted until its basis had been thoroughly calculated and the country and Parliament had shown themselves ready to accept it.[35] The 'Commission of Enquiry into the State of the Suffrage' was to make a thorough investigation lasting about two years, and subsequent to its report a bill might be drafted and presented towards the end of the Parliament. Russell and Brand hoped that the prospect of a bill would enable them

to manage the radicals and, next to there being no bill at all,
the establishment of a procrastinating Commission was the course
which was most likely to appease the Whigs and the members
for small boroughs.[36]

The Prime Minister had been warned, even before he made
his offer to Forster, that the radicals would not be content with
a Commission. They had intimated that they were willing to
proceed slowly, to await the collection of statistics by a committee of the House, and allow for lengthy consideration of the
drafting of the bill; but they would not permit the question to
be taken outside the House and deposited with an *ad hoc* body
whose report might be put aside. Stansfeld wanted a committee
of Cabinet to be formed as quickly as possible to gather electoral
statistics. 'The knowledge that some of us were so employed
would be the more perfect guarantee of your intentions', the
radicals' go-between, Sir Charles Wood, told Russell.[37]

On 16 November Lord John invited Forster to accept the
Under-Secretaryship for the Colonies:

> I made no hesitation, [Forster wrote in his diary] except on
> reform. He said Gladstone and he would bring in a bill. I
> stipulated for vertical extension. He assented, but said I might
> leave them if I did not like the details of the bill when I saw
> it. He used the word 'inquiry', and I said I trusted there would
> be no Commission, stating strong objections thereto. Upon
> that point he could not give me a distinct answer, so I agreed
> to call again on Saturday . . . after a Cabinet meeting.[38]

The Cabinet was apparently still averse to an immediate bill
because on Saturday 18th Russell was unable to assure Forster
that there would not be a Commission. 'My objections . . . he
heard very willingly [Forster recorded] and proposed I should
make my speech [at a coming Reform meeting at Bradford] and
he would write to me afterwards.'[39]

Russell was caught between his own preferences, which he
shared with the majority of his followers, and his necessity to
hold the support of his 'friends' below the gangway. But he was
swinging Forster's way. The latter felt bold enough to tell the
Prime Minister that, 'as he might not like what I said, I should
not think myself ill used if he then withdrew his offer'.[40]

Before the Reform meeting took place Forster received an
urgent letter from Brand imploring him not to commit himself

against a Commission of Enquiry and promising that it would be instituted in good faith and not meant for the purpose of delay. Forster replied that *any* Commission would entail delay and cast doubt upon the intentions of the Government; certainly it 'would be a wet-blanket to all support by reformers, and depend upon it anti-reformers are not to be conciliated or got round'.[41] The member for Bradford duly spoke at the meeting and called upon the Government to introduce a comprehensive Reform bill in the coming session.[42] On the following day, Russell received him cordially, and remarked that he had read his speech 'and like[d] it very much'. He then renewed the offer of the Under-Secretary-ship. The Prime Minister promised that the Cabinet would assemble its own information and so there was no more talk about the Commission. ' "You know",' he quoted Russell, ' "If you take office you must trust in Gladstone and me".'[43] Thus, after a month of searching for support, Lord John had once more come to terms with the Reformers. Although it may not have been clear to Russell at the time, and certainly it was not clear to the Palmerstonians in the Cabinet, Russell's abandonment of the Commission, with its potentialities for delay, meant that when figures were assembled there was nothing to hinder their forming the basis of an immediate bill.

Russell had already instructed the Poor Law Office in October to begin the collection of information for the projected Commission. This was partly because Russell believed it to be the proper procedure, and partly because he wanted to forestall Elcho and the Adullamites, who were threatening to press for it. The Poor Law Office was to ascertain the numbers of ratepayers in parliamentary boroughs at each one pound level from ten pounds down to six, and the numbers of county ratepayers and occupiers at £12, £15 and £20.[44] A clear annual value of £6 was his lowest limit, and Russell never once contemplated giving the vote below that level. He cheerfully assured Sir George Grey that the figures would be complete by the end of January.[45]

Despite his lifelong preoccupation with electoral reform, Russell was still far from comprehending the almost infinite variety of local rating arrangements. The disparities increased as the levels approached £6 and began to entwine with the mesh of compounding systems. However, Russell knew from his investigations in 1860 that inequalities in the suffrage qualifications did stem from rating differences, and as a way to uniformity he

considered reviving his 1860 plan of basing the borough qualification on net rental. Sir Charles Wood quickly dissuaded him by
pointing out that a rental condition would be even more variable
and open to abuse, especially if claims were to be founded on
rent receipt-books, and registers had to be compiled independently of the rate-books.[46] The old system of basing a national
administrative arrangement upon a localized sub-structure was
proving unworkable under the pressure of numbers and the
desire for uniformity; but the idea of a centrally directed registration and rating system was still unthinkable, outside Ireland. This
exchange between Russell and Wood was typical of the former's
attitude throughout his second premiership. Gladstone already
had a much closer knowledge of the difficulties surrounding the
rating figures but, except in periods of immediate crisis, Russell
tended to consult with his Whig cronies rather than confide in
his Chancellor of the Exchequer.

On 10 December Russell rejected a final bid from the Whigs
for a postponement. He told Sir George Grey that he could not
consent to the latter's moving for an Enquiry because 'such a
motion . . . would be prompted not by a desire for information,
but by a desire to evade the question'. Instead, he announced the
principles of his Reform Bill, though the returns were still far
from complete. The Bill was to contain a £6 borough rating
qualification and a small redistribution, though Russell added
by way of conciliation that there would be no outright disfranchisement. 'Bright would [not] have any chance of carrying
a large measure for re-distribution . . . after such a Bill was
carried', he explained, in an effort to mollify the Whigs. He
offered a further reassurance by pointing out that it would take
a year to pass the Bill and two more years to define the new
boundaries and compile the registers, and so there could not be a
fresh election until 1868 at least.[47]

While the Prime Minister happily issued orders about the main
features of the Bill, the task of preparing its details fell to
Gladstone, and Lord John apparently gave him little help.
Although Russell had informed Grey of the £6 level on 10 December, he confirmed it to Gladstone only on New Year's Day, 1866.
Gladstone had to reply accepting the £6 for ordinary ratepayers,
but pointing out that it could not apply to compounders, who
would have to come in at £8 to assimilate their part-rates to the
level of those who paid in full.[48] Gladstone wanted to proceed

slowly and surely. He was keen to work on his budget, but found himself toiling day and night with the returns, for it was becoming obvious, as they accumulated, that they were both defective and startling in their information.[49]

Others were doing their homework, too:

> The more I think of it [Wood wrote to de Grey] the more difficult I think it is to hit the right point, which will satisfy the H. of C. I might almost say, satisfy ourselves. It is extraordinary how difficult it is to obtain really accurate information. I have been 3 weeks in trying to get from Sheffield a very simple account of a small number of tenements and have not got it right yet.[50]

Charles Adderley, the Conservative, met with M. T. Bass, the radical, just after the latter had collated the statistics for Burton and Derby and found that with a £6 franchise 78 per cent of the electorate would be workingmen. 'Bass is in great terror of the amiable working class', he told Disraeli. But the member for Derby still wanted the suffrage lowered to £6: 'Bass's hope is that a lower franchise wld reach a Class of W'm more under their Masters' influence. He says the present £10 W'm are intolerable.'[51]

At the end of the first week in January the whole question of a bill was thrown back into flux. It had become clear that there was a huge and totally unsuspected number of £10 working-class men already on the rolls, and that the number in houses valued between £6 and £10 was very great.[52]

The news aggravated the existing discord in the Cabinet. The majority, Lord Clarendon, Sir George Grey, the Earl de Grey, the Duke of Somerset, Cardwell and Lord Stanley of Alderley, wanted either to ignore Reform altogether or shelve it with a Commission, while the rest, Gladstone, Villiers, Gibson and the Duke of Argyll wanted to make a timetable for a genuine settlement. The Palmerstonians now redoubled their attempts to force Russell to drop the Bill. He moved to strengthen his hand by promoting a young, moderate Reformer, G. J. Goschen, to the Cabinet as Chancellor of the Duchy of Lancaster. The appointment aroused great hostility in the party. Goschen had only been in Parliament for three years and he had German mercantile antecedents. The Whigs in the Cabinet were furious that Russell should try to out-manoeuvre them, and that the Marquis of Hartington should have been passed over; Russell was obliged to promote him in the following month. 'The Göschen business was done in the most thoro'ly Johnian style,' Clarendon told Lady Salisbury. 'Nobody was thought of *by* John *but* John. He believed it would improve his position and he cared nothing for the feelings of others.'[53]

Russell failed in his purpose. Goschen proved a broken reed in the Cabinet and usually sided with the Palmerstonians against Reform. The promotion only damaged party morale for the crisis ahead. The Barings, A. H. Layard, and Knatchbull-Hugessen were all disaffected by the move. Knatchbull-Hugessen, who had already had one blunt demand for a place ignored, began to plan the downfall of the Ministry in a secret correspondence with the chief Conservative agent.[54]

Meanwhile the Reformers in the Cabinet were being peppered with instructions from Bright. He was insistent that the Bill should have a 'solid basis' of £6 in the boroughs and £10 in the counties, or even household suffrage with strict residence qualifications. He wanted the Bill to be a 'single-barrelled one', dealing only with the suffrage, for in that form it would draw less opposition from those who feared a redistribution. Besides, redistribution could 'be dealt with much better in a Parliament elected on the wider suffrage'.[55]

Bright's well-publicized demand for a single-barrelled bill put Russell and the Ministerial Reformers in a dilemma. Russell wanted to round off the Bill with a minimal redistribution, both to spike the radicals' guns and to make a settlement, while Sir George Grey and the Palmerstonians wanted no redistribution at all. But this was the course Russell feared most, for it would give the country the impression that he and his Government were captive to the radicals. 'I feel grave doubts about the proposal not to touch the Seats,' he wrote to Grey. 'Bright has shown his cards, and if we follow suit we shall be considered his partners.'[56] In fact, the Bill emerged without a redistribution scheme, although this arose not as the outcome of a definite decision, but because Gladstone was too busy to prepare one.[57]

The Bill was promised for 12 March, but the nearer that day approached the greater became the difficulties and embarrassments which beset the Government. January and February saw the worst months of the Cattle Plague which afflicted nearly the whole kingdom, and the spread of the bitter controversy about Governor Eyre. When the House met in February the members were preoccupied with the amount of compensation to be paid for the losses caused by the Plague.

We don't think much yet about reform, [Clarendon wrote to Bloomfield on the 14th] because we are exclusively occupied with the Cattle plague. When one considers how large a rôle land plays in both Houses and the sore abatement in rents that must take place, it is not wonderful that agriculturalists should weep and refuse to be comforted.[58]

The Ministry was also confronted with a rival Reform Bill. The radical, James Clay, the lifelong friend of Disraeli, had introduced a Bill to extend the borough suffrage by providing for an educational test, rather than by reducing the rating or rental level. Clay and his odd bevy of Tory, Palmerstonian and radical supporters may have been perfectly genuine in their assertion that an examination in 'writing from dictation . . . simple addition, subtraction, multiplication and division of money',[59] was a more apt test for the personal and citizenship qualities of the prospective voter than the rating level of the house he occupied. The real function of the examination, Clay argued, was not to try the candidate's learning but the self-improvement he had undergone in preparing himself for it.[60] (Clay's test, incidentally, was harder than the Civil Service examination for clerkships.) Cranborne, Horsman and Elcho espoused it as a respectable way of embarrassing the Government,[61] and Clay's own motives may not have been the highest, for he had already begun to negotiate secretly with Disraeli for Tory support.[62] Clay's scheme was practicable and, as befitted the brain-child of the great authority on whist, much more logical and likely to endure than an arbitrary line imposed upon an ill-defined legalism related to property. He may have hoped that by forestalling the Government he could make them incorporate the examination principle into their Bill. Still, the move coincided with the tactics of the Adullamites and Tories.

The Government's own Bill, meanwhile, was lurching through a series of crises and hasty transformations which afflicted it almost until the day of its début in the House. Russell and Gladstone were constant in their intention that the Bill should make a sizeable addition to the working-class proportion of the electorate, yet not threaten the supremacy of the upper classes: so they set out to control the extension very precisely, but soon found that they could rely on the statistics only to the extent of fixing the general limits of the enfranchisement. The changes which the Bill underwent reflected the successive discoveries of gaps and errors in the information. The Ministers at the Cabinet of 11 January were shocked by the numbers of workingmen found to be already enrolled; they abandoned the levels Russell had decided upon and agreed not to fix any new ones until more information was to hand.[63] A fortnight later Russell and Gladstone agreed to discard rental as the ground of the borough qualification, and to settle for a £6 rating, 'as being, in so far as our present knowledge goes, decidedly the best . . . basis on which we can take our stand'.[64]

Early in February, John Lambert, the Poor Law Board official responsible for collecting the statistics, submitted a memorandum to the Cabinet showing that it was impossible to calculate accurately the effects of a £6 rating suffrage and that the rating levels were so uneven as to make almost any rating franchise scheme unworkable. On the 12th Argyll informed the Cabinet that because of the peculiar valuation and ratal system operating in Scotland and the very low rates that resulted from it, the Bill would be inoperative north of the Tweed. Gladstone, Milner-Gibson, Russell and Argyll thereupon decided to switch to a rental franchise. The other wing of the Cabinet—Grey, Stanley of Alderley and Somerset—angrily opposed the change. They seized the opportunity to point out that this hasty alteration was but one more proof that the whole undertaking was premature, and that the original plan for a Commission should be persevered with.[65] Thenceforth they washed their hands of the Bill, and at the meeting of 24 February they walked out when Gladstone, Russell and Milner-Gibson ignored their objections, and decided to confirm the basis of the Bill at £7 gross estimated rental.[66]

On 1 March Lambert presented a second memorandum describing the difficulties of collecting the numbers of potential voters. In twelve houses in the Strand, the rents of the occupancies varied between 1s. 6d. and 5s. 6d. a week, depending upon the floor on which they were situated, their size, condition and appurtenances. The houses had each, on average, four separate tenants, and most of the tenancies were sub-let, which meant that the occupiers' names did not appear on the rate-books. Even the names of the primary lessees were usually not entered, as the rates were paid by the owner, or commonly, his agent.

There were two other sets of information necessary for calculating the effects of an extension of the franchise which the rate-books could hardly provide at all. The frequent omission of the tenant's name opposite the occupancy column meant that it was impossible to make a confident estimate of the number of female householders, and the entries gave no indication of the length of the householder's period of residence. Lambert guessed that up to a half of the occupiers between £7 and £10 were female, and that a further third of the total would not fulfil the twelve months' residence requirement. And if he found it 'impossible . . . to arrive at any estimate . . . of the increase which would take place in the several Metropolitan Constituencies', where the rating systems were comparatively straightforward, he would have had even less chance of calculating the increase in boroughs like Exeter, Birmingham, Oxford, Sheffield and York, where the collecting and compounding arrangements were very strange and intricate.[67]

In the midst of these troubles, Gladstone was being hectored by Bright, who told him what he already knew, that the Cabinet's delay in settling the principles of the Bill and bringing it before the House was gravely damaging the prospects of both the Bill and the Government: 'Bouverie & all who are angry at being left out of your office arrangements, will do all the mischief they can, & the whole concern will become disorganized before the Bill is before us.' His diagnosis was apt, if unfair as it applied to Gladstone. He continued:

> You have had 3 months in which to frame a Bill, which any man knowing anything of the subject could have done in a week—& the Bill is not only not drawn, but its very purpose & extent are not yet determined.
>
> You have been hunting for figures from Parish officers to prove how many working men are now Electors—as if a great question like this were to be decided in a huckstering spirit, & as if a few thousands of Electors more or less were of the smallest consequence.[68]

The Cabinet was still wrangling between rental or rating only five days before the Bill was due to be introduced. Russell was afraid, apparently, of calling his Ministers together, and resorted to circularizing them with a memorandum setting out the advantages of a £7 gross estimated rental qualification, as suggested by Milner-Gibson:

It would be sufficient, to show that £7 . . . rental is a fair test
of what a good workman could afford to pay for his house, &
that the numbers thereby added would be a [strictly?] limited
addition to the £10 householders now on the register, & would
not give any preponderance of power to the working classes.
In fact except in some five boroughs the middle classes,
strengthen'd by the best of the artisans would still have the
preponderance of power.[69]

Gladstone, Milner-Gibson and the Duke of Argyll supported the
proposal and Sir George Grey, Lord Stanley of Alderley, Lord
Clarendon and the Duke of Somerset vehemently opposed it.[70]
The position was desperate; Russell overruled their objections and
instructed Gladstone and Thring to proceed with the final drafting. Amidst all the haste, at least one copy of the Bill was
printed and published with 'six' pounds instead of 'seven' as the
qualification.[71]

So, after months of indecision, the Russell Government was
embarked on the mighty task of improving the British Constitution. The Government had been returned in support of a leader
who since 1832 had been opposed or lukewarm to Reform, and
who had not mentioned it in his nomination speech. Indeed, by
ignoring Reform, Palmerston had implicitly dismissed it from his
future programme. Most of his supporters had taken a similar
negative stand, and they had been endorsed by the country. The
Government was launched into Reform despite the early plans
of its new leader and against the wishes of the majority of the
Cabinet. The Ministers were without the information they
believed to be necessary for the design of the Bill, and like their
followers in the House, they were without unanimity and
enthusiasm when it came to defending it. Indeed, like many of
their followers, they were looking forward to its demise. Few
government bills of such importance can have had such contin-
gent and inauspicious origins.

II The Franchise Bill

Gladstone introduced the Reform Bill of 1866 with unwonted
diffidence. He commended the measure, not by invoking its prospective enfranchisement, but by emphasizing the ways in which
it would uphold the *status quo*. The defensive cast of his speech
reflected the trouble he had had in using the returns and his

qualms about the hasty manner in which the Bill had been considered in the Cabinet. The returns should have formed the matrix of his argument but by showing that 126,000 or 26 per cent, of the borough constituency were workingmen they robbed him of his main justification for the Bill, while their imperfections denied him the chance of presenting it as statistically foolproof. The figures were only useful to him where they demonstrated the Government's conservative intentions: as when he explained the switch from £6 to £7 by showing that the lower qualification would admit too many artisans. There were 488,000 men on the English and Welsh borough registers, 362,000 of whom were of the upper classes, and the remainder workingmen. A £6 rental qualification would admit about 242,000 men, nearly all working-class, and that 'would place the working class in a clear majority upon the constituency. Well . . . I do not think . . . we are called upon by any . . . sufficient consideration . . . to give over the majority of town constituencies into the hands of the working class. We propose, therefore, to take the figure next above . . . namely a clear annual value of £7'.[72] This would add 156,000, of whom only 144,000 were workingmen.

Gladstone went on to argue that the proposed £7 level would mean, in effect, a much higher outlay by the prospective voter. 'Seven pounds clear annual value' represented the gross estimated rental exclusive of local rates and surcharges for furniture and repairs. These usually amounted to 60 per cent of the gross estimated rental, that is, £4. 4s. 0d. at £7, so that the gross annual outlay by a £7 householder was £11. 4s. 0d. On the assumption that an artisan spent one-sixth of his income on his residence, this would represent an annual income of £67. 4s. 0d., or 26s. a week. So Gladstone arrived at the selection mechanism. Twenty-six shillings a week was 'unattainable by the peasantry or mere hand labourers, except under very favourable circumstances [while] it is . . . an income very generally attainable by the artisans and skilled labourers of our towns'.[73] He made the 26s. level seem more embracing than it would perhaps have been, for it would have excluded all but those included in Dudley Baxter's 'Higher Skilled Labour and Manufacturers' division'.[74]

The rest of the Bill was shaped from the measures of 1852 and 1854. The Government planned to solve the compounder difficulty by allowing them to claim to have their names entered in the rate-books. Gladstone asserted, apparently quite arbitrarily, that this amendment would allow about 60,000 householders to qualify.[75] The Bill also contained two of the fancy franchises of 1854. In the boroughs there was to be a £10 lodger qualification and in the counties one for a £50 savings bank deposit. Gladstone estimated that the savings bank clause would extend the vote to 10,000 or 15,000 men, but he admitted that he had no statistics at all for lodgers and refused even to guess at the numbers who would qualify. But, as it was 'a middle-class rather than a lower-class enfranchisement', it was undoubtedly safe.[76]

In the counties the Government proposed to reduce the occupation franchise from £50 to £14, and to allow county leaseholders and copyholders resident in parliamentary boroughs to vote in the county in which their holding was situated. As in the Bill of 1854, the clause provided that the occupation had to be in house and land. The reduction was designed to admit 172,000 middle-class voters. Once again, Gladstone justified the change, not by the number of men it would enfranchise, but by the fact that a £14 level would still exclude the great bulk of the workingmen:

> The number of persons properly belonging to the working classes and having a £14 rental . . . will be so very small . . . as not to be worth taking into calculation. Or at the least . . . that . . . portion of the newly enfranchised . . . as may belong to the labouring class, will be tenants of small holdings of land in immediate connection with the landed class.[77]

But this was disguising the issue. As in 1852 and 1854, the Liberals were attempting, through the occupation clause, to give county votes to likely Liberal supporters in the boroughs. Nevertheless, their motives were not completely partial. They were trying to stabilize a constituency which was normally a decreasing one, and to make the county representation reflect the range of interests which the counties had come to contain.

In general, the Bill was meant to enfranchise about 400,000 men, half of whom were thought to be of the gentry and professional classes and half working-class. 172,000 voters were to be added to the county constituency of 550,000 and 204,000 were to be added to the boroughs, while the remaining 24,000 new voters were to qualify by the fancy franchises. The existing borough constituency of 488,000 represented about 36 per cent of the total male occupiers in boroughs, and the new total of 692,000 would still only amount to about 51 per cent of them.

Even assuming that the 204,000 new borough voters were all workingmen, the working-class share of the electorate would only be 330,000, and leave about 588,000 working-class borough occupiers still unenfranchised. There were 5,300,000 adult males in England and Wales in 1865, and the Bill was intended to create an aggregate constituency of 1,300,000; one man in four would have had the vote instead of one in five—it was hardly an extravagant enfranchisement.

In the early stages of the debate no Palmerstonian rose to support the Bill. C. P. Villiers was the only Minister, apart from Gladstone, who essayed to defend it, and he was half-hearted. He neglected its virtues and instead cited Catholic Emancipation and the Repeal of the Corn Laws as instances of changes that had been forced on Parliament by outside pressure, after it had failed to legislate in time.[78] His speech had little to do with the Bill, but it was an apt piece of prophecy. Among the moderate Liberals, only T. D. Acland, the philanthropic squire and friend of Gladstone, commended it. He approved the admission of a limited number of deserving artisans and was 'glad to say that the measure would . . . strengthen the Liberal party in the county representation'.[79]

The radicals were disappointed that the Bill did not go as far as household suffrage and the ballot, but McLaren spoke for them when he accepted the £7 level as the lowest which the House would be likely to carry.[80]

The Palmerstonian and Tory opponents of the Bill used the weaknesses in the returns as the basis for their assertion that the Bill would neither filter the prospective voters finely enough nor uphold the balance of classes. Samuel Laing, the shrewd and cantankerous Palmerstonian from Wick, cut to the heart of the Bill by arguing that the Government's proposed rental qualification was too indiscriminate a mechanism to ensure the selection of the best of the artisans. Instead, he wanted the occupation level to be kept at £10 and 'the franchise [to be] . . . extended by plans based upon intelligence and providence', which meant Clay's Bill.[81] The burden of Gladstone's speech had been the preservation of the exclusive electorate. Laing used the variations in rent given in the returns to prove to the Palmerstonians and Tories that a £7 qualification was a dangerous way of attempting it. As the Tory Butler-Johnstone explained, before they could vote for the Bill they had 'to know what share the working classes were to have . . . and ought not to be told to take a leap in the dark'.[82]

The Conservatives had joined the attack slowly and cautiously. Initially their role was played for them by the dissident Palmerstonians and played more effectively than they themselves could have done. Like the Liberals, they were divided and virtually leaderless. Derby had almost retired after his blunder over the Roman Catholics in the 1865 election and he had persuaded himself that the Conservatives would never again enjoy office in his lifetime. He was sixty-six, increasingly subject to the gout, and after spending most of the last thirty years as a member of a fragmented minority party, he was tired of politics. Yet he was loath to surrender the leadership he had held for twenty years, and so he continued at the head of his party without meeting his followers collectively and without consulting with his senior colleagues except for occasional correspondence with Disraeli about general tactics.

So the back-bench Tories were allowed to drag the party into disadvantageous positions on the Malt Tax, Cattle Plague Compensation and the suspension of Governor Eyre. Derby seemed also to be ready to let the party drift on Reform, for he ignored Carnarvon's early attempts to goad him into announcing his opposition to the Bill. Carnarvon feared that Derby would let the Bill through if it promised to bury the question with a conservative settlement. Such quietism had been safe enough while Palmerston was in charge, but Carnarvon saw that it was hazardous with Johnny Russell. He told Malmesbury:

> that some fuller communication from Lord D., at least as to his wishes and intentions, is necessary if things are to go on. No meetings are ever held . . . and though all this was possible . . . with Palmerston . . . it will be very . . . dangerous, to pursue the same course now, when everything is . . . changed.

Malmesbury agreed and remarked that, 'the real misfortune is the almost total want of hearty communication between him and Disraeli. The latter does not court it, the former is too proud to press it'.[83] Carnarvon was half Derby's age and his Toryism was a curious blend of romanticism and tough-mindedness. He believed in the paternalism of the medieval nobility and he was resolved that their descendents in the nineteenth century should retain their power in Parliament in order that they might continue their protection of the Church and the landed interest. He determined to organize a Tory opposition to the Bill.[84]

It was not until 8 March, a month after the session had begun, that Derby was induced to call a meeting of his followers. He alone addressed it and advised his men to withhold judgment on the forthcoming Bill and not to commit themselves against Reform. Earlier, he had rejected an approach from the Palmerstonian, Lord Elcho, backed by Disraeli, asking that the Conservatives support him in pressing for a commission.[85] Later that day Disraeli, Northcote, Cranborne, Sir William Heathcote and Spencer Walpole met secretly at the House of Commons and agreed to speak in support of Elcho and Lowe when they attacked the Bill on the following Monday.[86] Thus the decision to oppose Russell's Bill was taken against the probable intention of the party leader and without the acquiescence of the general body of the party.

The initiative for the secret meeting came, apparently, from Carnarvon. He had been warned that two influential Tories, Henley and Walpole, the rebels of 1859, were disposed to support the Bill if it should promise a restrictive settlement. This, coming upon his suspicion of his leader's intentions, determined him to save the party. He wrote to Sir William Heathcote to urge him to dissuade Walpole, and added that 'Lord D. and D. . . . are . . . doing everything they can to wreck the ship'. Heathcote's reply must have rattled him, for the former was known as a sound High Tory, but Heathcote confessed that he too would be relieved to see the question closed.[87] Carnarvon had thus to commit his leaders against the Bill before it entered the House and won acceptance. After Derby's indecisive speech of that morning, he was free to nobble Walpole and Heathcote without finding himself forced to lead an open revolt.

Before and during the party meeting on 8 March Disraeli moved cautiously on Reform, whilst waiting to see the ways Derby and the young magnates might take. His position in the party was still insecure, and he was dependent upon Derby as a bulwark against the squires, especially the Peelite-Conservatives. Only six months earlier he had nearly lost the leadership in the Commons, and survived mainly because the possible alternatives, General Peel and Lord Stanley, cancelled each other out. The back benchers would have supported Peel, but he refused to come forward and then spoilt Stanley's chances by declaring that he would not serve under him.[88] Disraeli's one concern with Reform was the protection of the landed interest: the extension of the franchise in the towns was but one more unit in the political game. Already he had sponsored a Reform measure to strengthen the landed interest in 1859 and opposed a Bill which threatened it in 1860. It suited his ambitions to fight Russell's Bill, but he waited until Derby had again renounced any aggressive role for the Conservatives and the young lords had moved against the Bill before he sided with them.

He was also persuaded to oppose the Bill by the likelihood of a major split among the Liberals for now that Palmerston was gone the alliance of gentry and commercial men was likely to break. He quickly appreciated that he could use the Palmerstonians to smash Russell's majority, bring down the Ministry and come into office himself. Since early February he had been savouring the prospect of inviting Lowe and Horsman to join his Cabinet.[89] But he needed the assurance that the Whig magnates would move against the Bill before he dared make himself independent of Derby and set out to defeat Russell. Cranborne, who had conferred with Elcho, brought to the secret meeting the assurance 'that Lord Grosvenor was trying to get a meeting of moderate Whigs against the Reform Bill'. 'Dis. thinks this very important,' Northcote recorded. 'He says Lord D. will now do nearly as he is told.'[90]

The Conservative Party was not informed that they were to oppose the Bill until 16 March. Derby, again stricken with gout, was absent from the meeting and Disraeli addressed the members in his stead. According to Northcote:

> Dis. made a capital speech . . . throwing all the blame of the present agitation upon W.E.G.; objecting principally to the county franchise proposed in this bill,—especially the admission of copyholders and leaseholders in boroughs to vote for the counties, and still more to the fragmentary character of the measure. He said it was obviously our duty unanimously to oppose the bill . . . but that we must leave it to our leaders to decide in what form the opposition had better be made, having reference . . . to the . . . dispositions of our friends on the other side.[91]

The back benchers were glad to be given a lead that accorded with their prejudices. The county men were reassured of the defence of their constituencies, and the borough members were heartened by Disraeli's promise to fight the suffrage extension and redistribution. Equally important, Disraeli had produced a scapegoat and held out the prospect of a Conservative victory in the House for the first time in years. The members came from the meeting cheered, and ready for battle.[92]

Their determination to defend the counties was consistent with their stand since 1830. The county seats were inadequate as a source of a parliamentary majority and the Conservative electoral strength in them was being increasingly challenged by urban intrusion, but the Conservative gentlemen desperately clung to them as the last preserve of the landed interest. When they learned of the contents of the Bill the proprietors were horrified by the £14 level and the leasehold clause, as these threatened to swell enormously the shopkeeper and artisan voting element in the market towns. Lord Robert Montagu told the House that in Huntingdonshire 'there were five large towns, [only] one of which was a borough. By the proposed reduction . . . the Chancellor of the Exchequer would be handing the power over entirely from the rich farmers . . . to the small shopkeepers'.[93] Montagu and Cranborne joined in demanding a redistribution bill similar to the Tories' Bill of 1859, to take the town voters out of the county constituencies and seal off the rural parts of the counties.[94]

The Conservatives were deeply perturbed by the revelation that nine borough constituencies already contained working-class majorities and that the Bill would add to the lower-class numbers without providing a demonstrably safe compensation of upper-class votes. They soon learned from Lowe and Cranborne that the Bill would annihilate the power of the gentry and inaugurate the decline of parliamentary government. Their prognostications were derived from their theory of the role of individuals in politics: that each voted rationally and selfishly to protect his immediate interests. Because individuals of the lower orders lacked wealth and social standing, they would combine to use their electoral power to take wealth from the upper classes and to diminish the social privileges of their betters. Charles Schreiber, for example, argued that if the workingmen gained the vote they would begin to imitate middle-class standards of food and dress; to help keep themselves in their new style the workingmen would press for the reduction of indirect taxation and would ally themselves with the mercantile interest to agitate for direct taxation on 'the only things direct taxes could be levied on—land and income'. Unless Reform were stopped, 'the fantastic experiments of . . . the Liverpool Financial Reform Association' would become realities, and the workingmen would get above themselves by evading their fair contribution to the national expenses.[95]

Cranborne believed that the lowly educational and economic condition of the workingmen inhibited their understanding of the laws of political economy. If they achieved power they would violate the laws in a vain attempt to hasten the betterment of their class. They would impose protection, curb the free supply of labour, and ruin agriculture, in particular, by demanding a minimum wage of 8s. a week. Moreover, on economic grounds, they had no right to power, for they contributed far less than the upper classes in direct taxation, and the total sum of indirect taxation paid by them, considering their vast numbers, was disproportionately small. Cranborne visualized the State as akin to a joint stock company in which those who had proved their eligibility by holding the greatest number of shares also held the voting rights: 'The main object [of the House was] the management of finance, the collection and expenditure of taxes, and . . . an ideal . . . Constitution . . . would allow the people to vote in the expenditure of the taxes, somewhat in proportion to the amount they contribute.'[96] But behind these rational arguments lay an unreasoning fear of the masses and a determination not to yield power to them by any Reform. It was a dangerous call to preserve a caste system of government that had been rendered fragile by social change. Cranborne's implicit demand that the exclusive Constitution should be upheld by force ran counter the the trend of political development since 1830. The semblance of government by consent would be replaced by the realities of oligarchy.

At this early stage Cranborne and Montagu were unusual among the Conservatives in explicitly condemning the enfranchisement of workingmen. The back-benchers seem to have been at once more flexible and more practical in their objections. Meller, Whiteside and Banks Stanhope, for example, wanted a 'settlement' but they emphasized the dire effects this Bill would produce in the counties and dilated upon the uncertainties in the returns and the Ministry's precipitateness in bringing down legislation.[97]

Robert Lowe, the cold middle-class intellectual, emerged as
the spokesman for the landed opponents of the Bill. In his
magnificent orations of 1866 he gave the case against Reform a
universality and consistency that transcended the narrow interest
arguments of the gentry. While they appealed to tradition and
the worth of the landed classes, he brilliantly related his stand
to the contemporary progress of the nation. Lowe asserted that
the balance of classes in the representation was already perfect:
the great interests of the nation had since 1846 reached a condition in which none was predominant and each had to strive to
better itself and, in so doing, contribute to the general comfort.
The prosperity of British farming, the expansion of manufactures,
the growth of class harmony and the spread of British influence
abroad, all attested to the freedom of enterprise that existed
under the rule of enlightened men. Their rule was sustained by
the recently established equilibrium between the permanent
interest of the land and the volatile interests of commerce. The
equilibrium was delicate and to tamper with the parliamentary
system by reinforcing the commercial, urban interests with the
votes of the least instructed could lead only to the dominance of
this single interest and so to the decay of British greatness.

In Lowe's view, there was no overriding philosophical reason
why the franchise should be extended. In the existing Constitution one man might not have as much power as another, but
there had never been a State in which this had been so and,
given the purpose for which government existed, it never could
be so: 'Government does not deal with justice. It deals with
expediency. . . . We may violate any law of symmetry, equality,
or distributive justice in providing the proper machinery to
enable us to do what is required of us.'[98] No extension, however
minimal and perfectly calculated, and no allocation of dual votes
to the educated classes would survive as a permanent settlement once the existing balance was upset. The increase of
industrialization and prosperity made 'uniformity and democracy'
inevitable in the future: the only hope was to stay its onset by
defending the present Constitution. The qualification was better
left at £10, to compel those workingmen who wished to join the
exclusive electorate to elevate themselves by thrift.[99]

Government was the highest expression of the aspirations of
an ordered society. It existed to uphold the social hierarchy and
the possession of property, to manage the defence of the nation

and to protect learning and the arts. The efficiency with which these objects were pursued could be tested by the economy achieved by the administration and the degree to which it enabled private interests to contribute to the public good. Recent experience and the lessons of the past showed that governments performed these functions best when the educated and wealthy predominated in the Constitution. These orders alone possessed the intellectual and material freedom to take such decisions as best served all classes. Their sense of security, born of their superiority of station and learning, allowed them to sift public questions in a disinterested manner.

Men of the lower classes, on the other hand, because they had constantly to labour at manual tasks in order to survive, had no opportunity to acquire education, while their dependent status precluded them from exercising such qualities of free judgment and leadership as they might possess. The executive powers of government were based ultimately upon compulsion and necessarily involved the truncation of the liberty of every member of the society. Each vote represented a mortgage upon the property and liberty of every other member and for this reason the vote could not safely be handed over to any one class, especially the enormous class of the improvident, which would use its dominance to satisfy its own uncivilized desires. Governments had no call to meddle in those private economic and social arrangements between individuals which were subject to the natural laws of political economy and could find their most advantageous expression when they were untrammelled by legislation. But because of their relatively weaker bargaining position the working classes would seek restrictive legislation in these spheres to the detriment of the free market.

Lowe claimed that his arguments against Reform, unlike the 'sentimental, metaphysical . . . and abstract' pleas for it, were 'all . . . drawn . . . from considerations purely practical . . . on the Inductive method'.[1] There were available working models of popular governments, and by use of the inductive method it was possible to discover the tendencies inherent in States controlled by the populace and to predict the fate of Britain if Parliament surrendered to the Reformers. The lower orders held power in New South Wales, France and the United States, and all educated men knew the histories of Greece and Rome. In each case the populace had shown itself incapable of considering policy in a rational, informed and unselfish way. The lower orders were intolerant and violent, they had small understanding and were usually bellicose in foreign affairs, while in domestic matters they pursued their own apparent economic betterment at the expense of the common weal.

Lowe knew from his experience of New South Wales that the participation of the mob made elections rowdy, and that candidates sought the plaudits of the crowd by offering rash promises. The politicians bowed to the fact that the poorest classes directed their votes to the improvement of working conditions and to taxing the rich to pay for the increased expenditure on public works. So the demagogues of New South Wales had introduced Protection, and the other colonies ruled by the populace, Victoria and Canada and the United States, had done likewise.[2]

His picture of that colony was a travesty, but it passed largely uncontradicted in the House. New South Wales had not achieved responsible government when Lowe was there in the forties, the franchise had been highly restrictive, the official doctrine had been Free Trade, and to cap the irony, the 'White-headed Angel' had been one of the more irresponsible of the local demagogues. However, Lowe's account of democracy in the colony was endorsed by M. H. Marsh, the Whig member for Salisbury. Like Robert Lowe, he had made his fortune in the Antipodes and had returned home to enjoy the perquisites of a gentleman in an ordered class structure, and to use his fortune to join the House of Commons. His references to Australia, like those of Lowe, betray an uneasy mixture of affection for the land which had raised his condition, and of rancour towards the society he had forsaken because it could not support him in the style his ambition had led him to expect. He, too, had left the colony before it achieved responsible government, but he readily assumed the posture of an Old Colonial Hand, to dilate upon the evils which followed from an unselective voting system.

Marsh contended that the numerical predominance of the lower orders in the electorate had smashed the political and social control formerly exercised by the educated classes. Gentlemen had been replaced in the administration by ignorant, pushful workingmen, while the general incursion into the legislature of poorly-spoken, uncouth men had driven the representatives of the educated classes into retirement. The amorphous society of the colony, bereft of the leadership of its landed and professional classes, was slipping into chaos. The schools were perishing by neglect, the magistracy was recruited from the lowest classes, with the result that 'the fountain of justice . . . [was] poisoned'. The trade unions in New South Wales stood as dreadful warning to the Mother Country. They were similar to their counterparts in Britain in being led by agitators who paid no regard to political economy, but they possessed a further vice in that the agitators used them to mobilize the voting power of the lower orders to press for an eight-hour day.[3]

The arguments from Australian experience, because they related to a community that was still British, were compelling for those members who were averse to Reform, but the lessons from France and America aroused more immediate reactions. The members had travelled in France; she was still the national enemy and there had been a war scare only eight years before. Marsh pointed out that 'in France under universal suffrage at the present moment . . . the press was completely gagged' and civil freedom had everywhere been curtailed,[4] while Cranborne added that the experience of France after 1848 showed that once the workingmen achieved power they would tax the upper classes to pay for *ateliers nationaux*.[5] Both agreed that the course of French history, since the mob had overturned the traditional order in 1789, had demonstrated the instability of ministries subject to the masses and the inevitability of despotisms.

If the course of French democracy perhaps exemplified the political incapacity of the Latins, the case of the United States showed how a society of Anglo-Saxon origins could collapse into social equality and mob-rule. The issue of slavery and the Civil War placed America in the forefront of discussion in Britain in the sixties. The radical improvers generally backed the Union, while the ruling caste widely sympathized with the Confederacy. To the radicals, the North was the land of free endeavour, where there existed, according to John Bright, 'a free church, a free school, free land, a free vote, and a free career for the child of the humblest born in the land'. America was, in short, the model for a progressive, industrialized Britain.[6]

The opponents of Reform were obsessed with the example of American democracy partly because they knew of it, at least by hearsay, from a text which appeared to demonstrate universal laws about the tendencies of industrialized societies towards social equality, vulgarity, and governmental instability. Alexis de

Tocqueville's *Democracy in America,* in Reeve's misleading translation, together with his dogmatic notes,[7] demonstrated abundantly the evils of democratic government and the inevitability of their transference to Britain if the suffrage were extended. The opposition read Tocqueville as claiming that authority in America was diffuse and ineffectual. Separation of the executive and the legislature, the dependence of the judiciary, and the proliferation of the bureaucracy all reflected a community in which distinctions of rank had been erased. In America, those traditions of duty and deference, which sustained authority in Britain, had been destroyed. Thanks to the supremacy of the lower classes and their voting 'machines', the representatives of the educated and leisured classes had been driven—as in Australia—out of politics. Mill, Bagehot and Grey pointed to the poor quality of Congressional debates as evidence of the sorry education of American politicians. Such debates could hardly 'instruct' the nation as did those conducted in the House of Commons.[8] The ineptitude of lower-class politicians allowed the bureaucracy to usurp power on vital matters like taxation, and to become corrupt. The judiciary, which in Britain served as an unassailable buffer between the rulers and the ruled, was amenable to popular sentiment in America because it was elective, with the result that the independence and continuity of interpretation of the law was broken, and the equity which derived from it was lost. Democratic ministries, rendered unstable by their subjection to the whims of the multitude, were unable to learn from their mistakes. According to Cranborne:

> history was rich in lessons of the inability of a democratic community to profit by experience. Did Athens profit when she repeated at Syracuse the same ruinous mistake which she had made in Egypt? . . . Have America and Australia profited, when, in despite of science and experience, they are . . . building up systems of protection? . . . Aristocracies and monarchies have their traditions; but . . . a democracy is the most oblivious and inconstant of all governments, therefore the least able . . . to remember facts, to reason from these facts, and to adhere steadily to the lessons which they teach.[9]

The 'Americanization' of the Constitution would prove especially disastrous, the critics asserted, because Britain, unlike America, was an old country 'where the population was dense and the struggle for subsistence was great'. There was no land to spare and if the lower classes came to power in Britain they would resort to socialism in a desperate attempt to redistribute resources.[10]

The lessons of ancient Greece were less quoted because the splendours of Greek democracy constituted an embarrassment.[11] But nevertheless, 'that sublime Republic by which [they] were all unconsciously instructed', coloured the views of all members in an age when education was founded on the classics. On one occasion, at least, Lowe imagined the artisans as the Persians and himself as Callimachus at Marathon.[12]

Lowe and the anti-Reformers regarded the workingmen as a different order of beings; he and his companions were genteel and educated, while the workingmen, however well-meaning, were rough and uncouth. And as politics was a matter of intelligence rather than sentiment, this was the crucial fact. Their concern to perpetuate the rule of the chosen few reflected their belief that the structure of government necessarily mirrored the structure of society and that a cultural élite could be preserved only if the representatives of that élite held power in Parliament.

His isolation and ruthless intellectualism betrayed him into his worst blunder—his attack on the moral worth of the artisans:

> If you want venality, if you want ignorance, if you want drunkenness, and facility for being intimidated; or if . . . you want impulsive, unreflecting and violent people. . . . Do you go to the top or to the bottom?[13]

Lowe's remark was true and it delighted the Conservatives, but it was fatal to the chances of keeping agitation quiet. Lowe played only to the guardians he dimly perceived before him in the House of Commons: by equating the workingmen with brute force he failed to comprehend that they could be moved by an offence to their sensibilities.

The Adullamites and Tories tirelessly quarried the works of John Stuart Mill for admissions to bring against the Bill, but they never met the claim of Russell and Gladstone that the Bill was the most moderate adjustment that was still possible. Indeed, the examples brought forward by the anti-Reformers seem to be debating points which mask a deeper fear, a fear that is barely relevant to the content and probable results of the Bill of 1866. The magnificent perorations of Lowe and others who roused Tory cheers, instead of recapitulating the arguments about good government, were dismal metaphors of equality, 'that bare and level plain where every ant's nest is a mountain and every thistle a forest tree'.[14] Ultimately, Lowe's case rested upon an uncompromising belief in human inequality and its expression in exclusive institutions: 'It is the order of Providence that men should be unequal, and it is . . . the wisdom of the State to make its institutions conform to that order.'[15]

Bright took up the challenge. He seized upon the unusual vehemence of Lowe's and Marsh's attacks on New South Wales and remarked that 'from their former residence at the Antipodes, [they] . . . seem to take . . . a Botany Bay view of the character of the great bulk of their fellow countrymen'.[16] Such contempt jeopardized the peaceful social order, which depended upon the mutual confidence of the classes. No force in England could prevent the lower classes from overturning society if they were driven to do so by their total exclusion from representation. Concessions had to be made to retain and increase their respect for Parliament and the system of property that Parliament upheld. Bright saw, with much greater prescience than Lowe, that the process of electoral devolution had to continue as the working classes rose in social and intellectual standing and so came to demand a share in government. The alternative was a policy of immobility which could only lead to class isolation, and revolution:

> Now, if this Bill be rejected you will show that you are against all Reform. You will show that you have no confidence whatever even in that portion of the population which lives in houses between £10 and £7; whereas if you pass this Bill you will show that you are not cut off altogether from sympathy with the multitudes of your people. I say that there is peril in this, and that every day increases that peril. You have a population divorced almost entirely from the land and shut out from the possession of the franchise . . . I think if you do not moderate your tone . . . you will find some accident happening when you will have something more to do than you are asked to do to-night, under threats, and it may be under the infliction of violence.[17]

The accident was to begin four months later, with the Hyde Park riots.

He also more than repaid the attacks that the Palmerstonians had made upon him as the instigator of the Reform agitation. He flicked such humourless individuals as Elcho and Horsman with their due meed of ridicule by disposing them in the Cave of Adullam, the resort of 'every one that was in distress and every one that was discontented'.[18]

The speeches by Lowe and Bright carried the debate to the plane which was to make it one of the great oratorical contests in the history of the House of Commons. Rarely has the philosophy and practice of parliamentary government been discussed so profoundly and fervently. The debates vividly reflect the virtues and defects of English nineteenth-century education. They have a breadth of historical reference and an acuity and eloquence in expression that has probably never since been repeated in a Commons debate. Yet at the same time the speakers betray a patronizing ignorance and remoteness from the working classes that assorts ill with the confidence of their assertions about them.

Although Lowe and Elcho claimed to have recruited forty supporters from the Palmerstonians in the Commons, a defection large enough to wreck the Government, Disraeli sought to ensure that they had the backing of the Whig magnates in the Lords. But Derby's inactivity hindered him. Negotiations affecting the great lords had still to be conducted by the great lords themselves, while Disraeli knew he was still too much a parvenu to make overtures to them. He turned to Carnarvon: 'It's a case . . . for the intervention of Peers, and the support of Lord Westminster or the Duke of Cleveland would determine many in the House of Commons. But it is vain . . . to expect or even to ask anything from Lord Derby.'[19]

Among the Whig magnates there was considerable unrest awaiting exploitation. The Dukes of Cleveland and Sutherland and Lords Lichfield, Lansdowne and Spencer all expressed themselves in favour of removing Russell and his Bill and restoring the Palmerstonian peace.[20] Lords Suffolk and Carrington also 'tremble[d] for their boroughs' and were disaffected.[21] Within the Cabinet the Duke of Somerset, and Earl Grey and Lord Clarendon, had broken with Russell after his vacillation on the Enquiry and sudden capitulation to the radicals. They disliked the Bill because in Clarendon's words, 'the extension only had reference to numbers, & . . . education, intelligence & property were not sufficiently cared for'.[22] Clarendon early began to co-operate with the Cave and privately warned the Queen against the Bill.[23]

The magnates also distrusted Gladstone. Apart from his un-predictable Reform proclivities, they dreaded him as a future demagogue and leader of the radicals, and for his probable policy in Ireland. As far back as 1862 the Whigs of Northumber-land had refused to associate themselves with his Newcastle tour and had refused to attend the banquet in his honour.[24] He had signalled a change of opinion on the Irish Church in 1865, when, instead of straightforwardly opposing Dillwyn's motion for disestablishment, he described it as 'a question . . . for future consideration'.[25] The Marquess of Lansdowne, the Marquess of Clanricarde, the Duke of Devonshire and Earl Fitzwilliam were all great Irish landowners who were afraid that he would attack the Church, and introduce a bill allowing compensation for improvements, or that such a bill would certainly arise in a reformed Parliament. 'Clanricarde is very friendly to us,' Disraeli was informed, 'and very hostile to the Government; partly for the Reform Bill, and partly for their *Irish Land Bill.*'[26] And partly also, no doubt, because he had been Postmaster-General and Lord Privy Seal under Palmerston and had been dismissed from both offices by Russell.[27] Sir George Bowyer, the Palmerstonian member for Dundalk, and W. H. Gregory, the member for Gal-way County, the nomination seat of Lord Clanricarde, also supported the Cave against Gladstone because they feared for the agricultural cause in Ireland.[28] The opposition of Grey and Clarendon to the Bill was also fed by their views on the Irish situation. Both were greatly alarmed at the Fenian outbreaks and the prospect of Gladstone's handling them too leniently. Clarendon feared that if the Government weakened their hold there would be 'a bloody social revolution . . . actively promoted . . . by the socialist clergy'.[29] Grey, meanwhile, was attempting to forestall moves to disestablish the Irish church by sponsoring a measure to distribute tithes between the churches, and to avoid the introduction of compulsory compensation for improvements by pressing a bill to foster voluntary compensation agreements.[30] Had the Whigs felt that Gladstone was safe on Ireland the extent of their revolt in 1866 would probably have been insignificant: they would have accepted Reform with a bad grace, rather than allowed themselves to be mobilized to destroy it. The Reform Bill of 1866 began the disintegration of the Whig-Liberal alliance. Russell found himself caught between the old families and the

new men: his party had entered the first of the crises which were
to mark its transformation in the later nineteenth century.

Once it seemed clear that the Whig magnates would act,
Disraeli laid his plans to smash the Bill. The first move was to
force Russell to bring in a 'complete measure', to bring redistribution to the forefront and so unsettle the Whig proprietors and the
small borough men. On 15 March Derby, probably at Disraeli's
instigation, prepared an amendment to the effect that the other
part of a 'complete Bill', the seats plan, should be given to the
House before they proceeded to deal with any single part of the
Bill. This amendment was to be moved on the Second Reading
of the Suffrage Bill. 'This however is to be kept secret for the
present,' Stafford Northcote recorded. 'Disraeli hopes that Lord
Grosvenor may be induced either to move or second it, Stanley
to second or move it with him as the case may be.'[31] With the
help of Lowe and Elcho, the Conservative leaders persuaded
Grosvenor to move the amendment.[32] On 12 April, the first night
of the Second Reading debate, he moved:

> That this House, while ready to consider, with a view to its
> settlement, the question of Parliamentary Reform, is of opinion
> that it is inexpedient to discuss a Bill for the reduction of the
> Franchise in England and Wales until the House has before
> it the entire scheme contemplated by the Government for the
> amendment of the representation of the people.

'My resolution,' he declared, 'has not been framed or worded by
a Tory hand.' Lord Stanley seconded it.[33]

The amendment was ingeniously worded. It explicitly supported Reform and called for a wider measure than that proposed
by the Government, yet its whole purport was deadly to the Bill,
for it appealed to all those who saw their interests threatened by
a redistribution. And it was general enough to enable the
Opposition to bring a full range of argument against the Bill.
It allowed even the dullest country gentleman to swell the
chorus against Reform; Taylor, the Tory Whip, spent the recess
before the second reading 'drumming up people to prolong the
debate'.[34] It was the first instalment of Lord Derby's 'tit for tat
with Johnny Russell'.

Grosvenor's motion brought the statistics into play against
the Government. The anti-Reformers used them both to illustrate

the dangers in the Bill and to emphasize their unsoundness when Gladstone had recourse to them. The Adullamites and Tories argued that the distribution of new working-class electors could only be accurately known when the increases were calculated against the pattern of altered electorates.

Some Liberals tried to make a virtue of the weaknesses in the returns by arguing that the figures greatly overestimated the numbers of enrolled and potential working-class electors. Hodgkinson, from Newark, asserted that the return from his borough had had to be altered three times in as many weeks, successively reducing the estimate of qualifiers from 648 to 356 to 279 and

> still the use of such general designations as 'tailor', 'butcher', 'miller', 'joiner', left it altogether uncertain whether the persons so described were masters or only journeymen; and in fact all those so designated were left as belonging to the working classes. In one instance he knew of a voter who was left on the revised list as belonging to the working classes who paid a rent of over £100 a year.

He concluded by saying that men with local knowledge had made a careful analysis of the registers and had found that there were only sixty-eight enrolled working men in Newark.[35]

J. T. Hibbert and J. S. Mill demonstrated that the working-class portion of the constituency, although estimated at 26 per cent, had had no perceptible impact on the composition of the House or its policies. They defended the reduction of the qualification because they wanted to enable the artisans to elect members to represent their own class interests; but the evidence they produced to soothe the Opposition really showed that the working-class interest remained unrepresented, whether the working men had the vote or not. Hibbert carried the argument to its logical conclusion when he assured the members that the working-class representatives would not attempt to deal with questions of capital and labour in the House. Disputes on wages and hours, he explained, were private questions subject to the laws of political economy and 'must be fought outside the House, between capital and labour, and not by political discussion'.[36] Hibbert was a partner in Platt and Son, of Oldham, a company which was notorious for its opposition to trades unions in its mills.[37]

Gladstone made little effort to vindicate the returns. He demonstrated that the rate of increase of the borough enfranchisement between 1851 and 1865, 24 per cent, had lagged behind the borough population increase of 28.9 per cent, but he refused to enter into discussion about the numbers of working-class voters in individual boroughs, or to promise to place further statistics before the House. Such a proceeding, he said, would 'assume an invidious and offensive character'.[38] It was a convenient excuse, but nevertheless Gladstone is pre-eminent in the debate as speaking of the working classes as human beings.

The conclusion that he did claim to derive from the returns, though it did not follow from any of them and indeed was not measurable, was that the working classes were 'not represented in proportion to their intelligence, their virtue, or their loyalty'. He answered Lowe's sneer about their degradation with one word—'Lancashire'. 'Lancashire, associated with the sufferings of the last four years, so painful . . . in themselves to contemplate, but so nobly and gloriously borne.'[39] To Gladstone, the cotton famine and its relief was the first working model of that reciprocity between a self-disciplined, grateful working class and a beneficent duteous aristocracy which he sought to exemplify in his Bill.

His contention, as with so many of his elaborate glosses, proved too much. How could it justify the £7 level and the precisely arranged exclusion of so many members of such a deserving community? It emphasized that the qualification was arbitrarily related to the maintenance of upper-class voting power and not to the selection of the electorally worthy. This conundrum Gladstone never resolved. He always evaded the argument that 'worthiness of inclusion' perhaps inferred a 'right to inclusion', though, conveniently, his utterances seemed to mean the latter when he intended the former. It was treacherous ground:

> There are no elaborate calculations involved in the matter [he told one country gentleman who had complained that they were too difficult] all that is necessary to bear in mind is that a £12 rating is equivalent or very nearly so to a £14 rental. But I do object to the whole mode of dealing with this question of statistics, as adopted by Honourable Members. . . . They seem as if they were engaged in ascertaining the numbers of an invading army; but the persons to whom their remarks

apply are our fellow-subjects, our fellow-Christians, our own
flesh and blood, who have been lauded to the skies for their
good conduct . . . I cannot accede to the demand for information founded on a principle which I consider mischievous and
untrue [An Honourable Member: Untrue!] I speak of the
principle as untrue, which means unsound. I deny that
mathematical precision is necessary in giving information on
this question. . . . These voters between £14 and £50 will not
belong to the labouring class. [Mr Banks Stanhope: That is
what I want to know] There are certain facts . . . which do
not require to be made the subject of a statistical Return.[40]

The Cabinet again found itself at cross purposes over
Grosvenor's amendment. Russell could not accept it because it
was commonly regarded as an outright attack on the Bill, but
he retained his faith in a 'complete measure', partly to ward
off Bright, partly because the example of the Reform Act made
it the correct procedure and partly because the redistribution
was an integral component of the machinery for delimiting the
working-class vote. Somerset and Clarendon were keen to assent
to it, in the hope that the redistribution clauses it would bring
would arouse sufficient hostility to make Russell drop the Bill.[41]
Gladstone had already publicly committed the Ministry against
the amendment. During the Easter recess he had spoken at a
mass meeting at the Liverpool Amphitheatre. It was a significant
occasion, for it was the first time in British history that a Minister
of the Crown had canvassed support at a public meeting for
legislation he had before Parliament. He had promised that the
Government would fight uncompromisingly for its Suffrage Bill,
and declared that the old half-hearted dalliance with Reform
was at an end. 'We have crossed the Rubicon; we have broken
the bridges; and we have burnt the boats behind us.' His sense
of the movement of society convinced him of the necessity for
a wider distribution of votes. Peaceful political advance depended
upon the foresight of the nobility and its flexibility in the use
of privilege. Aristocratic intransigence in the face of the need
for change would surely lead to turmoil and democracy; the
aristocracy had 'to be wise in due season'. Grosvenor and Stanley,
the scions of two great houses, were placing themselves athwart
the current of peaceful advance, and if they persisted they would
breed a revolution which would destroy the order they represented.[42]

Brand viewed the extent of Grosvenor's support very ominously, and advised Gladstone to let it be known that the Government would treat the amendment as vital and resign if it were carried. He emphasized that the threat had to be one of resignation, not of dissolution. The lesser threat would sufficiently intimidate the Liberal waverers, but the very whisper of a new election would send them applying to Derby to take office without one. Brand also suggested that his leaders should trump the amendment with an immediate promise of a Redistribution Bill. They could not hold out much longer against the demand for it, the promise would show the Ministry's willingness to co-operate with the House, and prove their independence of Bright.[43] Brand was determined, as a shrewd partisan, to wring advantage from necessity. He was happy to give the Tories their seats bill because he had contrived a distribution which they would dislike, but be forced to swallow because they had demanded it.[44]

The Queen was also pressing Russell to bring in a redistribution bill, by way of compromise on the amendment. She was anxious about the rising hostility between Austria and Prussia and was bent upon keeping the Ministry in office so that she might have agents ready to mediate.

Russell duly decided to introduce a Redistribution Bill and the Scottish and Irish Franchise Bills before the House entered Committee on the Suffrage Bill.[45] To give the appearance of conciliation, without openly capitulating to Grosvenor, he offered to accept an earlier radical motion calling for a seats bill.[46]

The Opposition's true intentions were revealed when they persevered with Grosvenor's amendment after the Government had acceded to its demand. The climax of the debate saw the first of the thunderous clashes between Disraeli and Gladstone. Disraeli brilliantly surveyed the genesis of the Bill, showing that the Government had been returned unpledged on Reform, that its returns were inaccurate and incomplete, that the Bill was ill-drafted and uncertain in its results, that it would surely open the way to an 'American constitution' of constituencies and Parliament dominated by the working classes. He hardly mentioned the amendment, yet his speech was completely in the spirit of it, for it was by implication against all Reform. However, the real elegance of the speech lies not in its theme but in its counterpoint, for it contains a virulent exposition of Gladstone's woolly-mindedness, of his sentimental illogicalities, his half-

conscious evasions, and his self-righteousness. Disraeli enjoyed
himself and the House loved it. *Hubris* led him to taunt his
opponent with an amendment that he had moved against the
Reform Bill whilst an undergraduate at Christ Church. He
brought upon himself a majestic and devastating rebuke:

> The right hon. Gentleman, secure I suppose in the recollection
> of his own consistency, has taunted me with the political
> errors of my boyhood . . . I grant my youthful mind and
> imagination were impressed with the same idle and futile fears
> which still bewilder and distract the mature mind of the right
> hon. Gentleman . . . and the only difference between us is
> this . . . that having these views, I . . . moved the Oxford Union
> Debating Society to express them . . . plainly, forcibly in
> downright English, while the right hon. Gentleman does not
> dare to tell the nation what it is that he really thinks, and is
> content to skulk under the shelter of the meaningless Amend-
> ment which is proposed by the noble Lord.[47]

Gladstone drew on his intuitive grasp of the social forces of
his age and on his belief in the Providence that shaped his
political development to declare the realities of the situation:

> You may bury the Bill that we have introduced but . . . [you]
> cannot fight against the future. Time is on our side. The great
> social forces which move onwards in their might and majesty,
> and which the tumult of our debate does not for a moment
> impede or disturb—those great social forces are against you;
> they are marshalled on our side; and the banner which we
> now carry in this fight, though perhaps at some moment it may
> droop over our sinking heads, yet it soon again will float in
> the eye of heaven, and it will be borne by the firm hands of
> a united people . . . perhaps not to an easy, but to a certain
> and to a not distant victory.[48]

The division was one of the largest that the House had ever
known. The Government emerged with a majority of 5, with
313 members voting against them: the strength Palmerston had
won but nine months earlier had vanished.

> The Adullamites on the Ministerial benches, carried away by
> the delirium of the moment, waved their hats in sympathy with
> the Opposition, and cheered as loudly as any . . . [Lowe] stood
> up in the excitement . . . flushed, triumphant and avenged.
> His hair, brighter than silver, shone and glistened in the
> brilliant light. His complexion had deepened into . . . a

bishop's purple. . . . He waved [his hat] in wide circles over the heads of the very men who had just gone into the lobby against him. 'Who would have thought there was so much in Bob Lowe?' said one member to another; 'why, he was one of the cleverest men in Lord Palmerston's Government.'[49]

Thirty-five Liberals voted against the Bill and six more absented themselves from the division. The rebels came from the traditional core of the party. Twenty-one of them were the heirs or close kinsmen of Whig lords and at least three more, Lowe, Crosland and Laing, sat for boroughs influenced by Whig proprietors. Nearly all of them had described themselves as 'supporters of Lord Palmerston' in the 1865 election. Frederick Doulton, the earthenware manufacturer of Lambeth, and popularly regarded as the nominee of the Duke of Westminster, was the only man in the group who represented a large borough.[50]

One 'independent Conservative', R. J. Harvey, the young member for Thetford, voted with the Government. He explained, clear-sightedly enough, that the Bill 'rather lean[ed] towards Conservative ideas', and that it would answer the need for Reform while the demand remained quiet.[51] His impartial stance masked the fact that he was trying to auction his vote in return for a baronetcy, the sole object of his entering the House. He achieved his ambition in 1867, by opportunely surrendering his seat to the Tory Lord Advocate.[52]

The Cabinet had been advised to expect a majority of between fifteen and twenty,[53] and it was badly shaken by the result. On the day after the division the Ministers considered resigning, but, partly out of deference to the wishes to the Queen, partly in response to Russell's and Gladstone's determination to carry on, and partly because they believed that the withdrawal of the Government would strengthen the radicals, the Cabinet decided 'not to resign upon a side blow'.[54] These consideration, especially the stand taken by the Queen, constrained the Ministry to stay in office for a further two months.

The Ministers were divided, as usual, as to their future course. Sir George Grey wanted Russell to withdraw before he was pushed to a dissolution by the radicals.[55] Milner-Gibson, egged on by Bright, was calling for an immediate dissolution in the event of the Government's being defeated on the next amendment,[56] while Gladstone was completely opposed to the Government's vacating office unless and until they were decisively

defeated on the Bill. He told Russell that Grey was 'flatly wrong'
and that it would be 'a deplorable and egregious error' for the
Ministry to break faith with the country by abandoning the
Bill.[57] He announced his intention to commit the Government to
'the essential clauses', by which he meant the £7 rental qualification and the ancillary borough franchises.[58] Russell, as before,
wavered between them, but Gladstone's was the stronger personality and, during May, he supported him. Russell felt duty-
bound to the Queen to carry on her Government, and no doubt
was loath to abdicate the office which had been the goal of his
career. So he began to search for a compromise with the Adullamites which would both enable the Government to survive and
preserve enough of the Bill to satisfy Gladstone.

On the morning of Monday 30 April Russell prepared a letter
to be carried to Grosvenor, offering to take the Bills *pari passu*
and promising to appoint a Boundary Commission. Gladstone
refused to agree to his sending it. He argued that the Adullamites
would not be conciliated by the offer, while it would commit the
Government to a double bill, despite the reiterated opposition
of the Cabinet. That afternoon Gladstone's colleagues overruled
him, and on the evening of 30 April he announced to the House
that the Ministry intended to introduce a redistribution bill and
the Scottish and Irish Franchise Bills on the Monday following.[59]

The Government had survived the division, but it had lost the
Bill. The decision to introduce a seats bill was unavoidable in
train of the small majority and the unrest that it represented.
The anti-Reformers had scored a major tactical concession, for
they now had a wider front on which to operate and an excellent
chance of ensnaring those Liberals who feared for their pocket
boroughs.

III *The Redistribution Bill*

The Redistribution Bill gave its unwilling sponsors even more
trouble than its predecessor. The Palmerstonians fought for a
month to throw over Russell's scheme, and finally installed Sir
George Grey's and Brand's more innocuous one. The Bill was
ultimately botched together in the week prior to its introduction.

Brand had devised a plan that involved the grouping of single-
member boroughs of under 5,000 population and the removal
of the second member from boroughs of over 6,000 and under
8,000. His scheme would have done the minimum of harm to the

Liberal party and the maximum of damage to the Conservatives, for only fifteen of the thirty-six threatened single seats were held by Liberals and only twelve of the thirty-four double boroughs. This arrangement would also have left Brand's own constituency untouched. His disfranchisement provided forty-two seats; sufficient, he considered, to quiet the radicals.[60]

Russell intended to cut more deeply into the small boroughs, in order to make a settlement. He proposed to group all the single-member boroughs below 8,000 and to take the second member from the double boroughs of under 12,000. He calculated, somewhat haphazardly, that 69 seats would thus become available. It was a much more impartial scheme than Brand's, for 28 of the 42 members for double boroughs between 8,000 and 12,000 were Liberals.

Impartiality bred its difficulties. The twenty-eight Liberals, together with their fellows from the doomed single boroughs, would constitute a bloc of fifty-five potential Liberal opponents of the Bill. There might 'be a few patriots . . . among them', Brand warned, 'but not many'. Brand himself did not intend to be one. He was member for Lewes, which came within the 8,000-12,000 range and so would have lost a member. 'I could not . . . be a party to the introduction of a Bill which thus mutilated a Borough at my own door which I have represented for 14 years.'[61] The Whigs in the Cabinet rallied behind Brand. Sir George Grey, who had created a plan similar to Brand's, and conjoined it with the Whip's more knowledgeable one, argued that the 8,000 ceiling would sufficiently placate the radicals, yet keep the number of disaffected members small enough to prevent them from overturning the Government.[62]

The Cabinet wrangled over the details of the disfranchisement throughout April. The extra seats for the towns and counties had either to be created, or taken from existing boroughs. The Palmerstonians regarded the first alternative as unthinkable and the latter as distasteful: they shared the common opinion of the clubs that the House was already overcrowded and that the nation was already over-represented. So their discussions ranged about the least unpleasant way of encompassing disfranchisement. The majority of Cabinet opposed the outright disfranchisement of the smallest boroughs, and even more they opposed grouping.[63] According to Somerset: 'The reduction of the franchise will add to the Corruption of the corrupt boroughs

and tying a corrupt to an uncorrupt constituency is an un-
mitigated evil.'[64] The spreading of corruption was only the first,
explicit stage of their argument. Implicitly, it meant costlier
elections, the probability of interlopers buying in, and ultimately,
less control in proprietorial seats. Better, Grey suggested, to take
one member from double-member boroughs.

Russell, Gladstone, Stanley of Alderley, Argyll and Granville
were for grouping as against outright disfranchisement, and
Villiers wanted both. Grouping appeared to have least disadvan-
tages. As it would preserve the small boroughs from complete
annihilation Russell hoped that some of the threatened members
would be mollified by his attempt to prolong their tenure. Amal-
gamation also seemed to be an easy way of consolidating the
urban interests of small towns, and this, Russell assumed, would
please the radicals while it seemed harmless enough to reconcile
the Whig and Tory proprietors. Argyll contended that the Scottish
grouped boroughs showed that grouping tended to lessen bribery
and election costs.[65]

However, Brand pointed out the vital difficulty. Grouping
involved a multiplicity of local interests and it was doubtful
whether it could be instituted without a lengthy enquiry and a
succession of intricate compromises. The Government had to be
sure about the interests which it intended to placate, and even
more sure of those whom it would have to offend; but there was
not the time to make the necessary enquiries and adjustments.[66]

Villiers sought the total disfranchisement of 'certain insignificant places' and the allocation of their seats 'to counties & boros
which are increasing in property, trade & manufactures and
popln. & are inadequately represented'. He wanted the thirty
smallest boroughs to lose their members and fifteen more seats
to be made available by grouping other small places. He pointed
out that corruption was strongest in those old nomination
boroughs, like Totnes and Lancaster, where interlopers were
already breaking in, and that the Whigs were likely in any case
to lose the rest of their boroughs as the rise in prosperity enabled
'the monied classes & the London proprietors' to increase their
bids.[67]

Finally, on 30 April, there emerged a decision to group single
boroughs of under 9,000 and to take one member from double
boroughs under the same level. Only represented boroughs were
grouped. This was all that was possible in the available time and

it seemed the simplest way of avoiding the myriad problems inherent in the construction of parliamentary boroughs out of unrepresented towns. The plan thus created anomalies in place of those it was meant to abolish. And the existing anomalies had representatives ready to defend them.

Brand made the final draft of the Bill five days before it was due to be introduced. Apparently on his own initiative, he reduced the double-member limit to 8,000,[68] which preserved Earl Fitzwilliam's Malton, the only double borough between 8,000 and 9,000 with 2 Liberal representatives. His scheme provided for the reallocation of 49 seats. The grouped boroughs under 15,000 were to retain one member and those over 15,000 were to have two. His allocation was completely in the spirit of Russell's intentions, as outlined in 1853.[69] Each large county and borough was to have an extra member. This would give the appearance of fulfilling the demand for more representation for the great towns, whilst giving the Conservatives or Whigs a minority member in the great radical constituencies and the Whigs a minority member in the Tory counties. Each new Conservative or Whig town member would neutralize one radical vote in the House and the new Whig county members would be clear gain to the party. He had intended to use a boundary commission to confer an air of impartiality, while it nevertheless carried out the Government's orders in subdividing the counties and enlarging the manufacturing boroughs to siphon off the radical constituencies. Then the Whig and Conservative proprietors would be able to continue to negotiate or fight for the seats in straight contests. But the pressure of time once more forced him to adopt the cruder expedient of fixing the boundaries himself.[70]

Brand gave twenty-six of his forty-nine seats to the English counties, fifteen to the English boroughs, one to London University, and seven to Scotland. Ireland was left unchanged.[71] By contrast, the industrial towns were meanly treated. Manchester, Birmingham, Liverpool and Leeds were each to be visited with one extra member. Salford was to have one more, and the Hartle-pools, Middlesbrough, Dewsbury, Burnley, Stalybridge and Gravesend were each to become parliamentary boroughs with one representative. Tower Hamlets was to be divided with two additional members, and Chelsea-Kensington was to become a borough, also with two. The new boroughs were to be excised

from their counties, and all parliamentary boroughs were to be
extended to their municipal boundaries.[72]

As this outline shows, the proposals were consistent only in
the intention to arouse as little objection as possible from the
members. Brand meant his plan to reinforce the traditional
representative pattern, yet the demands of population change
led him to diverge widely from it—he followed the principle
of representation according to population and local wealth, and
yet tried not to show it openly. His scheme modified the worst
anomalies, but it left substantially unaltered the imbalance of
representation between the South of England and London, the
Midlands, the North and Scotland. The thirty-one seats retained
to Devonshire and Wiltshire still outweighed the seventeen
added to the Midlands and the North and the six given to
London.

The grouping proposals were wide open to attack and the
'dying swans' made the most of their chance. Goldsmid, the
Liberal member for Honiton, showed that it was nonsensical to
join Honiton and Bridport. They were twenty-one miles apart
and there was absolutely no community of interest between
them: Honiton was a market town, Bridport a sea town. Bewdley
and Droitwich were close and had a common interest, they were
both under 7,000, yet they were left ungrouped; Cirencester and
Evesham, twenty-five miles apart with a four and a half hours'
rail journey between them, were clumsily matched. Goldsmid
also touched disloyally on the fact that the Bill left untouched
boroughs between 8,000 and 10,000—they returned 14 Liberals
and only 4 Conservatives.[73] This latter criticism was hardly fair,
for it implied the need for a thoroughgoing redistribution according to population, and this Goldsmid and his friends would have
found much more obnoxious. But the substance of the attack
remained. Even a loyal Liberal like Arthur Peel, who supported
the scheme in principle, confessed that he could not defend the
groups as proposed because they ignored geography and local
interest.[74]

The manipulation of the double boroughs between 6,000 and
9,000 was especially arbitrary and partisan. Maldon, Dorchester,
Chippenham, Devizes, Cirencester and Ludlow were all under
8,000 and were to be grouped. Newport, Bridgnorth, Cockermouth, Buckingham, Marlow and Huntingdon, also under 8,000,
were to remain separate boroughs and lose one member.

Tavistock, Malton, Wycombe, Chichester, Guildford and Stamford were each just above the 8,000 limit and were to keep their two members. The first lot returned only one Government supporter out of twelve members, the second, four out of twelve, and those over 8,000, eight out of twelve.

Though the scheme was blatantly one-sided, the Conservative leaders wanted to block it without adverting too strongly to its unfairness and so giving the impression of a factious opposition. At a party meeting on 12 May Derby and Disraeli guided their followers to attack three chief vices in it. The Conservatives decided to object to the proposal to add a minority member to the counties, they denounced the grouping plan because it failed to take unrepresented towns out of the counties, and, thirdly, they agreed that the proposals for the rectification of borough boundaries were 'most objectionable'.[75]

Disraeli had previously ascertained from the Conservative agents that the municipal and parliamentary boundaries were co-terminous in the great majority of boroughs.[76] The real need was to extend parliamentary limits beyond the municipal ones, as the latter rarely represented the confines of urban settlement. The extension of municipal boundaries constantly lagged because property owners in the extra municipal parishes enjoyed lower rates and resisted attempts by the town to engulf them. Incorporation was voluntary, in that it was decided by the parish council or vestry board, and this method was to be preserved in the Bill. The point was of great importance to the Conservative county men. Halifax had 40,000 people residing in suburbs beyond its municipal limits. The environs of Manchester sprawled for three miles beyond the circumference of the municipal borough. Birmingham had 29,000 outside; Southampton, 23,000; Stoke, 21,000; Derby, 10,000; Cardiff, 7,900; Kidderminster, 6,000, and Hull, 2,000.[77] Many of these were villa dwellers who voted in the county, supposedly for Liberal candidates, and the steady increase of their numbers seemed inevitable. But the Bill gave no promise that they would be absorbed into the borough constituencies, or that machinery would be established to spread the borough boundaries automatically with the growth of the suburbs. Furthermore, the grouping plan threatened Conservative strength in the small boroughs and did nothing to take urban voters in unrepresented towns out of the county constituencies.

The Conservatives' opposition to the redistribution was of a part with their objections to the £14 county qualification and the new freehold and leasehold clauses. The county members believed that the £14 level would greatly extend the vote among the villa dwellers. Du Cane, from North Essex, feared that his constituency would be swamped by the new voters of Braintree, Halstead and Coggeshall. Scourfield was worried by the likely incursion of hundreds of Yarmouth freeholders into East Norfolk, while Sclater-Booth was angry that Lewisham, with 22,000 inhabitants, had not been excised from the constituency of West Kent and that Croydon had been left to dominate East Surrey.[78] Even if the Seats Bill induced local authorities to attach their suburbs to the boroughs, the freehold and leasehold clauses of the Suffrage Bill would neutralize the advantage for the Conservatives. Already, 100,000 voters, one-fifth of the county constituency, derived their vote from a borough freehold qualification.[79] In Middlesex 3,000 more suburban voters would become eligible by virtue of the leasehold clause alone.[80] Thus Disraeli had to smash vital sections in both Bills, yet not alienate members who wanted a settlement and not give the appearance of his being opposed to all Reform.

His catspaws among the Adullamites ensured his control of their thirty or so votes, but to be sure of a majority, he needed to capture a dozen of the Liberal waverers. This required alert manipulation. By contrast with Gladstone, Disraeli had extraordinary sensitivity to the current of back-bench opinion, and while Gladstone held aloof from the body of his followers and affected to ignore their views, Disraeli flattered the most insignificant member on his own side and cultivated restive supporters of the Government. In the friable party politics of 1866-7 Disraeli's management of the independent gentlemen was a fundamental factor in his success.

The anti-Reformers' triumph with Grosvenor's amendment seemed to make the defeat of the Government imminent, but two fortuitous events came to Russell's aid. His readiness to resign after the division on Grosvenor's motion had alarmed the Whig lords, who, though eager to force him to drop Reform, were even more determined to keep their relations and friends in office and avoid the expense and possible disaster of an election. Their hesitation was strengthened by the financial crisis and the growth of hostilities on the Continent.

The financial crisis broke on 10 May, three days after the introduction of the Redistribution Bill. Overend and Gurney had liabilities of £19 million when they closed, and the following day saw 'tremendous anxiety in the City', with Lombard Street and Birchin Lane thronged all day with apprehensive crowds.[81] Gladstone suspended the Bank Charter Act and the bank-rate rose to 10 per cent.[82] Meanwhile the news from Prussia suggested a rapid worsening of the situation and that the invasion of Holstein was imminent.

Earl Grosvenor was sufficiently perturbed by the state of the nation to cease temporarily his campaign against the Bill, thus upsetting Disraeli's strategy. The latter had depended upon the vain and unpredictable aristocrat to maintain the Whig front for the opposition, but Grosvenor did not enjoy being estranged from his party and he and W. B. Beaumont suddenly decided that £7 was not such a dangerous qualification after all, and that in any case the Whigs in the Ministry would allow the Bill to die in Committee.[83]

Disraeli had planned to strike at the Government through a young Whig member, Arthur Hayter, who sat for Wells. Hayter was disgruntled at the prospect of losing his seat in the redistribution and Disraeli intended to cast him as the bell-wether for other Liberals who occupied threatened boroughs. He was also the son of the former Whig Whip and Disraeli hoped that his name would attract some of the older Palmerstonians. Disraeli conducted his negotiations with Hayter through Ralph Earle, his private secretary. Earle was a clever, unscrupulous young man and during the crucial weeks of May and June Disraeli seems to have allowed him considerable independent authority.[84] He devised and managed three of the subsequent attacks on the Bill.

Earle had discovered that Hayter intended to give notice of an amendment on the second reading of the Redistribution Bill and Disraeli seized the opportunity:

> the young H. must be utilised, and it may do the business. . . .
> He must give notice of his resolution on Friday, and Lord D.
> must pledge his party to support it on Monday. If you can
> discreetly modify the language, well and good. It will, how-
> ever, be looked upon as his father's, and so gain confidence.[85]

Thereupon, Hayter moved that:

> This House, while ready to consider the general subject of a
> Re-distribution of Seats, is of opinion that the system of group-
> ing proposed by Her Majesty's Government is neither con-
> venient nor equitable, and that the scheme is otherwise not
> sufficiently matured to form the basis of a satisfactory
> measure.[86]

Unfortunately for Disraeli, Hayter and Earle bungled the
moving of the amendment. Hayter moved it as an amendment
to an instruction previously moved by E. P. Bouverie and W. B.
Beaumont, that the Bills be taken together through Committee
and combined into one Bill. Hayter should instead have introduced his resolution as a separate amendment to the motion
to enter Committee. When Derby learnt of the resolution he
pointed out to Disraeli that it would probably miscarry because
it transgressed the rules of the House, for it would be taken
after the instruction to combine the Bills and if, as seemed likely,
that motion succeeded, the Speaker would probably veto Hayter's
amendment because it did not refer to the Franchise Bill. This
would entail the Opposition, much as it approved Bouverie's
instruction, having to vote against it to keep the Bills separate.[87]
Earle replied rather superciliously that the old man was wrong
and an amendment to an instruction could only be vetoed if it
were moved on the motion for reading the Order of the Day.[88]
The essential problem was that Hayter's motion was without
precedent. Speaker Denison was inclined to rule it out because
it was 'not really an amendment to an Instruction but . . . rather
a Resolution relating to the merits of the two Bills and pro-
nouncing an opinion on their want of any merit'.[89] After a conference between the Speaker, Disraeli and Cairns, it was arranged
that Hayter's motion should apply to the question for the
Speaker leaving the chair.[90]

Earl Grosvenor refused to support the motion and openly
repudiated Lowe and Elcho, explaining that he dared not risk
turning the Government out in the existing state of affairs at
home and on the Continent.[91] It's likely, too, that he resented
direction from an upstart like Earle. Beaumont followed his
leader and also became hostile, especially after he discovered
that he and Bouverie had been double-crossed.

Bouverie was a truculent Palmerstonian whom Russell had
offended when he removed him from the Church Estates

Commission. He was quite ready to embarrass the Ministry, but, like Beaumont, he wanted to settle Reform, albeit as conservatively as possible.[92] He disliked the redistribution plan, not because it affected him personally, but because he believed that it would not make a viable settlement. By his move to take the Bills together he intended to ensure that the redistribution was weighed against the suffrage extension and, if necessary, adjusted. Earle had tried to persuade him to add a rider that 'the scheme was not mature enough to be a settlement', but he had refused, and must have been irritated to find the words tacked on to Hayter's interposed amendment. Beaumont had been drumming up Adullamites and 'dying swans' to vote for Bouverie and had secured thirty-four promises, only to learn of Hayter's resolution and his competing for the votes of the small borough men. He was incensed when he finally heard that Earle was marshalling Adullamites to defeat Bouverie's instruction if it should be put first.[93]

Derby also objected to the coda which Earle had attached to Hayter's resolution because he saw it as reviving the slippery phraseology Russell had used against him in 1859. He wanted instead a motion which followed the lines of Manners' memorandum; a forthright amendment which attacked the disfranchisement, grouping and method proposed for extending borough boundaries, and which demanded that unrepresented towns be excised from the counties.[94] But Disraeli believed that this approach might scare off as many as it would attract. He preferred vague resolutions which could win support because they were not outright attacks on the Government, while they left the Opposition uncommitted.

> I am very low, [Earle confided to Disraeli] B[eaumont] very unsatisfactory, ditto Grosvenor, who does not think he can vote against going into committee. I agree with Heathcote & Elcho in thinking this very bad behaviour . . . I enclose the text of the little Hayter's resolution as concocted with me—I don't think much of him, but Mitchell [Liberal member for Bridport, another grouped borough] backs him strongly—we had much discussion . . . (Elcho, Heathcote & I) as to whether it wd not be better to let Mitchell himself move, but we thought the name so important, that we left it in H's hands. I think it possible that he may bring 10 men, but with Grosvenor doubtful & Beaumont hostile, we can only expect some 12 or 15 Adullamites![95]

Disraeli and Earle were in a fix; they had committed themselves without first securing their support. Besides Derby, they
had alienated several influential Conservatives by their tactics.
Walpole, for example, when Disraeli had asked him to second
Hayter's motion, had refused because he considered it dishonest,
and added that he preferred to wait to see if the Bills reached
Committee, and then 'to propose amendments, so that the
Country may know our views'.[96] Disraeli could not afford a bad
defeat in the division, for that would lose him the support of
Whig place-hunters like the two Mackinnons and Lord Arthur
Clinton.[97] Yet they could not abandon Hayter and his friends, for
this would destroy their links with the small borough men. Earle
tried to whip up more support among the Liberals. He approached
James Clay and George Clive, the proponents of the 'educational
franchise', but they and their group proved difficult to snare.[98]

Clay was persisting with his Bill, which was to come up for its
second reading on 30 May, and he too was busily hunting up
votes. Earle prompted a deal whereby Clay would move a
motion to postpone the Government Bill, and the Tories would
not oppose his Franchise Bill. Earle had conceived the postponement as a face-saving way of averting a division on Hayter's
resolution. A motion to refer the Bill to a select committee, he
suggested to Disraeli, would be 'plausible & wd suit the cowards
[and] . . . if Clay wd do this, so much the better'.[99] Clay was
tempted, but he was too shrewd to accept. He realized that by
shelving Reform he would lessen the impact of his own measure
on the Government and so destroy its chance of being incorporated in the Bill; and all for no very definite reward from the
Tories.[1]

Considering the chaos behind the scenes, the anti-Reformers
put up a good show in the debate. Gladstone accepted Bouverie's
instruction without a division and Hayter's resolution came on
unhindered. The Opposition managed to prolong the discussion
for four nights. Anomalies were easy to find and the doomed
borough men spoke with fervour. But they were expending their
breath in a pointless performance, for from the time of Grosvenor's
defection, Disraeli, Cairns, Elcho and Lowe had agreed that 'a
bad division ought if possible to be avoided'. On the final night
Taylor, the Conservative Whip, counted the heads and advised
that a division would be 'suicidal', for the Opposition could
expect to be beaten by fifty or sixty votes.[2] Word was passed to

Hayter and he rose suddenly and withdrew his motion. Then there was uproar: the Liberals were shouting for a division while the Adullamites and Tories began to stampede from the chamber.

The Speaker was also caught unprepared by Hayter's announcement, and attempted to follow standing orders by forcing the House to divide upon the question of permission to withdraw.[3] This provoked the first exodus. Permission to withdraw was refused on the voices and the Speaker put Hayter's motion. This precipitated a frantic clash as more members tried to leave while Lowe and a few Conservatives battered their way through the crowd to re-enter the chamber to vote. Lowe was severely bruised. Gladstone quickly moved the adjournment and this set off a third stampede.[4] About two hundred members surged through the doors in less than three minutes. The members were having a foretaste of the confused divisions of 1867, while the permanent legacy of this episode are some rules of parliamentary decorum.

Disraeli was the more ready to abandon Hayter's motion because earlier that evening the Opposition had won their first division against the Government and to have lost the second would have destroyed the impact. Sir Rainald Knightley, a Tory squire from Northamptonshire, had moved an instruction to the committee to add clauses to the Bill for the better prevention of bribery and corruption.[5] He had drafted his motion in concert with Earle.[6] Knightley was doubtless worried about bribery, but had he been really concerned to obtain effective legislation he would have withheld his instruction and embodied it in a separate measure. His instruction made the Bill a great deal more vulnerable, for legislation against corruption always antagonized members, and it so lengthened and complicated the Bill as to make it near impossible for the Government to carry it in one session.

Moreover, Knightley's instruction was superfluous, for Hussey Vivian, a Liberal who had chaired two bribery investigations, had already given notice of a Bribery Bill. Hussey Vivian declared that he would not support Knightley's 'side-wind', for his own bill stood a chance only if the Reform Bills were cleared first.[7] Despite the patent falsity of the motion and Knightley's failure to indicate the kinds of methods the committee might adopt to prevent corruption, the instruction captured the votes of a few Liberals like Bernal Osborne, Staniland, and Captain Grosvenor, who were not Adullamites, but men genuinely perturbed about electoral venality and the Government's neglect of it in the Bill. The Government lost the division, 238 to 248.[8] Twenty-six nominal Liberals voted with the Opposition.[9]

Gladstone was disgusted by the anti-Reformers' victory on this 'most barefaced proposal'. It made his task immeasureably harder, he told Russell: 'The franchise Bill alone I might have managed, but to arrange, put into shape, & prepare for the Cabt. the multitude of points that arise upon the combined measure is physically as well as in every other way impossible for me.'[10] He found himself amazed by the lack of principle among the Adullamites and the chicanery of the Opposition. They obviously despised the workingmen, they were clearly bent on wrecking the Bill, yet they remained devious and unpredictable in their tactics. Gladstone hardened his resolve to make the House carry the Bill in one session. He threatened the members with an autumn sitting during the debate on Knightley's motion,[11] and reiterated the threat during the succeeding nights of debate, so that the remaining weeks of the Government's existence saw a growing estrangement between him and the country men of both sides. He appeared to be ignoring the wishes of the ordinary members of the Commons in a matter on which they were sensitive (their right as independent gentlemen to be consulted about their attendance at the House), especially if the shooting season were to be interrupted by debate on this tiresome, doomed Bill. Gladstone's implacable high-mindedness enabled the Opposition to make him the scapegoat for their own obstructive tactics, for they were able to switch from attacking the Bill to denouncing the man who sought to impose it.

After their failure to smash the Redistribution with Hayter's resolution, the Conservatives exploded a new mine. On the evening of 7 June, Lord Stanley completely surprised the Government by moving that Redistribution be taken first. This move had been planned some days earlier and had been kept a close secret. The Tory rank and file and the Adullamites had been asked to come early to the House, but they were not told of the intended action, the timing of which was left to be determined by the numbers.[12] The anti-Reformers assembled on Thursday evening expecting to support a Conservative motion to protect the counties, when Stanley suddenly intervened to move

his amendment before the county motion. Gladstone had to fili-
buster until Brand could summon the Liberals from their dinner
tables.[13] The Tories' calculations had been accurate enough, but
they emerged the losers by 27 votes: 260 to 287. The Adullamites
had once more let them down, for only 12 of them, including
the Grosvenors, voted with the Opposition, while 21 supported
the Government. Much as they wanted to be rid of the Bill, the
waverers seem to have been repelled by the shabbiness of the
manoeuvre.[14]

After the failure of Stanley's motion and because of Derby's
displeasure with Earle, Disraeli paused in his campaign and
allowed the Opposition to revert to the Manners-Walpole
strategy of open attack. Walpole moved to lift the proposed
county qualification from £14 to £20. There was 'no principle'
in a £14 suffrage, he argued, and a qualification which did not
represent a principle could not be a 'resting place'. Twenty
pounds was the lowest level at which county jurors were called,
and so involved a known civil duty. It followed that £20 occupiers
were persons who could be safely entrusted with the vote.[15] The
£20 level represented a further principle, Walpole claimed, in
that it was the figure at which the house tax began: a £20
suffrage thus recognized the bond between taxation and the
privilege of choosing parliamentary representatives. Walpole's
arguments sounded impressive, but their substance was poor.
The great 'principle' of the £20 qualification was unknown in
the Constitution, for the house rate could vary from year to
year and in Middlesex liability for jury service began at £30
rating occupancy.[16] Still, it is a measure of the respect in which
arguments of 'constitutional principle' were held that Gladstone
countered with another 'principle'. Fourteen pounds, he claimed,
marked a 'stopping place', and therefore it became a 'principle';
it was the limit, according to the returns, at which the enfranchisement of the county middle classes became complete, and
was, therefore, the 'main member' of the Government's plan to
diversify the interests embraced in the representation.[17]

Walpole had introduced his amendment as a straight-forward
limitation of the county suffrage, but during the course of the
debate it was made the head for a thoroughgoing assault on the
county provisions in the Bill. The speeches of the Tory county
men vividly convey their confused, truculent opposition. Banks

Stanhope and Adderley both declared that they and their friends would vote for the amendment, not to institute a £20 level, but to wreck the £14 clause. They held themselves free to oppose any reduction of the county qualification until the redistribution excised the towns from the counties.[18] It was the first of the Tory county revolts, which were to bedevil the politics of 1866 and 1867.

The Government won the division by only 14 votes: 297 to 283.[19] Twenty-five Liberals voted with the Opposition, nine of whom had previously voted with the Government against Stanley's motion; six of the nine sat for counties.[20] But more important than this fairly predictable switch, the vote of the unsteady Liberals for Walpole signalled a fresh regrouping in the Cave and a return to the co-operation with Disraeli that had broken down with Hayter's and Stanley's amendments. Disraeli and Earle had been too subtle. The Liberal waverers were prepared to vote for a direct modification of the Bill, but they were not sufficiently attracted by feint amendments which were not clearly aimed at removing or remedying it.

On 11 June the Opposition sprang a new trap. Ward Hunt, with only a few hours' private warning to Gladstone, moved to substitute 'ratal' for 'rental' in the county franchise clause.[21] Its effect would have been to raise the comparable rental to £16 a year. Hunt claimed that his amendment would assimilate the English and Welsh county registration system to the Irish one and so increase the uniformity of both the franchise level and the method of enrolment, but he was wrong on both counts. The Irish county rates were fixed by a national scale of valuations and deductions instituted by the Irish Registration and Rating Act of 1850.[22] There was no similar law in Great Britain, and certainly no uniformity. The amendment, had it succeeded, would have severely diminished the numbers enfranchised by the Bill, and brought the Government back to the position they had been forced to abandon when they were making it.

Gladstone explained the impracticability of the amendment, but the Tory county men rose in a steady succession to voice their approval of it. Their speeches give a fine impression of the brute defensiveness which Disraeli was to play upon in 1867. They were worried not only by the incursion of town voters, but by the higher electoral costs of the enlarged constituency. Colonel Loyd-Lindsay explained that:

To his own constituency in Berkshire there would be added 1,200 persons, drawn in a great measure from the towns. He did not believe that those 1,200 persons would be amenable to . . . bribery, as they were highly respectable persons of the middle classes; but . . . they would require that their funds should be subscribed to . . . which would add considerably to the expenses which Members . . . wished to abridge. And furthermore the new voters . . . would be in no way amenable to the influence of the landlords, which . . . seemed to him to be by no means a desirable provision.[23]

Those members from counties which were already suffering urban expansion were extremely frightened. Sir Charles Mordaunt, the member for South Warwickshire, told Lady Knightley that he believed the local Tory party was 'going to smash', and that 'neither he nor C. N. N. [Newdegate, the member for North Warwickshire] ha[d] a chance of winning . . . with the £14 franchise'.[24]

Their fears were based on prejudice rather than analysis. Dudley Baxter had made an elaborate investigation of the probable effects of the new county franchise and had concluded that it would improve the party's chances. On 12 June he sent a memorandum on the subject to Derby and Disraeli; they apparently found it too speculative and inconvenient, for they suppressed it.[25] At this stage of the battle they had all to play for and they could not risk alienating their county men by asking Hunt to withdraw his motion. It would be time enough for Disraeli to being to 'educate his party' when the legislation at stake was his and not Gladstone's.

Hunt's motion went to a division, from which the Government emerged with a majority cut to 7: 280 to 273. As with Walpole's motion, 25 Adullamites, 15 of them county members, voted with the Opposition.[26] The revolt was gathering the momentum that was soon to carry it to victory. Lord E. P. Clinton, Dering, Duff, Finlay, Mackie and Sheridan all either returned to the Cave, or voted with it for the first time.

The Tories were now in full cry and Banks Stanhope, the member for North Lincolnshire, immediately followed the division on Hunt's amendment with another attack on the county franchise provisions. He moved the deletion of the section which required the building to be worth a minimum of £6 a year where the qualifying premises consisted of a 'house' and land.[27] His contention in support of his amendment, that the Government's attempt to define the substance of the qualification was an invasion of the rights of property, was doubtless true, though it is hard to see how the existing county qualifications and the projected fancy franchises escaped the same offence. However, Banks Stanhope protested his belief that the county franchise was a 'property franchise' and that there was no 'peculiar social advantage in bricks'. Gladstone replied with a curious speech which reiterated the evils that had developed from 'the knocking up [of] worthless places', and gave time for the Whips to count the heads, for he concluded by 'cheerfully' acceding to the amendment.[28]

His cheerful concession dismayed the radicals. The loss of the section 'struck a fatal blow at the utility of the Bill', for it would retain to the landed caste one of their most effective ways of holding the counties.[29] White angrily accused Gladstone of reverting to the bad old Whig habit of abusing 'the feelings' of the radicals, 'who, like himself, thought it their duty to support and carry through this Bill, and had therefore voted on all occasions for the Government'.[30] Forlornly, the radicals pushed the motion to a division, upon which the Whigs and moderate Liberals voted with the Tories to overwhelm them: 361 to 74.[31]

The Opposition had now tried six amendments, and, considering that they had begun the session in a minority of seventy, they had done extraordinarily well. The members' general dislike of Reform and Gladstone's intransigence had wrought a change of fortune that had seemed utterly remote only ten months before; the Tories now had the prospect of office, and for the first time in seven years Derby found himself leading a keen, aggressive party. The Tories' crucial need was to aggravate Whig unrest and draw in some of those who hesitated to oppose the Bill actively, for fear of toppling the Administration. Should the Bill survive the Commons, Derby and Disraeli hoped to organize a massive revolt of the Whigs in the House of Lords. Disraeli and Taylor drew up a list of Whig and Tory nobles who might be invited to an anti-Reform meeting at Lord Lansdowne's, and sent it to Lord Derby to prompt him to round them up. Derby entered eagerly into the plan and returned the list to Disraeli with his own annotations:

Dukes:
    Grafton XX
    Wellington XX
    Newcastle X?
    Cleveland X?

Earls:
    Suffolk X?
    Shaftesbury X
    Scarborough X?
    Fitzwilliam X
    Spencer O
    Wicklow O
    Grey X?

Viscounts:
    Stratford de Redcliffe X
    Coalthorpe X?
    Carrington XX
    Glasgow X?

    Roseberry [*sic*] O
    Stratheden X

Marquesses:
    Lansdowne XXX
    Westminster XX
    Camden X

Earls:
    Harrowby X?
    Somers O
    Lichfield XXX
    Yarborough X
    Leicester X
    Zetland X
    Dudley XX
    Portman X?
    Vivian X?
    Overstone X
    Aveland XX
    Llanover X

[X = likely to support the Opposition, O = 'hopeless'.]

Derby added that he was disposed to include the Dukes of St Albans and Sutherland, Viscount Eversley, and Lords Churchill, Leigh and Chesham, as 'kindred Whigs, who might be inclined to take a practical view of . . . affairs'.[32] Derby was possibly too optimistic, but the list does give some indication of the very wide extent of aristocratic disaffection[33] and underlines the importance of Whig resistance in the defeat of Russell's Reform Bill. If we follow only the most obvious lines of influence, we find that nineteen at least of the Liberals who were to form Dunkellin's majority against the Government were directly related by birth or marriage to the Whig aristocracy and at least seven more were their clients in pocket boroughs.

The amendment which emerged from the Lansdowne meeting was a restatement of Hunt's rating motion, applied to the boroughs. It was left as vague as possible, although its 'rating principle' would provide a strong debating point. If it passed it would materially reduce the enfranchisement by raising the occupancy level, and so transform the Bill while leaving the shell intact. This would permit Russell to drop the Bill without too much humiliation, and so deny Gladstone the cause for a dissolution; the waverers could then be assured that they were not voting themselves into an election.

The man chosen to move the amendment was Lord Dunkellin, the heir to the rancorous Marquess of Clanricarde. Dunkellin was an excellent choice as figurehead; unlike his father, he was amiable and popular, and of sufficient standing to command a hearing. In the House he justified a ratal qualification as being 'easy, convenient and constitutional', and he instanced the working of the Irish ratal franchise, despite Gladstone's having already shown it to be inapplicable in Great Britain. The English rating levels had not a semblance of regularity. In the parishes of Liverpool, for example, the allowable deductions for repairs were 20 per cent in Everton and Kirkdale, up to 25 per cent in Toxteth, and at a fixed 10 per cent in Liverpool City. In two parishes of St John's, Oxford, the deductions were 20 per cent and 33.25 per cent and these were further adjusted at the discretion of the parish officers according to the condition of the building.[34]

The basic flaw in the argument for a rating qualification lay in the fact that the rate was calculated *from* the gross estimated rental column in the rate-books.[35] The gross estimated rental, as the first and most readily ascertainable entry, was the figure least open to cumulative error. But Dunkellin was right when he asserted that a rating franchise 'would interpose a barrier, steady and fixed, to the descent to universal suffrage', for it would make the rate-book the roll, and bar the way to the lodgers, who were technically not rate-payers, and compound-householders, whose names were rarely entered. A rating qualification would have excluded 60,000 of the 144,000 men whom the Government proposed to enfranchise in the boroughs.[36] It would also have materially raised the level of the occupancy, for rating estimates were arrived at after the usual deductions had been made from the gross estimated rental. The allowable deduction in Oldham, for example, was 33.33 per cent, and a man would have had to occupy a building at a gross estimated rental of £10. 10s. 0d. to qualify for a £7 suffrage. Dunkellin's amendment would thus have the odd result of disfranchising £10 voters.[37]

Although the logic of the case was plain, it was spiked with intricate detail. And as the detail accumulated during the debate it bored the members and served completely to obfuscate the issue. The Tory back-benchers quickly lost the pretence of justifying rating as a principle and resorted to irrelevant

outbursts against Reform: 'Was the House prepared to hand over
the Government . . . to the working classes?' asked Mr Greene, the
brewer from Bury St Edmunds. '. . . everybody knew that
the working classes were not the men to be entrusted with the
control of affairs.'[38] The moment of truth for Dunkellin came
towards the end of the debate. McEvoy, an Irish Liberal on the
fringe of the Cave, was apparently bemused by the claims and
counter-claims on rental and ratal, and asked Dunkellin if he
would enlarge his amendment to provide for the introduction
to Great Britain of the Irish valuation system. Dunkellin was
nonplussed and met the question with a clumsy refusal.[39]

The Government handled the amendment very badly: its
information was inadequate and its strategy timid. By succinct
demonstration with exact figures Gladstone could perhaps have
persuaded genuine waverers like McEvoy and Lord E. P.
Clinton that an even rating franchise was impossible. It was not
until a week after the defeat that Gladstone produced returns
which showed that it would be necessary to set a level above
£6 rating in 16 boroughs, at £6 in 39 boroughs, at £5 in 112,
at £4 in 21 and below £4 in 5 others, to achieve the enfranchisement offered by the £7 rental.[40]

The Cabinet had been told before the weekend that the Cave
and the Tories were whipping vigorously for Dunkellin, but at
the meeting on the Saturday before the 16th Russell and the
Palmerstonians decided against making the amendment a vital
issue and concocted an ambiguous Whip notice. This only encouraged those unsteady supporters who wanted to see the end
of the Bill but not the Government. It was not until the very
close of the debate that Gladstone intimated, apparently without
the permission of the Cabinet, that the Ministers might not
accept an adverse vote. Childers believed that if Gladstone had
made his announcement at eight p.m. instead of two a.m., the
Government would have won.[41]

The anti-Reformers emerged triumphant, with a majority of
11: 315 to 304. 'With the cheering of the adversary there was
shouting, violent flourishing of hats, and other manifestations
which I think novel and inappropriate,' Mr Gladstone recorded.[42]
The Opposition could afford to cheer. They had overcome a
Ministry which had wantonly deviated from the anti-Reform
truce to side with the radicals in an attempt to impose a disruptive measure on the House. They had held all but two of the

men who had voted for Grosvenor's amendment and had won
fifteen more Liberal supporters.[43] Still, in the midst of the cheering, it is worth emphasizing that over three hundred members of
the House had enough loyalty and good sense to vote for a Bill
which would have bettered the prospects of very few of them.

Russell never forgave the Liberal rebels. They had wrecked
his last administration and his last great legislative endeavour.
In his *Recollections* he declared that, though some doubtless
were honest, he had never in his long political life, 'known a
party so utterly destitute of consistent principle, or of patriotic
end'.[44] Lowe and Elcho acted consistently upon their convictions,
but many of the rest were as flotsam on the tide.

IV *The Resignation of the Government*

The defeat on Dunkellin's motion was the final blow to a
Ministry which had entered the struggle divided and reluctant,
and which had been seriously contemplating resigning since
Grosvenor's amendment in April. Once the Redistribution Bill
entered the committee stage, on 28 May, the Cabinet lived in
daily expectation of defeat.[45]

On 3 June Brand warned Russell that a deputation of important Whig members was intending to go to him to demand that
the Reform Bill be postponed. They would represent, Brand
explained, 'a general wish both inside the House & out of it that,
while the Bill is postponed, the Govt. should not resign'. This
would necessitate a vote of confidence and Brand informed
Russell that he had already begun to draft a suitable one. It was
to be a 'general' motion recommending delay and not mentioning
the franchise clauses, in order to win a 'general support'.[46]

Brand's letter was more an ultimatum than a warning. As the
Government's existence became increasingly precarious he had
emerged as one of the spokesmen for the Whig anti-Reform
group, and as one of the most influential men in the party. His
rise reflects the general breakdown of authority on the Liberal
side and Russell's inadequacy as leader. The Prime Minister
was tired, and too vacillating and fretful to cope with a party
broken between its Whig and radical wings.

Russell told Brand that he would receive the deputation but
that he would prefer to resign rather than accept any vote of
confidence which required the abandonment of the Bill. This
was in the spirit of Gladstone's declaration, but he concluded by

remarking that he would not 'insist' upon resigning, if his colleagues thought otherwise.[47] The following day, expecting defeat
on Hayter's amendment, he joined Brand in a frantic search for
a formula that would allow the Government to drop the Bill,
secure a creditable vote of confidence, and placate Gladstone.

Placating Gladstone was the difficult part of the task. Gladstone needed the Prime Minister's backing if he was to have his
way in the Cabinet and he was determined to keep Russell up
to the mark:

> Brand has spoken to me a good deal about floating ideas and
> schemes for getting rid of our Bill and at the same time keep-
> ing *up*, by means of some step to be taken after the division
> on Hayter's motion. Looking at the matter . . . I cannot . . .
> divest such . . . proposals of the aspect of dishonour. Our
> Bill is *not* crude.[48]

He was resolved to keep the Bill in the House, so that Reform
should be won or lost in full view of the country. Russell replied
that he intended to resign if defeated on the motion of confidence, or if he received an insufficient majority. Gladstone
agreed, and then proceeded to subject Russell's note to his own
peculiar kind of exegesis: in the event of a victory on Hayter's
motion Gladstone wanted: 'To take votes on the franchises. . . .
And if the House will not vote upon them & postpone in order
to avoid it, thereupon to resign forthwith.'[49]

As the crisis deepened with the narrow votes on Stanley's and
Walpole's amendments, the pressure mounted for the Government to drop the Bill. The Queen became exceedingly anxious
and virtually commanded Russell to postpone it so that his
Ministry might survive to deal with the Prussian-Austrian War.
Lord Lansdowne came as emissary from the conclave of Whig
peers with a last offer of compromise.[50] But compromise was
impossible so long as Gladstone refused to yield on the £7 level
and the continuance of the Bill. He remained unmoved by the
Queen's plea and curtly reminded Russell that she had wanted
Reform settled when the Government first raised it.[51] He moved
quickly to stiffen Russell and Granville against Lansdowne's
offer; and symptomatically Russell enclosed Gladstone's letter
with his reply to Lansdowne.[52]

The split in the Cabinet vitiated the Government's handling of
Dunkellin's amendment. Clarendon headed the group who

wished to avert it by bringing on a motion of confidence,[53] while Gladstone wanted to make the amendment an issue by which the Government 'would stand or fall'. But he knew a majority of Cabinet was against him, and that it might cause a party revolt. Instead, he earnestly, and perhaps disingenuously, told Russell that he thought he 'ought to say at the close of the debate that we can make *no promise to accept Dunkellin's amendment*'.[54] The irony was that he achieved nothing by this course except to leave everyone irritably puzzled.

When the Cabinet assembled on the day following their defeat on the amendment, they were confronted with a telegram from the Queen informing them that she considered 'it the bounden duty of her Government, in the present state of the Continent, to set aside all personal considerations, and to continue at their posts. In fact, knowing the impossibility of forming another Government, the Queen could not accept their resignations.'[55] Nevertheless, they decided to resign. Russell received an angry, exasperated reply from the Queen, reiterating her earlier message.[56] Her stand precipitated a week of chaotic manoeuvring. The Cabinet now found it as difficult to leave office as they had previously found it to stay in.

Gladstone was eager for a dissolution. He wrote a long letter to Russell vindicating his own role, and setting out his conception of Parliament as an instrument of national moral progress. It gives a vivid impression of his ruthlessness when he was pursuing what he believed to be right, and it was this kind of ruthlessness which made him both so strong and so vulnerable a politician:

> The reasons against Dissolution seem to lie on the surface—It would cause expense and annoyance—It would lessen the chance of reuniting . . . the seceders and the mass of the party. It would—according to Brand—somewhat diminish the gross number of the nominal supporters of your Government, on the other hand. It is truly the course most conformable to the principles and spirit of the Constitution. It would probably bring the great question of the Reform of Parliament nearer an issue—With a little *more* real strength we should have carried our point—with a little *less,* we should have been met and defeated in open field by our opponents. Either way the country would have [been?] set free from what is now likely to continue, as it has unhappily long been, a source alike of difficulty and of discredit.

I quite understand how those who are prepared further to curtail, on some future occasion, the enfranchisement we have proposed, or whose minds are not made up against such a course, should now . . . rationally enough recommend resignation.

It relieves them from any pledges to the Bill. It will give them the chance of concurring thereafter in some plan, docked to meet the views of Lord Grosvenor. . . .

I start from a different point; from the conviction that we have proposed what should be regarded as a *minimum* of enfranchisement. In common with the 300 men . . . who support the Bill and the Government . . . I should find myself again landed . . . in opposition to Lord Derby. But either that opposition would not be a reforming opposition at all—in which case the loss of the question would be immense—or else it would combine for reform on some principle of compromise i.e. of asking less than the least which we deem advisable. . . .

With regard to the diminution of the majority of 70, the real question is not as to our nominal muster-roll . . . but as to the amount of strength available for great public purposes. A general election, which should somewhat reduce the party, would be of great use, *if* it should also have the effect of [purging?] it.

I feel painfully that the history of the question of Reform, from 1850 to 1866, is the one discreditable and dishonouring chapter in the history of the Reformed Parliament. All other battles have been honourably fought. . . . [Thus] the two objects which . . . ought to outweigh the doubtful considerations of party convenience are

1. To keep faith with the people.
2. To redeem the honour of Parliament . . .

[and] it is through Dissolution that they are to be pursued.[57]

Brand had analysed the constituencies of England and Scotland and estimated 24 losses in a dissolution, nearly all of them threatened Whig boroughs in the South. Against this he predicted 16 gains, mostly for seats held by Adullamites. On the basis of Dunkellin's division the Government had 320 supporters; an election would reduce them to 312, or a minority in the House of Commons.

I feel bound to add [Brand wrote] my strong opinion that a Dissolution at the present crisis would be a fatal mistake. I believe that it would go far to destroy the popularity which justly attaches to the Govt., & that it would be the making of the Conservatives for many years.[58]

It was a persuasive analysis to Ministers who wanted to take the easy way out.

But the easy path of resignation was also temporarily barred. As long as the Queen refused their resignations the Ministers had to seek for some way of staying in office. Earl Grey hinted that the Government might accept rating as a basis for the qualification, but Russell, backed by Gladstone, considered it out of the question because of the difficulties and the humiliation it would entail.[59] As he was writing his letter to Russell on the dissolution, Gladstone was handed a note from the Queen desiring the Government to accept Dunkellin's amendment or drop the Bill. He was moved to make a half-hearted offer to resign, to clear the way, but he shrewdly entwined Russell in his offer: 'Would it be possible that those colleagues who are less rigid than I—and I believe than you—should comply with H.M.'s wish, and carry on the Government, letting the Bill stand over?'[60] Gladstone's retirement was perhaps the one way by which the Government might have survived; but neither he nor Russell took it.

This week of defeat and indecision saw a sudden quickening among the Reform movements in the country. They reacted indignantly to the final triumph of the Opposition and their insidious efforts to wreck the Bill. Motions of support flowed in to Gladstone from meetings at Manchester, Birmingham, Sheffield, Middlesbrough, Bristol and Leicester, among others, all calling for a dissolution.[61] The speakers at the meeting presented it as a clear-cut issue: the Opposition was trying to thwart the moral progress of the people, by attempting 'to perpetuate a wrong'.[62] A mighty head of moral steam was building up.

The radical M.P.s were busy in the movement. P. A. Taylor led the Leicester demonstrations, Bright was campaigning in Manchester and Birmingham, Mill, Fawcett, Crossley and T. B. Potter were active in London, Brighton, Halifax, Rochdale, and Bradford, while Wykeham-Martin and Trevelyan were occupied in trying to breast the waves of the agitation in their constituencies.[63] The Irish independent Liberals were ardent in the cause. Benjamin Whitworth, the member for Drogheda, told the Reform meeting at the Free Trade Hall that 'the Government had won

the hearts of the Irish people during this session by its action
on the Church question and on the great question of tenant
right'. And by way of warning to those Irish landowners among
the Adullamites, he added that there could be no hope of peace
in Ireland if the Cave and the Conservatives supplanted the
Government without an election.[64]

Bright returned to the charge with his own form of moral
pressure. He informed Gladstone:

> Resignation I only dread, or dread chiefly, in the fear that the
> Tory Government, if formed, might conspire with the '40
> thieves' to force a Reform Bill which would be worse than
> nothing. . . .
> Brand makes no allowance for the moral force of a contest
> through the country for a great principle and a great cause.
> Last Easter showed how much feeling your appeals could
> speedily rouse. A General Election for Reform and a Reform
> Government would bring an immense force of popular feeling
> into the field, and I do not believe in your being beaten.
> Besides there is something (far worse than a defeat), namely,
> to carry on your Government with a party poisoned and
> enfeebled by the baseness of the '40 traitors'.
> If all the 40 come back & if a few counties are lost, there will
> be gains in Ireland, & in Scotland, & in English boroughs. . . .
> In great emergencies, something must be risked. You will
> have a great party, well compacted together and a great future.
> Mr. Brand's figures should be forgotten for the moment.
> Forgive this opinion and this advice—I think *you* are in the
> great crisis of your career and you must not forget the con-
> cluding passage of your great speech on the 2d Reading of the
> Bill. Read it again to nerve you to your great duty.[65]

But there were other Liberals who were vehemently opposed
to a dissolution. Charles Buxton, who had scraped in for East
Surrey, told Gladstone that 'many' Liberals were 'dismayed' at
the prospect of a dissolution 'as they feel in very many cases,
almost certain of losing their seats. The plain truth is,' he added,
'our constituencies would much *prefer* a less reduction of the
borough and county franchise than the one proposed by the Government. . . .' The financial crisis had made a dissolution
especially unwelcome 'when so many are distressed by pecuniary
losses'.[66] Hussey Vivian was not personally afraid of a new
election as he controlled his seat in Glamorganshire, but he too
warned Gladstone:

nothing could be more fatal to our party . . . I hear nothing
but angry & bitter words from our oldest & staunchest men in
reference to it. . . . Many will permanently withdraw from . . .
[the party], many will not contest their seats, many will return
with secret bitterness in their hearts at all the trouble &
expense to which they have been put.[67]

T. D. Acland and R. W. Crawford were both friendly to Gladstone and the Bill, but they too wanted to avert an election and
a break-up of the party. Both notified Gladstone and Russell
of their intention to move confidence motions.[68]

The motions had to bridge the gulf between Gladstone and the
Adullamites, and yet stand a chance of winning a creditable
majority from the scattered Liberals in the House. Brand spent
his time scurrying between the factions trying them with various
permutations of phrases. They all agreed on the innocuous first
paragraph: 'That in the present State of affairs, at home & abroad
this House would see with regret a change in the Councils of
Her Majesty', but they disagreed absolutely on the second, which
dealt with Reform. Russell had approved a version which ran:

> That this House, however, is anxious for an early settlement
> of this important question, & with this in view will be ready
> to take into consideration any measure which H.M.'s Govern-
> ment may introduce in a future session founded on the
> principles and leading provisions of the measures introduced
> by H.M.'s Govt. during the present Session.

Brand took the draft to Earl Grey and Earl Grosvenor, who
refused to accept the phrase, 'leading provisions of the Bill'.[69]
Then, on his own authority, Brand altered the motion to please
Grosvenor. He deleted the 'leading provisions of the measures
. . . ,' etc., and secured a promise from Grosvenor that he would
advise his men to vote for it. Gladstone was furious. The alteration, he told Russell, would 'leave our *Bill* as dead as mutton'.[70]

Russell, meanwhile, was at Balmoral pleading with the Queen
to come to London. She refused, but compromised by coming to
Windsor.[71] Throughout the crisis, her Ministers had wearisome
journeys added to their unsatisfactory interviews with their
Sovereign. While Russell was travelling, Sir George Grey circulated a resolution which deemed it 'inexpedient' to proceed further
with the Bill, but which committed the House to giving 'its best
consideration' to a future measure introduced 'after full deliberation & such further inquiry as they might think advisable'.[72]

Gladstone refused this too. Grey and Russell subsequently drafted eight revisions and Gladstone rejected each in turn.[73]

Russell would have liked to have kept the 'leading provisions' in Brand's resolution, deeming them 'absolutely necessary', but he quickly introduced seemingly explicit, but ambiguous, substitutes, by altering the motion to read, after 'principles', 'of a reduction of the County & Borough franchise and of a transfer of seats from the smaller boroughs to populous Counties & Towns'.[74]

Brand was now desperate and was fighting more deviously than ever. He followed up his letter accepting Russell's modifications with the news that

> My draft of the Resolution . . . has got into other hands, and it, or something to the like effect, will be taken up by Crawford & others. I hope that Gladstone will upon further consideration acquiesce in the movement. We can, if we please, wash our hands of it at the last moment, but it would be a strange situation for a Govt. to resist the [Group?] & Parlt., which actually presses you by the resolution to proceed with Reform.[75]

He primed Sir George Grey to emphasize to Russell that he would not support Gladstone in demanding the retention of the 'leading provisions' and that he was completely opposed to a dissolution,[76] while Brand himself told Gladstone that he would refuse to manage the election if the latter forced it.[77]

The next day, the 25th, Brand cheerfully announced to Russell that there had been an unofficial meeting of Liberal members. The meeting had been 'unanimous and hearty' and had decided that the resolution 'which had got into other hands' would be moved by Crawford and seconded by W. H. F. Cogan.[78] This development was an example of Russell's and Gladstone's mismanagement of their followers. During the Reform debate they had called only one general party meeting, and throughout the crisis they left their men in ignorance: Brand found it easy to organize behind their backs.[79]

One hundred and seventy Liberals had attended the meeting, and, contrary to Brand's report, it had been neither unanimous nor hearty. Grosvenor and Dunkellin agreed to vote confidence, but baulked completely at any specific promise of future Reform. A. S. Ayrton and K. D. Hodgson refused to countenance any resolution without the Reform pledge. 'Some wanted it strong, others mild—& so the meeting broke up without agreeing to anything', Beaumont reported to Earle.[80]

In preparation for the Cabinet on the 25th, Russell revived a form of compromise which his colleagues had earlier dismissed as being too flimsy to stand. He proposed that the Government should accept Dunkellin's amendment where it applied to £6 rated houses and attach a proviso to include those £7 rental occupiers who would be excluded by a rate-paying qualification. The Cabinet was equally divided about it. Granville, Stanley, Villiers, Argyll, Gibson, Goschen and Gladstone supported it, while Somerset, de Grey, Cranworth, Sir George Grey, Hartington, Clarendon and Cardwell opposed it, and preferred the Brand-Crawford motion. The compromise survived by the Prime Minister's own decision.[81] Russell omitted to tell Crawford that the Cabinet had abandoned his motion, and Crawford was justifiably angry when he heard indirectly of the switch.[82] It was an extreme case of the breakdown of communication within the party and of the leaders' failure to acknowledge and foster the co-operation of even their most reliable supporters.

Russell and Gladstone were not the only men in the Cabinet who felt that their personal honour was at stake. After the Cabinet meeting Clarendon wrote to Russell to plead for the abandonment of the shabby strategem they had adopted to by-pass Dunkellin's amendment. He was deeply concerned for the responsibility of Ministers to Parliament and had come to believe that Gladstone's obstinacy had damaged that mutual confidence between the members of the House which made parliamentary government possible:

> The decision of today causes me such distress of mind that I cannot help asking you to consider whether some form of resolution cannot be found that will command a majority & at the same time satisfy I will not say the honour of the Govt., but the exigencies of Gladstone & they are distinct things— Neither you, or any of yr. colleagues except Gladstone wishes to humiliate the H.o.C. or is unprepared to make such reasonable concessions as are necessary where compromise & conciliation are honestly desired, but he wants a triumph over them to wh. they will not submit & therefore wants to put words in the resolution beyond what are required for the real interests of reform (with wh. measure I am the first to admit that our honour is linked) & wh. he knows men as honourable as himself cannot accept. I am as convinced as any

one can be of that wh. has not yet happened, that the indignation at our having refused such a resolution of confidence as
Craufurd[83] [*sic*] wd. have moved will be universal *& just*.

I have no personal interest in the matter—such as I have is
in favour of resignation for official life is most distasteful to me,
but I have very strong party feelings & I cannot bear the
thought that an act of ours shld. be the construction of a party
for Derby & Co. . . .

I have also . . . an equally strong feeling for your reputation
and I cannot bear that the last act of your official life should
be to break up the party by which you have been so long and
so faithfully supported—It cannot promote the cause of reasonable reform and, when the truth comes to be known it will be
fatal to Gladstone whose services and abilities would fit him to
guide the destinies of this country if his arrogant ill temper
did not repel the sympathies upon which a leader must rely
for support.

Until today I was unable to understand the feeling with
regard to him that he has created in the H.o.C. . . .[84]

Russell went to Windsor on the day after the Cabinet. His
interview was inconclusive. He refused to press the resolution
and the chance of continuing the Government, and insisted that
the question of resignation was entirely in the Queen's hands.
She sent him to consult again with the Cabinet, which was to
meet that evening to receive his report. They again decided
to resign and sent their decision by telegram to the Queen who
notified them of her acceptance on the same evening. That night
she wrote to Lord Derby to ask him to form a Government.[85]

The Ministers took their last decision as they had taken its
predecessors: at a bewildered impasse and without consulting
their supporters. Given the balance of forces in 1866 the outcome
perhaps could not have been different. Russell and Gladstone
found themselves crushed when they determined to adjust, however slightly, the representative basis which supported the power
of the ruling caste. For fifteen years Governments had been
forced to jettison their Reform Bills before they were sunk with
them. Russell and Gladstone had struggled to cling to theirs and
had destroyed their Government in the attempt. The magnates
and the squires needed to be frightened by a greater force than
the eloquence of Bright and Gladstone before they would give
way to Reform.

5

THE REFORM BILL OF 1867

I *The Conservative Government and the Hyde Park Riots*

The erratic course of politics in 1867 reflects the peculiar and inauspicious circumstances under which the Conservative Government had its origins and fought its struggle to survive. Lord Derby's administration was a stop-gap in an interval of civil war in the Liberal party and he and Disraeli held office only as long as their opponents persisted in their differences.

Derby became Prime Minister because the Adullamites bungled things after their victory. That they should have done so was probably inevitable, for they had revolted to achieve an impossible aim. They were the Old Believers of the Liberal party, resolved to maintain the Palmerstonian calm, but they failed to realize that the quiescent nation which had allowed it and the grand old man who had ruled it had passed for ever. Their tactics against the Bill had been desperate and negative and they had not counted beyond throwing it out and perhaps replacing Russell and Gladstone. Certainly they had not planned that the passionate, implacable Gladstone should not only hold to the Bill but carry the Government down with it. The place-hunters among them viewed the prospects of a Tory Ministry with hope,[1] but the more established Whigs, Lowe, Elcho, Grosvenor and Horsman, thoroughly disliked it. They had co-operated with Disraeli and Earle because they needed their tactical advice and the Conservative numbers, and not because they intended to place a tricky upstart like Disraeli in a position to become Chancellor of the Exchequer. They had persuaded themselves while they were plotting with Disraeli that they were upholding the party truce and utilizing the Tories for their proper purpose, as a convenient, acquiescent Opposition to be summoned whenever the Whigs needed help to subdue the radicals.

With the success of Dunkellin's amendment the Old Believers had restored the first part of the status quo. To complete the process they now had to supplant Russell and Gladstone with an amiable, do-nothing Whig who would manage the gentry's resistance to the radicals. It was no part of the truce to accept a subordinate position in a Conservative Government.

Disraeli had worked with the Adullamites because he believed he could use them to climb to power. For twenty years he had hoped and worked for a split in the Liberal majority and Lowe and Elcho had presented him with his first great opportunity. From the outset he was contemptuous of the abilities of the Adullamites and completely sure that he was using them for his own purposes; so much so that he dismissed the possibility that they might equally be using him for theirs.[2] When the 'Third party' had first displayed its talents in the debate on Clay's Bill, Disraeli described Gregory's speech as 'vulgar', Horsman's as 'shallow and unstatesmanlike', and he dismissed Elcho as 'pompous and deficient in taste'. He thought 'with dismay of having such empty fellows in the Cabinet', he told Northcote.[3] On the other side, Northcote had heard that Lowe had 'no dislike for Dis., but a good deal of contempt for him'.[4]

When the showdown came Disraeli found to his alarm that the Adullamites intended that both he and Derby should be replaced in a new régime based upon a coalition of the gentry. They demanded that Derby give way to Clarendon as Prime Minister and Disraeli abdicate the leadership of the Commons to Stanley.[5] Forty Adullamites were prepared to join Stanley but only ten or twelve were willing to follow Derby.[6] Earle had played on their hopes by telling Elcho and Grosvenor that Derby intended to decline office and would accept a minor place in a Whig-led coalition. This assurance, given without Disraeli's knowledge, makes the behaviour of the Adullamites more 'explicable' and 'defensible' than Monypenny and Buckle would have us believe.[7] 'The amiable and spirited Elcho has played his unconscious part in a long-matured intrigue', Disraeli told Derby after he uncovered the story.[8] Earlier he had written:

> The terms intimated by Lord Grosvenor are not consistent with the honor of the Conservative party, and are framed in ignorance, and misconception of its character.
>
> I am, and, as you know, ever since the last General Election have been, prepared to withdraw from the leadership of that

party in the House of Commons . . . but I have only been
ready so to act on two conditions:
  Firstly, that, whether in or out of office, you should be the
chief; and, secondly, that, in the event of your declining the
post, you should be succeeded by Lord Stanley.[9]

He had thus once more entwined Derby's and Stanley's fates with
his own. Earle's rash promise destroyed his political career.
Disraeli arranged his transfer to the Poor Law Board in the
hope that it would keep him quiet, but far from his being
'completely satisfied', he resigned that office in March 1867, and
became a bitter and dangerous enemy to the Government. He
did not contest his seat in 1868 and left England to become a
merchant in the Middle East.[10]

  The Queen's summons reached Derby on 27 June and after
twenty-four hours' deliberation he undertook to form a 'Liberal-
Conservative . . . Government which might obtain the confidence
. . . of Parliament, and hold out a prospect of permanency'.[11] He
was loath to take office. He was tired and sick and he still
resented the humiliation he had suffered as leader of a minority
Government in 1859. He wanted the assurance of strong Whig
support before he would undertake to form another administration, and his negotiations with the Adullamites had soon convinced him that he would not get it. At the end of the week he
was ready to return his commission.

  After his rebuff from Grosvenor and Elcho, he had offered seats
in the Cabinet to Clarendon and Somerset, and had backed his
approach to the former with a letter from the Queen.[12] But both
the Whigs refused. This setback forced Derby to turn to the
Lansdowne-Clanricarde faction. He offered them one Cabinet
place and two other posts, but they too, like Grosvenor and Elcho,
promised 'an independent support', but would not join his Government. They had already wrecked one ministry because it had
deviated from the anti-Reform truce and they were not going to
surrender themselves to men whom they trusted even less.[13]
'Difficulties are on the increase—', Derby wrote to Disraeli on
the 30th. 'No external assistance—no progress made—the Adullamites en masse decline office.'[14] He was only kept going by Disraeli, who was determined to take office. 'The question is not
Adullamite; it is national. You *must* take the Government; the
honor of your house and the necessity of the country alike require it.'[15]

Disraeli had to prop the old aristocrat in the leadership because only Derby could shield him from the group in the party
who wished to break him. They were headed by the Marquis of
Bath and included Lord Cadogan, Sir Rainald Knightley, Baillie
Cochrane, 'Big Ben' Bentinck, the Lowthers and Beresford Hope
—veterans of the attempt to remove Disraeli in 1860.[16] They,
too, were Old Believers who wanted a coalition of the gentry that
would slough off the unsteady men, Russell and Gladstone,
Derby and Disraeli, and enable Parliament to maintain a quiet
front of resistance. Disraeli sent Taylor, the Conservative Whip,
to sound the Marquis of Bath and to soften him towards the
formation of a Derby Ministry: 'He is more of a "frondeur" than
ever,' Taylor reported.

> He declares that he will denounce in unmeasured language
> any attempt of Lord Derby to form a government—I was
> powerless to change his mind—he says he is supported . . .
> by *many* of the Conservative party . . . & declared further
> that all the Adullamites agree with him.[17]

The Bath clique, emboldened by the three notable resignations
from the Government in 1867, became a continual hazard to
Disraeli's ambitions throughout 1867 and 1868.

Bath's reply highlighted the fundamental question facing the
Conservative party. If Derby and Disraeli remained, the party
would continue in its rediscovered role as an aggressive parliamentary force and a viable alternative Government; but if they
were overthrown and the party coalesced with the Whigs it
would lose its identity and disappear. In the event, of course,
the Whigs coalesced with it. But the Conservatives knew they
were at the turning point. As Northcote told Carnarvon during
the week of negotiations, there was no alternative remaining
'but a Derby or a Russell Government: and I am satisfied that if
Lord Derby does not accept Office our Party is broken up for
good or bad. Anything that can be done to keep him up to the
mark ought to be done.'[18]

Ultimately, Derby was forced to draw his ministers solely from
among his Conservative supporters. Disraeli took advantage of
his leader's irresolution to forward the claims of his own age
group and so Northcote, Gathorne-Hardy, Cranborne, Carnarvon and the Duke of Buckingham all entered the Cabinet.
He demanded Northcote's inclusion upon the threat of his own
resignation and he embarrassed Derby.[19] The promotion of these

new men thwarted the expectations of the party stalwarts and
Derby became flustered as he tried to placate everybody. 'The
construction of the Government is still incomplete', Northcote
wrote in his diary on 4 July:

> There is great dilatoriness and some blundering . . . Lord D
> has offered the Vice-Presidency of the Council both to Adder-
> ley and Corry, and both have accepted. It is not clear how he
> will get out of the scrape. Neither of them can well take the
> Vice-Presidency of the Board of Trade as both are senior to
> me [Northcote had been appointed President] . . . Adderley
> may perhaps be induced to take the Under Secretaryship of
> the Colonies.[20]

Adderley accepted the Colonies and once the places were
settled, Derby and Disraeli relaxed. There was no call to produce a policy until the session in the new year. The Liberals
were disorganized and the Adullamites, if not positively co-
operative, would at least refuse to help Russell in turning out
the Ministry. During the time the Government was being
assembled, Ralph Earle had discussed the situation with Lord
Grosvenor's lieutenant, W. B. Beaumont, and transmitted the
latter's opinions, embellished with his own emphases, to Disraeli. Beaumont was very sanguine of the Government's prospects:

> Great interests have been alarmed & they must rally round
> you. . . . The time of year is in your favour—You need make no
> declaration of policy until next February . . . The dread of
> Gladstone, the hatred of Reform, the fear of dissolution only
> [go?] to secure you a good long spell of office.[21]

Recalling that there was war in Italy and Germany, revolution
in Spain, the threat of invasion in Canada, violence in Ireland,
and a commercial depression in England, Beaumont's analysis
might seem complacent. However, the Government did achieve
a state of suspended animation until the end of the session and
maintained it, despite a bad outbreak of cholera in London,
Liverpool and Southampton in July and August, and the Hyde
Park Riots.

The cholera and the Riots were ominously reminiscent of
the visitations which had accompanied the Great Reform Bill.
The cholera carried off 8,000 people in London alone and it

deepened the horror of the economic distress in the East End.[22]
The Hyde Park Riots seemed to portend a return to the violence
of 1831, and although they did not precipitate the Cabinet into
preparing a Reform Bill they did disturb its hibernation.

The Hyde Park Riots have come to have a fortuitous notoriety,
partly because they appear in retrospect to have been instru-
mental in persuading the Government that the introduction of
a Reform Bill was urgent, and partly because Matthew Arnold
made them symbolic of disorder in *Culture and Anarchy*, but in
themselves the Riots were comparatively unimportant. There
were serious disturbances in Hyde Park in 1855 during the agitation against the Sunday Trading Bill, but these have been
almost forgotten. The Riots of 1866 were much less violent than
the Nottingham election affray of 1865, or the 'Murphy Riots'
which broke out in Birmingham, Ashton-under-Lyne and Manchester in 1867 and 1868. The disturbances in Hyde Park were
unique in a mass agitation which maintained an unprecedented
degree of order and made their mark because they were a
reversion to the kind of popular violence which men could
recall from the thirties and forties. Although, as Matthew
Arnold perceived, the Riots were incidental to the clash between
the Reform League and the Government, they served to emphasize the victory of the massed force of the artisans over
traditional authority.[23] And this in its turn changed the attitudes
of members, from regarding Reform as an abstract question for
debate to accepting it as an issue which needed settlement.

The Reform League was one of the principal successors to a
long line of ephemeral societies which had striven for electoral
reform and redistribution since the collapse of the Chartist
Movement and the disbanding of the Anti-Corn Law League.
The societies inherited the sectional differences of the older
organizations and their activities had been continually vitiated
by disagreement about their objectives. Some sections adhered to
the Chartist demands for the ballot, 'manhood suffrage' and the
abolition of property qualifications for members, while others
deriving from the Anti-Corn Law League stopped at 'household suffrage'.

The societies were strongest in London and the industrial
towns of the Midlands and North. In the provinces they were
sponsored by radical manufacturers as a gesture of co-operation
against the territorial interest, while the artisans formed the back-

bone of the membership and supplied the audiences at the
public meetings. Several associations flared into life during
Bright's campaign in 1858-9 and then gradually sank back into
quiescence, while their sponsors and adherents turned their
energies to working for the Northern States and demonstrating
for Garibaldi.[24] The London societies were fostered by the
Trades Delegates. They tended to be more militantly committed
to manhood suffrage, and were usually stronger than those of the
provinces. They also had the backing of a small but brilliant and
enthusiastic group of intellectuals, like Frederic Harrison and
E. S. Beesly, who were to prove invaluable in 1866-7.

The societies' various Reform agitations brought no immediate
results but they contributed to one positive and influential
change, for they inculcated among their followers a sense of the
social value and inevitability of Reform, and they trained their
members in the management of orderly mass meetings. The
procession which escorted Garibaldi in London in 1864 must
have been one of the very first occasions when a crowd of
30,000 gathered to honour an idol of radicalism and afterwards
dispersed peaceably.[25]

The League's weakness as a political force was shown in the
1865 election. Its members worked for Tom Hughes and J. S.
Mill in Lambeth and Westminster, but its one prominent candidate, Baxter Langley, was badly beaten in Greenwich and it did
not succeed in making Reform the central issue of the election.
While the Reform meetings clearly encouraged the radicals to
force Russell's hand early in 1866 and deepened Gladstone's
resolve to stand by Reform, they had no direct influences, as
we have seen, on the shaping of the Liberal Bill. The relation
between the Reform societies and the Liberal Government was
one of reciprocal impulse, but the societies gained more from
Gladstone's emergence as a committed Reformer and public
orator than they gave to the Government in the form of pressure
for the Bill.

The mass meetings in London did not begin until after the
shock of defeat on Dunkellin's amendment. Beales and his committee turned to open air demonstrations only very reluctantly.
The League's first small march in the West End, in May, developed from a meeting in Trafalgar Square which George
Lucraft had organized in defiance of the League officials.[26] The
first mass demonstration occurred after the Liberal Government

resigned on 29 June, when a crowd of 10,000 people marched from a meeting in Trafalgar Square to Carlton House Terrace to cheer at Mr Gladstone's house and to groan at Lord Elcho's and the Carlton Club. The League committee then decided to hold a monster meeting in Hyde Park. This was not a new departure, for Beales, Bradlaugh, Holyoake and others, in an earlier capacity had held a meeting there in 1859 to protest against the Conspiracy Bill.[27] The trouble developed when Spencer Walpole, the Home Secretary, without consulting the Cabinet, instructed the 70-year-old Commissioner of Police, Sir Richard Mayne, to forbid the meeting and prepare to enforce the prohibition.[28]

Hyde Park was a royal park and in 1855, after the Sunday Trading Bill riots, the crown law officers had advised that the public enjoyed entry to the Park by royal favour. Her Majesty's Government therefore had a legal right to close the gates in order to exclude people, and to prosecute for trespass. Cairns and Bovill upheld this advice in 1866 but emphasized the difficulty of removing people from the Park once they had entered, especially as the Government had no legal right to use force to disperse a peaceful public meeting.[29]

The Council of the League met to consider Walpole's order and Beales explained the legal position to the delegates and pointed out that there were legal rights on both sides. He and Cremer pleaded with the Council to obey the Government in order to avoid possible violence, but Bradlaugh led the majority to overrule them and it was decided that the Hyde Park meeting should go on.[30]

The radical M.P.s were disconcerted by the move. They liked the prospect of the Government's being embarrassed by the agitations and they hoped that the Reform cause would receive a great impetus from them, but they hesitated to identify themselves with a demonstration which had an attendant risk of bloodshed. Bright wrote an open letter supporting the League's claim to meet in the Park but he refused to attend. The easy way out was to blame the Government for its mishandling of the affair.[31]

It is difficult to get a clear picture of what happened at the Park gates and along the railings, for the accounts vary widely. It seems that the column of upwards of 20,000 men marched up Park Lane to the entrance, and began to crowd densely when the head of the column stopped. Edmond Beales, at the front

of the men, quietly demanded entry of the police-sergeant at
the gates and asserted the legal right of the people to do so.
The sergeant politely refused and Beales turned to lead the
march off towards Trafalgar Square. The chaos began when the
huge mass of people tried to change direction. Beales had his
watch and handkerchief stolen by a pickpocket, and Howell and
Odger were badly jostled before they escaped and moved off
towards the Square. But the pressure of the crowd was so great
on those against the railings that they were forced to grasp them
to stop themselves being crushed. The railings were loosely set
in decayed stone and within seconds they suddenly heaved
over or snapped, and the people began to scramble into the
Park to escape the crush. Even as they poured in, they were
careful to step lightly across the flower-beds. The police reinforcements who had been drawn up inside the Park broke ranks
and began to chase the intruders and to swing indiscriminately
with their truncheons. Most of the demonstrators escaped, but
the roughs stayed to do battle with the police with stones
and branches torn from trees. One policeman later died of his
injuries and over one hundred from both sides were seriously
hurt. As night fell the police withdrew and left the Park to the
mob.[32]

The following day, Tuesday 23rd, Lord John Manners persuaded the Duke of Cambridge to send a regiment of Life
Guards to clear the Park. Then, according to Manners,

> as evening wore on things became worse, and Mayne, after
> a severe engagement between the Police and the mob, cleared
> Park Lane and the Park by charges of Horse and Foot Guards,
> against whom the mob never thought of making the slightest
> resistance. In fact, though the Park was quite open, it was
> successfuly defended, and when I arrived at the Piccadilly
> entrance about 9.30 I found a single line of Foot Guards drawn
> across the entrance from Apsley House garden to the Lodge,
> the gates open, the mob, among whom I mingled, exchanging
> chaff with them, but never venturing or thinking to attack
> that single line.[33]

The arrival of the Cavalry could have turned the riots into
another Peterloo, but fortunately Park Lane and the Park itself
offered room for the crowd to fall back. Both sides enjoyed
the unusual excitement and there was little ill-will. The Guards
were heartily cheered when they arrived, and Mrs Disraeli,

watching from her window in Grosvenor Gate, noted that 'the people in general seem to be thoroughly enjoying themselves'.[34]

Walpole found the events a nightmare. He was under pressure to stop the meetings and he had the law on his side but he could only stop them by ordering the troops to fire. The leaders of the League had technically obeyed the prohibition; the destruction of the flower-beds and the violence within the Park were largely the work of the mob after the main body of Reform Leaguers had gone off to Trafalgar Square on the Monday. Walpole was a gentle, indecisive man and he asked the much tougher Manners to help him receive a deputation from the League on Wednesday, the 25th. Beales browbeat Walpole and blamed the Government for the damage. He demanded that the League be allowed to hold a meeting unhindered by the police on the following Monday, in order that it might vindicate itself. 'Don't ask me that,' Walpole pleaded. According to Manners, Walpole attempted to continue, but 'was then so much affected that after the second sentence he broke down and, burying his face in his hands, gave way for a minute or two'. Holyoake, who was a member of the deputation, specifically denied the story, but whether Walpole wept or not the League lost no time in publishing the story, and it was almost universally believed.[35] The League also won another point. 'In tearful accents', according to Manners, Walpole gave Beales permission to set up a platform in Hyde Park that evening, whence to dissuade his Leaguers from further unofficial assemblies. The police and military were to be held in reserve. This gained, the deputation withdrew. Manners was extremely angry and told Walpole that he had abdicated his responsibility to men who were unable to guarantee the peace of the city. Suddenly 'Mr. Beales, & three or four more' re-entered the room and 'without sitting down and in a most irregular way' proceeded to ask permission to hold another Reform meeting on the Monday, unhindered by the police. Manners, fearful that his colleague would give way, whispered hastily, 'say you will consider it'. Walpole then asked them to put their request in writing so that he could place it before the Cabinet.[36]

That evening Mason Jones and Colonel Dickson put up a stall in the Park and advised the crowd to leave quietly. A few strollers followed their advice, but the rest ignored them and continued to enjoy their unusual freedom to play leap-frog across the flower-beds and climb the trees.[37]

Beales subsequently addressed a rather hectoring letter to Walpole urging the necessity of allowing the meeting on the Monday to relieve 'the dangerous state of exasperation now existing in the public mind'.[38] Before the letter was answered, the Reform League had begun to post placards advertising the Monday meeting. It was this act of defiance which increased the Cabinet's determination to meet bluff with bluff, and in its written reply on the 26th the Cabinet forbade a meeting in Hyde Park and offered Primrose Hill instead.[39] The latter site would have kept the crowds away from the West End, and, as most artisans walked to the meetings, would have greatly lessened the attendance. Beales was apparently genuinely convinced that Walpole had tacitly given his permission for the meeting, and when the Government forbade it he worked desperately to dissuade the League Executive Committee from persevering with it. But despite Beales' threat to resign, Bradlaugh and the Trade Union members of the Council determined to hold the meeting. It was not until John Stuart Mill, who was not a member of the League, put his influence behind Beales that the League decided to abandon the Hyde Park project and hold the meeting in the Agricultural Hall instead.[40] Mill's success and his later tumultuous reception at the Agricultural Hall testify to his prestige among the London artisans. It is a little mentioned incident in his life, but it may have saved London from serious rioting.

The League committee was deeply embarrassed by the rowdyism and it was their deputation which suggested that the broken railings and loose stones be removed from the Park because they were an incitement to the mob.[41] General Cluseret, the international revolutionary, entirely misjudged the temper and purpose of the leaders when he approached them to propose an armed insurrection, for Odger and Cremer quickly rebuffed him.[42]

The Riots gained their vehemence not from the positive support for the aims of the League, but from anger at the social exclusion implied in the Government's prohibition which ran counter to the general inclusionist enthusiasm of the age. The *English Workman* denounced Walpole's order as showing a lack

of faith in the good intentions of the workingmen and the use
of the Cavalry 'as importing continental practices into London,
and degrading us to the level of despotic capitals'.[43] Marx wrote:

> If the railings—and it was touch and go—had been used
> offensively and defensively against the police and about twenty
> of the latter had been knocked dead the military would have
> had to 'intervene' instead of only parading. And then there
> would have been some fun.[44]

As Professor Briggs points out, the 'if' is vital. The Riots were a
protest against class isolation, not a symptom of class war. Unfair exclusion was the theme of the handbills distributed through
the East End calling for

> 10,000 Costermongers, Mounted on their Donkeys. To parade
> Rotten Row, to test the question as to whether this or any
> other portion of Hyde Park belongs to a class or to the entire
> people.[45]

Amongst the upper classes, the doctrine of class mutuality
was agreeable only when the working classes kept their place.
Emily Eden attempted to drive around the Park at this time
and became so 'indignant at the sight of' unpoliced roughs
wandering the lawns that she told Clarendon that she felt
'bloodthirsty'. 'As for Beales', she supposed 'the meekest of
babies would hang that man as soon as look at him'.[46]

This demonstration of working-class independence, and the
assertion of the right to enjoy public amenities and political
discussion equally with the upper classes, greatly disturbed
Arnold and Carlyle. They saw it as the signal of the final break
in the chain of deference which had enabled English society
to progress peaceably, devoid as it was of a common faith and
common ideals. The working classes had shown themselves
prone to anarchy, and the upper classes had revealed themselves
as having lost the will to rule. But Arnold misjudged the Riots
as much as Marx. The actual disturbances and the League's
isolation from the mob presaged the Reformers' failure to con-
vert the votes of the mob into a viable electoral power and of
the mob's failure to translate its aspirations into effective parliamentary action.

Disraeli remained outwardly unperturbed by the Riots and
they did not impel him towards introducing a Reform Bill. The
famous letter, dated 29 July, in which he threw up the suggestion

that the Government carry a modified version of the Liberal
Bill was probably written, or at least conceived, on the 21st,
before the Riots began. The letter is useful, not for demonstrating Disraeli's reaction, or lack of it, to the Riots, but because
it sketches the motives which were to guide his course when
he brought in a Reform Bill in the following year.

> This is . . . the result of my reflections . . . on what Gladstone
> said yesterday.
> Suppose, instead of discharging the order of the day on the
> Reform Bill, you took up the measure where it stops: £6
> *rating* for boroughs; £20 rating for counties, to be brought up
> on report; the northern boroughs to be enfranchised; no dis-
> franchisement of any kind.
> You could carry this in the present House, and rapidly. It
> would prevent all agitation in the recess; it would cut the
> ground entirely from under Gladstone; and it would smash
> the Bath Cabal, for there would be no dangerous questions
> ahead.[47]

The 29th was a Sunday and as the House did not sit on Satur-
days, Disraeli is almost certainly referring to Gladstone's
speech on Friday 20th, in which he prefaced his withdrawal of
the Liberal Reform Bills with an ostentatious taunt to the
Ministry to carry them.[48]

Disraeli's three reasons for his projected manoeuvre are in-
separable in explaining his tactics in 1867, although only the
first, the prevention of agitation, is usually emphasized. He saw
Reform as but one more pawn in the game against Gladstone,
and as the mine the old Tories could use to destroy his leadership. On both counts there was much to be gained by passing
a Bill quickly. But he mentioned neither the need for a settlement nor the social good that would follow from extending the
vote to the workingmen.

His scheme was too blatant, of course, and the session ended
without further action on Reform. But the debates of May and
June and the high excitement of the divisions, and Gladstone's
public meetings in April, had made Reform a leading issue in
public discussion. Any Ministry which succeeded the Russell
Administration in 1866 would have had to make some gesture
towards it; while there is no reason to suppose that the Riots led
the Government to introduce its Resolutions when it did, the
mass agitation, the apparent breakdown of authority and the

belief that the lower classes were ready to demand Reform did ultimately persuade many members that Reform was an urgent question, while the need for a settlement gave the Ministry a powerful coercive argument in the debates of 1867.

II *The Resolutions*

The initiative for the second Conservative venture into Reform came from Derby. He had disregarded the July meetings, but on 16 September, a fortnight after Bright had begun his triumphal Reform tour, he wrote to Disraeli that he was

> coming reluctantly to the conclusion that we shall have to deal with the question of Reform. I send a memorandum . . . containing a sketch of a Reform Bill drawn up by R. D. Baxter, who has the whole question at his fingers' ends. . . . But I wish you would consider whether, after all the failures which have taken place, we might not deal with the question in the shape of Resolutions, to form the basis of a future Bill. We *need* not make the adoption of any of the Resolutions a vital question; while, if we should be beaten on some great leading principle, we should have a definite issue on which to go to the country.[49]

The primary impulse to plan for some gesture towards Reform in the next session undoubtedly arose from the growing impressiveness of the mass meetings, but the necessity to take up the question also stemmed from the Government's minority position in the House. Derby was resolved not to repeat his experience of 1859. As he explained later he

> did not intend for a third time to be made a mere stop-gap until it should suit the convenience of the Liberal party to forget their dissensions and bring forward a measure which should oust us from office and replace them there; and I determined that I would take such a course as would convert, if possible, an existing minority into a practical majority . . . [by] carrying a measure . . . the agitation for which was standing in the way of every measure . . . of practical legislation.[50]

Disraeli expressed himself against the introduction of a bill in the new session, because it would divide the party and unite the Opposition.[51] But on the day on which he answered Derby he also wrote to Cranborne, to sound his views on future legislation for Reform. Cranborne replied that he favoured a bill to disfranchise a few of the more notoriously corrupt boroughs, so as to forestall demands for wider redistribution.[52]

Derby, meanwhile, had found a strong supporter in the Queen, who was urging that a settlement be made to quiet popular unrest. He moved to persuade Disraeli:

> I agree with you that . . . there is considerable difference of opinion among our friends on the policy: but I think the general feeling is that we cannot escape doing something. The Queen spoke to me about it the other day—She said she was very anxious to see it settled.[53]

The Queen had a clearer sense than her Ministers of the strength of popular feeling and the necessity to maintain social harmony. Her agency gave the agitations a much greater influence in the counsels of the Tory Government than they would otherwise have possessed.

Disraeli thus found the views of the Queen, Derby and Cranborne ranged against his programme of inaction. He made one final effort to institute it by suggesting that the Government issue a 'Commission for Boundaries Etc.'. Derby refused, and patiently explained the strategy of the Resolutions to his lieutenant; strategy for which Disraeli has received credit ever since:

> In the first place, by introducing them, we put an end to the cry that we are the opponents of all Reform; no inconsiderable advantage if we should be driven to appeal to the Country. In the next place there will . . . be less likelihood of the necessity for such an appeal; and the House of Commons will not be sorry for an excuse which will postpone, at least for a year, a dissolution and a general Election. Then we are less committed to each several Resolution than we should be on the main provisions of a Bill; and whatever may be the point, if of sufficient importance to justify us in dissolving, the issue will be plain and sensible, and the Opposition will have the credit of doing their best to obstruct legislation. If . . . we get the House pledged to our *principles*, we shall be in a much better position for hereafter discussing details; and it will be difficult for the Radicals, either to escape from Amendments, or so to frame them as not to clash with the moderate Liberals, and widen the existing breach.

He added that he had drawn up a list of resolutions, 'which if carried, would place us on velvet. . . . The Queen wants "*us*" to settle it'.[54]

Disraeli could hold out no longer. He gave his enthusiastic agreement, but was careful to phrase Derby's general point more precisely: 'I had no idea, when you first wrote to me about "resolutions", that you contemplated the possibility of not legislating the session they were passed. If we can succeed in that, we shall indeed be on velvet.'[55] Now that he was committed, Disraeli moved to isolate General Peel, Cranborne, Bath and the others who were likely to denounce the Resolutions as the first step towards a full Reform. So he persuaded Derby to keep discussion out of the Cabinet and to reserve to themselves their preparation.[56]

They had the Resolutions ready for the second Cabinet meeting on 8 November. At the previous meeting they had persuaded their colleagues to adopt the method of proceeding by resolutions to a commission, and so eventually to a bill. The Ministers had gone away to prepare their clauses and came to the second meeting only to be confronted by an elaborate set, 'which no one much liked, but . . . which Lord Derby and Disraeli forced through . . . [because] the resistance was so fragmentary and uncombined'.[57] Cranborne and Carnarvon had both been warned, and Lowe suspected, that Derby and Disraeli were plotting a coup on Reform.[58] But Cranborne and Carnarvon were not intimates and Disraeli had been careful to lull them by keeping his intentions vague. 'Mr. Disraeli . . . seems to be most in favour of Resolutions', Carnarvon recorded, after a conversation at Highclere, 'and perhaps a Commission appointed by Parliament founded on the Resolutions. . . . He . . . is obviously in an undecided state of mind.'[59] As late as 26 December, Disraeli wrote to Cranborne to assure him that he was 'throughout . . . against legislation', and artfully went on to dissociate himself from his leader:

> Lord Derby . . . thought it inevitable, but, as you know, his views are now modified.
> It's a difficult affair, but I think we shall pull thro'.[60]

Disraeli remained uncommitted about the enfranchisement of the artisans and was prepared at this stage to use or abandon it according to the needs of his career and the party. He was resolved that if the Conservatives ventured into Reform, they should do so under their own colours and frame the issue so that if need be it could become a useful election cry. Thus he smartly blocked a proposal from Earl Grey and the Queen to appoint a committee of the Privy Council to draw up a report as the basis of a non-party bill. Grey wanted the 'concurrence of parties for this object . . . made *openly* . . . to avoid all risk of its being

thought an aristocratic cabal',[61] while the Queen told Derby and
Stafford Northcote that she was ready to appeal to the Whigs to
back the committee.[62] But the Tory leaders disliked Grey's plan
because it took the drafting of the Bill out of the House of Commons. They knew that the members would never accept from an
outside body legislation which affected their electoral interests.[63]
Disraeli also pooh-poohed the Queen's suggestion:

> The royal project of gracious interposition with our rivals is a
> mere phantom . . . the only practical result is to convey to our
> rivals that we are . . . feeble and perplexed.
>   Our future . . . depends on the course we shall chalk out
> for ourselves.[64]

Disraeli, rather than co-operate with his rivals, had his own pet
scheme for upsetting them. It was a variation on the coup he
had proposed on the motion for the withdrawal of the Liberal
Bill in July. He suggested to Carnarvon on 27 October, 'as a
detail', that they omit all reference to Reform in the Queen's
Speech. This would provoke Gladstone into moving an amendment to the Address, which Disraeli would then trump by announcing the date on which Reform would be considered.
Carnarvon jibbed; it was 'a dodge from which nothing could be
gained', and Disraeli acquiesced. 'He then spoke,' Carnarvon
recorded, 'of the difficulties of Government and said he had
never been in a majority.'[65] Although he gave Carnarvon to
understand that he had dropped the idea, Disraeli was still
canvassing it with Derby three weeks later, in mid-November.
He also came up with an alternative, more elaborate plan for
achieving the same end. If, as seemed likely, the Cabinet would
settle for resolutions and eschew his more hazardous proposal,
the key to success lay in the substantiality of the Resolutions.
They had to raise issues large enough to provoke a long discussion and

> if the House . . . gets involved in the discussion, the Liberal
> party will then probably be broken up.
>   If as is more likely, Mr. Gladstone meets the Ministerial
> motion by a general resolution in favour of immediate legis-
> lation, it is not impossible he may be defeated, which will
> establish the Government. But if he succeed it will probably
> be by a narrow majority, and the dissolution will then take
> place on an issue between Bright's policy and our programme.[66]

Derby, less whimsical than Disraeli and more perturbed by
the difficulties of his situation, constantly reiterated his demand
that the elusive 'substantial grounds' be found, for, he argued,
a lengthy and convincing enquiry offered the 'only chance of
escaping Shipwreck'. Boundaries could provide an adequate
excuse and bribery would give plenty of work, although they
hardly constituted a '*dignus nodus*' for a Commission. Derby
was now in full cry and he robustly threw over Disraeli's hint
that they dispense with further Cabinet meetings until after
Christmas.[67]

The Ministers spent the next eight weeks looking for suitable
issues. They had as their starting point the Resolutions (in
Derby's handwriting) which he and Disraeli had secretly prepared, and forced through on 8 November:

This House having in the last Session of Parliament assented
nem. con. to the 2nd Reading of a Bill entitled 'A Bill to extend
the right of voting at Elections of Members of Parliament in
England and Wales', is of the opinion.
1. That the number of Electors for Counties and Boroughs
in England and Wales ought to be increased.
2. That such increase may be effected by both reducing the
value of the qualifying Tenements in Counties and Boroughs,
and by adding other franchises not dependent on such value.
3. That the occupation franchises for Counties and Boroughs
should be based upon the principle of rating.
4. That while it is desirable that a more direct representation
should be given to the Labouring Classes, it is contrary to the
Constitution of this realm to give to any one class or interest
a predominating power over the rest of the community.
5. That it is expedient to revise the existing distribution of
seats.
6. That it is not expedient absolutely to disfranchise any
Borough, except on proof that corrupt practices have exten-
sively prevailed therein.
7. That in revising the existing distribution of seats, this
House will acknowledge, as its main consideration, the expediency of supplying representation to places not at present
enfranchised, and which from their population and property,
or from special circumstances, may be considered entitled to
that privilege.
8. That it is expedient that the Population of every Borough
represented in Parliament should amount to at least (   )
persons.

9. That a humble Address be presented to H.M. praying H.M.
to issue a Royal Commission to enquire into the Boundaries of
Boroughs; so that, in the above case, as well as in that
of Boroughs where the population has outgrown the limits
assigned to them by the Reform Act, a scheme for new and
enlarged Boundaries may be prepared for the consideration
of Parliament.
10. That the said Royal Commission should also revise and
verify the Returns laid before Parliament in its last Session,
with respect to the possession of the franchise; and obtain
such further information as may be the ground for well-
considered legislation.
12. [Derby missed 11] That it is expedient that the system of
Registration of Voters in Counties should be revised, and be
assimilated, as far as possible, to that which prevails in
Boroughs.
13. That it shall be open to every Parliamentary Elector, if he
think fit to record his vote by means of a Polling Paper, duly
signed and verified.
14. That provision be made by means of additional Polling
places, for diminishing the distance which Voters have to travel
for the purpose of recording their votes.[68]

The detail of the Resolutions formed Derby's problem. The
clauses set out all the principles that were needful for a bill
and made a Commission superfluous. Derby knew what addition
of votes and how much redistribution he wanted, and how to
contrive it. The Commission could add little to the information
already known and would appear as only a cover for procras-
tination. What he needed was a really sticky, vaguely practicable
question with which to clog the Commission's deliberations. On
22 December, while pondering upon possible questions, he
hazarded as an afterthought the idea of household suffrage: 'Of
all possible Hares to start I do not know a better than the extension of household suffrage, *coupled with plurality of voting.*'[69]
There was a new note of urgency in his letter. The session was
approaching, the agitations had continued almost unabated, there
had been another mass demonstration in the West End, and the
Government had still not settled its plan of survival.

The demonstrations had become really formidable. Bright's
campaign was attracting enormous crowds. At Birmingham, it
was claimed that over 150,000 people went to the meetings
organized jointly by the National Reform Union and the Reform
League at Brookfields on 27 August. The veterans of 1831

declared that it was the largest meeting they had ever known, and as enthusiastic as any in the great old days.[70] At Leeds, the day of demonstration became a general holiday. The procession of civic dignitaries, of Trades, Chapel, Temperance, and Friendly Societies and Reform delegations from the neighbouring towns, took an hour to pass the main stand, and it was said that 150,000 went to the meeting at Woodhouse Moor.

At Manchester, on 24 September, 120,000 people marched in pouring rain and an estimated 80,000 assembled to hear the speeches. In the evening the Free Trade Hall was packed and the ecstatic crowd sang the chorus of 'Auld Lang Syne' over and over as Bright came on to the platform.[71] The procession in Glasgow on 16 October extended for five miles and the open air meeting attracted an estimated 130,000 people. The procession exemplified the heightened self-respect of the growing class of artisans. There were iron-moulders, blacksmiths, engineers, ship-wrights, masons, bricklayers, plasterers, painters, goldsmiths, coppersmiths, leather-workers, corkcutters, pipemakers, carters, and miners, many dressed in their work attire and carrying their tools of trade, each group with its trade banners and emblems mingled with those of the Temperance Leagues and Friendly Societies. They sang the Reform ballads as they marched to the pipers, while the marshals strode briskly beside them, each armed with his white baton of office.[72] 'No public meetings in the course of my life . . . equalled them in enthusiasm', Wemyss Reid recalled.[73]

The strength of the agitation derived from the temporary unity of the Reform movements and the seeming certainty that they were about to achieve the final breakthrough. The day meetings belonged to the League and the populace, and the soirées to the Union and the middle classes. The mayor often led the procession and usually chaired the evening meeting. In Leeds nearly 1,000 of the leading citizens paid 5s. each to attend the soirée. Each gathering indeed, in the North, represented all who were 'most important, most influential, omnipotent, within that town in which it was held'.[74] The might of provincial mercantile Britain was massed against the landocracy. The artisans' sense of their moral right to inclusion was the spring of enthusiam at the mass meetings.

> Gladstone has said—'O brother band,
> Our flesh and blood throughout the land,

Workmen, of England's State the strength,
Your right is, to the front at length.'
Your country, Queen, and Nobles too,
In proud affection yearn on you,
Respect your honest rights on earth,
And trust in Heaven to stamp your worth![75]

Lowe's fatal words decorated one of the leading banners in each procession and Bright never failed to quote them in his speeches.

At last, after his weary years of campaigning, Bright was seeing the might of popular opinion harnessed to the cause of Reform. Joyfully he told the people of Manchester that their demonstrations had ensured that the Government would not dare otherwise than take up the question. But they had to keep up the pressure: popular pressure had coerced an unwilling Tory Ministry to repeal the Corn Laws, and coercion would be needed again to make their successors carry Reform. In his practised way, he adumbrated a threat:

These great meetings . . . are meetings for demonstrations of opinion, and if you like . . . for an exhibition of force—an exhibition of force of opinion now, and if that force of opinion be despised and disregarded, it may become an exhibition of another kind of force.[76]

The vehemence of Bright's speeches and the size of the demonstrations appalled Gladstone and some of the radicals, and confirmed them in their opinion that the Government would have to deal with Reform. Gladstone told Brand: 'The reform movement is by degrees complicating the question. It is separating Bright from us, and in one sense thus clearing our way. But then it may become too strong for us; or at least too strong to be stayed with our bill of last year.'[77] Edward Baines publicly declined an invitation to a joint Reform League and Reform Union meeting because he disapproved of mass meetings, and because the organizers refused to restrict the motions explicitly to household suffrage.[78]

The alliance between the workingmen and the middle-class reformers was always brittle, and it worked on a basis of spasmodic collaboration at public meetings rather than in continuing private co-operation between the local leaders of the respective groups. Arthur Partridge, the friend of T. B. Potter, had put 'five years of hard work' into the Birmingham Liberal Association and had been the founder-chairman of the Birmingham branch of the

Reform League, but he resigned after the Hyde Park Riots and in weariness of the unending wrangling in the League over tactics. He sounded Mill as a replacement for Beales as the figurehead of the movement: 'The middle class *cannot* unite under a man lower than many of themselves and who is incapable of commanding the elements with which he would work.' Mill replied evasively that he tried 'to cooperate with all reform groups'.[79]

Throughout the autumn the Whigs held aloof from the meetings. Brand refused an invitation from the National Reform Union to attend a banquet in Manchester, and said bluntly in his reply that he did not want to commit the Liberal party to agitation until the Government's intentions were known.[80] Sir George Grey thought his decision was 'very wise'; for if the Whigs connected themselves with the meetings they would only add impetus to the demand for household suffrage and make it difficult for themselves to accept a 'reasonable Bill from Derby if it comes'.[81]

Brand's anxiety to dissociate the Whig Party from the agitations was a symptom of their effectiveness. After the Birmingham meeting, Russell told Amberley that he thought it had 'put the question of the reduction of the franchise beyond all doubt'.[82] Brand tried to stop the drift by pointing out to Russell that there was no strong feeling for Reform outside the industrial towns. He wanted Russell to play 'a waiting game': if they became embroiled in the agitations there was a danger that they would appear to be tied to Bright and his henchmen, which would provoke their gentry supporters to 'create a Cave of Adullam in every constituency'.[83]

But the agitation had grown beyond the stage where the Whigs could afford to stand apart, and several attended the Manchester banquet despite Brand's publicized abstention. The speeches were very temperate, but some of the diners remained uneasy. 'Oh! Why don't those foolish men let Lord Russell's Bill pass?', lamented one lady. 'It would be such a comfort to cease being a Radical!'[84] As the winter drew in and the demonstrations continued unabated, even the radicals became anxious. T. B. Potter and his wife regaled the Amberleys at breakfast with 'the revolutionary . . . state the country wd be in if Reform . . . were not carried'.[85]

The demonstration in the West End on 3 December was planned as the climax of Bright's campaign. The Union and

League were hoping to have 250,000 marchers in a procession which was to fill Trafalgar Square and Piccadilly, and then to move through the West End to the grounds of Beaufort House, which had been lent them for the day by Lord Ranelagh. The organizers had decided against another trial of strength about Hyde Park.[86] The projected size of the demonstration alarmed Derby. He was thinking of forbidding it altogether and risking 'a disturbance', but Disraeli apparently counselled his leader to let it continue and he was vindicated in the event. To have attempted to stop it would have been to risk a disastrous battle in the streets of London. Monday 3 December unfolded as a louring, drizzly day and only about 25,000 turned out to march. Even so, 25,000 is an impressive figure, and the column took over an hour to splash softly past the Carlton Club. The demonstration impressed the onlookers with its high seriousness and good order; 10,000 of the marchers were voluntary marshals. Disraeli had instructed Lord George Lennox and Ralph Earle to mingle with the crowds, and at 1.05 p.m. Lennox reported: 'It is difficult to decide about numbers but it certainly is a formidable demonstration. . . . The drilling & organization . . . have been a complete success . . .'[87] Beales, George Potter, Dickson, Lucraft and Holyoake spoke at the afternoon meeting and Bright addressed the soirée at St James's Hall. The meeting marked a new stage in the collaboration between the League and the Union, for none of the motions referred to manhood suffrage.[88]

Though the December procession failed to reach the expectations of its organizers, the quiet determination of the ranks made its impact. On the following day the Liberal *Daily News* declared:

> We . . . have passed into a new phase of political life, and the class so well represented yesterday must soon be formally admitted within the pale of the Constitution. When a Reform demonstration musters for a march within pistol-shot of one royal palace and in the courtyard of another, and within hail of Whitehall, it is surely a sign that the change that has come over our political life will soon be recognized in Parliament.[89]

The *Daily News* was unduly optimistic, for Derby and Disraeli, though quietly watchful of the agitations, were intent upon proceeding via their Resolutions. But the promise of unrest did cause at least one Minister, Sir John Pakington, to waver. On the day after the march he had written to Derby and Disraeli to tell them that he had come to the opinion that their plan of postponement would prove difficult, and that they might have to drop the Resolutions and bring in a bill. 'Men . . . are really anxious for a popular measure and early legislation. . . . Others who . . . would gladly see it postponed, may nevertheless be apprehensive of the consequences of another year of agitation, and may wish the question settled.' He went on to request that the Cabinet begin to consider schemes which would 'concede a wide extension of the franchise without overwhelming property by numbers', and thenceforth Pakington became a strong advocate of an immediate bill.[90] But Derby stood by his Resolutions as the means of keeping the Opposition divided: 'the less we set up any specific scheme . . . as a *cockshy,* the less chance there is of their coming together'.[91]

A week later Disraeli received letters containing opinions similar to Pakington's from G. S. Beecroft, a Tory back-bencher, and from a Nottinghamshire squire, W. N. Denison. The latter declared that the proposal to set up a Commission was a 'transparent . . . dodge' which would not gain anything for the party either in the House or in the country. Neither gentleman wanted Reform, but believed that a bill would have to come, and, as Denison put it, they 'would much rather see a moderate Bill from our Side than an immoderate one from Gladstone, Bright & Co. better . . . to be wise in time, and do with a good grace what will have to be submitted to.'[92] Stanley held the same view,[93] while Corry told Disraeli that he had 'been rather surprised at the unanimity with which all classes, in the provinces where I have been, desire a Reform Bill—from Lord Shaftesbury to the Shropshire rustic'.[94] Disraeli bided his time. He told Cranborne that he was against a bill, and in his correspondence he referred only to the Resolutions.[95] But he secretly instructed Dudley Baxter to calculate the effects of various permutations of suffrage qualifications.[96]

The Ministers spent two meetings in January wrangling over the Resolutions and by the end of the month were still disagreed about them. Manners wanted clauses which would bind the Commission to recommend the insulation of the county constituencies and the enlargement of the county representation.[97] Cranborne and Hardy both objected to the preamble and Cranborne was adamant against giving any directions as to principle: he wanted to restrict the Commission to the collection of statistics.[98] Naas also preferred to keep the franchise question beyond the competence of the Commission and thought that it should deal only with the enlargement of the borough boundaries.[99]

Stafford Northcote emerged as the conciliator. He agreed with Cranborne and Hardy that the preamble was not in harmony with the Resolutions in that it could be interpreted as committing the Government to an unqualified reduction, but he also pointed out that if they omitted all mention of reduction, Gladstone and the Opposition would meet them with an amendment and thus seize the initiative. It would, therefore, be impossible for them to take their stand upon the existing suffrage levels, 'however desirable that might be'.[1] The Government had to find a 'standpoint' and guard it by conditions. He believed that there was no standpoint short of household suffrage, but he wanted to leave it to the Commission to discover it. He also proposed to amend the tenth Resolution to provide for representation of minorities.[2] This helped to mollify Cranborne and, after a fortnight's further negotiations, the Cabinet adopted the Resolutions. The memoranda on the new clauses have a stolid ring about them and they may well be Northcote's own unprompted work, but Cranborne suspected that Disraeli was using Northcote to clear the ground for household suffrage; Northcote arrived to discuss the subject with him the day after Disraeli first broached it.[3]

Disraeli was leading each of his two strongest opponents at their own pace. He dealt with them separately outside the Cabinet chamber. Cranborne, hard-headed and austere, was the more difficult, and with him Disraeli was careful only to propose, very vaguely, that household suffrage be sent as a possible franchise level to the Commission. Even this 'alarmed' Cranborne. He told Disraeli: 'Such a course would make it easy for the other side to frame an amendment that should drive the waverers into their lobby, & would deprive your concession of all neutralizing safeguards . . . resolutions are only safe so long as they are general.'[4]

Disraeli ventured one step further with Carnarvon. They had an agreeable conversation about the Resolutions on 1 February and Disraeli apparently found it opportune to raise the question of a bill. Like Cranborne, Carnarvon was obviously left uncertain as to what Disraeli had actually proposed, and he subsequently wrote to clarify their interview. It was a bewildered, anxious letter; the agitations had placed all the Ministers—except Disraeli—in a dilemma.

> On thinking over our conversation of yesterday it has occurred to me that I hardly expressed myself with as much clearness on . . . Reform as I could desire. . . .
> 1. I understand that we are generally agreed upon an attempt at legislation provided that no unforeseen circumstances arise. In this I quite agree—I see no alternative.
> 2. My own view is to carry the borough franchise down to a considerable depth in order to get a ledge on which to rest. I believe an arbitrary reduction of £1, £2, or £3 to be of all measures the most fatal. For this reason, I do not as far as I understand . . . the problem . . . object to household franchise.
> 3. But such a reduction needs some very distinct checks. A residential qualification of three years with the payment of rates and taxes is excellent; but I feel some fear of depending on one single safeguard . . . must we not expect that the moment that the measure is passed, agitation against the restrictable portions of it will commence? If so, is it not probable that agitation will have a fairer chance of success if the restrictions . . . are narrowed to one single . . . point?[5]

Disraeli's set of restrictions, based on rates and taxes, was part of an ingenious scheme conceived by Dudley Baxter. They planned to copy the system of plural voting in parochial elections and introduce it into the parliamentary system. Plural voting had been in operation in the majority of English parishes since 1818; the system had worked smoothly and excited no widespread dissatisfaction.[6] According to Baxter: 'The poorer householders seldom complain of the power of the larger rent payers, and the latter are enabled to exercise in some degree a control over the expenditure of the parochial taxation.'[7] He realized that the parochial system was too unwieldy to be adopted entire, but he proposed that the Sturges Bourne scale be taken as the model. He dismissed as unworkable J. S. Mill's scheme for plural voting based on educational and economic qualifications: 'There wld be dissatisfaction & jealousy among the plural voters themselves; and the mob wld be just as impatient of being ruled by the Aristocracy of Examinations as by the Aristocracy of Wealth.'[8] Baxter's scheme went far towards providing an effective counterbalance to household suffrage. He estimated that a household-occupier qualification would create about 400,000 or 500,000 extra working-class voters, if the compounders were included.

But plural voting on rating would give 362,000 additional votes to property, or plural voting on the house tax, 338,000.

Derby and Carnarvon approved the scheme, but Walpole and Pakington distrusted it.[9] Pakington told Disraeli he believed 'that the boldest course will be the *safest* and . . . as we must adopt a novelty, it will . . . be better to take that which is *simple & effective,* rather than one which is complicated, invidious & incomplete'.[10] Walpole also wanted a simple system of exclusion. He favoured household suffrage based on residence and direct rating, which, he was convinced, would be 'most conservative', for it would exclude compounders.[11]

It was only after the leading Ministers had individually accepted the principle of household suffrage in the Resolutions that Disraeli suggested that Reform be specifically mentioned in the Queen's Speech. The decision was taken, as were most of the Government's decisions, by separate private discussions and not by the open agreement of the assembled Cabinet. Disraeli persuaded Cranborne and Carnarvon that 'to omit all reference to it would be to give Mr. G. too useful a subject for oratorial elaboration', and so a 'rather indeterminate' paragraph was inserted.[12] Certainly it did not commit the Government very far. It was ambiguous as to whether it referred solely to the Resolutions or to a possible Bill, and it laid down no time schedule.

Many of the Conservative peers and back-benchers were now eager for a settlement and they seized upon the Reform paragraph as a promise to bring in a Bill.[13] Graves, the ship-owning M.P. for Liverpool, told Disraeli he was 'delighted' with it. It was 'an immense relief to him; there was only one opinion out of doors; settlement of the question'. Disraeli lost no time in reporting the conversation to Derby.[14] The House generally approved the paragraph when the session opened on 5 February, although Gladstone still managed to orate elaborately on the necessity for a Bill.[15]

Derby and Disraeli did not place Baxter's plural voting scheme before the full Cabinet until the day after the Queen's Speech. Resolution Five had been mysteriously transformed to read:

That the principle of Plurality of Voting . . . as adopted for the purposes of Parochial Legislation, would allow of the safe extension of the Borough Franchise to all rated Householders: and that such extension, so guarded, affords the best prospect of a safe and satisfactory settlement.[16]

The Cabinet decided to omit the phrase 'as adopted for . . . Parochial Legislation', but apparently accepted the rest. However, on the following day, General Peel wrote to Derby threatening to resign unless the reference to household suffrage were deleted.[17]

Disraeli was keen to prevent a break-up right at the beginning of the session and coached Derby in his reply: 'Our great anxiety not to lose his services would make you agree to recast, and modify, the Resolution . . . which you might also take the occasion of making him understand was your own particular policy, and which you had . . . carefully considered.' Disraeli also supplied an amended version of the fifth Resolution, substantially as it was later approved by the Cabinet and introduced to the House:

> That the principle of plural voting, if adopted by Parliament, might lead to the adjustment of the borough franchise on a safe and permanent basis. The House and the country (more important) would understand this.
> If the Resolution be adopted, we could do without Peel.[18]

He then went to soothe the General and secure his approval for the new Resolution. He succeeded, and reported to Derby that Peel was 'very placable, except on the phrase "household suffrage", when his eye lights up with insanity'.[19] '

On Monday 11 February Disraeli introduced the Resolutions into the House.[20] He made a long, pointless speech which bored and dissatisfied even his own supporters.[21] He pleaded for co-operation from both sides of the House to effect a moderate settlement. Gladstone justifiably replied that it was impossible for the Liberals to promise to co-operate while they were left uncertain as to whether the Government meant its Resolutions to stand as the principles of a forthcoming bill or merely intended them to be submitted to the Commission and forgotten.[22] It became clear from this exchange that the Government would have to jettison the Resolutions if it was going to survive, for they offered no basis for keeping the initiative in the House.

III   *Lurching into Reform: the Household Suffrage and Ten Minutes Bills*

The Conservative Reform Bills of 1867 were launched on their bizarre career on Thursday 14 February, only two days after the Resolutions had been introduced. The launching arose from an inconsequential dialogue between Lord Robert Montagu, a Tory back-bencher, and Disraeli. Montagu asked the Chancellor: 'Whether the Government will endeavour, as early as possible in this Session, to bring in a Bill which will carry out whatever Resolutions may be passed by the Committee?'[23] The leading nature of the question suggests at first sight that it was part of a preconcerted move to hurry the Cabinet into settling for a Bill, but Montagu was an ally of General Peel's and Disraeli would hardly have selected him as a foil. The spontaneity of the exchange seems clearly reflected in the fumbling reply Disraeli gave, and in the obvious astonishment it provoked in Montagu. Disraeli began by alluding to 'the Bill which we might bring in', and then shifted, apparently unconsciously, to 'the Bill which we hope we may almost immediately introduce . . . after the passing of the Resolutions', to the assurance, 'that the moment the Resolutions are passed not a moment will be unnecessarily lost'. 'I should consider,' he went on, 'that to invite the House to discuss Resolutions upon a subject of this paramount importance, and in the event of their not being adopted, not to be prepared immediately to act upon them, would be disgracefully trifling with the House of Commons.' So much for being 'on velvet'. Montagu was staggered:

> The right hon. Gentleman has misunderstood my Question. I did not ask him whether he intended to bring in a Bill to carry out the Resolutions . . . but whether he honestly and sincerely desired to gather the opinion and wishes of the House and bring in a Bill to embody those wishes as expressed by the Resolutions of the Committee. I wish not to be told he will bring in a Bill to carry out a certain foregone conclusion of the Government.

Disraeli:

> I do not clearly understand the object of the noble Lord's second inquiry. I take it for granted that everybody who acts in this House is noble and sincere . . . I must repeat again, in the most distinct manner, that we brought forward these Resolutions as the basis of a Bill.[24]

Disraeli had spent so many months obscuring the purport of the Resolutions for his colleagues, that in the stress of the moment he had temporarily deceived himself. He had finally been engulfed by the various streams of pressure for a Reform Bill, and without warning, without the prior consultation or permission of his Cabinet, he had hazily committed the Government to the immediate production of a Bill. At no time before this announcement had the full Cabinet even formally discussed or entertained the proposal.[25] No wonder Cranborne and Carnarvon believed that they had been tricked.

When the Ministers met after the blunder, General Peel rebelled again. The usually accepted version of this meeting derives from Disraeli's sketch for his misleading report to the Queen.[26] Here Peel is presented as an illogical hot-head, a man who accepted Resolutions which were specifically amended to meet his views and then suddenly broke faith with his colleagues by refusing to assent to any reduction of the franchise. Peel *was* a hot-head, but he was also loyal, consistent and intelligent enough to be chosen twice as a Cabinet Minister amongst a party in which there was plenty of high-born competition. He opposed the unsanctioned declaration of a Bill, not the Resolutions. The Queen realized this, despite Disraeli's report, for she commented during her conversation with the latter that 'the Reform Bill . . . was more important than General Peel'.[27] When the three rebel ministers later came to present their resignations to the Queen, Peel was the only one with whom she would shake hands.[28]

In the sketch of his projected letter Disraeli also began to convince himself that the Cabinet had swung round to a Bill 'after Christmas', and that the change had been signalled by the inclusion of the Reform paragraph in the Queen's Speech. Within a fortnight he had managed to forget that it had not been inserted until at least the end of January.[29] The real interest of the letter is the light it throws on Disraeli's ability to turn private fantasy into historical myth: a faculty that was to be invaluable to him when later he was put to explaining the evolution of the 1867 Act.

On Friday the 15th, the day after his announcement in the House, Disraeli sketched out a Bill. He abandoned the simple plan of giving double votes to electors above £10, and sounded Cranborne with a scheme 'which [had] just occurred to him'. It was Baxter's parochial voting framework with fancy savings and taxation qualifications added, allowing up to four votes. Cranborne demurred to a household suffrage plan so uncertainly protected, and instead proposed a £5 base level. When the Bill was put before Cabinet on the Saturday, £5 appeared as the limit and the plurality was cut back again to two votes.[30] The reduction to £5 would allow in 300,000 artisans, but the plural votes would create 390,000 extra upper-class votes. 'We all accepted this . . . as a very conservative measure,' Carnarvon recorded.[31]

The £5 limit survived only until the next Cabinet meeting on the 19th when it was abandoned and the Ministers reverted to a qualification based on household suffrage. The Queen had meanwhile persuaded Peel to waive his objections to a reduction. She had told Derby, he informed the meeting, that she believed that 'the security of her throne was involved in the settlement of this question, and if possible by her present advisers'.[32] Derby and Disraeli obviously felt confident enough to press upon the Cabinet the scheme which offered the best chance of outbidding the Liberals. And they had succeeded: 'all was smooth', Hardy recorded of the meeting.[33] Disraeli had not produced any figures to show the effects of the reduction, and so the final discussion of the plan was fixed for Saturday 23rd.

Cranborne was disturbed by the reappearance of household suffrage and he began to take precautions. He sought out Carnarvon, and they had a long talk about Reform. Cranborne was 'sure that Disraeli was playing them false and had Ld. Derby in his hands', and he and Carnarvon resolved to collaborate to stop the drift.[34]

Baxter and Montagu Corry were working desperately to prepare statistics for Disraeli to use at the Cabinet on Saturday.[35] The qualifications and calculations presented all sorts of unexpected difficulties. The depositors in Post Office and Railway Savings Banks were not registered by locality and their term and place of residence could not be proved from their pass-books.[36] The banks' records did not distinguish between the sexes and it was impossible even to provide a reasonable guess at the number of male depositors.[37] The educational qualification specified 'Associate(s) in Arts', but this award was made only at Oxford, and it did not include a certificate that could be submitted in proof of claim. 'Ministers of Registered Chapels' were to qualify, but there was no general law by which chapels were registered. Clause 20 provided that the Savings Banks should issue certificates proving the amounts of claimants' deposits, but the Bill made no provision for the cost of drawing up, printing and issuing the certificates, and Disraeli saw that the Government could not possibly order the banks to carry the expense.[38] The direct taxpayers had to be estimated from the Return of 1861.[39] Baxter made a series of elaborate calculations from the House and Assessed Taxes for 1859 and ended with a guess that the qualification might create 170,000 additional votes, 'if 50% register'; but he scrawled at the foot of the page: 'Difficulty of return *almost* insurmountable'.[40] The nice adjustment of the electoral balance required an administrative competence and a fullness and precision of statistical information which did not exist in Victorian England.

Baxter also produced tables setting out the probable results of adopting the various rental and ratal levels of enfranchisement on the size of the counterpoise produced by plural voting. Both tables show the uncertainties underlying the computations. At each level Baxter had to guess at the proportion who would fulfil the residence and poor-rate conditions, and then to estimate the number likely to register. The further he went down the scale the more variable the estimate became. He concluded that below £4 ratal, it was 'impossible to compute the numbers . . . as so many are excused payment'. The problem was further bedevilled by the unknown, but very great, number of compounders. However, the final conclusion was clear enough: the plural voting scheme would have to be extended if it was to outweigh household suffrage. Like Russell in 1866, Disraeli had decided upon his Bill before he knew the figures. At £7 rental according to Baxter, the working classes would have a minority of 28,000 against the existing and new plural votes of the upper classes; but at £6 the working classes would have a majority of 59,000; at £5, a majority of 146,000; at £4, a majority of 218,000; and at household suffrage, they would have 335,000 more votes than the upper classes, or better than 2:1. The same pattern was true of a rating franchise, though it would operate more favourably to the upper classes because it was more restrictive: at £7 rating the working classes would be in a minority of 103,000; at £6 they would have a minority of 63,000; but at £5 they would have a majority of 37,000 votes, and at £4, 107,000 more votes than the upper classes. Disraeli found these revelations bad enough, but they appeared to be catastrophic when he realized that it was futile to hope for a weightier system of plural votes. The House disliked electoral novelties and he was doubtful as to whether he could lead it to pass even the simple scheme.

Baxter was in a panic and advised him to abandon household suffrage and settle for a £5 rating level with a straightforward plural vote on property. The members would accept it, Baxter added, once they realized that these provisions were necessary to ensure an upper-class preponderance in the constituencies.[41]

Baxter's calculations, with their simulated precision, demonstrated household suffrage as a certain danger, but Disraeli had other sources of information and comfort. He had a conversation with S. R. Graves which struck him enough to make him recount it to Derby, and it may have crystallized the deductions he drew from two other sources. Graves told him that he wanted 'a moderate settlement'. 'But what do you call moderate?' Disraeli asked. 'Oh! I should say, for myself, household suffrage founded on rating. That's the real thing; rating is better than any money qualification. There are 10,000 Parliamentary voters now in Liverpool who do not pay their rates—and never will.'[42]

Graves' comments gave new point to a letter which Derby had passed on to Disraeli a few days earlier. The letter was from A. J. Murray, who had been Registrar of Electoral Claims in South Australia. In the course of a detailed account of the working of manhood suffrage in the colony, Murray set out to refute the myth that it had led to the supremacy of the working-men and to their mass participation in politics. He claimed that after manhood suffrage had been introduced in 1851 there had been only five voluntary claims for registration in the working-class West Adelaide division. The agents had had to canvass the householders and exert considerable pressure to persuade them to enroll, for registration cost one shilling, and the men were uninterested in politics. Derby marked the first part and doubly marked the sentence about reluctant enrolment: 'Some of this *especially the first part,* is worth your looking at', he endorsed the letter before sending it to Disraeli.[43]

The third influence was a pamphlet by Edward J. Gibbs, a revising barrister from Wolverhampton.[44] The crux of Gibbs' argument appears on page 19 of the 1866 edition:

The real objections to ratepaying clauses depends on a belief that householders below a certain class will not pay rates or any form of direct taxation, and that if their admission to the franchise depends on such payment, they will not be admitted at all.

But this belief, well founded, will not be considered an argument by those who wish to *have qualified* rather than a *pre-
determined number of electors*. It is possible that a Bill giving
even household suffrage on proof of the full payment of rates
would not add more votes to the lists than Mr. Gladstone's
Bill.

The emphases are Disraeli's. He apparently wrote to Gibbs to
congratulate him on his pamphlet and to seek further information, and Gibbs sent him an elegantly bound copy of the second
edition with several pages of manuscript notes inserted at the
back. In the preface to the third edition, published on 5 March,
after the announcement of the Conservative Bill, Gibbs proudly
hinted that the Government was following his lead. His boast
may not have been vain, for 'personal rating' became the key-
stone of Disraeli's Bill.[45]

Thus, despite Baxter's figures, Derby and Disraeli decided to
retain the household suffrage basis of the Bill. It was too late
and too difficult to change, the even level offered the best potentialities in out-manoeuvring the Liberals in the House, and there
seemed to be a good possibility that many would fail to enrol,
especially if the registration provisions were kept awkward.
Their immediate problem was to commit their Ministerial colleagues to household suffrage without their learning too much
about Baxter's calculations. When he arrived at the meeting on
Saturday 23rd, Derby announced that it would have to be short
because he had another engagement. Disraeli rapidly outlined
the figures prepared by 'the ablest statistician of the age', and,
with hardly a pause, the Cabinet accepted household suffrage
allied with a plural voting scheme based on property. A bribery
bill was 'scrambled over', a redistribution plan was mentioned,
and Derby closed the meeting. There had been virtually no discussion.[46] 'The Cabinet unanimous for the great plan. Baxter
must stop to see me', Disraeli scribbled triumphantly to Corry.[47]

Disraeli's triumph was premature. Cranborne had also been
doing his sums and on the day before the meeting he had
already reached a disturbing conclusion which he was to sub-
stantiate on the following Sunday.[48] It is curious that he did not
speak up at the Cabinet meeting, but perhaps it moved too
fast. Perhaps, too, he was biding his time while he accumulated
the ammunition with which to blast Disraeli. He broke his usual
Sabbath observance and spent the day in calculating the scheme

in detail. That evening he took his results to Carnarvon. 'It appeared', the latter recorded, 'that Baxter had only taken the totals and that the distribution of the new voters in the Boroughs under 20,000 . . . would leave the counterpoise not quite equal to the net additions. . . . Thus a complete revolution would be effected in these boroughs'. Cranborne declared that he intended to enclose his resignation when he sent the figures to Derby, but Carnarvon persuaded him first to ask for a meeting of Ministers. They spent the night in anxious consultation with potential allies. 'After a few mouthfuls of dinner', Carnarvon sought out Gathorne-Hardy, explained his mission and brought him back to Cranborne's house for a further study of the figures. He then went to rouse General Peel, who emerged from his bedroom 'bare-legged and dressing-gowned'. Peel quickly accepted their conclusions and promised that he too would resign if Carnarvon or Cranborne decided to quit the Cabinet. Cranborne sent a note to Derby demanding a Cabinet for the morrow.[49]

In lumping the totals together and assuming an equal distribution of new voters throughout the boroughs, Baxter had overlooked the probability that the fancy qualifications and the plural property votes would be concentrated in the larger towns. Cranborne argued in his letter to Derby that, 'in small boroughs the addition is large and the counterpoise small, in the large boroughs, where we are hopelessly overmatched, the counterpoise is large and the addition small'.[50] The flaw derived from the haste with which the measure had been cobbled together. But Cranborne knew that the Government was committed to its Bill and that no alternative remained, for Disraeli's indiscretions had closed the retreat to the Resolutions and the Commission. But fatalist as Cranborne was, his letter to Derby offered no suggestions for tightening up the Bill or altering the tactics of the ministry. His fatalism was to be a great strength to him when in power, but in 1867-8 it helped to immobilize him as a possible leader of the malcontents against Disraeli.

Disraeli was still abed on Monday morning when a note arrived from Derby covering Cranborne's and Carnarvon's threatened resignations. 'The enclosed, just received, is utter ruin. What on earth are we to do?' Disraeli, never one to lose the initiative in a melodramatic situation, replied: 'This is stabbing in the back! I will come to you as soon as possible, but I am not up, being indisposed; but I shall rally immediately in such dangers. It seems like treachery.'[51] Hard upon his first note, Derby sent another alarmed scribble. He had just received a report from Baxter confirming Cranborne's results on the small boroughs. Later calculations showed that in the boroughs under 10,000 the number of sub-£10 working-class voters likely to register would be more than twice the upper-class votes created by duality.[52]

Derby planned to explain the Bill to the Conservative members at Downing Street at 2 p.m. and at 4.30 Disraeli was to introduce the Bill in the House. In response to Cranborne's demand, those Cabinet Ministers who could be found were summoned to Derby's house at 12.30 p.m. Pakington arrived soon after that time and found three or four there. Cranborne himself did not arrive until 1 p.m., so that Carnarvon, who had come on time, had to bear the brunt of the angry discussion. He stood by his threat to resign if household suffrage were not abandoned.

> No attempt was made . . . to contradict the accuracy of our case. Whilst Disraeli was white as a sheet, Lord Derby was very angry—broke in repeatedly using the strongest expressions of regret and dismay etc.
>
> At last when we had come to within half an hour of Lord Derby's meeting, and the Cabinet had in fact dissolved, Stanley proposed as a compromise, a £6 rating, but without any duality of voting. Vehement discussion followed on this and it was only within five minutes of Lord Derby's meeting that it was finally decided to take the £6 rating. . . .
>
> I proposed to abide by the original proposal, household rating and plurality of votes and direct tax, but apply it only to the larger boroughs . . . but . . . it was overruled . . . Peel, Cranborne and I were alone. Walpole sat in a corner of the room speechless. Naas, who came late into the room, and could not make out what we were discussing . . . thought . . . it was the suspension of the Habeas Corpus Act.[53]

The simple £6 franchise survived, for want of time to thrash out a better compromise. Derby and Disraeli supported it, but a majority of those present, Buckingham, Chelmsford, Hardy, Pakington, Northcote and Manners, spoke against it before they unhappily acceded to it.[54]

Disraeli ate nothing that afternoon. At 3 o'clock, after taking a single glass of wine at Downing Street, he went to the House to outline the truncated Bill. When the story of the £6 qualification later became known, the measure was tagged as the 'Ten

Minutes Bill'. The House was packed, with members seated on
the floor and the galleries crowded with distinguished visitors.
With an 'air of deprecation and depression', he began to describe
a set of qualifications not greatly dissimilar from those in the Bill
he had destroyed the year before: £6 rating in the boroughs, £20
in the counties, four fancy franchises, and no plurality of votes.
There was also to be a redistribution of thirty seats. Until the
very end of his speech, Disraeli referred almost exclusively to the
Resolutions which, despite his reply to Montagu, were technically
still before the House, and he concluded with a motion, not to
introduce the Bill, but to take the Resolutions into Committee.
It was an extraordinarily empty, confused performance and when
he sat down, Lowe and Bright proceeded to flay the Government:

> We had a speech which told us nothing; then we had Resolu-
> tions which told us little more than nothing; then we had the
> reasons (which came afterwards, instead of before) . . . why
> Resolutions were proposed instead of a Bill. . . . Is it business-
> like to introduce a number of abstract propositions, withhold-
> ing the concrete scheme, and to ask Parliament to waste its
> time in the discussion of theses almost too general to be sub-
> mitted to boys in a debating society?[55]

Bright found the whole affair 'ludicrously crude'. 'Why, under this
Bill, a ratcatcher who keeps four dogs would pay a direct tax
. . . of 20/- and, of course, would come into the new constituency
which the right hon. Gentleman says is to save this country from
destruction.'[56] When Disraeli rose to reply he was met with
cries of 'Withdraw! withdraw!'; he half withdrew some of the
Resolutions and offered to deal with the rest on the following
Thursday.[57]

Derby and Disraeli had been forced into a bad tactical error.
They had tried from the outset to give themselves as much freedom as possible by presenting abstract resolutions, and now the
very nebulosity of their proceedings had created an opening for
the Opposition. Gladstone was to address a party meeting on the
26th and he would be able to fill out and take over the Government measure. The Ministers had, therefore, to forestall him with
an effective bill: 'What must be done is best done without the
appearance of compulsion', Stanley advised Disraeli on the
morning of the 26th. He pointed out that Gladstone was sure
to receive strong backing if he opposed the Resolutions at the

Liberal meeting and 'to give way after their intention is announced will be humiliating. I would decide the question in
Cabinet this morning, and at half past four today announce the
abandonment of the resolutions, and your intention to propose
a bill'.[58]

Derby was panicky and reverted to his old hope of securing
Whig support, or a truce with Gladstone obtained through the
influence of the Queen. Disraeli wrote two letters in quick succession to strengthen him. He argued that Gladstone and the Whigs
would keep a truce only if they could dictate on the bill, and so
the Conservatives would lose the prestige of carrying their own
measure. Disraeli was determined to bring events to a fight.[59]

The Cabinet meeting on Tuesday the 26th was 'gloomy and
irritable'. The dissidents said very little, while Derby and Disraeli, supported by Pakington and Stanley, urged that the Resolutions be withdrawn and a bill be brought down in the
following week.[60] That evening Disraeli gracefully withdrew
the Resolutions, and so checkmated Gladstone, who had come
to the House prepared to move a motion to that effect.[61]

The smooth disappearance of the Resolutions helped to
disguise their role in the development of the Bill. Disraeli
subsequently found it easy to present them as the planned but
unimportant accompaniment to the paragraph in the Queen's
Speech, with the implication that together they formed the
introductory notices of a Bill which had been discussed, decided
and prepared simultaneously with them.[62] Salisbury offered a
belated correction to the myth when Kebbel presented it in 1882
in his collection of Disraeli's speeches, but Kebbel omitted it
and only published it years later as a 'curiosity'. 'The Resolutions
disappeared so rapidly,' Salisbury had written, 'that nobody
guessed the importance which the Cabinet originally attributed
to them, or the labour which it cost to draw them up.'[63]

The Conservative back-benchers generally supported the
Cabinet's decision to bring in a Bill, but they wanted one that
would make a settlement. On the Monday evening Graves had
collected a small group in the smoking room of the Carlton Club
and urged that the municipal suffrage was the only basis on
which 'the municipal Reform Bill could rest'. He found ready
support and the movement spread next morning. Three of his
friends, Laird, the shipbuilder M.P. for Birkenhead, Goldney,
the member for Chippenham, Jervis, the railway and shipping

magnate from Harwich, and Graves himself, were chosen to form
a deputation to convey the views of the movement to Disraeli.
He received them coldly and indicated that the Ministers were
resolved on the £6 Bill; the time had passed for major changes,
he added, and back-bench amendments would 'certainly upset
the Government'. Graves replied that 'the feeling was so strong
it would find vent in some embarrassing way'. Then, 'the Chancellor, throwing off the reserve which had thus far marked
[our] interview, said . . . he was free to admit he had long been
of the opinion that rating and residence were the true principles
for a Reform Bill, and added: "Lord Derby was also of his
opinion".' Graves saw his chance and undertook 'to give him
proof of the strength of feeling amongst the borough members'.[64]
He and Laird called a meeting at the Carlton Club and 150
attended on the Thursday.

The meeting was representative and influential. About four-
fifths of those present expressed themselves in favour of household suffrage, protected by three years' residence and personal
payment of rates. The minority, led by Beresford Hope, James
Lowther and George Bentinck, vehemently supported the £6
level, but they failed to persuade their fellows. Many members
were unhappy at the prospect of a reduction, but if one had to
be made it was better that it should be final. George Beecroft
and Colonel Hogg, for example, were worried about the impact
of household suffrage in their respective constituencies, Leeds
and Bath, and Hogg declared 'that any lowering would destroy
him', but they acquiesced with the majority view that the general
party advantage outweighed individual difficulties. 'It was
strongly felt', Disraeli's informant reported,

> that whatever characteristic touches your Bill received should
> be *made by Government*, not accepted from opponents. And
> household suffrage, thus protected, especially with the power
> of Cumulative voting, was urged as a *Conservative* measure—
> on the ground that it offered the best means of resisting farther
> and wilder changes. . . . *Graves* gave *important evidence*. In
> Liverpool there are 40,000 £10 householders. Of these only
> 21,000 vote. *Why?* Because 19,000 won't take the trouble to
> enfranchise themselves by *paying the rates*.[65]

The back-benchers did not press, as Buckle suggests, for a
'generous extension to a new and respectable class',[66] rather,
they wanted 'a successful Reform Bill': one which would impose

a safe and lasting limit to the downward extension of the franchise, and offer a base from which they could resist dangerous
amendments from Gladstone and the radicals. Banks Stanhope,
who supported Graves and Laird, wrote to emphasize to Derby
that, 'there [was] . . . one Principle of Vital Importance, *One*
Barrier against *Manhood* Suffrage, namely, "*Personal* Rating".
Upon some one Firm Basis we *must* make a stand against "Democracy".'[67] Gladstone had had 289 Liberals at his meeting and
he had to be checked. The Adullamites and the Palmerstonians
also realized the danger, and eighty of them met on the Thursday
and decided to plump for household suffrage and plurality of
votes as 'the only lasting basis upon which the . . . question can
be settled'.[68]

The Queen, influenced by General Grey, still preferred the £6
qualification but she wanted a settlement even more, and emphasized to Derby that she would back him at whatever qualification he might finally arrive. She also told him that if the three
dissidents continued to obstruct the way to a settlement they
would have to be removed.[69] The Queen's acquiescence in the
'larger measure' completed the line-up of forces against Cranborne and Carnarvon and the Ten Minutes Bill. They had failed
to win potential allies like Walpole and Hardy and the great
majority of the party had sided against them. Derby and Disraeli
now felt strong enough to force the issue at the Cabinet on
2 March. Derby had already instructed Baxter to return to the
preparation of a household rating franchise bill on the 28th, the
day on which he received the Queen's letter.[70] On 1 March he
informed Cranborne that he intended to ask the Cabinet to
revert to the larger Bill. Cranborne suavely agreed that he was
'taking the most expedient course'.[71]

Before Disraeli left for the Cabinet on the Saturday he received
a letter from Sir Henry Edwards, his lickspittle M.P. for
Beverley, who reported that 'the feeling of the party grows
stronger *every hour* in favour of your original scheme of Reform
and the hope is that Lord Derby may at the Cabinet Council
today get rid of the Dissentients at any risk to save us from
irretrievable ruin'.[72] The meeting lasted for a grim two hours.
Northcote, with Manners, who himself preferred the Ten Minutes
Bill, tried desperately to persuade Cranborne to accept the
change.[73] Peel and Carnarvon agreed to drop their objections if
Cranborne would, but he was adamant. At last Derby rose to

conclude the meeting: 'This is the end of the Conservative Party,' he remarked. As Cranborne left the table, Peel turned to him: 'Lord Cranborne, do you hear what Lord Derby says?' But Cranborne walked from the room without speaking. Derby sighed, closed his red despatch box, and murmured, 'The Tory Party is ruined!' 'Poor Tory Party,' added Disraeli, his object achieved.[74]

Three adherents of Disraeli and supporters of the household suffrage plan were promoted to the vacancies in the Cabinet. The Duke of Buckingham succeeded Carnarvon as Colonial Secretary, Pakington took Peel's place at the War Office, and Northcote followed Cranborne as Secretary for India. Their places at the Council, the Admiralty, and the Board of Trade were taken by the Duke of Marlborough, Henry Corry and the Duke of Richmond. Disraeli used his patronage carefully. Henry Corry was the father of his private secretary, and Marlborough and Richmond were powerful potential enemies. He even sounded George Bentinck, but this time it was Bentinck who refused.[75]

IV *The Transformation of the Suffrage Bill*

The Cabinet allowed themselves a fortnight to prepare the Bill. They announced 'personal payment of rates' as the leading principle, but this proved exceedingly difficult to embody in a clause. If payment was to be made directly and personally it had to be severed from occupation, and this ran athwart the usual system of collection and recording. Further, if direct payment was made mandatory for the qualification it would disfranchise those £10 compounders who were enrolled under the terms of Clay's Act. For them, Baxter left an escape clause whereby the compounder could retain his qualification by agreeing with his landlord to pay the full rate with his rent.[76] This clause conflicted with the theme of the Bill and negated several earlier provisions. But there was an even greater difficulty. Neither Baxter nor Disraeli could devise a way of preventing indirect payment and personation.[77] Personal rating also blocked the possibility of including a lodger qualification, yet Gladstone was sure to press for one. Lodgers in England and Wales did not even theoretically pay rates with their rent and they were not recognized in the rate-books. Disraeli pondered upon a qualification by which lodgers of two years' standing at £10 rental could ask to be assessed voluntarily and pay their rates with their rent and so be entered in the rate-books. But it was clearly impossible to establish proofs of residence and payment.[78] It emerged only later that there was not even a usable legal definition of a lodger.[79] The increase of votes in the small boroughs posed a special difficulty. Baxter and Disraeli considered a special £5 limit but realized that it was politically hopeless.

The prospects for the dual vote were not much better. It had the disability that it would gravely complicate the registration, and as it was an innovation likely to prove expensive, the House of Commons was ill-disposed towards it. Disraeli saw that it would be tactically disastrous to set it firmly in the Bill and argued strongly in the Cabinet for its abandonment. The Duke of Buckingham, Walpole and Hardy were all determined to retain it. Buckingham even threatened to vote against the Government if the Bill came to the Lords without it, and claimed that the influential Earl of Harrowby would go with him.[80] The dual vote thus survived for the time being, though Disraeli dropped it from the county clauses, and was quietly determined not to press it in the House.[81]

These squabbles in the Cabinet coincided with the new elections for those Ministers who had changed office. Sir John Pakington, who was a leading protagonist of the household suffrage plural voting scheme, revealed the story of the Ten Minutes Bill in his nomination speech at Droitwich. In its context, the speech was not a thoughtless indiscretion,[82] but a deliberate attempt to sway the issue in the Cabinet by cutting off any possibility of an official return to the £6 qualification. His speech was a careful vindication of the course he had pursued in relation to Reform since December, when he had arrived at the need for a household franchise bill perhaps earlier than anyone else in the Ministry.[83] He broadcast the account of the Cabinet break-up and the £6 rating in an effort to commit the new dissidents, Buckingham and his friends, to household suffrage.[84]

The fancy franchises also gave trouble continuously until 18 March, the day on which the Bill was to be introduced. The number of possible voters by the educational qualification was not estimated until the 16th, when it was discovered to be much less than Disraeli had hoped.[85] On the morning of the 18th Gathorne-Hardy raised a fundamental objection to the qualification based on the assessed taxes, by pointing out that they were variable, and likely to be reduced and soon repealed. If they were to become entangled with the franchise they would immediately be rendered less flexible and their repeal would become impossible. The assessed taxes were curious survivals of the old sumptuary laws. They were levied on inhabited houses, servants, carriages, horses, horse dealers' licences, armorial bearings, and hair powder; their payment scarcely formed a test of moral fitness. Hardy disliked them because they were 'a serious restriction upon the employment of domestic servants & certain other branches of trade'. He suggested that any man who paid assessed taxes would almost certainly qualify already in respect of his house rates, and if not by that, by his 20s. income tax. Few men with a yearly income of less than £120 could afford servants or carriages, yet £120 per annum, a flourishing shop-keeper's income, was the minimum amount necessary to realize 20s. tax.[86]

The income tax qualification had also been insufficiently explored. Disraeli intended it to make a middle-class counterpoise drawn from wealthier lodgers and other non-householders. He and Baxter had been careful to put the qualification well above the reach of the artisans, but in doing that they had forgotten that they were also excluding many deferential lower middle-class voters. Most people with incomes below £200 were assessed at twopence in the pound, but even assuming that they were assessed at the higher rate of fourpence, they would need an annual income of £120 in order to pay 20s., after the usual amount of £60 had been allowed for deductions. £120 a year meant effectively 8s. a day for 300 days, allowing for illness, holidays and unemployment, and 48s. a week was obtainable only by the very highest class of skilled overlookers and shopkeepers, people who were generally believed to be Liberal. The 20s. tax level excluded the commercial, banking and legal clerks who were thought to be Conservative and whom Disraeli had hoped to include. The clause as it stood fulfilled neither of its intended tactical functions: it tipped the balance the wrong way and it was too narrow to offer an adequate counter to the demand for a lodger franchise. The figures were not examined in detail until a week after the Bill had been introduced.[87]

The drafting of the Bill had been entrusted solely to Baxter, and he had botched it. Disraeli had resisted pressure from the Cabinet to call in Thring, the legal expert at the Home Office who normally helped to draft government measures. He had hoped, apparently, that he and Baxter could manipulate the Bill between them. When the draft was finally submitted to Thring, he pronounced it legally illiterate, whereupon Disraeli instructed Baxter to turn it over to Thring, and the statistician resigned in a tantrum.[88] Thring had only twenty-four hours in which to redraw the Bill. He worked all day Friday and the Bill was printed during the night.[89]

The convergence of the views of Ministers and back-benchers on household suffrage unified the party. The squires had at last a policy to fight for and a leader who seemed sympathetic to their views and competent for all emergencies. They were ready for action: 'Although I am wishing to stay here [Downham Market] till Monday week don't let that prevent your summoning me to the rescue if you want me to back up the Govt.,' W. Clive wrote to Taylor. 'I think Disraeli from the way he fights Gladstone & Co. deserves the best thanks of every Conservative in the land. I am quite sure we shall lose nothing by Household Suffrage . . . don't bother yourself to write unless you want me—you have *more than enough* to do I dare say.'[90] Similar letters came from W. T. Cox and Viscount Galway; rarely can a Whip's life have been so sweet.[91]

Derby and Disraeli decided to capitalize on the loyalty. They took the most unusual step of revealing the contents of the Bill to a general party meeting three days before it was introduced to the House. 195 members attended and 43 more sent messages of support. The move was completely successful. The back-benchers were flattered that their advice about household suffrage had apparently been accepted and that they were now invited into the confidence of the Cabinet. At the meeting Derby, Disraeli and the great venture were all enthusiastically applauded. Cranborne, Carnarvon, Peel, Heathcote, Tom Baring and Shaftesbury found themselves isolated, and none tried to speak out against the Bill.

By contrast with the Conservatives, the Liberals were in the doldrums. Throughout the latter half of 1866 they had remained divided, mutually suspicious, and fearful of the traps that Disraeli might spring in the New Year. Russell had been stealthily working for a reconstruction, as a preliminary to turning Derby out. He had asked Brand to 'ascertain quietly' from the Adullamites 'what kind . . . of Bill would not exceed their capacity of digestion'. He was half afraid that Disraeli would bring in an 'easy measure' that they would have to amend and carry, rather than throw out to regain office.[92]

Bright's campaign in the autumn widened the rifts in the party. The radicals became more outspoken in denouncing the Adullamites and the Whigs became increasingly distrustful and angry. Erskine May told Denison that as he travelled from one country house to the next in Scotland he found 'Whig Country Gentlemen & M.P.s becoming very conservative, sadly afraid of Bright, and democracy, & bitter against Gladstone'.[93] Sir George Grey was completely dispirited and intended to go on a long Continental tour in order to miss the next session; 'Bright has destroyed the prospects of union among the Liberal party', he told Brand.[94] His plans followed those of Gladstone, Argyll, Clarendon and Cardwell, who were all tired of the party strife, and had escaped to the Continent to evade the possibility of becoming embroiled in the agitations.

Gladstone returned at the end of January, but felt so unsure of himself that he refused to give the usual dinner for the party at the commencement of the session. 'He dares not ask Bright,' Granville told Halifax, 'and funks omitting him.'[95] There had been 'no marshalling of our host, (if we have any)', Dundas lamented.[96] The only political dinner on the Liberal side was given by Grosvenor to the Adullamites. The party seemed to be without a leader and without a policy. Russell wanted an immediate amendment to overthrow the Ministry, Gladstone remained noncommittal,[97] while the radicals were eager to throw out the Resolution and demand a bill.[98] Gladstone was waiting to see what the Government would do and how the moderate Liberals would react, and meanwhile he was quietly equipping himself to do battle if a bill should come. He had Lambert, the Poor Law official, coaching him in the intricacies of the Compounding Acts.[99]

His patience was rewarded when Disraeli projected the Ten Minutes Bill. It offended all sections of the Opposition. Adullamites, like Laing, who wanted a settlement, denounced it for its 'general want of finality'.[1] Moderate Liberals, like Warner, agreed with Laing, and Bright and the radicals found the proposed redistribution 'very incomplete and unsatisfactory'.[2] Gladstone himself devastated Disraeli's ill-prepared introduction and showed conclusively that his statistics were erroneous and misleading.[3] He shrewdly emphasized that Disraeli had evaded the question of the compounders and lodgers. Thus the Government's ineffectual Bill had had the effect of restoring a superficial unity to the

Opposition and had temporarily re-established Gladstone as leader. The Whigs realized for the first time that his earnest pursuit of a moderate settlement with middle-class predominance was their last chance of withstanding a more radical change: 'Gladstone is gaining ground every hour', Villiers reported to Delane; 'His judgment & moderation are astonishing everybody'.[4] From the radical wing Bright recorded: 'Party more united than for a year past'.[5]

Gladstone quickly summoned the first party meeting of the session and it passed off smoothly. Although the good temper of the members derived partly from the relief of discovering that the big questions were to be left undisturbed, the Whigs and radicals, in their common aversion to Disraeli and his Bill, ignored rather than resolved their differences. Grosvenor and Bright both condemned the Bill, but both left unstated the kind of bill they would prefer in its place.

Clay, the independent radical and proponent of the educational franchise, also spoke at the meeting. He outlined a course which ultimately by-passed Grosvenor, Gladstone, and Bright, to become the commanding tactic of the session. He wanted to avoid challenging amendments and to keep the Conservatives in office, in the belief that they would be found 'squeezable'. He argued that a minority Tory Government offered an extraordinary opportunity to the radicals to force the Reform deadlock, for it would nullify the resistance of the Whigs and reverse the anti-Reform position of the Tories.[6] 'If the Government were defeated,' he explained, 'there must be . . . a new Government, and there might . . . be a dissolution and . . . considerable delay. The Tory party, if placed again in Opposition, would probably be unwilling to concede so much as, now they were in office, they were willing to yield.'[7]

The success of the 'squeeze' was ultimately assured because it suited those members who feared a dissolution but wanted an extensive settlement. It was a matter of gently forcing Disraeli to give way by precise, limited amendments, while avoiding motions aimed generally against the Bill and the Government, which might cause a collision. As long as Disraeli was prepared to play, this strategy of 'non-party' give-and-take blocked Russell's hopes of toppling the Ministry and hamstrung Gladstone's attempts to remodel the Bill into a viable piece of legislation.

Gladstone saw the danger, should the Bill reach the Committee stage, of Disraeli jettisoning the safeguards one by one at the behest of the radicals, and of its emerging as a household suffrage measure, 'pure and simple'. He felt even more unhappy because he knew that he would have to destroy the safeguards of personal rating and dual voting, as dishonest innovations. He proposed to replace them with a plan to excuse the rates of all occupiers of premises below £5 annual rental and so exclude them from the rate-books. He explained, rather tortuously, to Argyll that: 'Those under £5 . . . would be fairly met by the reply that they were not called on to pay rates [and] therefore had not the same direct interest in the place as ratepayers while the continuous residence would exclude all the migratory and less respectable portion of the working classes'. But he realized from the start that Disraeli had nominally outbid him.[8] A hollow measure of household suffrage seemed to offer a better chance of a settlement than an arbitrary level contrived midway down the rental scale. His forebodings were confirmed by the reports from Brand and his fellow Whip, George Glyn, after they had toured Brooks's and the Reform Club. The Whips reported that the Liberal back-benchers were generally averse to opposing the Second Reading for fear that the Government would dissolve if beaten, and they dared not face the country after having defeated a household suffrage bill. So Brand strongly advised Gladstone not to oppose the Bill at that stage.[9]

Gladstone would not be persuaded. He began negotiations with the Tory dissidents with the object of working up a majority against the Second Reading; he hoped that the promise of support from the Tory benches would rally the Liberal 'middle men'.[10] Sir William Heathcote and Lord Henry Thynne gathered twenty-five to thirty votes, but Gladstone's 'middle men' were set on averting a dissolution and remained cold to the plan.[11]

On 18 March, midst a packed House, Disraeli introduced the Bill. It provided for household suffrage in the boroughs, hedged by personal payment of rates and two years' residence. There were also dual votes for property, and fancy franchises for those with educational qualifications, those who had £50 in the Funds or the Savings Bank, or who paid 20s. in direct taxation. The county occupation level was to be reduced from £50 to £15 and the redistribution remained at 15 seats. He suggested 237,000 as the total borough rating enfranchisement and 305,000 votes as the addition created by the fancy franchises, giving an aggregate borough electorate of over 1,000,000. The reduction of the county qualification would, he claimed, enfranchise 170,000 men, and the fancy franchises would add about 139,000 votes.[12]

It was an elaborate speech, aimed at Gladstone and his prospective £5 level, rather than commending the virtues of the Bill. Disraeli succeeded brilliantly in contrasting Gladstone's insecure, tricky limitation, with the Government's safe, frank bulwark against democracy. He embroidered his remarks with a series of grandiose equivocations which his hearers could interpret to suit their fancies:

> Our object is not only to maintain, but to strengthen, the character and functions of this House [by] . . . establish [ing] them on a broad popular basis. I know that there are some . . . in whose minds the epithet which I have . . . used may create a feeling of distrust; but I attribute the sentiment of alarm . . . associated with it to a misapprehension of its meaning, and to that perplexity of ideas which too often confounds popular privileges with democratic rights. They were not identical . . . they are contrary. Popular privileges are consistent with a state of society in which there is great inequality of condition. Democratic rights . . . demand that there should be equality of condition as the fundamental basis of the society which they regulate. If this Bill be a proposal that Her Majesty shall be enabled to concede to her subjects, with the advice and concurrence of her Parliament, a liberal measure of popular privileges, then . . . many of its provisions . . . will be regarded as prudent, wise, and essentially constitutional. [But] if . . . it be looked upon as a measure having for its object to confer democratic rights, then I admit much that it may contain may be . . . indefensible and unjust. We do not, however, live—and I trust it will never be the fate of this country to live—under a democracy.[13]

Disraeli projected personal payment as the cardinal principle of the Bill and lauded it as an ancient and fundamental part of the British Constitution: in spite of the fact that the existing rating qualification, particularly as defined in Clay's Act, had never insisted upon personal payment, and that the principle was unknown in the common law.

> We wish . . . [the] admission to take place in the spirit of our existing institutions, and with a due deference to the traditions

of an ancient State. . . . The person . . . to be intrusted with
a vote to elect members of Parliament should be one with
respect to whom there should be some guarantee . . . for the
regularity of his life and the general trustworthiness of his
conduct . . . and the . . . fact of a man being rated to the relief
of the poor and being able to pay his rates gave that fair
assurance which the state had a right to require.[14]

Gladstone sat fidgeting through the speech, and then rose to
demolish it. Disraeli, he said, had overstated his probable enfranchisement by 100,000. Three-quarters of the fancy franchise
statistics were 'wholly erroneous and visionary'.[15] Disraeli's vaun-
ted 237,000 took no account of those who would fail to qualify
by insufficient residence or excusal of rate. Personal payment was
an utterly new and false accretion to the Constitution and it
would exclude compounders, many of whom were already enrolled. Pertaining to their situation, there was a further crucial
difficulty under the Bill, for if they had to pay the difference between their composition and the full rate in order to come on
the rate-books, they were effectively 'fined' by that amount for
seeking the privilege of enrolling. And as the composition varied
from one parish to the next so would the 'fine'. This would leave
the question of enfranchisement in the quite improper condition
of its being decided by the local authorities; a vestry could
decide to adopt the Small Tenements Act and so disfranchise a
section of hostile voters in their parish. Gladstone failed to add
that that was already the existing situation.

He also fell upon the dual vote. This 'gigantic engine of fraud'
completely negated the purpose of Reform, which was to recognize the convergence of classes and to increase the equal participation of the workingmen in the choice of representatives. The
dual vote destroyed equality under the law; it would neutralize
the lower-class enfranchisement and lead to 'a war of classes'.
It had no foundation in the Constitution and was the most dishonest and hurtful of the innovations in the Bill, for it would
institute a rich new source of corruption. Small wonder that Disraeli had not given figures to show its probable results.

Gladstone found ten main defects in the Bill: it wanted a
lodger franchise, twelve months' residence, a wider redistribution, a lower county franchise, provisions to stop the corrupt
payment of rates, the amendment of the existing disqualifications
on compound householders. He condemned the dual vote, the

fancy franchises, the provisions for voting papers, and the additional hindrance to compounders.[16] His demonstration of the shortcomings of the Bill was irrefutable, but his vehemence and very accuracy only scared his followers the more. Roebuck set the tenor for the reply of the Liberal 'middle men' by asking that the dual vote be abandoned and that the rest of the Bill be tidied up and allowed to pass. Indeed it had to pass; 'the country [was] in a state of disquietude'; anarchy would result if they obstructed the Bill, and Gladstone's demands were 'obstructions.'[17]

The Tory dissentients, bitter in the knowledge of their isolation, savaged Disraeli and the Bill. They argued that Disraeli, having led the House to defeat the Liberal Bill, was morally precluded from attempting to carry a more extensive measure. Their attacks only served to damage their cause for, by supporting Gladstone, they gave the impression that they would forsake the Government and join him in destroying the Bill. Thus they alienated the waverers on their own side and confirmed them in their allegiance to Disraeli, while at the same time they deepened the radicals', and the uncommitted Liberals' suspicions of Gladstone. Disraeli had won the day. He had fixed the division between Gladstone and the radicals, Cranborne and his friends had isolated themselves, and still the £5 limit remained hypothetical. He could now afford to shed the dual vote, which Henley and other influential Tory independents had rightly criticized as an impractical 'mischief'.

This opening debate set the pattern which was to obtain throughout 1867. Disraeli had to fight on two fronts. On one side he had to outbid Gladstone and persuade his men of his fighting qualities and of the opportunities for parliamentary success inherent in the Bill; and on the other, he had to combat Cranborne's and Lowe's penetrating analyses of the measure and re-assure the House that it would make a conservative settlement. He could win as long as he could keep these ends confused and the opposing forces divided. The genius of his achievement in 1867 was that he managed to do all these things and, amidst the petty-mindedness and ignorance on both sides of the House, contrived to give the appearance of logical consistency and high purpose to the ignoble scramble to settle the question.

The Bill was riddled with anomalies, which Gladstone took pleasure in exposing. They were partly the outcome of Baxter's legal inexperience and Disraeli's ignorance of local rating law, and partly the inevitable result of having to couple a national franchise system to a complicated series of local property laws enmeshed in a tangle of local custom. Somewhat by design but mostly from the haste and ignorance with which it was prepared, the Bill was not congruent with the 1832 Act: £10 household voters needed only one year's residence while those below £10 needed two; men above £10 qualified in respect of a 'building', whether a house, shop or other structure, whereas those under £10 qualified only in respect of a dwelling house; those over £10 could qualify by occupying a part of a house while those below (and the clause was ambiguous) seemed to need to occupy the entire dwelling.

Disraeli's 'principle' for excluding the compounders rested upon 'personal payment', yet the Court of Queen's Bench had held only two years earlier that a compounding tenant paid the full rate assessed upon his occupation with his rent to his landlord and that it was the compounding landlord who paid the reduced rate to the parish.[18] Yet, under clause 34 the compounding tenant who wished to register would have to make up the 'full' rate to the parish. Few tenants would bother to go before the revising barristers to tender a claim that had to be repeated annually and pay the difference between the composition and the full rate; unless, of course, the rate was paid for them by the local party agent. The clause would work arbitrarily wherever compounding systems were in operation. In towns where the Small Tenements Act applied only those few tenants who, for some uncommon reason, paid their rates direct would qualify. In Carlisle, for example, calculating from the number of occupied houses and the estimated number of adult male inhabitants, 406 would qualify while 3,571 would be excluded; in Dudley 232 would come in while 6,315 would be excluded; in Calne 25 would qualify and 695 would fail. In the aggregate, 25,064 occupiers under £10 in the Small Tenements Act towns would qualify and 139,377 would be excluded. In the 98 boroughs where the Act had been adopted only for certain of the poorer parishes, the numbers would be 106,467 included and 249,472 left out. In Aylesbury, for instance, 446 would qualify and 3,514 would fail; in Frome 38 and 1,363; in Kingston-upon-Hull 64 and 12,026. In these boroughs the Bill would have had the crazy effect of en-franchising the occupiers on one side of a street along a parish boundary and leaving voteless their equally rented neighbours on the opposite side. In those towns which used Local Rating Acts the results would be similar. They contained 329,000 male occupiers, nearly one quarter of the total in England and Wales. In Brighton 14 would qualify and 2,553 would be excluded; in Kidderminster 24 and 2,343; in Birmingham 2,300 and 36,177. A total of 10,638 would be included in such towns and 87,774 would be excluded.[19]

Far from Disraeli's grandiose 237,000, the total borough rating enfranchisement was likely to be only about 120,000. The uneven effects of the Bill would deprive it of any utility as a test of 'moral fitness' to vote. Gladstone laboured all these points in his speech, but he had lost the House long before he came to the end of his analysis. He bored the members with his statistics and abstruse legal niceties. Gathorne-Hardy showed how little he understood the point when he declared that the compounding tenant would be able to deduct from his next rent to his landlord the difference between his composition and the full rate which he had paid to qualify. In fact, the Bill contained no such provision. Roundell Palmer, the eminent Liberal lawyer, pointed out that if it were so, it would upset the existing common law which held that a landlord was not liable for refund of the difference.[20]

The foundations of the Bill had taken a tremendous battering, but Disraeli calmly set out to defend it and produced one of the greatest speeches of his career. He blandly admitted its defects, but, apart from the dual vote, he conceded nothing; he was truculent in rejecting Gladstone's demands, yet conciliatory to the radicals and his own followers. He agreed that only 120,000 would be admitted and adduced it as a proof of the Ministry's conservative intentions. He refused Gladstone's ultimatum for a lodger qualification and a more extensive redistribution, but offered to consider these amendments if they derived from another source in the House. Deftly he widened the gap between Gladstone, the Whigs and the radicals. He completely side-stepped the difficulties inherent in personal payment of rates, but by emphasizing at once its 'principle' and its 'extensiveness' he made it impossible for Gladstone to move against him.[21] 'It was the most wonderful piece of acting & the most extraordinary exhibition of talent I have ever heard,' one Liberal back-bencher wrote to his wife. 'He pitched into everybody, he abandoned all his principles, & all through he delighted and amused the

House.'[22] Edward Russell declared that it 'was the speech of
the session, though hardly ten lines of it will be remembered;
and men who have heard Mr. Disraeli throughout his career
agree that never did he show such mastery over his audience, such
boundless histrionic resource'.[23]

Disraeli had hit exactly the right note in his Second Reading
speech: he captured Liberal backbenchers like Saunderson, who
were bored with Reform, who wanted to see Gladstone humbled,
and to have the assurance that the Bill, *a* bill, would finally
remove the problem. Gladstone and Lowe had intended to oppose
the Second Reading, but they found themselves unable to carry
an angry party meeting.[24] Beresford Hope and Heathcote were
unavailing in their efforts to persuade the Tory loyalists to throw
over Disraeli and the Bill. So 27 March saw the droll situation
of Disraeli carrying the Second Reading of his Bill without a
division, though it was incomplete and unsatisfactory in every
way, and nearly all the House distrusted it. Bernal Osborne, the
Liberal wit, remarked that he had 'bamboozled' Parliament and
led it to suffer a Bill 'which no ten members in their secret
hearts like'.[25]

Gladstone called a second party meeting on 5 April and 250
Liberals attended. He made a last desperate plea to them to support him in introducing a fixed rating level into the Bill, and
had ready an Instruction for the Committee of the House:

> That they have power to alter the law of rating; And to provide
> that in every parliamentary borough the occupiers of tene-
> ments below a given rateable value will be relieved from
> liability to personal rating; with a view to fix a line for the
> borough franchise; at which all occupiers shall be entered on
> the rate-book, and shall have equal facilities for the enjoyment
> of such franchise as a residential occupation franchise.[26]

The Instruction was consistent with Gladstone's aim throughout
1866 and 1867—to extend the suffrage genuinely to those who
passed a defined test of social and moral worth. 'It was meant,'
he said, 'to carry out the principle that the franchise should be
enjoyed equally by those in a condition of life and a position of
independence which will give them a title to the franchise.'[27]

He had taken care to express his clause as an amplification
of the Bill and not as a destructive motion which Disraeli could
turn into a vote of confidence. Given his own doubts about the

leadership and the splintered condition of the party, it is unlikely that he intended it, wholly consciously at least, as a lever
with which to turn out the Ministry as Russell had done in 1859.
But certainly the brief on the Instruction that he prepared for
himself shows that he intended to turn the Bill inside out by
amending every clause but the first two.[28]

The radicals were outspoken in their opposition. Locke wanted
to maim the Instruction by deleting everything after the first
sentence. Clay, who a fortnight earlier had resumed his secret
negotiations with Disraeli, gave his opinion, 'with the deepest
sincerity, that the Instruction [was] fatal to the Bill, whereas
[they] might make a good Bill if [they] contented themselves
with the first line only'. Gladstone, supported by Bright, refused
to accept their proposal and the meeting broke up in an uneasy
stalemate.[29] Two radicals, L. L. Dillwyn, the iron-master from
Swansea, and Harvey Lewis, the member for Marylebone, refused even to attend the meeting. They told Acland that Gladstone always monopolized the discussion and that they had 'never
been asked to give [their] opinion'. They wanted a meeting
where those who wished could speak for a few minutes each,
and all could sit equally rather than have to stand in a crowd
while Gladstone orated from the staircase at Carlton House
Terrace.[30]

On the day after the meeting, Clay wrote to Disraeli to sound
him as to whether the Government would back a radical motion
to omit the second part of the Instruction. He added that he
had already secured about 40 Liberal votes and envisaged 150
if he could give his fellows a promise that the Government would
not leave them to be beaten in a division.[31] Disraeli apparently
gave the signal to proceed and Clay and his allies held a conference at the Reform Club on Sunday afternoon, 7 April. Nearly
forty attended. They agreed that Locke should move and Torrens
second an amendment to delete the second part. Torrens quickly
informed the Conservative Whip that the trap was set.[32]

Disraeli, meanwhile, had been trying to persuade the Speaker
to rule the Instruction out of order, on the grounds that it
constituted a negation of the Bill. Denison, however, perhaps
unfortunately for Gladstone, ruled in its favour on the argument
that it necessarily preceded the changes in the rating franchises
which Gladstone had foreshadowed.[33]

The Liberal dissidents held a further meeting in the tea-room of the House of Commons on Monday the 8th. The meeting crystallized from the unrest in the party: Locke, Clay and Seely prompted it, but it had no central organizer and grew 'by one Member telling another'. About fifty attended and another thirty sent their adherence. The gathering split between the group led by Clay, Locke, Torrens and Lewis, which wanted to throw out the Instruction altogether, and Candlish, Dillwyn, Potter and Dent, who wanted to reaffirm allegiance to Gladstone by accepting it and reserving judgment on the £5 limit. It was only after a strong demand from Potter that the majority consented to select a deputation to take their views to Gladstone; the rebels had been prepared to let him crash without warning. Fawcett, Jackson, Seely, Crossley and Hanmer went immediately to Gladstone to present the view of the majority that the second part of the Instruction should be dropped. He acquiesced, upon the understanding that the Government should accept the first sentence on rating.[34]

The tea-room meeting was composed of a heterogeneous collection of radicals from English industrial and commercial boroughs, Scottish members, English small borough men, mostly Palmerstonians, and a few Irish pocket-borough representatives.[35] Radicals and the Scottish members (in the cases of McLaren, Grant Duff, Dalglish and Oliphant, the terms were synonomous) saw the Bill as a unique opportunity to secure a really wide redistribution. Some of them also found themselves confronted with the possible materialization of their slogans. They were suddenly afraid of the agitations, which threatened to sweep the adjustment of power beyond the point of supremacy of the commercial middle classes. Locke told the House that he had been fighting for household suffrage for years, but equally his 'struggles against manhood suffrage had been both continuous and severe'. Now that household suffrage was within grasp it would be 'dangerous' to tamper with the Bill, and so risk toppling into manhood suffrage.[36] Seely was heard at a dinner party to declare that he 'and . . . many like him' would support the Government because it was 'better to have the question settled by [Disraeli] and Lord Derby than by Beales and Potter'. He was 'very sore with Bright and the League', the informant continued, 'and quoted Potter's speech recommending the working men to cease work for one week—The effect of that . . . wld be that the trade of England would not only be suspended but ruined, because there is but one week's consumption of coal above ground'.[37]

The Irish members were pocket-borough men who were interested in averting a dissolution and in securing a restrictive settlement for Ireland. As Roman Catholics, they wanted to keep the present English Bill because it offered the best chance, in Reardon's words, of 'direct influence and powers of self-protection [to] thousands of Catholic Irishmen in this country'.[38]

Beyond these sectional interests, however, the tea-roomers shared a general distrust of Gladstone and desire for a settlement. Henry Seymour spoke for many of them when he explained that he had been prepared to follow Gladstone until he became threatening and drew up the Instruction. This, he argued, would only have repeated the collapse of 1859, with the difference that the country would now be plunged into a wild general election. And even after an election there would be no guarantee that the musical chairs game on Reform would not start again. The question had to be settled before a 'catastrophe or revolution occurred', which would destroy the chance of 'moderate progress'.[39] Yet, as the group's subsequent voting pattern shows, it was a temporary combination of men, some of whom believed that the Bill offered the best prospect of leaving their borough unscathed, others that it offered the best opportunity for forcing an extensive Reform, but all of whom were agreed that Gladstone threatened its survival. Once the tea-room movement achieved the withdrawal of the Instruction it disintegrated.

That evening Locke and Disraeli went smoothly through their charade and the Instruction was dropped. Disraeli airily declared that the Instruction was superfluous, as, 'of course the Committee [had] power to alter the law of rating'. Coleridge, the rising Liberal lawyer who was to move the Instruction, was dumbfounded; he had not discovered that Gladstone had agreed to withdraw the second part, and Clay's bargain with Disraeli over the first part completed the surprise. Gladstone sat 'lowering and gloomy'. Disraeli had given way to his demand, but had circumvented him.[40]

Gladstone counter-attacked with a series of crafty amendments which would have had the same effect as that part of the Instruction he had agreed to delete. They referred explicitly only to compounding and registration and would have had the result of allowing the tenant to qualify whether he paid his rate personally or not; implicitly, they prepared the way for a £5 limit. Their wording was vague, partly to attract the widest possible range of support, and partly to avoid giving too direct a negative to the 'principle' of the Bill. Yet in this very vagueness lay his undoing. Gladstone pursued his own devious course in 1866 and 1867 but he seemed fated to be thought subservient to the schemes of unwelcome allies. In 1866 it had been Bright; now it was Gros-venor.[41] The Adullamite chief had already foreshadowed an amendment for a £5 barrier. He had concocted it, not in collu-sion with Gladstone, but with Elcho and Disraeli, when the latter thought that he might need a second line of defence.[42]

Disraeli was still fighting desperately to hold the Cabinet intact while he prepared them for the approaching succession of failures. The agreement with Clay was the first collapse; the inutility of the fancy franchises was already apparent; it was proving impossible to devise a workable system of plural voting, and plural voting was unlikely to survive in the House anyway. The Duke of Buckingham, Hardy and Walpole were all at the point of resignation at various times during these weeks. The loss of any one of them would probably have toppled the Govern-ment. The Duke wanted to cling to plural voting, while the other two became very angry when Disraeli sought to rationalize personal payment a little.[43] Their worries were not made any easier by the threat of imminent war between Prussia and France, although the crisis perhaps helped to keep the Cabinet together.[44] The Tories were beginning to reap the penalties of their minority position and their brash venture into Reform.

The House was looking forward to the Easter recess and was utterly weary of compounding and its intricacies. Disraeli and the Adullamites feared that the moderate Liberals and recalci-trant Tories would combine to pass Gladstone's amendments in the hope of finding a safe limit and ridding themselves of the problem before the House rose. But Gladstone's proposals would have thwarted Grosvenor's projected move for a £5 level and so the Tory Whips put up Grosvenor, Elcho and Clay to talk out the amendments until after Easter.[45] Corry used Clay more subtly than the others and had him try to shunt the debate on to the bribery provisions. He also had Clay insinuate that there might be a dissolution if Gladstone's motions were carried. Bright observed venomously, and correctly, that Clay 'generally manage[d] on these occasions to say something . . . very service-able to the Chancellor of the Exchequer'.[46] However, Clay failed to draw off the rest of the tea-roomers, who wanted to carry the amendments and get on with the Bill. When it became clear that Grosvenor's adjournment motion would fail, Disraeli gave him a hint and he dutifully withdrew it.[47]

Gladstone's amendments offered the only chance of avoiding the queer patchwork of enfranchisement which the Bill would create. Such a capricious system could never become a 'solid . . . wall . . . to stem the tide of agitation'. Once more Gladstone had offered a brilliant, searching analysis and the best remedy, but he had had to apologize for 'the mingled difficulty and dry-ness of the subject' as the members dozed or crept out of the chamber. They were too bored to care or understand: the only argument that held weight with them was the *argumentum ad desperationem*.[48] At one point the debate had almost lapsed for want of a speaker and Kendall, a Tory squire from East Corn-wall, had risen to fill the gap. His rambling discourse conveys the attitude of the Tory back-benchers very vividly. In his view the present trouble had begun when Lord Palmerston died and left no one to check the radicals. Russell and Gladstone had attempted to force Reform on the House and had provoked the Hyde Park Riots, which had led the members into their present unhappy necessity. Kendall did not like the Bill, he was sorry that Lord Derby had ventured into Reform, but now that he had done so, he would support him. He disliked household suffrage, but 'there was this . . . to be said for [it] . . . it presented some-thing simple and intelligible'. He hoped that the Government 'would stick to their colours', and accused Gladstone of trying to 'mystify' the issue and make a 'Dutch auction' of the franchise. The benighted loyalty represented by this speech shows how the country gentlemen remained immune to the sophisticated argu-ment of Gladstone and Cranborne; but it well served the purposes of Disraeli.[49]

Gladstone's move to by-pass personal payment was bedevilled by an amendment introduced by J. T. Hibbert, the M.P. for Oldham, and supported by many of the tea-roomers. Hibbert wanted to retain personal payment and the two-years' residence, but still to allow the tenant to qualify if he paid only the amount of his former composition rate. In this way the 'fine' would be avoided and the bulwarks against an indiscriminate reduction would be kept free of attack. The amendment was as ambigious and impracticable as the clause it was intended to replace, for it made no provision for reducing the rent by the amount of rates the tenant was to pay directly. It was inherently unlikely—and 1868 proved it so—that landlords would voluntarily and uniformly lower their rents. It was equally unlikely that vestries would permit the composition to continue once they lost the advantage it was meant to reward; that is, the cheaper and surer payment from one landlord rather than the hazardous collection from individually rated tenants.

Hibbert's amendment deepened the split in the Cabinet. Disraeli wanted to accept it as a way around the unworkable clause in the Bill. It also presented an opportune diversion from Gladstone's amendment, on which the Whips had advised him that the Government was likely to be defeated. Hardy and Walpole saw Hibbert's motion as a mine which would explode the restrictive working of personal payment, and threatened to resign rather than accept it. Their resistance to Disraeli reflected the leaderless state of the Cabinet, for since the beginning of April, Derby had been confined to his bed by an attack of gout. Disraeli badly missed his support, for the meetings of 11 and 12 April degenerated into long, bitter wrangles and the two sides remained implacable. Finally Hardy, Walpole, Buckingham and Stanley overrode Disraeli and Northcote, and committed the Government to stand by its original clause.[50]

This decision left Disraeli in a predicament because during that second week of April he had promised the tea-room leaders that the Government would accept Hibbert's amendment. He could rely upon Grosvenor's men in a possible division against Gladstone, but, as usual, he needed to snare some of the radicals and 'independent Liberals' if he was to be certain of a majority. He now resorted to the threat of a dissolution, which he effected by the unusual course of writing to *The Times* to intimate that the Government would drop the Bill if Gladstone's amendments were carried.[51] The announcement was ostensibly a private letter to his supporters but *The Times* received it before they did.[52] Disraeli had now not only ignored the House, but had even by-passed his own party and Cabinet to attain his tactical objective.

The complement to the threat was an inducement to the tea-room leaders to believe that they could pin the Bill to household suffrage. On the evening of the 12th, as the members entered the

House, Dillwyn and Seely were busy stalking recruits in the
lobby, armed with a memorandum from Taylor to the effect that
Derby and Disraeli would carry Hibbert's amendment if the tea-
roomers helped to defeat Gladstone. At eleven o'clock, as the
House filled after dinner, Brand put up Bernal Osborne to reveal
the stratagem. Disraeli immediately denied all knowledge of the
agreement, and remarked that as Lord Derby was ill he could
not possibly have assented to it and added superfluously, that
he had lately 'thought it best not to trouble him with . . . business
of any kind'. In fact Derby was not named in the memorandum.
It seems improbable that a Tory Whip would commit his leaders
to a total change of policy without their permission, especially
when, as the Disraeli Papers reveal, Taylor was in almost hourly
communication with his chief. At least, Disraeli's Cabinet colleagues thought so: Hardy recorded that, 'Stanley evidently
thought this [Disraeli's denial] untrue, and after some words
between us, he got up on the part of the Government, declared
us unpledged, and demanded . . . a division of the merits.'[53] This,
of course, was only re-stating the policy affirmed by the Cabinet
that very morning. These manoeuvres illuminate the 'sagacious
advice' Disraeli gave to Gathorne-Hardy before he was to speak:

> Permit me to intimate that, without in the slightest degree
> compromising your convictions, it is expedient not to make an
> unnecessarily uncompromising speech tonight; and with regard
> to the question over which the Cabinet was so divided this
> morning, it seems to me unnecessary to touch on it.[54]

Hardy took the advice. He was of great service to Disraeli in
the debates of these first weeks. He rigorously expounded the
restrictive clauses and so reassured the country gentlemen.
Although he doubtless believed that these clauses would be
adhered to, he always managed to stop short of declaring whether
the Government would stand or fall by the particular safeguard
under discussion.[55]

Disraeli wound up the debate with the same kind of grandilo-
quent vacuity and precise personal attack as he had used earlier.
He avoided any analysis of the differences between the Bill and
the amendment and painted the latter as a wrecking move
inspired by Gladstone's personal ambition:

> The right hon. Gentleman suddenly placed upon the paper a
> declaration of war . . . I acknowledge the right hon. Gentle-
> man's position and talents—that he is perfectly justified in

attacking the Government; but do not let us misunderstand the
motive or the conduct of the right hon. Gentleman . . . It is a
party attack.

Once again Disraeli trailed the ambiguity he had used throughout the debate:

> I wish, on the part of Her Majesty's Government . . . to say
> that in dealing with this question Her Majesty's Government
> have never for a moment swerved from those sentiments
> which, with the full concurrence and desire of my Colleagues,
> I have often expressed in this House—namely we are most
> anxious to co-operate with the House in bringing this question
> of Parliamentary Reform to a satisfactory settlement, and
> although we could not swerve with respect to the borough
> franchise from those principles which we regard as vital—
> namely, personal payment of rates and residence—still with
> regard to almost every other point—we are most anxious, in
> Committee, after a fair deliberation, and after an interchange
> of opinion, to adopt that course which the House in its wisdom
> may think most expedient and desirable . . . But when the right
> hon. Gentleman comes forward suddenly with a counter propo-
> sition to the main proposals of the Government it is impossible
> for me to close my eyes to the nature of the movement; I
> must say to the right hon. Gentleman that I cannot in any way
> agree to the propositions he has made.[56]

In effect, Disraeli offered to accept almost any amendment provided it did not come from the leader of the Opposition. It was
a brazen and successful attempt to complete Gladstone's isolation
from the tea-room men. 'There is a real difference in principle',
Acland told his wife,

> but owing to Dizzy's extraordinary ingenuity and a certain
> kind of tactics . . . he has outwitted us and made it very
> difficult for the principles to show themselves.
>   Gladstone is hampered by three sets of people:
>   1. Radicals who will vote for household suffrage and
>   don't want it carried.
>   2. Whigs (aristocrats) who won't risk a collision with the
>   Government, and hope that very little Reform will be
>   carried, and want to discredit Gladstone.
>   3. A large body who care for nothing except to avoid a
>   dissolution.[57]

Finally, as Big Ben struck two, the House divided on Gladstone's
amendment. The Government emerged with a majority of twenty-

one, 310:289. Forty-five Liberals had voted or paired for the Government.

> When the numbers were read out . . . the hurrahs rose again and again . . . and all the Tory country gentlemen rose from their seats and rushed to shake hands with the leader who was said to have betrayed them.[58]

He briefly joined the party at the Carlton Club afterwards and Sir Matthew Ridley proposed a toast which summed up the situation more aptly than he perhaps realized: 'Here's the man who rode the race, who took the time, who kept the time, and who did the trick!' Then, tired but triumphant, Disraeli hastened home to Mary Anne and the famous Fortnum and Mason's pie.[59]

Gladstone was astounded at his defeat and dismayed by what he assumed to be the venality and stupidity of his unfaithful followers. He told himself in his diary that it was a 'smash perhaps without example', and contemplated resigning the leadership.[60] Brand divided the forty-five renegades into four classes: Grosvenor's men; 'advanced Liberals in favour of Household Suffrage'; men desiring to save the Bill or the Government; and a final category of 'Men voting in fear of a dissolution or from worse motives'. He put nineteen in the first class:

Visct. Andover	Lord Dunkellin	C. W. Martin
Hon. Maj. Anson	Lord Elcho	M. H. Marsh
Lord C. Browne	Hon. C. W. W. Fitzwilliam	J. Pim
Lord E. Bruce	H. W. Foley	O. Stock
Sir R. Bulkeley	Earl Grosvenor	A. Smith?
Lord A. Clinton	Lord R. Grosvenor	[Brand's query]
F. Doulton	Hon. G. H. Heathcote	

All except Martin and Smith had been Adullamites in 1866. Brand put only four men in the second group; a significantly small number when one considers the usual description of the tea-roomers as men bent on household suffrage: Dalglish, Dillwyn, Crum-Ewing? (Brand's query), Steel. There were twelve men in the third class:

E. Akroyd	M. E. Corbally	J. A. Roebuck
M. A. Bass	E. James	H. F. Vernon
M. T. Bass	E. McEvoy	H. H. Vivian
J. I. Briscoe	J. Pritchard	G. H. Whalley

The two Basses, Roebuck, Vivian and Whalley were usually considered to be wild radicals, James was a Palmerstonian who had scraped in for Manchester, and Corbally and McEvoy were Irishmen who may have been carrying out their side of the bargain mentioned above. Brand set ten members in the lowest circle:

J. Brady	J. Lamont	L. B. Mackinnon
T. Chambers	H. Lewis	W. A. Mackinnon
G. Hodgkinson		T. A. Mitchell
[he queried whether he should have put		T. Parry
him with the household suffrage group]		D. J. Reardon

Mitchell and the Mackinnons were Palmerstonians, Chambers, Lewis and Hodgkinson called themselves advanced Liberals, while Reardon and Brady had their own sectarian reasons. There were also seventeen Liberals who were absent and unpaired: seven said they were ill, and of the rest, eight were Palmerstonians, and two were radicals, Hibbert and Platt, the mover and seconder of the prospective rival amendment to Gladstone's.[61]

The list shows clearly that the smash was not a result of the tea-room mutiny, for there were only nine tea-roomers amongst the forty-five; the rest voted solidly, if unenthusiastically, for the amendment.[62] Instead, it reflected the revival of the Adullamite wing of the previous year, allied with a motley collection of Palmerstonians and unimportant radicals and Irishmen. The Grosvenor faction, from their mulish distrust of Gladstone, had destroyed their one opportunity of entrenching the restrictions they wanted to preserve in the Bill. The contributing factor to the Liberal smash was the ineffectiveness of the Cranborne rebels. His aide-de-camp, Sir William Heathcote, could only prevail upon four Tories to follow Cranborne and himself in voting against the Government: A. H. Baring, J. B. Beresford Hope, Ralph Earle, and J. G. Hubbard. Even such confirmed Dizzy-haters as General Peel, James Lowther, G. M. Sandford, and the erstwhile organizer of the Cranborne 'cave', Lord Henry Thynne, could not bring themselves to vote with Gladstone. He weighed the situation accurately when he told Russell that they had 'been thrown overboard—not by the Radicals . . . but by the timid men, the Adullamites and the "moderate" Conservatives'.[63]

There was plenty to reflect upon during the Easter vacation. The Tory back-benchers were at once delighted and apprehensive at Disraeli's extraordinary success. Rear-Admiral Octavius Duncombe sent his 'hearty congratulations. You now have the whip hand of your . . . antagonist completely'. The rear-admiral promised his full support, but ended with a pathetic postscript: 'I feel somewhat afraid of the *Lodger* franchise'.[64] They liked winning, but wished they were winning with a different horse. 'For my part, I think D'israeli's plan and Gladstone's plan equally objectionable,' wrote Lord Ilchester,

> either will end in Chaos, and pure democracy in 2 or 3 years . . . and this being the case, I stick to my colours, by which I mean the Government—Gladstone's conduct is unaccountable, never has there been such a failure, as his, or such a triumphant course as that of Disraeli with every sort of difficulty to contend with, he gains strength every day, and it is refreshing to observe the tact, cleverness, and temper, with which he overcomes all obstacles—and the promptness with which he pounces upon every favourable position—he is a great man.[65]

Ilchester's letter is symptomatic of a tremendous shift of opinion in the Tory party in 1867. Disraeli's followers changed from regarding him as a necessary evil, as a shrewd debater speaking for a party that was perpetually in Opposition, to admiring him as the brilliant commander of an aggressive parliamentary force. As the popular riddle went: 'Why is Mr. Gladstone like a telescope? Because Dizzy draws him out, sees through him and shuts him up'. His triumphs of 1867 laid the foundations of his subsequent career.

V   *The Transformation Completed*

When the House resumed after Easter Duncombe's apprehensions began to be fulfilled. A. S. Ayrton, the Liberal member for Tower Hamlets, moved to secure a uniform residence qualification of twelve months, and in less than an hour, with hardly any debate, the first of the 'vital safeguards' had been smashed. It was symptomatic of the state of the parties that the success of the amendment was largely accidental.

Gladstone had virtually surrendered the leadership. He had decided that the necessary modifications of the Bill would only win Liberal support if they were moved by unofficial members. Ayrton's was the first amendment in line with his proposed revision of the Bill, for he had withdrawn a similar motion of his own.[66]

The two years' residence clause in the Bill had been adapted from the clause which Lord John Russell had introduced into his 1854 measure,[67] which he in turn had taken from section IX of the Municipal Corporations Act. This provision was quite different from the residence qualification in the Reform Act (sections XXVI-XXVII). The Reform Act required twelve months 'occupation', while the Corporations Act, because it was founded on the principle of 'local interests' and its franchises were intricately linked with rating, demanded 'local residence' in addition to 'occupation'. Baxter had incorporated almost the complete provision, with the result that the under £10 voters were to be required to have a two-year residence while the ten-pounders could continue to enrol after twelve months' occupation.

The residence question badly divided the Conservatives. One stalwart was 'convinced . . . that great *dis*satisfaction will be felt and expressed by many of our best men if [the] government does not adhere to the *two years* residence'.[68] On the other hand, Colonel Gilpin and W. E. Welby both claimed that the 'best men' wanted to give way on the two years requirement. Welby believed that the difference would create 'an invidious distinction & source of agitation for years to come', and added, 'I know the additional number enfranchised by the "12 months" will be very large, but I do not fear that so much as the possible consequences of a fresh agitation'.[69] Taylor and his fellow Whips were convinced that the Government could not win a division against the amendment, as the Liberal renegades would not dare to vote against it and many of the Adullamites and Tories would support it to ensure a settlement. Taylor suggested that the only feasible way out of the dilemma was to deprive the clause of the status of a vital issue and chance it in a division. If the Government won unexpectedly, so much the better for morale, and if it lost they could blame Gladstone and the 'two years' supporters would save their wrath for him.[70] Disraeli urged this course in the Cabinet but he met vehement opposition from 'Hardy & Co.' The key to their opposition was the fact that residence was an integral part of the rating barrier: Hardy argued that 'if the term [were] reduced to one year then probably a single payment of rates would enable a man to be placed upon the register . . . this would really open the way to corrupt payment of rates and would bring us to the verge of household suffrage'.[71]

Ayrton's amendment came on early in the evening while the House was still half empty. The members were expecting a long debate on an amendment which Grosvenor was to move, to establish a £5 limit. But, when Grosvenor rose, he withdrew his proposal and offered an incoherent apology which was apparently meant to express his sudden realization that the House would not support him.[72] Ayrton's amendment thus came on early and caught everyone unprepared. There was virtually no debate. He justified his motion on the grounds that it would provide an even, certain settlement which would exclude 'the migratory' part of the population. He 'never entertained for a moment the idea that it was expedient to admit every person to . . . the franchise because he happened to be a man'.[73] Only Pakington and Karslake spoke for the Government and neither offered a very lively opposition. The division saw the Government defeated by 81 votes: 197 to 278. Seven Conservatives voted against the Government and about fifty more were absent from the division, probably because they were still at dinner.[74] The next day Disraeli complacently accepted the result and expressed his regret that the debate on the amendment had been 'of so brief a character'.[75] This comment could mean that the Ministers were taken by surprise when Grosvenor withdrew his motion. But Grosvenor rarely moved without prompting and his flustered explanation suggests that he was carrying out an unexpected order. Certainly his withdrawal permitted the inevitable to be disposed of before the 'two year' men could get up a debate.

This beginning of the transformation of the borough qualification coincided with a sharp renewal of anxiety about the Reform agitations in London. The leaders of the League were planning to repeat their defiance of the Government by calling another meeting in Hyde Park. They were hoping to produce a climactic demonstration which would stampede the Parliament into liberalizing the Bill. The League's challenging stance was also in part a desperate attempt to revive interest, for attendances at the weekly meetings had fallen off as the artisans had become bored with the sameness and apparent futility of the speeches and motions.

The new series of meetings had begun with a comparative failure when only about 20,000, instead of the hoped-for 100,000, had turned out for a rally in Trafalgar Square timed to coincide with the introduction of the Resolutions. The procession had been the usual sober, well-managed affair. The marchers had cheered the Prince of Wales, the Duke of Edinburgh, the Archbishop of York and Charles Dickens, as they distinguished them among the gentry who were watching from the balconies of the clubs.[76]

The announcement of the Bill, with its exclusive residence clause and dual voting provisions, had aroused the extremists in the London Working Men's Association and the League to emphasize the divergence between the interests of the ruling caste and those of 'the people' and openly to threaten violence. Bradlaugh hinted at a mass campaign to refuse payment of taxes and declared that: 'they intended to take away the government from the hands of those who had held it so long, and were determined that it should no longer be an heirloom, descending from . . . Derby to Derby'.[77] Nuttall told the League rally in Birmingham that:

> not the Tories only but the House of Commons, hated Reform and would never grant it until they could not withhold it. (hear hear). The land lords, army lords, navy lords, and law lords, who looked eagerly for a share of the taxes for themselves and their dependents, would never let the people's nose from the grindstone if they could help it. But the people had the power in their hands if they only knew how to use it. Let them set their backs up, and show their bristles, and they would get the Reform Bill they wanted (We'll do it!). They must show they were prepared to burst open the doors of the House of Commons should they be kept persistently closed against them (cheers). He hoped that they were not coming to the end of a peaceful agitation. . . . But when an aristocracy declared that the people should not be heard in the counsels of the nation . . . that was a very dangerous and criminal thing (hear hear) for should the people rise in their might and majesty—(and they ought). If like the raging sea, they should sweep on in their righteous indignation, every barrier set up against them—the aristocracy itself—might be swept into oblivion forever.[78]

Under the stress of apparent trickery and possible defeat Beales' and Applegarth's demands for an equitable, orderly inclusion were becoming submerged in a call, especially in London, to over-run the exclusive Parliament and capture power for the working classes. Nevertheless, the agitation was still moved primarily by abstract ethical ideas rather than by overt sectional economic or political aims. The speakers still concentrated upon the need for the vote as an end in itself, as an attribute of citizen dignity, and rarely discussed the objects for which the artisans might use their votes when they achieved them. But the arguments were becoming more tense.

Gladstone's move to abrogate the apparent household suffrage of the Bill provoked the London spokesmen into breaking their compact with the Reform Union and returning to their demand for manhood suffrage. George Mantle, the old Chartist and aggressive representative of the London Working Men's Association, went with a deputation of Reform League men to Disraeli and embarrassed them by declaring that the 'League and Reform movement' favoured manhood suffrage

> based on the principle of a vote for a man because he was a man, and . . . that in regard to the rate-paying clauses the Government had no more right to inquire into the pecuniary relations between a man and his parish, than between a house-holder and his cats-meat man.[79]

The demonstration at Leeds was split in two when Beales, Ernest Jones and George Potter demanded manhood suffrage at the open-air rally in the afternoon and W. E. Forster, Edward Baines and James Stansfeld heavily emphasized household suffrage at the soirée. The break-up of the League-Union alliance seemed likely to end the great meetings.[80]

On 18 April the League executive met and unanimously condemned the Bill as 'partial and oppressive'. Bradlaugh raised the question of holding a giant rally in Hyde Park, and his proposal caused an angry debate. Despite Beales' pleading, the executive voted five to three in favour of calling the meeting, and the League went ahead and posted placards advertising a demonstration for 6 May.[81]

The Cabinet considered these developments on the 1st, and found themselves in the same predicament as they had been in 1866, for they had since neglected to legislate to prohibit meetings in the Park. Walpole's proclamation aptly illustrated their dilemma:

> Whereas it has been publicly announced that a meeting will be held in Hyde Park on Monday the sixth day of May next, for the purpose of political discussion:
> And whereas the use of the Park for the purpose aforesaid is illegal, and interferes with the enjoyment of the Park by the people, and is calculated to endanger the public peace:
> Now all persons are hereby warned and admonished that they will attend any such meeting at their peril, and all Her Majesty's loyal and faithful subjects are required to abstain

from attending, aiding, or taking part in any such meeting, or from entering the Park with a view to attend, aid, or take part in any such meeting.

By Order

S. Walpole.[82]

The notice which Derby read to the House a week later differed from the one on the placards, for it was shorn of its first sentence to render it less ambiguous.[83] After his weak showing the year before, this episode finally destroyed Walpole's political career.

Bradlaugh forced the issue, as Lucraft had done in 1866, at a meeting in Trafalgar Square. The Home Secretary made a crashing blunder by instructing the police to issue the prohibition to Bradlaugh while at the rally; he immediately broadcast it to the crowd and turned the meeting against any compliance with the legally flimsy, and politically unenforceable, proclamation.[84]

The House was greatly disturbed by the League's show of defiance. Members on both sides attacked Walpole and the radicals associated with the League. R. J. Harvey, the Conservative, and Arthur Hayter, the Whig, both assumed that the Government would not attempt to stop the meeting and demanded that special constables be sworn and the cavalry be brought up 'to protect life and order'. Elcho and Selwyn, the Tory member for Cambridge University, both stirred the House by recalling 1848, and the latter offered to serve again as a special constable.[85] P. A. Taylor restored sanity to the discussion by suggesting that the Government knew that the demonstration would be orderly, they knew that they could not prevent it without bloodshed, and they would best help themselves if they offered police to assist the marshals.[86]

Taylor's remarks cut through to the real concern of the members. They were more anxious about appearing to give way to the demonstration than they were about possible disorder resulting from it. They knew that they were slipping towards an unguarded, possibly catastrophic enfranchisement, yet they wanted to keep the pose of control. When Bright taunted them with having reached their present position on Reform only with 'the assistance of those great demonstrations of public opinion', the House met him with hollow laughter. The Government's capitulation on the Park seemed utterly ignominious to its supporters. One busy-body wrote from the Carlton Club to inform

Disraeli 'how strong and outspoken . . . the feeling of the Members [was] against any symptom of giving way on the part of the Govt.', but he and his friends had no positive suggestion to offer for preventing the meeting.[87]

The demonstration was held, and passed off quietly. The police and special constables were mainly kept busy protecting the marchers from pickpockets, while the troops from Aldershot spent an uneventful day guarding the West End and the nearby railway stations. It was the League's most signal victory; never before had a lower-class agitation successfully defied parliamentary authority and managed to keep such good order. Walpole resigned a week later, and never held office again. His belated 'Meetings in Royal Parks Bill', which subjected the holding of meetings to the permission of the Queen-in-Council and provided penalties for non-compliance, had not even had its second reading.[88] It was a year too late, for the agitation it was designed to suppress had all but achieved its object; the May meeting proved to be the last demonstration in Hyde Park in the Second Reform Period.

The agitations were to hasten the modification of the Bill which had begun with Ayrton's amendment. The motion by Hibbert to allow the tenant to qualify by paying only his former composition rate was the next to come on. Disraeli had used it to foil Gladstone's move to ease the difficulties facing the compounders, and now he set out to foil Hibbert by moving that the phrase 'rated as an ordinary occupier' be inserted in the borough franchise clause, and that section III of Clay's Act be repealed.[89] This last was the provision which allowed compounders to register while paying the composition rate, and was the very section on which Hibbert had based his amendment. Disraeli's motion would have retained the 'fine' in a new guise, and it made no provision for compounders to 'de-compound'. He explained the amendment to a gathering of the party, but it passed over their heads.[90]

In fact, Disraeli himself was out of his depth. Robert Upperton, a Conservative agent of twenty years' experience, wrote urgently to point out that Disraeli's amendments would be inoperative because 'rated' normally meant 'assessed', and compounders were already 'assessed at the full rate' because their landlord's composition was calculated from it. The amendment was a clumsy last-minute attempt to give some substance to the

'principle' of the measure: even so, personal payment was still
not defined, there was no machinery provided to implement it,
and the words did not appear in the Bill.

It is difficult to see how 'personal payment' could be worked
in, taking Upperton's description of the system by which compounders were registered in Brighton. There the rates were struck
in July, the last day for payment was the fifth of January following, and because the collection was never complete by then, the
date was customarily extended to April. The party agents waited
until March, and then canvassed the £10 compounders with
printed forms on which the tenant applied 'to pay or tender' his
rates. The compounder usually signed, because in most cases his
landlord or landlord's agent had paid the rate for the occupancy
in January. The parish officials, usually Liberals, who already
had their moneys collected, were content to accept the applications as proof of readiness to pay and entered the tenants' names
in the rate-books, and so on to the electoral roll. Thus, even
Clay's Act had not ensured 'personal payment'. The method had
placed 1,500 on the Brighton register, and once the tenants'
names came into the rate-books they generally stayed, because
the collectors never visited them and rarely learnt of changes in
occupancy. Personation was rife. Much the same situation, apparently, obtained in Birmingham, Manchester, Rochdale, Sheffield, Exeter and Oxford, and altogether there were 25,004
non-rated occupiers on the rolls in 1867.[91] Upperton was greatly
perturbed, for, if Hibbert's amendment were carried it would
extend the present system below the ten-pounders and by swamp-
ing the constituencies with 'all the refuse of the land' it would
enormously increase the costs of 'nursing' a borough. 'We shall
be wrecked upon this compound question if we don't take care'.[92]

Some of the misconceptions about 'personal payment' are nicely
illustrated in the brush over its definition between the lawyers,
Denman and Gathorne-Hardy. The courts had held that the
tenant's payment of rates through his landlord or landlord's agent
constituted bona fide 'personal payment'.[93] Denman wished to
insert words to maintain this interpretation against the Government's clause which would be held to mean that the tenant
wishing to register would personally have to hand his rate to the
collector. Hardy airily dismissed the amendment as 'idle words',
and declared that the phrase 'personal payment', as it was not in
the Bill, 'was a description rather of the Government's intention

. . . that a man should be responsible for his rate'. He accepted that part of Denman's motion referring to 'bona fide' payment because it was legally meaningless, but rejected 'or cause to be paid', which was equally otiose in the light of his explanation. Clearly, he had not seen Upperton's letter, and his statement 'that a man should be responsible for his rates' ignored the principle established by the Small Tenements Act, which held the landlord ultimately liable for the payment of all rates levied on his properties.[94]

Hibbert pounced on the defects in Disraeli's counter-amendment and claimed that they would have the effect of raising rents and causing general social dislocation. Reliable, long-established tenants would de-compound in order to register, leaving their poorer, transitory fellows to continue to compound. Landlords would thus suffer a diminution of their rating rebates, and be left with the worse tenants; inevitably, they would raise their rents to cover their losses and try to coerce those tenants who wanted to de-compound. Whole communities would have their housing and local financial arrangements upset. In Hull, for example, there were 12,026 compounders and only 64 directly rated occupiers under £10; in Manchester, 33,013 compounders and 2,862 directly rated tenants. Birmingham and Leeds had similar figures. However, these objections were hypothetical, for the difficulties confronting the compounders who wished to register would have made the clause a dead letter.[95]

Hibbert did not make much impact because the members were fed up with 'fantastic objections' on compounders. It was oppressively hot, the effluvium of the Thames wafted through the House, many, including Gladstone, slept through the speeches, while others stretched and scratched in their heavy black clothes. They carried Disraeli's amendment by 66 votes, 322 to 256, with 25 Adullamites and 26 of the Dillwyn-Seely group voting for the Government and once more turning the balance. Disraeli had concluded his speech by emphasizing 'how critical the state of affairs would be' if his amendment were rejected in favour of Hibbert's. Once more he mastered the cowards, and gulled those who least wanted household suffrage into defeating an amendment that offered a real chance of containing it.[96]

The fragmentation of party, the confusion of principle, the pressing desire to be rid of the Bill and to avoid a dissolution, all contributed to the drift of votes in the successive divisions.

After the Liberals' defeat on Hibbert's amendment, Tom Hughes exploded to de Grey:

> Did ever mortal man ever read or hear or conceive of the sort of trivial meanness which governs the votes of a whole lot of our so called liberals? Why last night one little skunk was lobbying about just before I went . . . to dinner & blowing his penny whistle against Hibbert & his amendment, & lo when I get back at 10 he is all back again & going to vote for us— which he did—I found the conversion to have arisen (he confided the fact to Trevelyan . . .) that Gladstone had fallen in with him on the stairs & had *ridden up to dinner in his brougham!* How in heaven's name are we going to advance the new jerusalem by wise legislation . . . when this kind of critter has his oar in & may catch a crab at any moment . . .— There is not only an utter absence of political thought & principle about a lot of our men, & the presence of meanness & petty self-interested motives, but what is almost worse, no shame whatever at avowing the springs of their action.[97]

A month after he had spurned the proposal for a lodger franchise from Gladstone, Disraeli accepted it from Torrens, the radical member for Finsbury. Torrens moved for a qualification based on a twelve months' sole occupation and a six months' sole residence of 'a part of a dwelling house' let unfurnished at £10 a year.[98] This level would have almost completely excluded the artisans, whose highest rents in the London area, according to Tom Hughes, were 3s. 6d. to 4s. a week. Disraeli had been briefed that only lodgers of the professional class in London and the South Coast resorts would benefit by the clause and he was not unduly worried by it: 'I wish . . . you would get up an anti-lodger speech, or a speech on the subject either way,' he wrote to Stanley. He knew his man: 'I am so deeply pledged to the principle,' Stanley replied, 'that I cannot speak against it; but we may fix the limit where we please. I think £15 would do no harm. It would swamp only constituencies which are already as radical as they well can be.'[99] So Disraeli initiated a secret conference with Torrens to seek a compromise at £15. But Torrens held to £10, for he knew that he could outbid Disraeli for the freebooters' votes.[1]

Disraeli staved off a division on the first night of the debate, and when it was resumed a week later Goldney, a Conservative backbencher, had ready an amendment to rise the level to £15.

This would have taken the qualification well beyond the range
of the artisans. Workingmen who paid 6s. a week almost uniformly sub-let or shared their lodgings and so could not qualify
as sole occupiers. Bright intervened to suggest the figure in the
Bill of 1866, '£10 annual value', which meant the rating value of
the unfurnished lodging, representing an actual rental of almost
£15 when charges for furnishings and service were added. Disraeli quickly accepted the bargain.[2]

Thus, without a division, the Government adopted a motion
which cut right across the declared principle of their Bill. The
lodger qualification negated the theory of personal payment as
a test of citizen worthiness. Sir Rainald Knightley angrily denounced the Ministry for their tergiversation. That very evening,
he said, Disraeli had repeated the 'oft told tale'.

> But they were now adopting a hard and fast line, and abolish-
> ing the personal or any payment of rates.

Disraeli gave the retort courteous:

> An hon. Baronet . . . who sits on this side of the House—who
> still does us that honour—has indulged in invective which
> by repetition becomes more perfect . . . [He] is not for a
> moment, I suppose, prepared to contend that the payment of
> rates is the entire principle of this Bill (Laughter) . . . what
> we all said, was, that with regard to the . . . borough franchise
> —we were of opinion that it should be founded on the personal
> payment of rates. That is a principle which is not relinquished,
> and which we shall not relinquish.[3]

Goldney went on to seek a further concession, by proposing
to extend the residence period to twelve months. The requirement seemed innocuous, but its effect was intended to nullify
the qualification. Persons who could afford to live in a 6s. apartment could, Goldney and his supporters believed, afford to take
annual holidays. Usually the tenant legally 'surrendered' his
apartment because, while he was absent, he paid a retainer only,
consisting of the rental less service charges. However, unless
the lodger paid the full rent throughout and ensured that his
apartment was not let during his absence he could not swear to
twelve months' sole occupancy at '£10 annual value'. Torrens
had specifically drafted his clause to overcome this difficulty and
refused to give way.[4] The Liberals lost the division by 63 votes,
145 to 208.[5] Ten Adullamites and ten freebooters voted with the
Government, but the defeat sprang from the abstention of about

130 Whigs and Palmerstonians, who liked the prospect of enlarging a potentially independent, radical electorate as little as
the Conservatives.

Lambert was set to calculate the probable enrolment resulting
from the amendment, but found it impossible. Landlords and
tenants refused to disclose their rentals, and whether the lodgings
were shared. But, given the high rental level, the stiff residence
qualification and the necessity for the voter to repeat his claim
annually before a revising barrister, Lambert was sure that the
figure would not be large.[6] He proved correct, for by 1869 only
about 12,000 lodgers were registered, and over 8,000 of them
were in Marylebone and Westminster. Liverpool had 529, but
no other commercial or industrial centre had more than 100:
Manchester had 28, Birmingham had one.[7] And few of these,
apparently, were workingmen. 'The Journeyman Engineer' explained that the lodger voter of 1868 was 'really a householder
. . . holding an apartment, and that the "true lodger", the single
working man, who occupied one room at a much lower rent
did not qualify'.[8]

By defeating Hibbert's amendment, Disraeli had brought the
question of personal payment to an impasse. Hibbert's amendment had offered the last viable opportunity of keeping the existing compounding arrangements by leaving on the rolls those £10
compounders who had registered under Clay's Act, and of retain-
ing some semblance of selection among the under-£10 compounders. The back-benchers on both sides were now desperate
and Bright feared that they would sever the borough qualification from its rating framework and let it collapse into manhood
suffrage. He drew on his local political knowledge to devise

a mode of getting out of the difficulty of the late division. . . .
In Rochdale there is no Small Tenements Act & no Compounding Acts, but generally thro' the Town, the Landlords or
Owners of Cottages pay the rates, & are repaid in the rents
charged to the occupiers. The occupiers' names are on the Rate
Book, the *full sum of the Rate is paid,* by Tenant or Owner, as
the case may be, & the Franchise is preserved. In Rochdale
therefore the vote will be 'Household' & yet the *occupier* will
have all the advantages of the system of Compounding.
In Birmingham, there is no Small Tenements Act, but there
are Compounding Acts, one of which goes up to Houses rated
as high as £12—or about £16 rental. The *full rate* is not paid

and the occupiers generally are not entered on the Rate Book, excepting those who have been enfranchised under the 3rd section of Clay's Act, & are now to be disfranchised.

What is wanted is, not to disturb the plan of paying the rate by the Landlord, but to abolish the 'Composition' . . . so that the *occupier* would have still the advantage of the system of compounding. His name being on the Rate Book, & *his full rate paid,* whether by himself or his landlord, he would appear on the Register of Voters.

Under this plan the payment by the owner would be voluntary, as in Rochdale. He would get no allowance from the Parish, & therefore he *would not pay for empty houses.* But he would undertake the payment as a Convenience to his Tenants, & he would have no difficulty in repaying himself . . . by an addition of 3d per week.

Bright thought that his scheme had no chance as an amendment, and suggested to Gladstone that the members would more readily accept it as a separate Bill after the Franchise Bill was carried.

The Bill should repeal all the powers given by existing acts to make *allowance to Landlords* who undertake to pay the Rate . . . It should leave parishes & owners the power to arrange for payment by the owners, but *of the full rate only,* and thus abolish the 'composition' or . . . disenfranchising rate.[9]

The famous amendment which Grosvenor Hodgkinson, 'the insignificant solicitor from Newark', moved on 17 May, was a crude variant of Bright's scheme. He moved, as a proviso to the borough franchise clause:

That, except as hereinafter provided, no person other than the occupier shall, after the passing of this Act, be rated to parochial rates in respect of premises occupied by him within the limits of a Parliamentary Borough, all Acts to the contrary now in force notwithstanding.[10]

Hodgkinson had been elected as a 'Liberal'. He believed, he said, in the wide enfranchisement of the artisan class, provided the balance of power was preserved in the constituencies, and he was utterly opposed to manhood suffrage. He had held aloof even from the National Reform Union. In his explanation of his amendment Hodgkinson carefully avoided any suggestion that his motion would revolutionize the Bill. Rather, his amendment 'was essential to the satisfactory and permanent working of the leading principle—the personal payment of rates . . . [and] it would . . . get rid of . . . "the residuum" ' because they never paid them.[11]

Hodgkinson's motion and speech echo Bright's letter, but the evidence suggests that his motion was not instigated by Bright, as Trevelyan assumed.[12] Bright wanted to have the occupier assessed to the full rate, but equally he wanted to preserve the system whereby the landlord paid the rates for the occupancy by agreement with his tenant. Hodgkinson's motion ignored the second part.

Bright's scheme was in fact introduced as a separate amendment, after Gladstone had received a deputation of radical M.P.s and manufacturers from London, the Midlands and the North, who urged that Bright's plan be adopted as an official Liberal amendment.[13] The outcome was a motion moved by Childers. He was a faithful, moderate colleague of Gladstone's, and much more in the counsels of the Liberal leadership than Hodgkinson, who was a nonentity and, moreover, a freebooter who had previously voted against Gladstone's and Hibbert's amendments. When Gladstone spoke on Hodgkinson's motion he explicitly stated his preference for Childer's foreshadowed amendment; he clearly was little concerned for the survival of Hodgkinson's scheme, for he left the chamber immediately after his speech and was not present to hear Disraeli accept it.

Moreover, the freebooters had met secretly to discuss the compounder difficulty and it seems certain that Hodgkinson's motion was the outcome.[14] Two of their ringleaders, M. T. Bass and Thomas Chambers, supported the motion in the House, and Bass came equipped with some rating statistics which purported to show that the direct payment which would result from Hodgkinson's amendment would increase revenue.[15] Hodgkinson himself revealed the typical freebooter attitude when he confessed himself 'nauseated' by the compounders and anxious to be rid of them before they caused the collapse of the Bill.[16]

His motion came on shortly after eight o'clock, and by nine, with less than one hundred members in the House, Disraeli had accepted it without a division.

To those at the clubs the electric wire soon sent the news, and at a hundred tables there were surprise . . . and consternation, the like of which has seldom been seen. Many a snug dinner party was prematurely broken up . . . and by half-past [nine] the House was . . . full. As the members rushed across the

lobby, astonishment sat upon . . . their faces. Is it true? . . .
was everywhere asked . . . 'True, disgracefully true!' exclaimed
. . . a . . . Lord of the old Tory race.[17]

It was the quickest way out of the maze, but Disraeli could
instead have acceded to Childers' amendment which promised
less disruption in the parishes. But he believed that Childers was
the cipher for Gladstone and he rashly seized upon the alternative
motion as a shift to further outbid and confound his rival. He
accepted the amendment with a speech which beautifully dis-
plays his parliamentary genius: his audacity and almost endless
resource of plausible equivocation:

> The proposal . . . was not at all opposed to the principle upon
> which the Bill . . . is founded. . . . On the contrary, it must be
> evident that if the policy recommended by this clause should
> be brought into action, it would enforce the policy which we
> recommend, give strength to the principles which we have
> been impressing upon the House as those which are the best
> foundations for the franchise, and give completeness to the
> measure we have introduced . . . there must be something in
> this principle . . . which has received such signal corroboration.

He concluded by warning his followers against rejecting the
amendment; he subtly blamed the agitation, and hence the necessity for passing the clause, on Gladstone, and ended by denying
that the House accepted it from fear of further unrest.[18] Just
seven days earlier, he had denounced as 'rash counsel' Gladstone's
advocacy of Hibbert's less sweeping amendment.[19]

Hodgkinson had worded his motion very clumsily and even as
he accepted it Disraeli managed to adumbrate a saving clause to
permit existing agreements to continue voluntarily; in fact,
towards the system which Childers' motion would have introduced. Hodgkinson and White, the radical who seconded the
motion, ingenuously swallowed his assurances, while the Attorney-
General and another Tory lawyer, William Brett, joyfully interpreted his remarks to mean that the concession had not been
made at all. J. S. Mill thought so too, and quickly pinned Disraeli
to a statement that he would introduce a separate rating bill
before he carried the Reform Bill.[20]

The House was now filling rapidly, and Disraeli was striving to
close the discussion before the Tory rebels could have their say
and drag the question to a division. Sandford managed to express
the consternation of his friends when he asked if the concession

had had the approval of Cabinet, especially as the Government's followers had been assured that the compounding acts would be retained, while Cranborne declared Disraeli's sudden admission of '500,000 people' to be 'entirely an abnegation of all the principles of his party'.[21] It emerged later that the Conservatives had been whipped to come that evening to defeat 'an Amendment of vital importance'.[22]

Sandford was right in his surmise that Disraeli had accepted the amendment without prior consultation with his Ministers. Disraeli moved quickly to secure Gathorne-Hardy, the strong man among the likely critics in the Cabinet. He wrote him a placatory letter, to Osborne, whence Hardy had gone to receive the seals of the Home Office in place of Walpole, and once more he used Gladstone as the scapegoat:

My dear Hardy,

I have had great difficulties about the Reform Bill since we parted, and have terribly missed your aid and counsel.

On Thursday night Dalglish gave notice of a motion for a Committee on Compound Householders wh if carried wd have 'hung up' the Bill, and wh, as it was to have been supported by the independent Liberals and many of our own men, would certainly have been carried. I prevailed on him yesterday morning to give this intention up, but he informed me at the same time that he and all his friends, and many of ours, as we knew, must support Hodgkinson's amendment for the repeal of the Small Tenements Act. I sent off to you, but you had gone to Osborne. Lord Barrington, however, told me that you had mentioned to him that you were not unfavourable to the repeal in itself.

I sent for Lambert, who after long consultation with myself and Thring, said if required he could effect the repeal of the Rating Bill in five clauses, and was in favour of it; two months ago such a repeal was impossible but a very great change had occurred in the public mind on this matter. Two months ago Gladstone would have placed himself at the head of the Vestries and 'civilization' [Gladstone had frequently defended compounding as a means of social improvement and class mutuality]—now—we were secretly informed that he intended to reorganize on the principle of repeal of local Acts [Childers' Amendment] In this state of doubt and difficulty I went down to the House—and about 9 o'clock, being quite alone on our bench, & only 45 men on our side, some of whom were going to vote for Hodgkinson, the amendment was moved, and as I had been led somewhat to believe, Gladstone got up (his benches with about 100 men) & made his meditated coup, which you will read.

I tried to get up some debate, or rather I waited for it . . . but it was impossible. His 'appeal' to me prevented any one but Bass and Co. speaking, and they were for Hodgkinson. I waited till the question was put when, having revolved everything in my mind, I felt that the critical moment had arrived when, without in the least degree receding from our principle and position of a rating and residential franchise, we might take a step which would destroy the present agitation and extinguish Gladstone & Co. I therefore accepted the spirit of H's amendment. . . .

I have no reason to doubt the adhesion of the Cabinet, with the exception of the Duke of Buckingham . . . if the Cabinet is united to-day all will go right.

Gathorne-Hardy duly agreed with Disraeli that he had taken 'the logical & consistent course'.[23]

The compromise with Dalglish was probably linked with the squabble over the redistribution for Scotland. The Scottish members among the freebooters, Dalglish, Crum-Ewing, Kinnaird and McLaren, threatened to throw over the Government if it did not engage to produce more seats for Scotland. Disraeli had prevailed upon Dalglish to drop their plan to obstruct the Bill with a committee on compounders,[24] but whether he gave him any firm undertaking is doubtful, for Dalglish was not well placed to bargain: certainly the Scottish radicals were treated badly in the eventual redistribution.[25]

Hodgkinson's ineffectual wording of his motion was revealed when Disraeli introduced the changes he had promised. His clauses first restricted the abolition of compounding only as it applied to the poor rate, then made provision for entering the ratepaying occupier's name in the rate-book and, finally, made provision for the continuance of compounding by voluntary agreement between landlord and tenant.[26] The first point was essential, for to tamper with the arrangements for collecting the highway, watch, lighting, paving and cleansing rates was to invite complete chaos. The nub of the deviation from Hodgkinson's intentions lay in the third part which, by allowing voluntary compounding to continue, would have allowed landlord and agents to dictate the registration. The tenant who wished to de-compound and register would have found the whole of local authority combined against him, for it had a stake in making him continue to compound for his rates.[27] Russell saw through Disraeli's clauses immediately, and warned Gladstone 'that they [would] never do—They revive all the evils of the compound householder in a more insidious shape—Hodgkinson should with the assistance of R. Palmer, frame a clause to the effect of his amendment'.[28] The solicitor from Newark had his revised amendment ready when Disraeli's clauses came on, and stoutly declared that they were 'quite untenable'. Then followed an extraordinary sequence of amendment and counter-amendment, which culminated with Gaselee roaring 'that it was quite impossible to know what was going on'.[29] Disraeli finally gave way and deleted the section allowing voluntary agreement.

Before the clause was carried, Ayrton made a last attempt at salvage. He knew that the abolition promised trouble and wanted at least to leave the owner ultimately responsible for recovery of rates. But the House shouted him down; they had had enough of this 'dry and wearisome' subject.[30] Disraeli sat tight, although he had received a flood of letters from vestry clerks in the 192 boroughs which would be affected, declaring that abolition would cause an immense loss and pleading that it be reconsidered.[31] The clerk of Whitechapel, for example, wrote that tenants were 'here today and gone tomorrow', and that it was 'almost *impossible* to get rates from them', let alone keep an up-to-date list of names. Whitechapel already had two special sessions to hear cases against over two hundred defaulters each year. The abolition of compounding, the clerk continued, would mean that collectors would 'have to go with demands for Rates in one hand & warrants for distress in the other'. Already the rates were collected in four portions and the collectors had to call three or four times to screw each portion out of the tenant.[32]

The vestry clerks had not exaggerated, for when the October quarter came due, the collectors in Lambeth, Whitechapel, Bethnal Green and Southwark found it almost impossible to extract rates at all: landlords refused to pay, and many tenants believed that Parliament had abolished rates.[33] Tenants frequently told the collector that they would 'see him damned' before they paid.[34] In Birmingham, 25,000 summonses were issued and after that some parishes gave up the attempt.[35] Before the end of 1867, in boroughs of over 20,000 inhabitants, 137,000 summonses and 29,000 distress warrants had been issued.[36] The tangle persisted until 1869, when it was largely cleared by Goschen's Poor Rate Assessment Act.[37] This measure displaced the 'great principle' of the Second Reform Act by allowing compounders under £8, and outside the four great cities, to register upon their production of a written rent agreement with their landlord. In London the level was set inclusively at £20, in Liverpool at £13, and at £10 in Manchester and Birmingham and, as many landlords were unwilling to make written agreements with their tenants, the Act had its intended winnowing effect.[38] This last gesture towards independent payment quickly became a source of local contention and was, with fitting irony, finally abolished by the Disraeli Ministry of 1878.[39]

Disraeli and Hodgkinson had been careful not to mention any figures, but it had been commonly assumed that the amendment would enfranchise 500,000 borough householders.[40] In 1867 there were about 1,367,000 adult male occupiers in the parliamentary boroughs of England and Wales: among these there were 570,704 compound householders, 94,111 at or above the £10 line and 476,593 below it.[41] Homersham Cox assumed that 50 per cent of the over ten-pounders would register, in addition to the 25 per cent already enrolled, and that 55 per cent of the under ten-pounders might enrol. Thus:

$$50 \text{ per cent of } 94,111 = 47,055$$
$$55 \text{ per cent of } 476,593 = 262,126$$
$$\overline{\phantom{55 \text{ per cent of }} 309,181}$$

Cox then added the original increase intended by Disraeli, as he calculated it, 118,400, and concluded that Hodgkinson's amendment increased the enfranchisement 'almost four times as much as was originally contemplated'.[42]

Cox was a shrewd observer and his estimates deserve respect, although they are probably too conservative. He allowed for a large number of former compounders who would not pay their poor rate and we know that by December 1867 at least 165,000 adult male occupiers had been excused or were unable to tender their full rates.[43] But if we assume that all of these were former compounders under £10 and set them beside his projected enrolment of 262,000, we are 50,000 short of 476,593. Some of these 50,000 may have registered, but probably most were excused and were not counted in the return of excusals, which essayed only to cover boroughs with over 20,000 inhabitants. But there remain the 47,000, the other 50 per cent of ex-compounders over £10 and it seems that a much higher proportion of these came on the registers than Cox allowed. There were arrangements, notably in Liverpool, by which the local Tories disfranchised occupiers by having the corporation collect part of the rate from their landlord. But evidence from other boroughs suggests that the more substantial ex-compounders came freely onto the rolls.[44]

If this impression is correct, it suggests that registration became much easier. Cox and his contemporaries presupposed that the initiative for enrolment would continue to lie with the party agents and the individual qualifier, and this was so with lodgers, but the evidence given to the Select Committees on Rates and Registration implies that Hodgkinson's amendment had the effect of making registration largely automatic.[45] The direct collection of rates, as required by section VII of the Second Reform Act, meant that collectors had to visit each occupancy, enter the name of an occupier in the book and try to exact the full rate. The administrative burden of new assessments caused vestries to tighten their methods of collection. In Norwich, for example, there were 12,000 new assessments and the overseers had to appoint salaried collectors to do the work formerly done voluntarily and negligently by themselves. In Birmingham there were over 30,000 new entries and 15 additional collectors had to be appointed, while the Manchester vestry had also to employ extra staff to cope with 22,000 more assessments.[46] Through 1867-8 the revenue in most boroughs, outside those of the metropolis, seems to have exceeded the old levels, even beyond the saving on landlords' compound rebates. This, coupled with the often tiny proportion of excusals, suggests that more occupiers found themselves paying rates than ever before. And upon surrender of the full rate, over the period of a year, male occupiers, many of whose names appeared in the rate-books for the first time, found their names transcribed independently into the electoral register. The exaction of the full rate was especially rigorous in Sheffield, Oldham, Stockport and Manchester and these are among the boroughs which record the highest increases in enrolments between 1865 and 1868. Thus, Hodgkinson's amendment not only enabled over 400,000 compounders to qualify, but also led to the situation in which 'household suffrage' became a reality and the

borough constituency of England and Wales increased by almost
1,000,000 between 1865 and 1874.

The defeatist mood of the House did not carry the members as
far as giving a vote to women. On 20 May, John Stuart Mill
moved that 'person' be substituted for 'man' in the Bill. He carefully defended his proposal on the grounds of 'expediency'.
Women had the same qualifications for the franchise as the male
artisans they were admitting, for women were no longer illiterate
servants of confined outlook, but had elevated themselves to
become the 'companions' of men and to share their interests and
views on public policy. As tax-payers, women had as much claim
as men to the franchise, and if artisans were to have the vote to
express their particular interests, so should women, for they had
a vital interest in the reform of property law, the law of domestic
relations, and the regulations governing entry to the universities
and professions. Their improvement gave them as much 'moral
right' to the franchise as workingmen and unfitness or public
danger had equally to be proved against their enfranchisement if
it were to be objectively opposed. It was a brilliant, persuasive
speech which delighted the ladies in the gallery and was
rewarded with the undreamed of total of 73 votes.

Still, as the 196 Tory and Whig votes against the amendment
showed, more than rational argument was needed to sway the
House of Commons. As Laird confessed: 'although they might
not be able to give a single argument for their opinion he would
back their instincts against the logic of the hon. Member.' And
women's suffrage *was* a public danger, for only ambitious and
aggressive females would want to vote: 'who', he asked, 'was most
likely to be a[n] . . . elector . . . Cordelia or . . . Goneril or
Regan?' By enfranchising women, the House was thereby depri-
ving them of the source of their moral influence, 'their gentleness
. . . affection and . . . domesticity'.[47]

Ironically, Mill might have achieved his object if he had kept
silent. As the Bill stood, women ratepayers could have legally
challenged the right of returning officers to exclude them when
the next registration was made. Baxter and Thring had used 'man'
instead of 'male person' throughout the Bill, although 'male
person' was believed to be the only definition which the Courts
would have accepted.[48] The House subsequently agreed to
amend the third clause to read 'male person', but, curiously,

this refinement never emerged in the Act. One woman, whose name slipped into the register, did vote in Manchester in November 1867, and some women voted in Finsbury, Ashford and Ormskirk in 1868. When 2,300 more challenged their exclusion from the rolls in 1868 the Court of Common Pleas had to fall back on the Registration Act of 1843, which referred to 'male person', as the ground for refusing to hear their appeals.[49]

Half the session was gone and the House had only now reached the county franchise clauses. The impatient Liberals hustled to transform them. C. R. Colvile, the member for South Derbyshire, moved that holders of copyholds rated at £5 a year should qualify.[50] The figure in the Bill was £10, in continuation of the level created in 1832. The Attorney-General opposed the amendment, as 'nothing had occurred since 1832' to make them reduce the limit. Colvile had not only M. T. Bass and the freebooters keen for 'reasonable . . . concession [s]', but Tory county members like W. H. Barrow, who supported the motion because it was 'based upon the . . . desirability of giving property some influence'. He carried his amendment by 44 votes, 201 to 157, with 10 Tory county members voting against the Government.

In their eagerness to secure this small extension of votes among their tenantry, the Tory county members forgot that the copyhold qualification was associated with the leasehold franchise in the Reform Act, and that if the one were altered the amendment of the other would surely follow. The leasehold franchise was exercised predominantly by men who occupied cottages on land on the outskirts of towns, and they were commonly believed to be independent and to vote Liberal. Hussey Vivian, from Glamorganshire, duly moved that the leaseholder qualification be reduced to £5.[51] It was hopeless for Disraeli to divide against the amendment, with the Liberals united behind it, and many of his followers willing to back their judgment of their cottagers and vote for it, so he interposed to neutralize the motion. He offered to accept it, provided that it retained the condition of 1832 that leaseholders who qualified for the borough roll by reason of their borough occupancy should exercise their vote in the borough, and be excluded from the county constituency.

When the Act emerged it was discovered that the copyholders were also subject to the proviso of 1832, though this was neither included in Colvile's amendment nor raised during the discussion on it. This was a deft piece of salvage by Thring and Disraeli.[52]

But the clause remained so tangled that even the revising barristers found it obscure. Section LIX of the Second Reform Act specifically incorporated sections XXIV and XXV of the First Reform Act, but made no provision for the fact that they applied only to £10 holdings. Thus Disraeli's machinations went awry, for only copy and leaseholders at £10 and over could be compelled to vote in the boroughs, as before.[53]

The usual pattern of cross-voting re-emerged when Sir Edward Colebrooke, the Liberal member for Lanarkshire, introduced an amendment to prevent the creation of faggot-votes. He moved the deletion of the words, 'premises of any tenure', from the franchise clause, and the substitution of 'a dwelling-house or other building':[54] this amendment followed the provisions in Russell's Bills of 1854, 1860 and 1866. Lord John Manners duly opposed it because it would 'subvert that which had hitherto been . . . the basis of the county franchise'. The members divided 196 to 193 in favour of deleting the original words, and then voted 212 to 209 against inserting the new ones.[55] The House was in uproar, when Gathorne-Hardy filled the gap with an ingenious improvisation, by moving that 'lands or tenements' be inserted. The phrase was technically meaningless, and completely evaded the point of Colebrooke's motion, that the 'tenement' should be substantial enough to be 'a dwelling house'.[56] When the re-worded clause came up again four days later, it was carried by one vote, 255 to 254. The Adullamites and freebooters once again swayed the result, for eight freebooters and twelve Adullamites voted with the Government, and over twenty more were absent.[57] Thus selfish, ill-considered cross-voting encumbered the statute book with one more empty phrase and perpetuated a main source of corruption.

The final extension of the county qualification came with Locke King's motion to reduce the proposed level from £15 to £10. Disraeli offered a bargain at £12 and Locke King gratefully accepted it. The transaction measured the general success of the landed interest in their rearguard action. For fifteen years Locke King had fought for a £10 county level and even at the height of the triumph of Reform he and his friends could not exact more than £12, and then receive it by the gracious permission of 'the cavaliers of that House'.[58] Like so many of the major changes in the Bill it came about with very little debate and without a

division; Disraeli preferred to confront his back-benchers with a
fait accompli rather than let them run amok in a division.

Of the original suffrage clauses, there now remained only the
fancy franchises, and these were soon dispatched. The lodger
franchise and Hodgkinson's amendment had made the educational qualification superfluous. Fawcett pleaded with the
Government to keep it as a test of electoral worth, but members
from both sides derided it as being unworkable and expensive,
and 'unconstitutional' because it was not linked with local citizenship. Disraeli withdrew it. The savings, tax and funds qualifications and the dual vote all suffered the same criticisms and the
same fate. Disraeli cheerfully abandoned them 'in deference to
the . . . reactionary party'. [59] The fancy franchises were probably
unworkable and certainly would have been expensive to adminis-
ter, but they were thrown out because the House was suspicious
of their novelty and the mass electorate had supervened, not
because their impractibility had been demonstrated in debate. So,
within the space of an hour, the results of fifteen years' work to
devise a set of qualifications supplementary to the old tests of
occupation and citizenship were scrapped, and with their disappearance went the last chance of introducing counterweights
within a mass electorate.

The prospect of the inclusive electorate prompted two other
interesting amendments. The first slightly re-phrased clause
XXXVII, which repealed the laws of 1706 by which a Minister
had to vacate his seat and seek re-election upon his transferring
office.[60] A few Whig and Tory die-hards opposed it because it
contracted the sovereignty of the electorate, but Cranborne and
Gladstone combined to point out that the provision was already
a dead letter, as it had become customary for the Opposition to
allow Ministers to be re-elected unopposed. The amendment was
then swiftly carried. Nevertheless, the repeal was of some con-
sequence in decreasing the costs of office and in helping to
increase the insulation of Ministers from the country and the
House of Commons. It destroyed a mechanism which could have
developed into a rudimentary form of plebiscite in the age of
mass politics.

The other important motion was Henry Fawcett's attempt to
have election expenses defrayed from the local rates. He argued
that the public payment of expenses was a necessary concomitant
to the extension of the suffrage, if the representative principle was

to be taken to its proper conclusion and artisans were to have a fair chance of entering Parliament.[61] The returns gave the candidates' average expenses in a borough election as £70, which represented a year's wages for a skilled artisan. J. S. Mill endorsed this case with the argument, from *Representative Government*, that the morality of the choice of the electors could only be at its optimum when they were allowed to choose among the widest range of candidates. He thought it 'strange that elections should . . . be run by taxing candidates . . . it was like asking a judge to pay for justice'. The Tories dismissed election costs as 'a trifling expense', and Lord Hotham remarked that Fawcett's proposal would induce men to 'stand out of mischief'. The last criticism was reasonable in an age of open elections and decoy candidates, but Hotham went on to use the radicals' own slogans to defend his notion of an exclusive Parliament. Candidatures and parliamentary service were 'a matter of free trade—of supply and demand', and it would be wrong to increase the rates in order to support candidates who could not keep appropriate state if they were elected. Samuel Laing, the Adullamite railway magnate, showed that the logical result of Fawcett's motion would be payment of members, which he regarded 'with more horror than . . . the most extreme extension of the suffrage' because it would allow 'Chartist orators and local agitators' to become candidates. This was too much for the gentlemen, and they defeated the motion by 106 votes, 248 to 142.[62] The calamities of the Reform League candidates in 1868 sprang directly from their lack of funds,[63] and the later difficulties of the trade union candidates of the seventies and eighties suggest that the defeat of Fawcett's amendment helped to delay the advent of a parliamentary Labour party for a generation.[64]

The third reading of the Bill occasioned an angry valedictory debate. The foiled Tory rebels bitterly attacked Disraeli and his Bill, while the Liberals were determined not to let it go without highlighting its defects. Few important measures can have suffered such unanimous condemnation as they emerged from the Commons. Cranborne declared that Disraeli's tactics had undermined that trust and stability of purpose upon which executive government depended. Once he had climbed into office he had repudiated all his party stood for, had deceived his Cabinet colleagues, and swept the nation into peril: his capitulations to the radicals amounted to 'a political betrayal which has no parallel in our Parliamentary annals'.[65] Beresford Hope, W. H. Brown, G. M. W. Sandford and Lord Eustace Cecil all agreed that the vast extension of the borough franchise had created a lower class pressure which would soon demand the opening of the counties and a further redistribution. The way had been cleared for a malignant alliance between wealthy parvenus and the populace, which would drive men of ancient family out of public life.[66]

Disraeli sat smiling through the abuse. Cranborne and the rest could not harm him now: the majority of Tory back-benchers were committed to him and the Bill. He rose, and calmly and elegantly affirmed his devotion to Conservative paternalism and his confidence in the deference of the lower orders. The Bill passed without a division. Jauntily, the Tories shook hands among themselves while the Liberals gave a tired cheer.[67]

VI *The Bill in the House of Lords and the Cumulative Voting Clause*

Disraeli's triumph in the Commons cut the ground from under the Tories in the House of Lords. The intellectuals of both sides, Carnarvon, Cairns, Grey and Russell, set out to persuade their colleagues to lift the franchise qualifications and counteract the popular character of the new electorate by restoring the small boroughs and introducing voting papers. But they failed to produce a consistent line of attack. Some, like Carnarvon and Grey, wanted to reject the Bill or transform it utterly, others, like Cairns and Salisbury wanted to tighten it and be rid of it. Russell wanted to reinstate the dual vote and fancy franchises.[68] But there was no imperious, unpredictable Gladstone to provide a focus for their discontents, and they were faced by a Commons and a public press resolved upon a settlement. The intellectuals did have the support of a few Tory die-hards like Lord Ellenborough, repeating his stand of 1832, the Earl of Selkirk, and the Dukes of Portland and Buccleuch, but they failed to upset Derby's control of the main body of his followers. Carnarvon did not have the standing to lead a revolt of his elders, Cairns was an outsider, Grey was disliked as a crotchety Whig and Russell was suspected for his factious spite. Moreover, the Tory peers were enjoying a rare and, for many of them, a new experience, for they were reviewing important legislation sent up by a Tory Government. Their attendance was about twenty to thirty higher than normal during the mid-sixties, while the Whigs, including several of the leading rebels of 1866, largely absented themselves.

On the day of the Bill's appearance in the Lords, Grey and Carnarvon moved a general critical resolution as preliminary to opening the Bill to detailed amendment. By declaring that the Bill would 'not make a settlement or promote future good Government', they hoped to gather in those restive peers who had particular objections to the measure.[69] But Derby checkmated them by summoning his followers and warning them against falling into the traps of the Whigs and repeating the collapse of 1859. He made Russell the scapegoat and, indeed, Lord John was planning to use his motion on the fancy franchises as a lever to turn out the Government. Support for Carnarvon and the Whigs, Derby added, could only lead to a repetition of the split of 1846 and another twenty years in the wilderness.[70]

The peers learnt their lesson. They dared not join in a wholesale remodelling of the Bill. Although Carnarvon and Grey eloquently denounced the Bill for its democratic import, they found themselves isolated in the House. Potential supporters such as Lord Shaftesbury confessed that it was 'somewhat difficult to argue against a Bill which we do not wish to reject, and which it seems next to impossible that we can amend'.[71] Others, like Earl Beauchamp and Lord Feversham, remarked that the need for a settlement was so urgent, and the undesirability of a quarrel with the Commons so patent, that the House could not afford to be swayed by 'hobgoblin' arguments. Feversham consoled himself by trusting to 'the intelligence, and the enlightened patriotism of his fellow countrymen'. By 'admitting them in larger numbers within the pale of the constitution' he hoped that Parliament was 'strengthening their attachment to the institutions under which they lived'.[72]

Still the Lords were keen to modify the Bill in ways that would not give great offence, and their opportunity came when Derby again fell sick with gout. While he was away the intellectuals and die-hards of both sides proceeded, against the pleas of the weak Lord Chancellor, Chelmsford, to tinker with the Bill. They instituted voting papers for both boroughs and counties, they altered the County qualification to make the creation of faggot votes easy again, they increased the borough qualification, and they introduced the cumulative vote.[73] Two constitutional amendments of some importance were also carried. Grey secured the complete abandonment of the law which required Ministers to seek re-election after accepting or changing office.[74] And Earl Stanhope had a clause inserted which removed the necessity for Parliament to dissolve upon the death of the Sovereign.[75]

The peers' comments were guarded and the debates were short, but clearly that they would have liked to smash the Bill. De Grey and Harrowby spoke for them when they described themselves as defending property and the hereditary principle against an irresponsible Commons and the levelling tendencies of the age. Now that the bulwarks of the Commons had been breached it behoved the Lords to stand firm in defence of traditionary sovereignty. Once undermine the influence of the peerage in the country and there would follow diffusion of power, instability in society and the distribution of property. With the equal electorates and mass constituency promised by this Bill, everything would be brought to a dead level.[76] But the revolt subsided with Derby's return. He made his men abandon all but two of their amendments touching the franchise, and only one of these, the cumulative vote, survived the reconsideration of the Bill in the Commons. His unruffled mastery contrasts significantly with Russell's uncertain relations with his followers.

Of the amendments which failed to survive, the most insidious was that introduced by the Whig rebel, the Earl of Lichfield. This sought to include the payment of the borough and county rates with the poor rate, as a prerequisite of registration. The amendment semed to touch on a mere technicality and it passed without discussion. But it was later revealed that the borough rates included the municipal levies for lighting, paving, etc., and as they were often twice the poor rate, they were even more frequently partially levied, excused or evaded. Dudley Baxter, who possibly conceived this amendment, estimated that it would have disfranchised 20 per cent of the potential borough electorate. W. E. Forster had the clause removed when the Bill returned to the Commons.[77]

Thus the freebooters' hopes that the Tories would prove 'squeezable' were triumphantly fulfilled. In an atmosphere that was peaceful by comparison with that of 1831-2, Russell would never have been able to coerce the Tory majority in the Lords into carrying a Bill, and the revolt of his 'noble friends' in 1866 had shown the kind of virulent and unyielding opposition a Bill would have met from his own side of the House. Yet Derby was able to lead nearly all the active Tory peers and several of the Whigs to acquiesce in a much more extensive measure. It is a strange irony that the first Reform Bill to reach the Lords since 1832 should arrive in a form that would have been unthinkable at any time during the preceding fifteen years, and then be passed so easily.

The Lords' amendment which did pass into law was Cairns' motion for the cumulative vote in three-member constituencies.[78] Voters in these electorates were to have a maximum of two votes when all three seats were contested. In this way, Cairns argued, those minorities in the great cities who possessed 'the greatest amount of property and intelligence' would gain representation. The members returned by them would compensate for the loss of the small borough representatives and provide a 'steadying element' in the House to counteract the men elected by the populace. Russell, who had included similar provisions in his Bills of 1854 and 1860, led a large section of the Whigs to support the amendment; it passed, 142 to 51.[79]

The minority representation scheme had already been raised in the Commons, in two distinct proposals, one from Mill for proportional representation and the other from Lowe for plural voting. Both motions had split the House across party divisions and revealed a curious alliance of Liberal and Tory intellectuals against the traditionally minded parliamentarians of both followings.

Mill, Fawcett and Hughes had been working to propagate Hare's scheme since the early fifties,[80] but the parliamentarians still found the system easy to ridicule. Hare's plan for a national constituency, electing a national list of candidates upon a quota allocation of votes, ignored existing political and regional interests. It offered no defence against the party agents who would arrange expensive elections on a national scale and manipulate the various regions to secure a strong overall vote. The system undervalued the candidate, the members argued, and superseded that clash of loyalties and interests in localities which provided the vital element in the representative system. The weaknesses they discerned in Hare's scheme would perhaps be inevitable in any system of mass politics and it is likely that a national list of candidates would have made members even more remote from their constituencies than they already were. The system could have raised the quality of candidates, but irrespective of its possible merits or demerits, the plan was much too speculative and careless of local loyalties to survive the prejudices of the members.[81]

Lowe's proposal was the corollary to Horsfall's amendment for the third member, and it was the scheme which Cairns later introduced in the Lords. Lowe wanted to protect the intellectual candidate who, as he saw it, would inevitably be rejected by the ignorant majority; while Mill and Fawcett backed the amendment for the opposite reason that it would encourage the minority to participate and so activate the majority. Mill argued that there was no simple majority and minority but that each arose from fluctuating coalitions of interest groups, and so the general good would best be discovered when the optimum number of electors was enabled to vote in some hope of furthering their particular interest. In this way the majority coalition would be broadened and rendered more enlightened. Fawcett added:

> every opinion would . . . be fairly discussed, every side of a question would be advocated by able men, truth would then be victorious, and the will of the majority would predominate, not by trampling and despising the minority, but by giving to every class of opinion . . . its just . . . and proportionate interest.[82]

Bright launched a tremendous onslaught on this scheme of 'peculiar crotchets and dreamy propositions'. It deviated from the spirit of the ancient Constitution in assuming that minorities were more likely to be right than majorities; it would fragment parties, weaken majorities in the House of Commons and create unstable executives. But he left unsaid his basic objection, that it threatened to diminish by half the effective voting strength of the great towns in the House of Commons. Disraeli finally demolished the motion with a superb piece of mockery in which he demonstrated to his followers that, as the innovation was only to apply in eight constituencies, it was almost worthless in terms of future party advantage. The ensuing division was extraordinarily confused. Disraeli, Gladstone, Manners and Bright were among the 314 who formed the majority against the amendment, while about 100 Tories, 50 Whigs and Adullamites and 20 radicals, most of them young men, composed the 173 who voted for it.[83]

When Cairns' motion came down from the Lords, Disraeli must have worried as to how he could eliminate it without exposing a rift in his party. But Gladstone solved his problem by energetically attacking the motion because it admitted 'the principle of numbers' and thereby paved the way to equal electorates.[84] Thereupon Disraeli turned it into a party question: faithfully attended by over 100 of his followers who had previously voted against cumulative voting, by the Adullamites, and by the little band of philosophers, he marched into the lobby to support a proposal he despised, and emerged victorious, 253 to 204.[85] So the minority vote, embodying an aim subversive of the prime electoral principle of the Constitution, that of single vote majority rule, entered upon its brief role in the British electoral system. Professor Hanham has calculated that the clause cost the Conservatives about six members, and that its 'approximate effect in a division in the House of Commons was to give the Liberals an extra three votes in 1868, an extra eight in 1874 and an extra four in 1880'.[86] Its practical importance probably lies in the way in which it forced on party organization in the constituencies, especially in the counties.[87]

VII   *The Redistribution Bill and the Reform Acts for Scotland and Ireland*

The Conservatives' Redistribution Bill was consistent with their aim throughout the period. As in 1859, they planned to preserve the Conservative small rural boroughs and to insulate the counties from the suburbs by consolidating the urban boroughs. Disraeli had had Baxter and Spofforth working on the problem in relation to the Bill of 1866 and so they were able to draw upon detailed statistical knowledge when producing the scheme for 1867.[88]

The plan which Disraeli introduced in February 1867 was thus, unlike Brand's Bill in 1866, well matured and nicely adjusted to its purpose. It proposed the re-allocation of thirty seats; seven were to come from the four boroughs recently declared corrupt,[89] and twenty-three from double seats under 7,000 population. Fourteen of the seats were to go to the new boroughs carved out of the counties.[90] The counties were to receive fifteen, and some of the more populous of them were to be divided to obtain 'a pure county population'. London University was to have one representative.[91]

The measure was devised to give the minimum of offence to the small borough men and was neatly adapted to the restrictive enfranchisement envisaged when it was drawn up. But when the Redistribution Bill came on at the end of May, the enfranchisement had been so distended that most Liberals and many Tories had come to believe that the scheme was much too puny to effect a settlement.

Thus it came about that the first amendment to expand the redistribution was moved by Samuel Laing, who twelve months before had opposed his own party's Bill because he thought it too drastic. He was far from wanting the 'representation . . . to be based entirely on mere arithmetical computations', but he did want to remove the worst inequalities, as for example, between Honiton and Manchester, so that the redistribution would 'satisfy the wants of the age'. He moved that the limit at which double boroughs should lose their second member be raised to 10,000, and that seven seats be made available by grouping eight of the smallest boroughs. His plan provided 52 seats; a radical prologue to a very conservative re-allocation. He revived Russell's proposal of 1854 to give a third member to the six cities of over 150,000; the four single-member towns of over 50,000 were to receive a second representative; and sixteen more seats were to go to the counties of over 150,000.[92]

Sergeant Gaselee, the Liberal member for Portsmouth, rose 'boiling with indignation'. He had moved an amendment to disfranchise boroughs under 5,000 and to re-allocate their seats to large boroughs, including London. He had given his notice before Laing, yet the latter's motion had come on first.[93] The motions had been switched by Disraeli and Laing in concert, to forestall the more sweeping amendment.[94]

Baillie Cochrane from Honiton spoke up for the small borough men, but he realized that the cause was lost, for the House was ready to throw over the small boroughs in its quest for a settlement.[95] They were the more despondent because their natural allies, the county members, leapt eagerly at the bait of additional county seats.[96] Disraeli, with his followers thus divided, warily opposed the amendment, and with good cause, for the Government was beaten by 127 votes: 306 to 179; the Tory county men voting with the Opposition. Although he spoke against it, Disraeli had helped to bring the motion on, and had ordered Spofforth to whip for it among the county members. All

would have gone well had not one of the doomed men caught
him at it. Lord Henry Lennox, M.P. for Chichester, with 8,000,
informed Disraeli that his 'Political existence was cut short by
the Vote of Friday last'. He added that, 'while you as organ of
the Govt., were speaking against Mr. Laing's Amendment, Mr.
Spofforth . . . was diligently whipping in favour of it, and with
considerable audacity, asserting that the Govt. wished to be
beaten on the point'.[97]

Robert Lowe, in typical *après moi* vein, summed up the
motives which induced the conservatives to muster in support
of Laing. He told Lady Salisbury that he had voted for the
semi-disfranchisement of boroughs under 10,000, 'and should
most likely vote for disfranchising all boroughs under 5,000
(Calne is 5,150)':

> with this new franchise these places are quite indefensible
> and must be dens of corruption of the lowest order. The
> same is true of Calne but I can't in honour vote to disfran-
> chise that . . . As it has pleased the House to make a Revolu-
> tion we must adapt our institutions to what has been done.[98]

Laing's success led Gaselee to persevere with his motion, but
the small borough men of both sides rallied enough support to
defeat it. Disraeli again spoke tortuously, but ended by taking
his stand on 'no disfranchisement'. He had weighed the forces
aright, for the amendment was beaten by 52 votes: 269 to 217.[99]

On 13 June Disraeli brought in a revised scheme which incorporated Laing's amendment. He now had forty-five seats to
re-allocate: he gave nineteen to the new boroughs; twenty-five
to the counties; and one to London University. The landed
interest was thus still richly served, while the great towns and
Scotland received no extra seats at all. He had thus evaded the
main point of Laing's amendment. The latter returned to the
fight with a fresh motion to give third members to the six
boroughs (excluding the metropolitan ones) of over 150,000,
and to take the seats from grouped small boroughs. Disraeli
opposed the motion, he said, because it too greatly emphasized
population as the ruling principle of distribution and so opened
the way to equal electorates. Furthermore, it would only add to
the commercial, industrial phalanx returned by the great towns,
because the diverse interests of 'property and intelligence' could
never be fairly represented in an urban dominated system.

Cumulative voting, the projected corollary of the three-member plan, was a 'fantastic scheme' which might help to secure representation for the propertied minority, but could never replace the real strength of the landed interest which lay in its representation in the countryside. Disraeli's argument was a curious amalgam of blindness as to the direction of social change and the latent strength of Conservatism in the towns, and brilliant foresight into the actual working of the minority vote. Cranborne countered his leader with a speech that exactly reversed the assumptions. He wanted the triple seats and cumulative vote precisely because he saw that the Conservatives would have to increase their representation outside the countryside, and that electoral innovation offered them the best chance of winning a foothold in the great towns. At this point of transition in the Conservative party it was the hard-headed Cranborne who was educating his leader.[1] Nevertheless, Laing's motion was rejected by 8 votes: 247 to 239. There was much cross-voting, reflecting the members' confusions about the import of the cumulative voting scheme.[2]

Some days later Horsfall and Graves, the members for Liverpool, introduced a modified version of Laing's amendment. They proposed to give an extra member to the three northern cities of over 250,000. Disraeli was sitting with Adderley, and put him up to answer Horsfall. While Adderley was expatiating on the representation of localities and interests rather than mere population, Disraeli anxiously conferred with Taylor. He then rose and casually accepted the amendment, together with an extra member for Leeds, which Baines demanded. Adderley, looking 'exceedingly miserable', hurried from the House, as the Redistribution Bill passed its second reading: 297 to 63.[3] The minority consisted of Tories, some of whom wanted more country seats, with others wanting to fight to the end for their pocket boroughs, while a few, including Cranborne, Carnarvon, General Peel and Henley angrily refused to vote at all.[4]

When he accepted Horsfall's amendment, Disraeli had been careful to add that he held to the policy of non-disenfranchisement of the small boroughs and that the four seats would have to be taken from the new boroughs. He mumbled this reservation across the table and few heard it, so when he later announced that St Helens, Keighley, Luton and Barnsley were to forfeit their prospective members a tremendous row broke out.

Gladstone and Bright demanded that four seats be taken from the counties; whereas the Tory county men were determined to keep the new boroughs to ensure that their voters were removed from the counties. R. T. Gilpin, from Bedfordshire, moved that seats be provided by the semi-disenfranchisement of the four boroughs next above 10,000, and the threatened representatives of Tiverton, Tamworth and Warwick hastened to defend their seats. But the small borough men had the numbers: they kept their places intact by 29 votes: 244 to 195. Thus, with Disraeli's connivance, they had levelled out Laing's amendment.[5]

In addition to his tireless complaisance in the House, Disraeli was busy privately charming rebels into acquiesence. He managed to quell an impending mutiny by the Welsh county Tories, who wanted an extra member for counties of over 50,000.[6] Lord George Gordon Lennox wrote to inform him that if the family borough of Lymington were partially disfranchised, 'with household suffrage no Cons. candidate would have the ghost of a chance', and added later he held himself 'totally independent & at liberty' to act as he considered best for his constituency. But within two days he was fawning on Disraeli:

> How can I sufficiently thank you for your kind letter . . . I hasten to assure you that I shall cheerfully support you in the struggle that is now at hand and I heartily wish you success.
>   Even if the place I now represent were to be totally disfranchised, I should stand by you, feeling sure that you would do all in your power that I should have a seat in [one?] of the newly made constituencies. As I told you the other day when I had the pleasure of seeing you in the House . . . I have spent large sums of money to keep the Conservatives in the ascendant though I could ill afford to do so—but this and other points I shall leave in your hands.[7]

Lymington duly lost its second member, but was preserved with its boundaries intact, and Lennox went on to represent the declining borough until 1874.

Arabella Darby Griffith wrote to protest against the semi-disfranchisement of the family borough of Devizes, because, she said, this would force the local proprietors into 'cutting each others throat' to secure the remaining seat. Disraeli soon disarmed her: 'It is so kind of you to have replied to me yourself

... I have full confidence that you will do what is possible'.[8] Her husband remained dutiful as a back-bencher, but Disraeli's assurance went for little in the 1868 election when Darby Griffith was crushingly defeated by two other local gentlemen.

The Government's intentions on redistribution were carried further by the Commissioners appointed to redraw the electoral boundaries. Disraeli had seen to it that they were predominantly Conservative country gentlemen, and even after Bright had led the Liberals to reject two of his initial appointees, the Commission remained biased towards the traditional interest. Viscount Eversley became chairman, and the other members were Russell Gurney, the Recorder of London and Tory member for Southampton, J. T. Buller Duckworth, a former Tory M.P., John Walter, a Whig and former county member, and Sir Francis Crossley.[9]

Their commission was adapted from that issued in 1832, and like their predecessors, the Commissioners were both precluded from decreasing the size of any borough, and ordered to incorporate into the parliamentary boroughs all premises which by 'situation or local circumstances' were associated with them.[10] To this end the Commissioners were supplied with Baxter's maps and memoranda of 1866. As their deliberations went forward, their recommendations were supplied to a sub-committee of Cabinet, comprising Derby and Disraeli, Buckingham, Hardy, Stafford Northcote and Manners, which studied their possible effects on family interests and then passed them on to Baxter for analysis of the likely tendencies of their constituencies.[11] By 11 June the Commissioners' work was advanced enough for the Cabinet to summon a secret meeting of Tory agents to consider the report.[12]

The Commissioners had interpreted their instructions very liberally and recommended not only the inclusion of adjoining suburbs in industrial boroughs, but also the incorporation of a large number of independent villages which seemed likely to develop into suburbs. Manchester parliamentary borough for example, was to be enlarged to take in 8,000 voters in Crumpsall Green, Rusholme and Moss-Side, though these centres were self-contained and still separated by fields from the built up area.[13] Aston Manor and Balsall Heath, at this time separate housing estates with 2,200 county voters, were to be added to

Birmingham.[14] The Commission exactly followed the plan submitted by the local Conservative agents for Bristol in selecting patches from among the outlying parishes to add 386 county voters and 2,500 under-£12 occupiers to the borough.[15] The proposed boundaries of Middlesbrough, Birkenhead and Gateshead were extended to take in fields that were likely to be built upon.[16] The suggested expansion of Nottingham would have taken 200 'shopkeeper' voters out of the county.[17] Tynemouth was to incorporate the separate towns of Howden Pans and Willington Quay, which together contained 300 'blacksmiths and shipwrights', many of whom already voted in the Southern Division of Northumberland.[18] Jarrow, with 250 £12 occupiers, was also taken out of Durham county and coupled with South Shields.[19] Ince-in-Makerfield, containing about 1,600 potential borough voters, was to be added to Wigan, and Gosport, with a strong Liberal constituency, was excised from Hampshire and combined with Portsmouth.[20] In each case the protests of the local Liberals were ignored.[21] The Commission's recommendations, with the exception of those relating to the West Riding, where Crossley's concerns were involved, were blatantly one-sided.

The Conservative agents were content with the *Report,* but the country gentlemen were far from convinced that the counties had been sufficiently scoured. They resented the meddling of Disraeli's secretariat in spheres which their families had controlled for generations. Banks Stanhope, Chaplin, and Hamilton met and 'settled' the division of North Lincolnshire by decisively altering the boundary which Baxter had suggested to the Commission. The gentlemen wanted to transfer the wapentakes of Aslacoe and Well to the Southern Division in order to rid their division of two knots of Liberal voters, but their proposed boundary was so irregular that Baxter was sure that it would 'not be very defensible in the House'.[22] Nevertheless, Well duly appeared in the Mid Division in the schedule of the Bill, for which Banks Stanhope ecstatically thanked 'Dear Mr. D'Israeli'.[23]

The Tory county men were willing to try any means that would offset the impact of urbanization in the shires. S. T. Kekewich of Devonshire demanded that Baxter's plan for his county, which sectioned it according to its highway pattern, should be recast to preserve the old division by hundreds. The roads basis would only 'make for greater expense' by easing access to the poll. Kekewich succeeded, with the result that the divisions continued to bear no relation to the system of communications and local association in the county.[24] C. Freville-Surtees of County Durham worked to have the limits of Darlington extended to take in Blackwell,[25] while W. H. Gore-Langton wanted 'the town element' of Ilminster, Chard, Wellington, Longport and Yeovil all taken out of West Somerset. Their proposals were both politically indefensible, for Blackwell was still a distinct agricultural hamlet and the Somerset towns would, according to Gore-Langton's plan, necessarily have been grouped with Taunton and Bridgewater.[26]

Henry Selwin and Lord Eustace Cecil were busy urging Disraeli to have Stratford and West Ham excised from South Essex. Their county, they insisted, was 'agricultural and therefore a Conservative constituency', but, if the proper excisions were not made 'before long it will be overpowered by the urban element'. Meanwhile, Charles Du Cane, of North Essex, was fighting to have Braintree and Witham, with their Liberal majorities, transposed into South Essex. Their demands were equally impracticable and their neat cancellation of each other allowed Disraeli and Baxter to ignore them.[27] The Tory proprietors of Norfolk held a 'private meeting' to decide the boundaries of the division, but 'as no two appeared to agree as to how it should be done' they finally left 'such arrangements to the Boundary Commissioners'.[28] Disraeli and Baxter had a less easy passage with the Tory agent for North Staffordshire, who resigned in protest against outside interference after Spofforth upheld Baxter's plan against that of the agent and the local proprietors.[29]

The other group of members whose political futures were bound with the niceties of redistribution, the small borough men, were equally importunate with Disraeli. They were keen to make their boroughs viable against the population limits and to keep out rival interests. B. T. Woodd and T. Collins wanted Knaresborough to be extended to incorporate the neighbouring parishes in order to carry it above the 10,000 population level, but they were also insistent that any proposal to include Harrogate should be rejected. They must have been gratified by the *Report*, which recommended that Harrogate, despite the fact that its population had increased by 2,000 in the preceding 15 years, should remain in the county.[30] The Honourable Egremont Lascelles demanded that Northallerton take in its surrounding

villages, but 'go no further, [as] *any scheme of extension including* the *town of Bedale . . . would be decidedly adverse'*.
Bedale was the centre of influence of the Peirse family who were
the principal electoral rivals of the Harewoods for the Northallerton seat. The two families had shared the representation
before 1832, but after Northallerton had been preserved as a
single-member borough, the Peirse family had generally managed
to exclude their opponents. Lascelles' re-capture of the seat in
1866 was the first time the Harewoods had held it in thirty years
and so his request, though hopeless, is understandable. The
borough already extended over six miles from north to south
and five miles from east to west, and its population had declined since 1832. Any extension which did not take in Bedale
would have been indefensible in the House. The Commission
recommended that the boundaries remain unchanged.[31]

Those Tories who had been unruly in the past could now only
plead or threaten. R. J. Harvey, the young go-getter from Thetford, realized that he was being excluded from the discussions
about his 'little borough' and humbly wrote to Disraeli to offer
'valuable suggestions', which seem to have gone unheard.[32] The
little borough remained unexpanded and duly lost one representative. G. M. W. Sandford was very angry when he discovered
that Disraeli and Baxter planned to alter the boundaries of
Maldon without consulting him and refused to attend a meeting
with Disraeli arranged by one of his country colleagues 'to
smoothe over their differences'. The borough boundaries did,
ultimately, remain unaltered, and Maldon, with little above
6,000 population also lost one member.[33]

The Whig magnates' boundary plans were largely checkmated
by the Conservatives' dominance of the Commission. Only in the
West Riding do they seem to have prevailed. Baxter had divided
the county so as to keep the Northern Division 'Agricultural
with a few Manufactures', the Mid Division, 'Entirely Manufacturing and homogeneous', and the Southern Division, 'Manufacturing & Fitzwilliamite'. This would have strengthened the
Conservative grip on the Northern Division and confined the
Whigs to the other two,[34] and moreover it would have given
the Whigs a population of 330,000 in the Southern Division, or
126,000 more than the Tories would have in the North. Crossley
apparently informed the Beaumonts of the plan, for H. F. Beaumont quickly came up with a scheme which transposed West

Morley and the Bradford parishes, with 76,000 industrial inhabitants and 3,449 county voters, from his Southern Division into
the Mid Division. This alteration would not have changed the
party control of the divisions, but Beaumont argued that the
numbers should be made more nearly equal in the divisions, to
spread electoral costs. The Whigs had a conference with Spofforth, who, upon Baxter's assurance that Beaumont's plan would
leave the Northern Division safe, allowed it to go to the Commissioners. As far as the Conservative bureaucrats were concerned, it was a gratifying compromise, but at least one local
Tory gentleman was angry:

> We are smashed . . . in Yorkshire of all the D—d mistakes ever
> made . . . it was D'Is—li's to put Ld Halifax's right hand man,
> Sir F. Crosley on as Boundary Commissioner & what vexes
> me is that S[pofforth] went over Ld Halifaxe's . . . divisions
> with Dudley Baxter & told him . . . that such divisions must
> return 3 of Ld Halifaxe's men—there is not a particle of doubt
> that these divisions were drawn out by D. of Devonshire
> Lord Halifax & Sir F. Crosley & Co.

He ended with a refusal to subscribe future registration costs in
the county.[35]

Yorkshire was not the only county where the Commissioners
and Disraeli's men had transgressed local opinion, and when
their *Report* was tabled in May 1868 it met with hostility from
both sides of the House. The Commissioners advised the extension of eighty-one boroughs, the same number as in 1832. Conservatives like Walpole disapproved its bias and its wholesale
retrenchment of the county constituencies, while the Liberals,
led by Gladstone and Hibbert, were already armed with a
wrecking amendment. Their common objection—and the main
source of protest from the parishes—was the enormous dislocation of rating, especially compounding, that would ensue from
the inclusion of extra municipal areas in parliamentary boroughs.
Disraeli hedged briefly but eventually he proffered a select
committee to study the more contentious of the Commission's
findings.[36]

The Select Committee, headed by Walpole, with one other
Tory and three Liberals, sat for four days consecutively and
had its report ready by the first week in June. It had no time

to consider the problem in detail, for 10 June was set as the last day for registration before the coming dissolution. 'Having regard to situation and local circumstances', the Select Committee proposed a return to the *status quo* for Liverpool, Manchester, Birmingham, Lambeth and Marylebone, whereas the Commissioners' extensions would have swollen each of these boroughs to over 400,000 and left their neighbouring county divisions with under 100,000. The Select Committee also advised that those additions of 'no possible co-interest' with Tynemouth, South Shields, Gateshead, Birkenhead, Warwick and Portsmouth, should be returned to the counties. The extensions to Bristol and Nottingham were likewise to be cut back to avoid the disfranchisement of county freeholders living on the outskirts, while the 'upper class residential areas with no sympathies with the town' around Reading and Wigan were restored to their counties.

Thus the recommendations of the Select Committee, though applying to only fifteen boroughs, destroyed the crucial part of the Conservative's redistribution. The Tory agent in Birkenhead pleaded with Disraeli to uphold the Commissioners who had given 'exactly what we wanted', while their man in the North-East reported that if the old limits of Gateshead were retained the effect on South Shields would be 'fatal', and if Middlesbrough were reduced 'both North Riding Seats [would be] gone for ever'.[37] But their colleagues from Warwick, Oldham, Hastings, Reading and other boroughs were either resigned or generally pleased with the reduction of their numbers. The agent in Lambeth, for example, thought that the contraction of his borough would be 'highly serviceable'.[38]

Disraeli was at first disposed to reject the Select Committee's report and cling to the Commission's findings, as embodied in his Boundaries Bill. But he misjudged the temper of the Liberals and the fears of the Tory county men, who now realized that the enormous transfer of numbers out of their constituencies undermined their claims for extra county representation. Disraeli and Gathorne-Hardy forced to a division a radical motion upholding the Select Committee's reassessment and found themselves defeated: 184 to 148. Thereupon, they gave in and incorporated the revised boundaries into the Bill, which was then hurried through both Houses.[39]

Despite this last minute redress, the redistribution still favoured the traditional ruling interests. In 1870 the rural South and West still had many more seats than the Midlands and the North. The South-Western region with 76,612 borough electors, had 45 representatives, while the North-Western with 232,431 had 32; the South-Eastern with 80,177 had 41, while the Metropolitan with 263,991 had 22. If the representation had been spread according even to the number of electors, the Metropolitan boroughs would have received 63 more members.[40] This maldistribution, together with the incorporation into the boroughs of 100,000 suburban dwellers, buttressed the landed interest in both the counties and rural boroughs for another seventeen years.[41] But ultimately this enfranchisement of labourers in incorporated villages served to heighten the anomalous unenfranchisement of their fellows in the counties and make it indefensible.

The redistribution also preserved the economical spread of the Conservative vote in relation to its capacity to return representatives. In 1874 the Conservatives polled 38.32 per cent of the registered electors of England and Wales and returned 154 members, while the Liberals polled 37.39 per cent and returned only 116. And in relation to population the Conservatives were much better placed. In 1868, 101 of their members were returned by boroughs in the United Kingdom with just over 2 million people, while 263 Liberals were returned from boroughs containing 8.5 millions.[42] Indeed, the Conservatives were to have the best of both worlds, for even where the redistribution violated their plans to segregate the suburbs it did not harm their electoral chances: in subsequent elections, especially 1874 and 1885, suburban voters emerged as a solid Conservative force.

In March 1867 Disraeli had promised to introduce Reform Bills for Scotland and Ireland, and on 13 May he brought in the Reform Bill for Scotland. The Irish Bill was first stated to be delayed and then, in June, postponed indefinitely. Disraeli gave as excuse the impossibility of implementing a Reform in the midst of the outbreak of Fenianism in that country. Nevertheless, he made the announcement after receiving a private deputation of influential Irish supporters, who had demanded that the Irish Bill be dropped as a condition of their supporting the English and Scottish Bills.[43] Eventually, the Irish Bill came on with the Scottish Bill in 1868.

The Reform Bill for Scotland contained the same qualifications as the English Bill, with the exception that it had no lodger franchise. Lodgers had qualified in Scotland since 1832 because there they were legally tenants. Disraeli introduced it four days before Hodgkinson's amendment, and he expatiated on the virtues of personal payment of rates as a test of worth as a citizen. But personal payment would have been even more unreal in Scotland than it was in England, for there was no compounding, although most tenants who paid rates paid them through their landlords. Tenants of premises rated under £4 were almost uniformly excused, and so, as the Bill stood, it would have introduced universal male suffrage above £4. More anomalous still was the fact that in many rural parishes the poor rates were levied and collected voluntarily and no proper rate-books were kept. In Greenock, for instance, the houses were not even assessed to the poor rate and alms were paid by custom. In the 1832 Reform Act for Scotland the difficulty had been met by requiring payment of the assessed taxes instead of the poor rate and this provision was incongruously retained in the 1868 Act for those over £10.[44]

The members could do little to restrict the Scottish influx after the collapse on the English Bill. The radicals had been given an effectively lower qualification than they had hoped for, and the Conservatives had to accept a *fait accompli* and put their trust in the redistribution. 'Who, when Lord John Russell came in . . . dreamt that we were coming to what we had?' asked Grant Duff exultantly, and a little alarmed. 'The truth was events had been too strong for men . . . the majority of the House were conjugating to themselves, "I don't want, thou dost not want, he does not want". . . . And yet who did not see that the old £6 limit was "gone, frozen, dead for ever?"'[45]

The real fight centred on the redistribution. Disraeli offered the Scottish members seven seats, to add to the fifty-three they had possessed since 1832. The counties did well out of the proposed allocation: Lanarkshire, Ayrshire and Aberdeenshire were each divided with one extra seat for every new division. Glasgow was to be split, with two additional members, and the two remaining seats were to be shared by the universities. The redistribution was partisan enough, but the real sting lay in the thoroughgoing excision of towns from the counties and their being lumped together with existing Liberal boroughs.[46] The Scottish Liberals were infuriated by this scheme. The seven extra members, even if they had been fairly allocated among the boroughs, hardly compensated Scotland for the twenty-two she would have received had her representation been made equal with that of England and Wales in terms of population, or 'wealth, intelligence and inhabitants', as the Scottish Liberals preferred to express it. McLaren and his colleagues felt themselves to have been cheated: Disraeli's plan to make the counties even more impregnably Tory by rendering them 'purely agricultural reserves', seemed to be poor thanks for the support they had given him on the English Bill.[47] Gladstone artfully lit another fuse by casually hinting that the Government might provide the seven seats by taking them from Ireland. The Irish members of both parties immediately declared war and Disraeli hastily had to announce that the Government planned to enlarge the House by seven seats. But the Gaels remained unappeased and on 29 July he withdrew the Bill and promised to introduce a revised version in the next session.[48]

The new Bill was brought down in February 1868. The redistribution was slightly altered, but it retained its conservative character. The universities and the counties kept their five seats, Glasgow was to remain undivided and received one extra member to make it a three-member borough, and one seat went to a composite borough of towns carved from the counties.[49]

The Scottish Liberals strove mightily to alter the redistribution and to protect Glasgow from the minority clause. They failed in the latter endeavour, but they did succeed in cracking the insulation of the counties by having the boundaries of some boroughs redefined. Their main achievement was to force the Government to take the seven seats of the smallest English boroughs rather than create them as an addition to the House.[50] The Irish members had backed this move by way of insurance, and the Whigs and Liberals had voted for it as a means of settling the question. But no one was prepared to follow the Scottish members in attempting to remodel the redistribution, and so the Bill passed as a triumph for Conservative rearguard action.

The story of the Irish Reform Bill is similar. The Government set out to add to the county representation but dropped the proposal in the face of united Liberal opposition.

The borough qualification was reduced from £8 to £4 and the county franchise was maintained at the 1850 level of £12. The planned increase of voters was negligible, only 9,000, and once the members threw out the redistribution, they hurriedly passed the rest in two nights in a hot, sultry June.[51] The crazy maldistribution of seats in Ireland was to survive unaltered until 1885. The House was preparing for the coming dissolution and the Reform Bills for the fringe areas came as tiresome echoes of a question which they had rid themselves of a year before. The 'independent members' of the House of Commons in the 1860s never acted so typically as when they carried these two important measures with a minimum of interested, informed discussion and a maximum of irresponsible contempt.

6

CONCLUSION

The Reform Bill of 1867 survived because a majority of the members of both Houses of Parliament dared not throw it out. They did not want it, they did not like it, they feared what it might do, but they passed it. For the first time in the Second Reform period a majority of members felt an imperative need to make a settlement.

There were three new elements in the situation which decisively swung the balance of forces in the House of Commons. The first was the mass agitation which had sprung up after the defeat of the Liberal Bill, and which kept up its importunity until the borough suffrage provisions of the Conservative Bill were transformed and safe. The second was Disraeli's resolve to carry the Reform Bill, *a* Reform Bill, to consolidate his leadership and to humiliate Gladstone. His determination to cling to the Bill neutralized the traditional Conservative opposition to any wide-ranging Reform and left the Whigs without their natural allies against the radicals. The third element was latent throughout the period, but it only wreaked its full havoc in 1867. It was the mixture of boredom and confused disillusionment that set in as some of the members gradually realized, during the interminable debates on the rating laws, that the safe, limited enfranchisement of the artisan élite was a fantasy appropriate only to those dear, dead days when Reform was not urgent. The central themes of the long and brilliant debate of the period, the worth of the artisans and the machinery for effecting their admittance, gradually faded into irrelevance.

The collapse of the borough qualification was inevitable from the time that Disraeli decided, in his ignorance, to use 'personal payment' as the restrictive mechanism. It worked brilliantly as a political ruse, for it deceived his own supporters and made Gladstone appear a humbug when he tried to explode it. But Disraeli, with a minority behind him, could not impose his will on the House in the shaping of the Bill: instead, he could only play on the Liberals' distrust of Gladstone, on their dread of further agitation and on their fears of a dissolution. He was helped by the agitations, which quickened the need for a settlement and reduced the details of the Bills to petty-seeming hindrances. Whenever Gladstone sought to grapple with the technical difficulties in the measures, to ensure that they would fulfill their ostensible purpose of a restrictive Reform, Disraeli could isolate him by claiming that he was trying to obstruct a settlement. The great changes in the Bill—the lodger franchise, Hodgkinson's amendment, the enlarged redistribution—were all made after a minimum of debate, and the first two without even a division. Disraeli led his country gentlemen to accept anything as long as they appeared to be winning. The acceptance of Reform by the country gentlemen reflected their underlying confidence in the submissiveness of the workingmen—a confidence founded on the economic and social stability of the previous eighteen years.

Lowe's arguments against 'democracy' had been a powerful stimulus to those Whigs and Tories who had joined to smash the Bill of 1866, but that success makes the Adullamites' ineffectiveness in 1867 all the more striking. Apart from the amendment instituting a cumulative voting arrangement in the 'triangular' constituencies, the Opposition case of 1866 would seem to have been forgotten. It was forgotten, midst the haste to find a settlement, because Disraeli took over the Reformers' arguments and used them to isolate the Adullamite and Tory incorruptibles, and thereby induce his bemused country gentlemen to swallow the Liberals' amendments.

The bogies of Australian and American democracy had been largely disposed of by the Liberals. Childers, who knew more about Victoria than Marsh or Lowe, vigorously defended the colony by asserting that it had a viable economy, that its patriotism and class harmony were proven by its corps of volunteers, and that its government aided the building of churches of all denominations and made grants for education.[1] He was supported by Charles H. Pearson in *Essays on Reform*, which appeared in March 1867. Pearson emphasized the high standard of the judicial system, the honesty with which the people paid their taxes and the rate of attendance at schools, which was much higher than in the Old Country.[2]

W. E. Baxter, the Scots radical, used Tocqueville's description of the vitality of American life to argue that the strength and variety of American government derived from the participation of the whole people. The open system of government gave a sense of interest, and roused the wealthy classes to work to retain their influence, because they knew that they could not rest on privilege. By comparison with their British counterparts, the American voters of the lower classes were informed and honest, precisely because they participated in the representative system as independent citizens.[3] Leslie Stephen, in his contribution to *Essays on Reform,* claimed that the lack of refinement in America and the abuses in politics had their origin, not in the equalitarian social structure, but in the newness of American society.[4] He pointed out that the argument by analogy from Australia and America ignored the opposed patterns of historical evolution as between the colonies and the Mother Country. The colonies had begun without fixed social distinctions founded on the possession of land, while the intricately ranked Home society was the 'product of a set of immensely complicated social variations'. The development of social organisms, like that of natural organisms, was a specialized response to environment, a process which eradicated their original common features.

After it became apparent that the fancy franchises and dual votes for the upper classes were doomed and that the Conservative Bill would pass with a much enlarged and un-counter-weighted borough enfranchisement, some Conservatives adopted the theme that Britain's unique social development would protect her from the infection of American uniformity. C. B. Adderley, for example, the Under Secretary of State for the Colonies in 1867, published a widely quoted pamphlet, in which he argued that the distinctive characteristics of societies could be traced to the conditions peculiar to their origins and growth. Laws of development might then be established which precluded the growth of certain forms of society if the necessary conditions for these forms were absent. Thus Britain, which had progressed through tribalism to feudalism to ranked, harmonious classes under 'aristocratic chieftainship' based on the possession of land, could never become 'democratic' like America, where these pre-conditions did not exist:

Even if the thousand elements which combine to make up American democracy could be introduced into [Great Britain]

. . . the inveterate habits of the centuries, the ligaments and fibres of long associations . . . and attachments would have to be wholly cleared away to give space for the new creation.[5]

Gradually, in self-justification, the Tories and Adullamites took over Russell's and Gladstone's arguments for the strengthening of the Constitution by the enlargement of the working-class share. The Tory Lord Ravensworth accepted the presidency of the Workingmen's Conservative Association in Newcastle-on-Tyne.[6] Lord Derby visited a meeting of a similar body in Liverpool, to tell the artisans, amidst cheers, that he believed that they had 'as much Conservative feeling, as much respect for property, as much respect for education and as much respect for social position . . . as . . . the middle classes'.[7] That cantankerous Adullamite, Lord Elcho, found himself compelled to accept the Act as a 'resting place' and to announce his trust in the deference of the British workingmen.[8]

Disraeli, who had attacked Russell's and Gladstone's Bill of 1866 as heralding the replacement of the 'prescriptive spell [of] . . . families of historic lineage', by 'the sway of turbulent multitudes',[9] could, once the Bill was secure, forsake these auguries for the happier ones expounded by Gladstone and the radicals:

We are told that 'democracy is triumphant', [he remarked in defending his acceptance of Hodgkinson's amendment] . . . and who are those people to whom you are offering the franchise? . . . They are Englishmen, who have been born and bred under the influence of the laws . . . the manners and customs of the country.[10]

After the Bill had passed with its huge borough enfranchisement, Disraeli proceeded to elaborate the radical case into the myth of Tory democracy:

It is said we are on the verge of a great democratic change. My lords and gentlemen, believe me the elements of democracy do not exist in England (cheers). England is a country of classes, and the change impending in the country will only make those classes more united, more content, more complete and more cordial (cheers). We are warned of the example of America and against entering upon the course pursued by the United States. I say there is no similarity of position of the United Kingdom and the United States. The United States were colonies and they still are colonies. . . . They have settlements of democracy in America; they have unbounded possession of land, and they have no traditions. We, on the contrary, have a very limited portion of land, and a vast, numerous, artificial and complicated state of society, entirely governed and sustained by its traditionary influences. Therefore I have no fear of England.[11]

The essential premiss, that the ranked society would continue as long as it remained an open one, regardless of how many workingmen had the vote, had been put forward by Bernard Cracroft in *Essays on Reform*. This hard-headed student of politics suggested that the enfranchised working classes would behave much as the middle classes had done since 1832: as long as the working classes could continue to assimilate their manners and aspirations to those of the upper classes and as long as there appeared to be the opportunity for them to rise in wealth, the working classes would continue to expect the upper classes to set their standards. The granting of the vote would help to erode class consciousness among the lower orders.[12] As Disraeli explained, his Bill was a 'bulwark against democracy', for it would strengthen the exclusive character of Parliament by founding it 'on a broad popular basis'. 'Popular privileges,' he added, 'are consistent with a state of society in which there is great inequality of condition.'[13]

His rationalizations were a comfort to his backbenchers. C. N. N. Newdegate, who had attacked the Bill of 1866 because it threatened to wipe out the representation of rural England, announced during the third reading of the Bill of 1867 that he 'had no want of confidence in his countrymen and . . . trusted the result would be advantageous'.[14] The same Henry Selwin who had arraigned the Bill of 1866 as being 'disastrous to the well-being of the country' by opening the way to 'democracy . . . and the rule of the lowest' could claim in 1867 that 'ever since his election he had strongly and consistently advocated a large extension of the franchise, because in his opinion the extension of education and the increasing population had made it a necessity'.[15] No wonder that Mr Greene confessed: 'in that House he had been taught that black was not always black, or white always white, but that black might be white . . . on occasion . . . He did not see why, the residuum . . . being allowed to sink to the bottom, the intelligent workingmen should not be allowed to . . . vote'; although twelve months earlier he had asserted that workingmen were incapable of understanding political affairs.[16]

The Tory backbenchers were willing to be led by the nose. Disraeli had also to utilize the Adullamites and those Liberal waverers who were afraid of a dissolution. He completely deceived Grosvenor and his friends with the restrictive façade of the Bill and he had only to hint at a dissolution to send twenty or thirty 'independent' Liberals scurrying to the Conservative lobby. Every important division which destroyed the Bill of 1866 and shaped its successor was decided by an unpredictable floating vote composed of these individuals entering one lobby or the other according to their whim or muddled understanding of the question. The weakening of the Bill reflected the weakening of party. The debate of 1866 and 1867 set going the transformation of the old 'associative' gentry parties into the Whig-Conservative and Liberal-radical groupings which were to play out the issues of the late Victorian age.

Disraeli also partly ensnared, and was himself partly ensnared by, the small group of radicals who seized the opportunity to break down the borough qualification and extend the redistribution. The amendment of the Bill marked a new break-through for them. It laid the foundation of their enlarged influence in the House and the country, and inaugurated the rapid achievement of several of their long-term aims: the abolition of compulsory church-rates, the abolition of public hanging, the introduction of the ballot and the rest.

Nevertheless, the radicals' success would have been impossible without their backing from the agitations which swept London and the industrial towns. The demonstrations were the triumphant outcome of the growth of urban population and wealth which marked the Second Reform period. The intermittent trickles of opinion apparent in the fifties and early sixties, artisan pride, provincial assertion, Nonconformist political endeavour, middle-class professional and academic idealism, all suddenly coalesced to produce the great meetings. Their class co-operation, their seriousness, their massive good order, made them the expression of the best aspirations of their age. Yet the motivation behind the meetings as expressed in the speeches and the petitions served to narrow their impact on the Bill. The workingmen turned out to demonstrate their respectability, to demand 'to be deal with on the square', to prove their moral right to be entrusted with the borough franchise. And they achieved the franchise, though more through the Government's ill construction of its Bill

than by their importunity. While they finally forced the issue by
intimidating enough members into accepting the Bill, they did
not precipitate it and they had no direct influence in shaping it.[17]
The Reform League's demand for the franchise as a symbol of
social recognition, rather than as an instrument to coerce Parliament and rearrange society, reflected their general lack of
concern for the questions of power which were raised by the Bill,
and in their clamor for the suffrage they ignored the redistribution. The Act emerged with its chaotic borough qualifications as
the only component which adequately represented the social
change in the country. The other parts, the high county qualification, the limited redistribution, the minority clause, reflected
the gentry's success in preserving the foundations of their
parliamentary supremacy.

Disraeli, who continued to orate upon Tory concern for the
artisans, refused to attend the tea parties of the Conservative
Workingmen's Associations although his refusals were always
eloquently regretful.[18] He was beholden to no one; he had carried
the first important measure of his career and consolidated his
place in the Tory hierarchy. He knew that the workingmen lacked
the money and the independence to enter the House of Commons.
At most, in the foreseeable future, they would become a nuisance
to the radicals in the towns. And, even there, until 1880 their
presence was hardly felt. The artisans' spokesmen and the Reform
League continued to preach social harmony, the balance of
classes and the virtues of deference. They exercised their vote as
a 'popular privilege', as Disraeli called it, as humble contributors,
not leaders of the political process. In 1867 the Reform League
officially accepted the Hare-Fawcett-Mill scheme of proportional
representation, in order to avert an over-representation of the
lower classes.[19] The League advised working-class electors in the
1868 election not to back candidates of any particular class or
party, however ingratiating they might be, but to vote for men
who would benefit 'not only yourselves but the whole nation . . .
[by] reducing the enormous expenditure and taxation'.[20] Several
League candidates were withdrawn when it appeared likely that
they would endanger the return of upper-class candidates from
the Liberal Party.[21] Gladstone and Disraeli were vindicated. The
working classes had been brought within the pale of the Constitution and had proved themselves 'safe'.

The exact numbers enfranchised by the Act will probably never be known. We have no wholly reliable base figures for 1865, and the estimates and returns for 1868, 1869 and 1873 are all incomplete. In 1868 the registers in large new boroughs like Chelsea-Kensington were unfinished at the time of the election. In 1869 the returning officers in Stafford, Thirsk, Stockton, Chelsea and Southwark, returned 'no information', their colleagues at Aylesbury and Canterbury had omitted to count double entries, and in 1873 there were 'no records' in Shrewsbury and Stockport.[22] Probably the most carefully calculated figures for 1866 and 1868 are those given by Dudley Baxter, and these are presented in the table below:

		Boroughs	Counties	Total
England	1866	499,668	501,979	1,001,647
	1868	1,169,112	728,270	1,897,382
Wales	1866	14,358	40.654	55,012
	1868	55,930	62,983	118,913
Scotland	1866	55,515	49,979	105,494
	1868	152,312	74,978	227,290
Ireland	1866	30,958	164,408	195,366
	1868	53,070	180,090	233,160
United Kingdom	1866	600,499	757,020	1,357,519
	1868	1,430,424	1,046,321	2,476,745
Increase United Kingdom 1866–1868		829,925	289,301	1,119,226
% Increase		138	38	82.5

Thus, according to Baxter, the total increase of new borough votes was about 830,000. The official returns suggest an increase of about 818,000. It is perhaps worth recalling at this point that the English and Welsh borough enfranchisement intended by the 1866 Bill, about 200,000, was denounced as 'too sweeping'. Thus, of approximately three million adult male occupiers in the boroughs of the United Kingdom, about 1,430,000, or 47 per cent, were registered in 1868.[23]

This vast enfranchisement came about solely from the registration of occupiers. The ancillary lodger franchise was almost inoperative, because the registration of lodgers presented almost insuperable difficulties. The working-class lodger who wanted to register faced the prospect of losing wages, for he had to appear before a revising barrister, and they would only hear lodgers' claims during business hours: in Sunderland, for example, there were five hundred qualified workingmen lodgers, but only twenty were enrolled. Objections were free, even if unsustained, and so the working man stood to lose not only his wages, but legal costs and probably his vote as well, for objections were commonly upheld. The landlord's 'profession' had to be given on the application and 'landlady' was often held not to be a profession. The landlord had also to be described and the description was disallowed if it erred in detail. If the working man did not know his landlord, it followed that he could not even apply. The application forms were also ambiguous and some revising barristers required three signatures, including that of the landlord, others two.[24]

However, by 1874 there were 1,399,745 single entry voters registered in the English and Welsh boroughs, giving an increase of 175,000 on the 1868 total.[25] The Tory victories and greatly improved polls in Lancashire, Leeds and the Metropolitan boroughs in the General Elections of 1868[26] and 1874 suggest that the mid-Victorian anti-Liberal forces had much stronger support among the urban working classes than most contemporary Conservatives realized, and most historians have believed.[27] Perhaps even more important, in explaining the steady Conservative vote in the later decades of the century, is Dickens' prediction that the admission of the workingmen would activate the middle-class voters. Dickens believed in 1868 that the change effected by the Act would be 'very gradual . . . and quite wholesome. Numbers of the middle class who seldom or never voted before, will vote now; and the greater part of the new voters will . . . be wiser as to their electoral responsibilities'. Simply by reaction, the exclusive electorate may have held its own longer than contemporary Jeremiahs feared.[28]

The largest proportionate increases between 1866 and 1877 occurred in the big industrial boroughs; while most of the smaller boroughs, after doubling between 1866 and 1868, remained stationary. This development emphasized the trend which Baxter and Disraeli had predicted, that the heaviest increase would take place in radical strongholds, and would exacerbate the radicals' difficulties in coping with their overgrown constituencies. The increase in Sheffield alone between 1865 and 1877 was twice the aggregate constituency of the ten smallest boroughs. Thus twelve of the boroughs present the following contrast:[29]

				General election			
				1868		1874	
	1865–6	*1868*	*1877*	Lib.	Cons.	Lib.	Cons.
Birmingham	14,997	42,840	61,756	3	—	3	—
Finsbury	25,600	31,759	41,196	2	—	2	—
Leeds	7,217	35,510	49,300	2	1	1	2
Liverpool	20,618	39,645	59,667	1	2	1	2
Manchester	21,542	48,256	63,938	2	1	1	2
Sheffield	8,389	29,995	40,543	2	—	2	—
	98,363	228,005	316,400	12	4	10	6

				General election			
				1868		1874	
	1865–6	*1868*	*1877*	Lib.	Cons.	Lib.	Cons.
Andover	255	775	805	1	—	—	1
Knaresborough	272	747	709	1	—	—	1
Midhurst	309	995	985	—	1	—	1
Northallerton	442	807	846	—	1	—	1
Petersfield	296	750	795	1	—	—	1
St Ives	486	1,414	1,330	1	—	—	1
	2,060	5,488	5,470	4	2	0	6

So, in 1874, the members of six small boroughs neutralized the Liberal representation of six other boroughs with over 300,000 more electors; but, equally important, the Conservatives made a significant inroad into the representation of the great towns themselves.

The process of accumulation in the urban vote was also intensified by the re-arrangement of the borough boundaries and the creation of new boroughs. Lambert estimated that by 1870, 30,000 had come on the borough rolls after their districts had been incorporated into the boroughs from the counties, and 70,000 new voters had been created by the elevation of their towns into parliamentary boroughs. Registration was difficult and inefficient in these boroughs, where the rolls had to be compiled from

scratch.[30] The elaboration of the local party electoral machinery
was a direct outcome of the necessity to organize vast numbers of
apathetic occupiers and to overcome the hindrances to registration. The existing municipal methods of handling electors were
increasingly adapted to parliamentary elections, as in Birmingham, Liverpool and Oxford, for example.[31] It was the added
expense and difficulty of coping with the newly swollen electorates which converted or reconciled members to the ballot.

In the counties, by comparison with the boroughs, change was
less dramatic: whereas in 1868 the borough constituency was
increased more than four times that of 1832, the county constituency was only slightly more than doubled, and it then remained
stable for the next decade. The Tories' success in maintaining the
exclusive electorate in the counties is even better shown by the
figures for Scotland and Ireland:[32]

	County population		County voters			
	1831	*1871**	*1832*	*1866†*	*1868†*	*1877*
England	8,280,000	11,270,415	345,000	501,979	728,270	785,343
Wales	598,000	789,428	26,000	40,654	62,983	65,243
Scotland	1,485,000	1,873,078	33,000	49,979	74,978	89,750
Ireland	7,000,000	4,546,021	61,000	164,408	180,090	173,919

* Exclusive of represented boroughs   † R. D. Baxter's figures

By contrast with the ratios in the boroughs between population
and electors,[33] the county vote was still a sparsely distributed
privilege:

	County electors		Borough electors	
	1832	*1868*	*1832*	*1868*
England	1 in 24	1 in 15	1 in 17	1 in 8
Wales	1 in 23	1 in 13	1 in 17	1 in 8
Scotland	1 in 45	1 in 24	1 in 27	1 in 9
Ireland	1 in 115	1 in 26	1 in 22	1 in 16

In the redistribution, the South and West, as at the start of the
period, still had more representation than London or the Midlands and the North. The 23 smallest boroughs, for example, with
about 28,000 electors in 1868 returned 45 members, while

Edinburgh, with an equal constituency, returned only 2. The 19 largest boroughs with a population of about 5 million possessed 46 members, while the 68 under 20,000 each with an aggregate population of 420,000, had 68. The 19 boroughs between 50,000 and 100,000 with a total of 1,385,000 had 36 representatives, while the 49 boroughs between 10,000 and 20,000 had 81. In general there were 168 boroughs under 50,000 with 226 members and 48 over 50,000 with 82. This capricious system was to continue for another 17 years before it was decisively altered, and even then the wastage of Liberal votes by urban accumulation proved impossible to re-arrange.[34]

Although the redistribution renewed the principle of the First Reform Bill, the reduction of the borough qualification marked a decisive break with it. The collapse all but wrecked the mechanism which sustained the localized, exclusive electorate. The First Reform Bill had systematized, rather than abolished, the tie between local citizenship privileges and duties and the parliamentary franchise. But in establishing common qualifications and in intervening in the municipal electoral system, Parliament began a process towards simplification and uniformity and towards emancipating the suffrage qualifications from local custom. It was a process that was irreversible under conditions of increasing population and spreading prosperity. The levelling of borough rating and residence requirements and the introduction of the lodger franchise instituted the principle that the voter might hold his franchise irrespective of his economic, educational and citizen standing, and that the sole test of his fitness to vote were 'objective' criteria of sex, age, insanity, public office, and imprisonment. The county franchises also followed this pattern of devolution, though they remained intricate and exclusive.

The minority clause was the one part of the Bill which sought to reverse the trend towards single votes of equal weight. Yet by its very principle and method, it too broke with the past. By providing a representative for the upper-class minority in the great towns and counties, the clause implicitly denied the old theory that members represented the total range of interests in their locality. It broke also with the principle that the representatives elected by the majority enjoyed their right to speak for the whole constituency, and that their independence to vote in the House as they thought best arose by virtue of a majority of their constituents having freely and directly chosen them.

Finally, the minority clause accelerated the movement towards the representation of numbers rather than localities. This highly conservative-seeming dodge, as Disraeli pointed out, was revolutionary in its implications.[35] It curiously coincided with the Hare system of proportional representation which Mill supported in the House and the Reform League championed outside.[36] Both schemes were desperate attempts to preserve the balance of class interest in the constituency by minimizing the pressure of the mob.

The success of the agitations and the collapse of the Bill caused the gentry to lose confidence in their ability to preserve the old exclusiveness. It was this loss of confidence, apparently signalled by the mishandling of the Hyde Park Riots, and the loss of disciplined, intellectual leadership in public life epitomized in the triumph of Derby and Disraeli, which so alarmed Matthew Arnold, Coventry Patmore, George Eliot and Thomas Carlyle. Each saw the educated upper classes as the guardians of culture against the 'philistine' middle-class Dissenters and the ignorant and brutal mob. George Eliot appealed to the workingmen to continue their deference to the higher orders, and held out a mild assurance that they would do so.[37] Bagehot was hopeful, too, and together with the historians and jurists—Stubbs, Freeman and James Fitzjames Stephen—began to seek precepts for the distinction of intellectuals and the privileges of the owning classes in the usages of ancient communities and the law of Darwinian competition.[38] And like most of their educated contemporaries, they looked to a nation-wide system of primary education to inculcate deference in the children of the lower classes and equip them to receive instructions from their betters. The Education Act of 1870 is the only piece of social legislation which arises directly from the Second Reform Act.

More passionate intellectuals, like Patmore and Carlyle, who despaired of the multitude's being governed by principle or of its respecting learning, found release in vituperation:

> In the year of the great crime,
> When the false English Nobles and their Jew,
> By God demented, slew
> The Trust they stood twice pledged to keep from wrong,
>
> .   .   .
>
> Ye outlaw'd Best, who yet are bright
> With the sunken light,

Whose common style
Is Virtue at her gracious ease,
The flower of olden sanctities,
Ye haply trust, by love's benignant guile,
To lure the dark and selfish brood
To their own hated good;

. . .

But, when the sordid Trader caught
The loose-held sceptre from your hands distraught,
And soon, to the Mechanic vain,
Sold the proud toy for naught,
Your charm was broke, your task was sped,
Your beauty, with your honour, dead . . .[39]

Carlyle was even more rabid:

> Manhood Suffrage . . . universal 'glorious liberty', count of
> Heads, the . . . Devil-appointed way . . . the equality of men,
> any man equal to any other; Quashee Nigger to Socrates or
> Shakespeare; Judas Iscariot to Jesus Christ.[40]

It was attacks such as these which Disraeli sought to counter
in his public speeches after the Bill was passed. He successfully
propagated his myth that the Bill had been conceived in its
entirety at the outset, and that the successive alterations in it had
been the result of a deliberate plan by Derby and himself. Far
from giving way to pressure, he had progressively 'educated his
party'.[41] Disraeli saw the events of life and politics as a stream of
exciting fragments, to be moulded according to aesthetic fancy
and the expediency of his struggle to succeed in public life. He
created the 'Tory faith in the people' almost as a by-product, by
emphasizing the necessity for the traditional ruling class to continue to lead and by appropriating from the radicals the doctrine
of social unity. This return to the theories he had earlier
advocated in *Sybil* has served to obscure the anti-popular trend
of his actions in the fifties and sixties, and has enabled his apolo-
gists to invest his political career with a false consistency in the
Second Reform period.

Disraeli, the political genius and chronicler of the English
aristocracy as a ruling caste, saw more clearly than the poets and
theoreticians that though the upper classes might cease to rule so
obviously, they would continue to enjoy enormous advantages of
wealth, tradition, connection and education and—equally important—that the lower classes would largely continue to defer to

them. But the poets, together with Lowe and Mill, sensed more acutely than Disraeli the real opposition between civic liberalism, with its emphasis on the development of the individual irrespective of his social environment, and the approaching conformist anonymity of public life and culture. They divined correctly that the Second Reform Act had opened the way to the mass politics of another age.

ABBREVIATIONS

Hansard	Hansard, *Parliamentary Debates,* Third Series
L.Q.V.	G. E. Buckle (ed.), *The Letters of Queen Victoria* Second Series, 2 vols, London, 1926
P.P.	*Parliamentary Papers*

NOTES

INTRODUCTION

1 *A History of the Reform Bills of 1866 and 1867.*
2 *The English Reform Bill of 1867.*
3 *Hansard*, CLXXXVI, 15.
4 See especially the essays by Hutton and Harrison.
5 *Hansard*, CLXXXVII, 416, Grant Duff.

1 THE EMERGENCE OF THE LABOUR ARISTOCRACY

1 H. Parkes, *Australian Views of England—Eleven Letters written in the Years 1861 and 1862* (London, 1869), p. 40.

2 G. M. Young and W. D. Handcock, *English Historical Documents 1833-1874* (London, 1956), pp. 208-15; Beesly, *Letters to the Working Classes*, pp. 3-4; *1851 Census Report*, pp. cxxii ff.; *1871 Census Report*, p. xliii.

3 Baxter, *National Income*, Appendix IV.

4 'A Journeyman Engineer' [Thomas Wright], *Some Habits and Customs of the Working Classes*, p. 258; see also Pollard, *A History of Labour in Sheffield*, p. 22; H. J. Dyos, *Victorian Suburb: A Study of the Growth of Camberwell* (Leicester, 1961), pp. 85 ff.

5 Ludlow and Jones, *Progress of the Working Classes*, pp. 186-7, 221; T. Cooper, *Life of Thomas Cooper. Written by himself* (London, 4th ed., 1873), p. 393; see also A. E. Musson, *The Typographical Association. Origins and History up to 1949* (London, 1954), pp. 89 ff.

6 W. E. Gladstone, 'Speech in answer to an address from the printers and compositors of Newton-le-Willows, Lancashire', *Speeches and Addresses delivered at the Election of 1865* (London, 1865), p. 37.

7 S. Pollard, 'Nineteenth Century Co-operation: From Community to Shopkeeping', *Essays in Labour History*, ed. Asa Briggs and John Saville (London, 1960), pp. 97-8.

8 S. J. Price, *Building Societies Their Origin and History* (London, 1958), pp. 155-7; also Ludlow and Jones, op. cit., p. 138.

9 Price, *Building Societies*, p. 140.

10 *P.P.*, 1868-9, vol. LXII, p. 250.

11 C. Kingsley, 'Preface to the Undergraduates of Cambridge', [1862] in *Alton Locke*, with a prefatory Memoir by Thomas Hughes, 2 vols, (London, 1881); see also Robert Potter Berry, *A History of the Formation and Development of the Volunteer Infantry* (London and Huddersfield, 1903).

12 *The Times*, 11 July 1865.

[13] Beales, *Speech . . . at the Meeting at St. Martin's Hall, in support of the [Reform] League, May 13, 1865*, p. 12.

[14] W. E. Gladstone, *Speeches on Parliamentary Reform in 1866*, p. 333, speech on Baines' Borough Suffrage Bill, 1864; see also W. O. Henderson, *The Lancashire Cotton Famine* (Manchester, 1934).

2   THE SYSTEM OF REPRESENTATION

[1] *Hansard* CLXXXIII, 1818; see also Bernard Cracroft, 'The Analysis of the House of Commons, or Indirect Representation', in *Essays on Reform*; Edward Wilson, 'Principles of Representation', *Fortnightly Review*, vol. 4, 1866, p. 428.

[2] Cf. Norman Gash, *Politics in the Age of Peel* (London, 1953), part I.

[3] Lord Hobart, 'Parliamentary Reform', *Macmillan's Magazine*, January 1866.

[4] *Dod's Parliamentary Companion*, 'New Parliament', 1865.

[5] Cracroft, 'Analysis of the House of Commons', *Essays on Reform*, p. 164. For corrections to this essay, see *Athenaeum*, 23 March 1867.

[6] Hanham, *Elections and Party Management*, pp. 273 ff.

[7] 11 and 12 Vict. c. 90.

[8] 14 and 15 Vict. c. 14; also *Hansard* CXIV, 820 ff. and CXV, 901 ff.

[9] J. Lambert, Secretary to the Poor Law Board, 'Confidential Cabinet Memorandum', 1 March 1866, Disraeli Papers, B.XI.L.2.

[10] 2 and 3 Will. IV c. 88; 13 and 14 Vict. c. 69.

[11] *P.P.*, 1866, vol. VII, *Electoral Returns*.

[12] *P.P.*, 1865, vol. XLVII, no. 195.

[13] *P.P.*, 1867, vol. VI, no. 120.

[14] *Hansard* CLXXV, 285 ff.

[15] *P.P.*, 1866, vol. VII, *Electoral Returns 1866*, 'Actual Number of Persons Entitled to Vote'.

[16] Cf. Baxter, *The New Reform Bill*, p. 20. *Hansard* CLXXXIII, 145-6.

[17] They were respectively: H. W. Eaton, silk merchant, and M. Treherne, gentleman barrister, both Conservative (Coventry); M. A. Bass, brewer, Liberal, and Walter Meller, gentleman, Conservative (Stafford); G. M. W. Sandford, Conservative gentleman, and Ralph Earle, Disraeli's private secretary (Maldon); W. S. Allen, Liberal, and Edmund Buckley, a Conservative, both gentlemen (Newcastle-under-Lyme); Sir Henry Edwards and Christopher Sykes, both Conservative industrialists (Beverley); Alderman Salomons, Liberal merchant banker, and Sir Charles Bright, Liberal engineer (Greenwich); and Henry Paull, the Conservative son of a merchant (St Ives). In sum, nine Conservatives out of fourteen members and only Bass can be doubtfully classed as a radical Liberal.

[18] Cracroft, 'Analysis of the House of Commons', *Essays on Reform*, pp. 175-6.

[19] Bright, *Speeches on Parliamentary Reform*, p. 387, Manchester, 20 November 1866.

[20] Leech (ed.), *The Public Letters of the Right Hon. John Bright*, p. 76, 17 May 1857.

[21] W. Robertson, *Life and Times of the Right Hon. John Bright* (London, 1883), p. 383, speech at Leeds, 11 December 1860; cf. *Hansard* CLXXXII, 883-4, P. A. Taylor.

22 *Financial Reformer,* 1 February 1866.

23 Quoted by R. Masheder, *The Right Hon. Wm. Ewart Gladstone, M.P.* (London, 1865), p. 197.

24 Aytoun, *Parliamentary Reform and The Way To Obtain It,* p. 11.

25 Beales, *Speech . . . at the Meeting at St. Martin's Hall in Support of the League, May 13, 1865,* p. 9.

26 *Hansard* CLXXXII, 2128.

27 J. B. Mackie, *Life of Duncan McLaren,* 2 vols, (Edinburgh, 1888), vol. 2, p. 154, January 1866; cf. Hutton, 'The Political Character of the Working Classes', in *Essays on Reform.*

28 *Hansard* CLXXXII, 1707-8.

29 *Hansard* CLXXXII, 1259; cf. Frederic Harrison, 'Our Venetian Constitution', *Fortnightly Review,* March 1867, pp. 275-6.

30 *Hansard* CLXXXV, 1901.

31 *Hansard* CLXXXII, 1407-8; also 865 ff., Platt.

32 G. Barnett Smith, *The Life and Speeches of the Right Hon. John Bright, M.P.,* 2 vols, (London, 1881), vol. 1, 220.

33 *Hansard* CLXXXIV, 613, 18 June 1866; cf. 'What right have you to assume to be more Conservative in intention than I am? I have a business which is more liable to injury from any disturbance of the public peace than your property. . . . I believe that in reality I am infinitely more Conservative, if you will cast your eyes twenty or thirty years forward', *Hansard* CLIII, 791, 25 March 1859.

34 Cf. T. C. Anstey, *Plea of the Unrepresented Commons for Restitution of Franchise,* and Bright, Speech at Reform Conference in Manchester, 20 November 1866, Robertson, *Life . . . of . . . John Bright,* p. 439.

35 'J.S.', *The Reformer's Year-Book and Political Annual 1867,* p. 19.

36 Cf. *Hansard* CLXXXII, 61, Marsh.

37 *The Times,* 17 July 1865.

38 *Hansard* CLXXV, 324.

3 THE SECOND REFORM PERIOD, 1851-1865

1 The Bills are summarized in Young and Handcock, *English Historical Documents* (London, 1956), pp. 121-3. The borough qualification in the Bill of 1860 should read '£6 Gross Annual Rental', and the redistribution, 'twenty-five smaller boroughs', instead of 'twenty-two'. The Bills are reprinted in *P.P.,* 1866, vol. LVII.

2 *Hansard* CXIV, 851 ff.

3 *Hansard* CXIV, 857 ff.

4 *Hansard* CXIV, 863-4.

5 *Hansard* CXIV, 870-1.

6 *Hansard* CXVIII, 374-5.

7 *Hansard* CXV, 916.

8 *Hansard* CXV, 940.

9 *Hansard* CXVIII, 356, 370.

10 *Hansard* CXV, 935-6.

11 S. Walpole, *The Life of Lord John Russell,* 2 vols, (London, 1889), vol. 2, p. 130.

[12] See pp. 214, 238.

[13] Walpole, *Russell,* vol. 2, p. 130.

[14] *Hansard* cxix, 252-3.

[15] *Hansard* cxix, 261-5.

[16] *Hansard* cxix, 267.

[17] *Hansard* cxix, 269-70; 284-5; 296.

[18] *Hansard* cxix, 273-4, Sir John Walsh; 278, Sir R. H. Inglis; 295, C. N. Newdegate.

[19] *Hansard* cxix, 971-3, 12 March 1852.

[20] L. Strachey and R. Fulford (eds), *The Greville Memoirs, 1814-1860,* 7 vols, (London, 1938), vol. 6, p. 356, 11 August 1852.

[21] *Hansard* cxix, 270.

[22] G. M. Trevelyan, *The Life of John Bright* (London, 1913), p. 201, 15 July 1852.

[23] Walpole, *Russell,* vol. 2, p. 195.

[24] N. W. B. Pemberton, *Palmerston* (London, 1954), pp. 215-17.

[25] Russell to Palmerston, 16 November 1853, Walpole, *Russell,* vol. 2, pp. 196-7.

[26] *Hansard* cxxx, 405-8.

[27] *Hansard* cxxx, 411.

[28] *Hansard* cxxx, 506.

[29] *Hansard* cxxx, 502.

[30] H. Oliver Horne, *A History of Savings Banks* (London, 1947), pp. 231-2; also Ludlow and Jones, *Progress of the Working Classes,* p. 119.

[31] Russell referred specifically to Fox's great speech of 1797, *Hansard* cxxx, 505-6; cf. *Parliamentary History,* xxxiii, 726.

[32] *Hansard* cxxx, 498; cf. J. S. Mill, 'Thoughts on Parliamentary Reform', February 1859, reprinted in *Dissertations and Discussions,* vol. 3, and J. H. Burns, 'J. S. Mill and Democracy', *Political Studies,* vol. 5, 1957.

[33] *Hansard* cxxx, 526, Hume; 527, Murrough; cxxxii, 851, Bright.

[34] *Hansard* cxxxi, 282.

[35] *Hansard* cxxxii, 843.

[36] *Hansard* cxxxii, 839.

[37] *Hansard* cxliv, 841-63. The Government's majority against the motion was only 13, composed of office-holders and Tories. Russell voted for it, against Palmerston.

[38] W. F. Monypenny and G. E. Buckle, *The Life of Benjamin Disraeli, Earl of Beaconsfield,* 2 vols, (London, 1929), vol. 1, p. 1479, 21 April 1857. Jones' assertion that Derby took the initiative in this move towards legislation on Reform is not borne out by the dates and contents of the letters as printed in M. and B. Derby's letter of 24 April 1857 is clearly a reply to Disraeli's of 21 April. Jones, *Lord Derby and Victorian Conservatism,* p. 244.

[39] *Hansard* cxlix, 43, 1 March 1858.

[40] *Hansard* cl, 1857-81, 2289-91.

[41] M. and B., *Disraeli,* vol. 1, pp. 1584-5.

[42] Robertson, *The Life and Times of the Right Hon. John Bright,* p. 259.

[43] *Mr. Bright's Reform Bill,* cf. J. B. Mackie, *The Life and Work of Duncan McLaren,* vol. 2, p. 151.

44 Robertson, *The Life . . . of John Bright,* p. 364.

45 Reduction of Franchise—Epitome of Information Collected. n.d. Disraeli Papers, B.XI.C.27. The Disraeli Papers were being re-sorted during the period I was reading them. Where possible I have given the new classification.

46 Reform Memorandum, 24 January 1859, Disraeli Papers, B.XI. C. 32.

47 Ibid.

48 *Hansard* CLII, 985 ff. It was during the course of this debate that Bright invented the label, 'fancy franchises', for those proposed qualifications which did not derive from local occupancy (*Hansard* CLII, 1025).

49 *Hansard* CLII, 999-1001.

50 *Hansard* CLII, 1016, Lord John Russell; CLIII, 473, Newdegate; 559, Byng; 568, Banks Stanhope; 579, Knightley; CLII, 1038, Disraeli.

51 *Hansard* CLII, 1037, Bentinck; CLIII, 457-8, Horsman; 556-7, Bulwer-Lytton; 753 ff., Walpole; 932, Elcho; 1212, Henley.

52 *Hansard* CLII, 1061-3, Walpole; 1064-8, Henley; see also Henley to Derby, 14 July 1867, Disraeli Papers 'General Correspondence'.

53 *Hansard* CLII, 1015, Fox; CLIII, 539, Wilson.

54 *Hansard* CLIII, 405.

55 *Hansard* CLIII, 462, Horsman; 929 ff., Beaumont; 932 ff., Elcho.

56 *Hansard* CLIII, 332-3, Roebuck; 333, Cox, M.P. for Finsbury; CLII, 1031 ff., Crossley.

57 Palmerston to Russell n.d. [late 1859], Walpole, *Russell,* vol. 2, p. 330.

58 *Hansard* CLVI, 6, 24 January 1860.

59 *Hansard* CLVI, 2051.

60 *The Greville Memoirs,* op. cit., vol. 7, p. 462, 7 March 1860.

61 *Hansard* CLVI, 895 ff., Bright; 1081 ff., Crossley; 2144 ff., James; 848 ff., Disraeli.

62 *Greville Memoirs,* vol. 7, p. 479, 15 June 1860.

63 *Hansard* CLXI, 15 ff., Derby; 92 ff., Russell.

64 July 1850 Locke King's Bill for extension of the suffrage. Ayes 100, Noes 159. *Hansard* CXII, 1184-6.
July 1851 Berkeley's motion for the ballot. Ayes 87, Noes 50. *Hansard* CXVIII, 374-5.
March 1852 Hume's motion for Parliamentary Reform. Ayes 89, Noes 244. *Hansard* CXX, 169-71.
June 1853 Berkeley's motion for the ballot. Ayes 172, Noes 232. *Hansard* CXXVIII, 229-31.
June 1854 Berkeley's motion for the ballot. Ayes 157, Noes 194. *Hansard* CXXXIV, 114-16.
May 1855 Berkeley's motion for the ballot. Ayes 166, Noes 218. *Hansard* CXXXVIII, 946-9.
May 1856 Berkeley's motion for the ballot. Ayes 111, Noes 151. *Hansard* CXLII, 450-1.
June 1857 Berkeley's motion for the ballot. Ayes 189, Noes 257. *Hansard* CXLVI, 682-5.
March 1860 Berkeley's motion for the ballot. Ayes 147, Noes 254. *Hansard* CLVII, 957-60.

65 Cf. W. E. Williams, *The Rise of Gladstone to the Leadership of the Liberal Party 1859 to 1868* (Cambridge, 1934).

66 *Hansard* CLIII, 1045 ff., 1258.

[67] *Hansard* CLVIII, 633.

[68] J. Morley, *The Life of William Ewart Gladstone*, 3 vols, (London, 1903), vol. 2, p. 133.

[69] *Hansard* CLXXV, 326-7, 11 May 1864.

[70] *Hansard* CLXXVIII, 1691 ff., Disraeli; 1423 ff., Lowe.

[71] The future Adullamites included: Hon. A. H. A. Anson; H. B. Baring; Lord J. T. Browne; Maj. C. Bruce; Sir R. Bulkeley; Sir M. J. Cholmeley; R. W. Duff; Lord Dunkellin; A. S. Finlay; Hon. C. W. W. Fitzwilliam; W. H. Gregory; Earl Grosvenor; Lord R. Grosvenor; Hon. G. H. Heathcote; R. Lowe; J. Mackie; T. Mainwaring; M. H. Marsh; Col. G. Packe; *Hansard* CLXXVIII, 1707-9.

4 THE REFORM BILL OF 1866

I *The Origins of the Bill of 1866*

[1] *The Times*, 7, 13 July 1865; *Hansard* CLXXXII, 1665.

[2] *The Times*, 1 July 1865, Cecil, South Essex; 15 July, Montagu and Egerton, South Lancashire.

[3] *The Times*, 1 July 1865, Fane, Oxfordshire; 3 July 1865, Bailey, Hertfordshire; 14 July 1865, Du Pré, Buckinghamshire; 15 July 1865, Palk and Kekewich, South Devon.

[4] *The Times*, 3, 4, 13 July 1865.

[5] *The Times*, 1 July 1865; also Lusk and Torrens, 10, 12 July 1865.

[6] Speech at the Royal Amphitheatre, Liverpool, *The Times*, 19 July 1865.

[7] *The Times*, 5, 13 July 1865.

[8] *The Times*, 10 July 1865.

[9] *The Times*, 5, 13, 14, 24 July 1865.

[10] *The Times*, 24 July 1865.

[11] E. Hodder, *The Life of Samuel Morley* (London, 1887), pp. 208 ff.; *The Times*, 5, 13, 14 July 1865.

[12] Cf. Hanham, *Elections and Party Management*, pp. 39 ff.

[13] E.g., James Clay to Disraeli, 8 January 1866, Disraeli Papers, 'Clay'; Kinnear, *Principles of Reform: Political and Legal*.

[14] *The Times*, 25 July 1865.

[15] 64 of the new men described themselves as 'Liberal-Conservatives', 'Conservatives', or 'supporters of Lord Derby'; 75 called themselves 'Whigs', 'Liberals', or 'supporters of Lord Palmerston', while 20 described themselves as 'advanced Liberals' or 'radicals'. In 1859 there had been 78 new members and in 1868 there were to be over 200: *Dod's Parliamentary Companion*, 'New Parliament', 1859, 1865, 1868.

[16] Derby to Disraeli, 24 July 1865, Disraeli Papers, '14 Derby'.

[17] Palmerston to Brand, 3 August 1865, Hampden Papers.

[18] Dowager Duchess of Argyll (ed.), *George Douglas, Eighth Duke of Argyll. Autobiography and Memoirs*, 2 vols, (London, 1906), vol. 2, p. 229.

[19] Algernon West, *Recollections*, 2 vols, (London, 1899), vol. 1, p. 306: quoting Sir Charles Wood.

[20] Gladstone to Russell, 18 October 1865, Morley, *Gladstone*, vol. 2, p. 151.

[21] Russell to Gladstone, 20 October 1865, Gladstone Papers, B.M. Add. MSS. 44292.

[22] Monypenny and Buckle, *Disraeli,* vol. 2, p. 158.

[23] Clarendon to Granville, 21 October 1865, Granville Papers, P.R.O. 30/29/29A.

[24] Russell, Personal Memorandum, 23 October 1865, Russell Papers, P.R.O. 30/22/15.

[25] Russell, Personal Memorandum, 24 October 1865, Russell Papers, P.R.O. 30/22/15.

[26] Lady Gregory (ed.), *William Henry Gregory, An Autobiography* (London, 1894), p. 240.

[27] Granville to Russell, 26 March 1866, Granville Papers, P.R.O. 30/29/22A; also Walpole, *Russell,* vol. 2, p. 409.

[28] Sir Arthur Hardinge, *The Life of Henry Howard Molyneux Herbert, Fourth Earl of Carnarvon 1831-90,* 3 vols, (Oxford, 1925), vol. 1, p. 337, Carnarvon's Journal, 26 December 1866; also A. P. Martin, *Life and Letters of the Right Honourable Robert Lowe Viscount Sherbrooke, G.C.B., D.C.L.,* 2 vols, (London, 1893), vol. 2, p. 251. (Lowe to Henry Sherbrooke, 6 December 1865) and Gladstone to Russell, 6 December 1865, Granville Papers, P.R.O. 30/29/29A.

[29] Stanley to Disraeli, 4 November 1865, Disraeli Papers, '15 Derby'.

[30] Stanley to Disraeli, 8 November 1865, Disraeli Papers, '15 Derby'.

[31] Stanley to Disraeli, 16 November 1865, Disraeli Papers, '15 Derby'.

[32] Disraeli to Earle, 6 November 1865, M. and B., *Disraeli,* vol. 2, p. 159.

[33] Disraeli to Derby, 24 November 1865, M. and B., *Disraeli,* vol. 2, p. 160.

[34] Russell to the Queen, 11 November 1865, Copy, Russell Papers, P.R.O. 30/22/15.

[35] *Hansard* CLXI, 92-3, 1861. Also the famous 'Rest and be Thankful' speech at Blairgowrie, 1863. Walpole, *Russell,* vol. 2, p. 402.

[36] Sir Charles Wood to Russell, 3, 23 November 1865, Russell Papers, P.R.O. 30/22/15.

[37] Wood to Russell, 3 November 1865, Russell Papers, P.R.O. 30/22/15.

[38] T. Wemyss Reid, *Life of the Right Honourable William Edward Forster* (London, 1889), p. 207.

[39] Ibid., p. 208.

[40] Ibid.

[41] Forster to Brand, 20 November 1865, ibid., pp. 208-9.

[42] Ibid., pp. 209-10, 22 November 1865.

[43] Forster to his wife, 24 November 1865, ibid., pp. 210-11; *Leeds Mercury,* 29 November 1865; Stanley to Disraeli, reporting conversation with Russell, 16 November 1865, Disraeli Papers, '15 Derby'.

[44] Russell to Sir George Grey, 31 October 1865, enclosing copy of instructions to Poor Law Office; Russell Papers, 30/22/15. Since this book went to press, an incisive account of these negotiations has been published by Mr Maurice Cowling, 'Disraeli, Derby and Fusion, October 1865 to July 1866', *Historical Journal,* vol. 8, no. 1, 1965. Mr Cowling probably overstates Russell's early enthusiam for a bill (pp. 40-1). Russell's main concern was to hold his following together: as shown by his letter to Grey (sent before Elcho's letter was read to the Cabinet) he was ready to proceed by Commission, which would have mollified the Whigs. But while he was feeling

his way he supported a Commission in his correspondence with Grey and Wood and, as quoted by Mr Cowling, criticized the proposal in a letter to Gladstone. No doubt he was acting deviously, but the general impression given by his correspondence at this time is that he had slightly lost his grip on affairs.

⁴⁵ Russell to Grey, 10 December 1865, Russell Papers, P.R.O. 30/22/15.

⁴⁶ Wood to Russell, 7 November 1865, Russell Papers, P.R.O. 30/22/15.

⁴⁷ Russell to Sir George Grey, 10 December 1865, Russell Papers, P.R.O. 30/22/15.

⁴⁸ Russell to Gladstone, 1 January 1866, Gladstone to Russell, 3 January 1866, Gladstone Papers, B.M. Add. MSS. 44293.

⁴⁹ Gladstone to Villiers, 5 January 1866, Gladstone Papers, B.M. Add. MSS. 44409.

⁵⁰ Wood to de Grey, 9 January 1866, Ripon Papers, B.M. Add. MSS. 43529.

⁵¹ C. B. Adderley to Disraeli, 25 January 1866, Disraeli Papers, 'Adderley'.

⁵² Sir George Grey to Russell, 6 January 1866, Russell Papers, P.R.O. 30/22/16 and Russell to Grey, 7 January 1866 in G. P. Gooch (ed.), *Later Correspondence of Lord John Russell*, 2 vols, (London, 1925), vol. 2, p. 342.

⁵³ Brand to Sir Charles Wood, 11 January 1866; de Grey to Wood, 11 January 1866; Clarendon to Lady Salisbury, 15 January 1866: quoted by Sir Herbert Maxwell, *Life and Letters of George William Frederick, Fourth Earl of Clarendon*, 2 vols, (London, 1913), vol. 2, pp. 304-5.

⁵⁴ Layard to Clarendon, 10 January 1866 (draft), Layard Papers, B.M. Add. MSS. 38992; also Gordon Waterfield, *Layard of Nineveh* (London, 1963), pp. 304-5; Knatchbull-Hugessen to Russell, 23 October 1865, Russell Papers, P.R.O. 30/22/15; Spofforth to Disraeli, 9 January 1866; Knatchbull-Hugessen to Spofforth, 25 January 1866, Disraeli Papers, 'Spofforth'.

⁵⁵ Bright to Villiers, n.d. [December 1865?], Russell Papers, P.R.O. 30/22/15; also Bright to Villiers, 27 July 1865, quoted in Trevelyan, *Bright*, p. 345.

⁵⁶ Russell to Sir George Grey, 7 January 1866, in Gooch, *Later Correspondence . . .*, vol. 2, p. 342.

⁵⁷ Lord Fitzmaurice, *Life of Granville George Leveson-Gower, Second Earl Granville, K.G.*, 2 vols, (London, 1905), vol. 1, p. 500; also Gladstone to Russell, early January 1866, Russell Papers, P.R.O. 30/22/16.

⁵⁸ Lord Clarendon to Lord Bloomfield, 14 February 1866, Clarendon Papers, c. 145.

⁵⁹ *Hansard* CLXXXIII, 1482.

⁶⁰ *Hansard* CLXXXI, 828.

⁶¹ *Hansard* CLXXXI, 832, Gregory; 838 ff., Elcho; 841 ff., Horsman; also Stafford Northcote, Diary, 20 February 1866, Lang, *Stafford Northcote*, p. 145.

⁶² Clay to Disraeli, 8 January 1866, Disraeli Papers, 'Clay'.

⁶³ Milner-Gibson to Bright, 11 January 1866, Bright Papers, B.M. Add. MSS. 43388; W. E. Forster to his wife, 11 January 1866, Wemyss Reid, *Forster*, p. 216.

⁶⁴ Gladstone to Russell, 25 January 1866, Russell Papers, P.R.O. 30/22/16.

65 Russell, Cabinet Memorandum, 12 February 1866, (outlines Lambert's memorandum); Cabinet Minutes, 12 February 1866, Russell Papers, P.R.O. 30/22/16.

66 Stafford Northcote, Diary, 17, 20, 28 February 1866, Lang, *Stafford Northcote,* pp. 144-9.

67 J. Lambert, Confidential Cabinet Memo, 1 March 1866, Disraeli Papers, B. XI. L. 2; also Lefevre, *The Personal Payment of Rates.*

68 Hon. E. P. Bouverie, Member for Kilmarnock burghs. Although he did not join the 'Cave', Bouverie became a tepid supporter of the Government in 1866. Bright to Gladstone, 10 February 1866, Gladstone Papers, B.M. Add. MSS. 44112.

69 Russell, Memo. 7 March 1866, Russell Papers, P.R.O. 30/22/16.

70 Russell, Memo. n.d. [7 March? 1866], Gladstone to Russell, 6 March 1866, Russell Papers, P.R.O. 30/22/16.

71 Stafford Northcote, Diary, 16 March 1866, Lang, *Northcote,* p. 154.

II *The Franchise Bill*

72 *Hansard* CLXXXII, 52-3.

73 *Hansard* CLXXXII, 54-5.

74 See p. 2; also Baxter, *National Income,* pp. 88-9.

75 *Hansard* CLXXXII, 43-6. The Bill is printed in *P.P.,* 1866, vol. LVII, pp. 87-100.

76 *Hansard* CLXXXII, 47.

77 *Hansard* CLXXXII, 30.

78 *Hansard* CLXXXII, 176-7.

79 *Hansard* CLXXXII, 189.

80 *Hansard* CLXXXII, 864-5; also 200 ff., Fawcett and *English Leader,* 7 April 1866, Joseph Cowen.

81 *Hansard* CLXXXII, 83.

82 *Hansard* CLXXXIII, 32.

83 Carnarvon to Malmesbury, 20 October 1865, Malmesbury to Carnarvon, 23 October 1865, Hardinge, *Carnarvon,* vol. 1, p. 272.

84 Northcote to Disraeli, 29 January 1866, Iddesleigh Papers, B.M. Add. MSS. 50014.

85 Derby to Disraeli, n.d. [late February 1866?], Disraeli Papers, '14 Derby' Stafford Northcote, Diary, 8 March 1866, Lang, *Northcote,* p. 152.

86 Hardinge, *Carnarvon,* vol. 1, p. 277.

87 Carnarvon to Heathcote, 6 March 1866, Heathcote to Carnarvon, 6 March 1866, Hardinge, *Carnarvon,* vol. 1, pp. 275-6.

88 Hardinge, *Carnarvon,* quoting Stafford Northcote, 10 March 1866, vol. 1, p. 277.

89 Stafford Northcote, Diary, 3 February 1866, Lang, *Northcote,* pp. 138-9.

90 Ibid., 8 March 1866, p. 153.

91 Ibid., 16 March 1866, p. 154.

92 A. E. Gathorne-Hardy, *Gathorne Hardy, First Earl of Cranbrook, A Memoir,* 2 vols, (London, 1910), vol. 1, p. 185, Diary, 17 March 1866.

93 *Hansard* CLXXXII, 74.

94 *Hansard* CLXXXII, 74; 227 ff,

95 *Hansard* CLXXXII, 185.

96 *Hansard* CLXXXII, 231

97 *Hansard* CLXXXII, 187-8, Meller; 190-200, 1904-39, Whiteside; 856-61, 1212-20, Banks Stanhope.

98 *Hansard* CLXXXII, 154.

99 *Hansard* CLXXXIII, 1640 ff.

1 Lowe, *Speeches and Letters on Reform; with a Preface*, p. 3.

2 *Hansard* CLXXXII, 2105 ff.

3 *Hansard* CLXXXII, 61 ff.

4 *Hansard* CLXXXII, 61.

5 *Hansard* CLXXXII, 233.

6 Speech at Birmingham 18 December 1862, Rogers (ed.), *Speeches...by John Bright M.P.*, vol. 1, p. 223; see also Henry Pelling, *America and the British Left* (London, 1956), p. 7 ff.

7 Alexis de Tocqueville, *Democracy in America*, with an introductory notice by the translator, 2 vols, (London, new ed. 1862).

8 Mill, *Representative Government*, pp. 266-7; W. Bagehot, *The English Constitution* (London, 1891 ed.), pp. 170-1. [First published *Fortnightly Review*, 1865-66]; Earl Grey, *Hansard* CLXXXV, 1905-6; CLXXXVII, 1816-17; see also 'An Ex-M.P.', 'The Extension of the Franchise', *Contemporary Review*, vol. 3, December 1866, pp. 437-8.

9 [Lord Cranborne], 'Reform Essays', *Quarterly Review*, vol. CXXIII, July 1867, p. 255; also *Hansard* CLIII, 740, Marsh, 24 March 1859.

10 Cf. *Hansard* CLXXXII, 1244-5, Bulwer-Lytton; also CLIII, 740, Beresford Hope.

11 Cf. *Hansard* CLVIII, 157, Bulwer-Lytton.

12 Williams, *The Rise of Gladstone . . .* , p. 149.

13 *Hansard* CLXXXII, 147-8.

14 *Hansard* CLXXIII, 1650.

15 *Hansard* CLXXXVI, 62.

16 *Hansard* CLXXXII, 221.

17 *Hansard* CLXXXII, 223-4.

18 *Hansard* CLXXXII, 219.

19 Hardinge, *Carnarvon*, vol. 1, p. 278.

20 Emily Eden to Clarendon [January?] 1866, Sir Herbert Maxwell, *Life . . . of Clarendon* (London, 1913), vol. 2, p. 307; also the Earl of Malmesbury, *Memoirs of an Ex-Minister*, 2 vols, (London, 1884), vol. 2, p. 350.

21 Brand to Russell, 23 March 1866, Russell Papers, P.R.O. 30/22/16.

22 Clarendon to Russell, 5 September 1866, Russell Papers, P.R.O. 30/22/16; cf. *Hansard* CLXXXV, 1908, Grey.

23 Russell, Memo of Conversation with Queen, 24 March 1866, Russell Papers, P.R.O. 30/22/16.

24 Wemyss Reid, *Memoirs*, p. 54.

25 *Hansard* CLXXVIII, 422, 28 March 1865; cf. Morley, *Gladstone*, vol. 2, pp. 141-2.

26 Derby to Disraeli, n.d. [22 June? 1866], Disraeli Papers, '14 Derby'.

27 Cf. W. M. Torrens, *Twenty Years in Parliament* (London, 1893), p. 37.

28 Sir George Bowyer to Disraeli, 5 July 1866, Disraeli Papers, 'Bowyer'; W. H. Gregory, *Autobiography*, pp. 222-3.

29 Clarendon to Odo Russell, 23 April 1866. Clarendon Dep. C. 143. Bodleian Library.

30 *Hansard* CLXXXII, 358 ff.

31 Diary, 15 March [1866], Iddesleigh Papers, B.M. Add. MSS. 50063A.

32 Lowe to Mrs Billyard, 25 March 1866, Martin, *Sherbrooke*, vol. 2, p. 277; see also Grosvenor to Baxter, 26 March 1866, M. D. Baxter, *In Memoriam, R. D. Baxter, M.A.* (London, 1878), pp. 34-5.

33 *Hansard* CLXXXII, 1156.

34 Taylor to Disraeli, 3 April 1866, Disraeli Papers, 'Taylor'.

35 *Hansard* CLXXXII, 2121. The want of a sociological framework is reflected in the instructions issued to the Poor Law officials responsible for gathering the returns: 'The Board do not intend that the return should be exclusively confined to journeymen who are employed by masters at daily or weekly wages; but that it should include men who work daily at their own handicraft trade without a master and even sometimes employ a journeyman . . . provided they derive their chief support from their own hand-labour, and not from the labour of others, or the profits arising from the employment of capital, or the supply of materials. No artisan, mechanic or labourer is to be excluded because he has a shop which is kept by his wife or *other* member of the family; but it must be distinctly understood that, as a general rule, shopkeepers and their assistants are not to be inserted. Overlookers, superintendents, foremen . . . are not to be included, unless actually employed in daily manual labour in the same manner in every respect as the men who are under them.' Charles Knight, *The British Almanac* . . . (London, 1867), p. 108.

36 *Hansard* CLXXXIII, 50-1; CLXXXII, 1256-7, Mill.

37 J. B. Jeffreys, *The Story of the Engineers, 1800-1945* (London, 1945), p. 69.

38 *Hansard* CLXXXIII, 126.

39 *Hansard* CLXXXIII, 147.

40 *Hansard* CLXXXII, 873-4.

41 Sir George Grey to Russell, 25 April 1866, Russell Papers, P.R.O. 30/22/16.

42 Gladstone, *Reform Speeches*, pp. 89-90.

43 Brand to Gladstone, 22 March 1866, Gladstone Papers, B.M. Add. MSS. 44193.

44 Brand to Russell, 29 March 1866, Gooch (ed.), *Later Correspondence . . . of Russell,* vol. 2, p. 344.

45 Russell to the Queen, 23 March 1866, *L.Q.V.*, vol. 1, p. 306.

46 *The Times,* 22 March 1866 (notice of motion by A. W. Kinglake).

47 *Hansard* CLXXXIII, 129-30.

48 *Hansard* CLXXXIII, 152.

49 J. Irving, *Annals of our Time, 1837-71,* quoted by Martin, *Sherbrooke,* vol. 2, pp. 292-3.

50 The men from the Government benches who voted for Grosvenor's amendment were: Capt. the Hon. L. G. F. Agar Ellis, heir to Lord Dover, Kilkenny Co; Viscount Andover, heir to the Earl of Suffolk, Malmesbury;* Hon. A. H. A. Anson, second son of the Earl of Lichfield, Lichfield;* H. B. Baring, son-in-law to the Earl of Cardigan, Marlborough;* W. B. Beaumont, son-in-law to the Marquess of Clanricarde, Northumberland South; Lord

E. A. C. B. Bruce, second son of the Marquess of Ailesbury, Marl-borough;* Major C. L. C. Bruce, son of the Earl of Elgin, Elgin and Nairn;* Sir R. B. W. Bulkeley, Angleseyshire;* Earl of Brecknock, heir to the Marquess of Camden, Brecon Boroughs;* Hon. C. R. Carrington, heir to Lord Carrington, Wycombe; Lord A. P. Clinton, third son of the Duke of Newcastle, Newark;* Lt-Col. T. P. Crosland, Huddersfield;* Frederick Doulton, Lambeth; Robert W. Duff, Banff Co;* Lord Dunkellin, heir to the Marquess of Clanricarde, Galway Co;* Lord Elcho, heir to the Earl of Wemyss, Haddington Co;* Hon. W. Fitzwilliam, heir to the Earl Fitz-william, Malton;* W. H. Gregory, Galway Co;* Earl Grosvenor, heir to the Marquess of Westminster, Chester;* Lord Richard Grosvenor, son of the Marquess of Westminster, Flintshire;* Hon. G. H. Heathcote, heir to Lord Aveland, Rutlandshire;* Rt. Hon. E. Horsman, nephew to the Earl of Stair, Stroud; Samuel Laing, Wick;* Robert Lowe, Calne;* J. Mackie, Kirkcud-bright Stewart; J. N. McKenna, Youghal;* P. McLagan, Linlithgow Co;* T. Mainwaring, Denbigh; M. H. Marsh, Salisbury; Col. C. H. Packe, Lincolnshire South;* Jonathan Pim, Dublin; E. Saunderson, son-in-law to Lord Farnham, Cavan Co;* T. O. Stock, Carlow;* G. Tomline, Shrewsbury;* Hon. C. R. D. Hanbury-Tracey, second son of Lord Sudeley, Montgomery. The six absent were: M. E. Corbally, Meath Co; A. S. Finlay, Argyle Co; A. W. F. Greville, son-in-law to the Duke of Montrose, Westmeath;* Sir T. D. Lloyd, Cardiganshire; A. Matheson, Inverness; George Traill, Caithness Co. [Traill was ill].
* Seats under strong family influence.

Hansard CLXXXIII, 153-6; *Dod's Parliamentary Companion* 'New Parliament 1865'.

⁵¹ *Hansard* CLXXXIII, 69.

⁵² John, First Earl of Kimberley, 'A Journal of Events During the Glad-stone Ministry 1868-74', ed. Ethel Drus. *Camden Miscellany,* vol. 21, 1958, p. 17.

⁵³ Brand to Russell, 22 April 1866, Russell Papers, P.R.O. 30/22/16.

⁵⁴ Clarendon to Lord A. Loftus, 28 April 1866, MS. Clarendon Dep. C. 145, Bodleian Library; Russell to the Queen, 19, 28 April 1866; the Queen to Russell, 25, 29 April 1866, *L.Q.V.,* vol. 1, pp. 319-24; Granville to General Grey, 24 April 1866, Fitzmaurice, *Granville,* vol. 1, pp. 503-4.

⁵⁵ Sir George Grey to Russell, 29 April 1866, Russell Papers, P.R.O. 30/22/16.

⁵⁶ Milner-Gibson to Bright, 30 April 1866, Bright Papers, B.M. Add. MSS. 43388.

⁵⁷ Gladstone to Russell, 30 April 1866, Russell Papers, P.R.O. 30/22/16.

⁵⁸ Gladstone to Russell, 8 May 1866, Gooch (ed.), *Later Correspondence . . . of Russell,* vol. 2, p. 347.

⁵⁹ Russell to Granville, 30 April 1866, Granville Papers, P.R.O. G.D. 29/18; Gladstone to Russell, 30 April 1866, Russell Papers, P.R.O. 30/22/16; *Hansard* CLXXXIII, 163-72.

III *The Redistribution Bill*

⁶⁰ Brand to Russell, 1 April 1866, Russell Papers, P.R.O. 30/22/16.

⁶¹ Brand to Russell, 1 April 1866, Russell Papers, P.R.O. 30/22/16.

⁶² Sir George Grey to Russell, 5 April 1866, Russell Papers, P.R.O. 30/22/16.

⁶³ Sir George Grey, Cabinet Memo., n.d., [29 April? 1866], Russell Papers, P.R.O. 30/22/16.

64 The Duke of Somerset, Cabinet Memo., 29 April 1866, Russell Papers, P.R.O. 30/22/16; Earl de Grey, Memo., 29 April 1866, Russell Papers, P.R.O. 30/22/16.

65 Duke of Argyll, Cabinet Memo., n.d., [29 April? 1866], Russell Papers, P.R.O. 30/22/16.

66 Sir George Grey, Cabinet Memo., n.d., [29 April? 1866], Russell Papers, P.R.O. 30/22/16.

67 C. P. Villiers, Cabinet Memo., 30 April 1866, Russell Papers, P.R.O. 30/22/16.

68 Brand to Gladstone, 2 May 1866, Gladstone Papers, B.M. Add. MSS. 44193.

69 See p. 35.

70 Brand to Russell, 2 April 1866, Russell Papers, P.R.O. 30/22/16.

71 The following boroughs were to be grouped: Woodstock, Wallingford, Abingdon—2 members; Bodmin, Liskeard, Launceston—2 members; Totnes, Dartmouth, Ashburton—1 member; Bridport, Honiton, Lyme Regis—1 member; Dorchester, Wareham—1 member; Maldon, Harwich—1 member; Cirencester, Tewkesbury, Evesham—2 members; Andover, Lymington—1 member; Ludlow, Leominster—1 member; Eye, Thetford—1 member; Horsham, Midhurst, Petersfield, Arundel—2 members; Chippenham, Malmesbury, Calne—2 members; Westbury, Wells—1 member; Devizes, Marlborough —1 member; Ripon, Knaresborough, Thirsk—2 members; Richmond, Northallerton—1 member; Eight towns under 8,000 were left ungrouped: Bridgnorth, Buckingham, Cockermouth, Hertford, Huntingdon, Lichfield, Marlow, Newport. South Lancashire was to be divided into the West Derby and Salford divisions, each with 3 members. The other 23 seats were distributed as one extra seat to each of the counties and divisions of counties with over 150,000 population: Lincolnshire; Northern Division of Chester; Southern Division of Chester; Western Division of Cornwall; Northern Division of Derby; Northern Division of Devon; Southern Division of Devon; Northern Division of Durham; Southern Division of Durham; Northern Division of Essex; Southern Division of Essex; Eastern Division of Kent; Western Division of Kent; Northern Division of Lancaster; Western Division of Norfolk; Eastern Division of Somerset; Western Division of Somerset; Northern Division of Stafford; Southern Division of Stafford; Eastern Division of Surrey; North Riding of York; Northern Division of West Riding of York; Southern Division of West Riding of York. Middlesex was excluded: 'We do not propose,' explained Gladstone, 'to give to the metropolis the extraordinarily large number of Members which it would be entitled to claim if it were dealt with in respect to its population alone.' *Hansard* CLXXXIII, 193-6.

72 *Hansard* CLXXXIII, 493-6.

73 *Hansard* CLXXXIII, 1555-7.

74 *Hansard* CLXXXIII, 1746-7.

75 Derby to Adderley, 10 May 1866, William S. Childe-Pemberton, *Life of Lord Norton* (London, 1909), p. 194.

76 Baxter to Disraeli, 11 April 1866, Disraeli Papers, B.XI.D.21.

77 Reports from Agents of Boroughs, n.d., [April? 1866], Disraeli Papers, B.XI.F.4; cf. Baxter, *Redistribution of Seats and the Counties.*

78 *Hansard* CLXXXIII, 1620; 1595; 1373.

79 Baxter, *Redistribution*, p. 4.

80 Colleton Rennie to Disraeli, Monday, 14 May [1866], Disraeli Papers, B.XI.D.52.

[81] *The Annual Register,* 1866, p. 184.

[82] It continued at 10 per cent until mid-August and by the end of the year there had still been no real recovery. The crisis coincided with the portent of the first bad harvest of the 1860s, after particularly good ones in 1864 and 1865. There was sporadic unemployment in what had been the boom industries, shipbuilding, engineering and railways. Share prices remained low throughout 1867 and the bank-note did not return to 2 per cent until 1868, *The Annual Register,* 1866; 1867; see also Viscount Goschen, *Essays and Addresses on Economic Questions* (London, 1905), pp. 49-50; T. Wright, *The Bane of a Life,* 3 vols, (London, 1870), describes the impact of the depression on the artisans in the Thames-side shipbuilding industry.

[83] Derby to Disraeli, 'Sunday ev.', [20 May? 1866], Disraeli Papers, '14 Derby'; Earle to Disraeli, 23 May 1866, Disraeli Papers, 'Earle'.

[84] See G. B. Henderson, 'Ralph Anstruther Earle', *Crimean War Diplomacy and Other Historical Essays* (Glasgow, 1947).

[85] Disraeli to Earle, 19 May 1866, M. and B., *Disraeli,* vol. 2, p. 170.

[86] *Hansard* CLXXXIII, 1348.

[87] Disraeli to Earle, [27 May? 1866], M. and B. *Disraeli,* vol. 2, p. 170; cf. T. Erskine May, *A Treatise of the Law, Privileges, and Usage of Parliament* (London, 5th ed., 1863), pp. 262, 365-6.

[88] Earle to Disraeli, [27 May? 1866], Disraeli Papers, 'Earle' (Standing Orders, 1852, 1854).

[89] Denison to Disraeli, 28 May 1866, Disraeli Papers, 'Denison'; see also John Evelyn Denison, *Notes from My Journal* (London, 1900), pp. 196-8.

[90] Erskine May, *Parliament* (6th ed., 1868), p. 465.

[91] *Hansard* CLXXXIII, 1812.

[92] *Hansard* CLXXXIII, 509.

[93] Earle to Disraeli, n.d. [20 May? 1866], Disraeli Papers, 'Earle'.

[94] Derby to Disraeli, 'Tuesday night', [22 May? 1866], Disraeli Papers, '14 Derby'.

[95] Earle to Disraeli, 23 May 1866, Disraeli Papers, 'Earle'.

[96] Walpole to Noel, 25 May 1866, Disraeli Papers, 'Walpole'.

[97] Lord George Gordon Lennox to Disraeli, 9 April 1867, Disraeli Papers, 'Gen. Correspondence', (discussing the Mackinnons' claims on Disraeli for services rendered) and 10 January 1868, (discussing Lord Alfred Clinton's financial straits and his competition with Lennox for the hand of a Rothschild heiress).

[98] Earle to Disraeli, 27 May 1866, Disraeli Papers, 'Earle'.

[99] Earle to Disraeli, 27 May 1866, Disraeli Papers, 'Earle'.

[1] Clay to Earle, 26 May 1866, and Earle to Disraeli [26? May 1866], Disraeli Papers, 'Earle'; Clay to Disraeli, 26 May 1866, Disraeli Papers, 'Clay'.

[2] Taylor to Disraeli, 'Monday night', [28 May? 1866], Disraeli Papers, '14 Derby'.

[3] Cf. Erskine May, *Parliament* (5th ed.), p. 262: 'Withdrawal [of amendments] can only be made without a negative voice, otherwise there must be a division'.

[4] *Hansard* CLXXXIII, 1913-17.

[5] *Hansard* CLXXXIII, 1320.

6 Earle to Disraeli, n.d. [21 May? 1866], Disraeli Papers, 'Earle'.

7 *Hansard* CLXXXIII, 1330.

8 *Hansard* CLXXXIII, 1333, Staniland; 1323-4, Osborne.

9 *Hansard* CLXXXIII, 1344-7. The Liberals were: Hon. A. H. A. Anson; H. B. Baring; W. B. Beaumont; Sir G. Bowyer; Lord J. T. Browne; Lord E. Bruce; Sir M. J. Cholmeley; J. Clay; Lord A. P. Clinton; G. Clive; F. Doulton; Lord Elcho; H. J. Foley; Capt. R. W. Grosvenor; A. Hayter; Hon. G. W. Heathcote; E. Heneage; E. Horsman; R. Lowe; T. Mainwaring; M. H. Marsh; T. A. Mitchell, R. B. Osborne; Sir R. Peel; R. B. Sheridan; M. Stanliland. This division was the only occasion in the Reform debates of 1866 when Bowyer, Clay, Capt. Grosvenor, Hayter, Mitchell, Osborne and Stanliland voted against the Government. While the Elcho-Lowe group voted solidly for the amendment, most of the 'Grosvenor gang' voted for the Government: Earl Grosvenor; R. M. Biddulph; T. P. Crosland; Sir E. C. Dering, R. W. Duff, A. S. Finlay, Hon. C. W. W. Fitzwilliam, W. H. Gregory, Lord R. Grosvenor, Col. G. M. Packe and E. Saunderson.

10 Gladstone to Russell, 28 May 1866, Gladstone Papers, B.M. Add. MSS. 44293.

11 *Hansard* CLXXXIII, 1323.

12 *Birmingham Daily Post,* 11 June 1866, W. H. White; see also *Hansard* CLXXXIV, 668, Earl Granville.

13 *Hansard* CLXXXIII, 2057-75.

14 Adullamites who voted with the Opposition: Hon. A. H. A. Anson; H. B. Baring; Sir M. J. Cholmeley; Lord A. P. Clinton; Lord Elcho; Hon. C. W. W. Fitzwilliam; Earl Grosvenor; Lord R. Grosvenor; Hon. G. H. Heathcote; E. Horsman; R. Lowe; G. Tomline. Adullamites who voted with the Government: W. B. Beaumont; R. M. Biddulph; M. Biddulph; Lord J. T. Browne; Lord C. Bruce; Hon. C. R. Carrington; Lord E. P. Clinton T. P. Crosland; Sir E. C. Dering; F. Doulton; R. W. Duff; Lord Dunkellin; A. S. Finlay; W. H. Gregory; E. Heneage; J. Mackie; P. McLagan; M. H. Marsh; Col. G. M. Packe; J. Pim; R. B. Sheridan; *Hansard* CLXXXIII, 2072-4.

15 *Hansard* CLXXXIII, 2075-83.

16 *Hansard* CLXXXIII, 2083 ff., Villiers; 2110 ff., Sir George Grey.

17 *Hansard* CLXXXIII, 2043 ff.

18 *Hansard* CLXXXIII, 2102-10.

19 *Hansard* CLXXXIII, 2129-33. The majorities given by Monypenny and Buckle for this division, and for that on Stanley's motion, are incorrect. M. and B., *Disraeli,* vol. 2, p. 171.

20 Hon. A. H. A. Anson; H. Baring; R. M. Biddulph;* M. Biddulph;* Lord J. T. Browne;* Lord E. Bruce; Maj. C. Bruce; Sir R. Bulkeley; Hon. C. R. Carrington; Sir M. J. Cholmeley; Lord A. P. Clinton; G. Clive; Lord Dunkellin;* Lord Elcho; Hon. C. W. W. Fitzwilliam; R. Fort; W. H. Gregory;* Earl Grosvenor; Lord R. Grosvenor; Hon. G. H. Heathcote; R. Lowe; M. H. Marsh; Col. G. M. Packe;* E. Saunderson; G. Tomline.
* County members who had previously voted with the Government.

21 *Hansard* CLXXXIV, 176 ff.

22 13 and 14 Vict. c. 69.

23 *Hansard* CLXXXIV, 386.

24 Julia Cartwright (ed.), *The Journal of Lady Knightley of Fawsley* (London, 1915), p. 123, 12 June 1866. Newdegate was returned top of the poll in 1868 and went on to hold the county till 1885. Mordaunt retired in 1868 in favour of John Hardy.

[25] Baxter had sorted the county occupiers into six groups, as follows:

	Counties	Towns and Parishes above 5,000	Proportion
£14 and under £20	101,000	36,000	1/3
£20 and under £50	185,000	61,000	1/3
£50 and upwards	202,000	36,000	1/6

'It may be taken,' he wrote, 'that the larger the town the less likely it is to be Conservative. I found this from an analysis of all the English Boroughs. . . . The smaller the place the more agricultural and Conservative.

Hence the *least* Conservative parts are the Towns of 5,000 and upwards population. . . . But the more Rent a man pays the more likely he is to be Conservative. And the £20 to £50 occupiers, even in the 5,000 Towns, are likely to have a Conservative majority. Hence we need only fear the £14 to £20 occupiers in those towns. But they are only 1/3rd of the total occupiers of that class. And the remaining 2/3rds are in Conservative districts and likely to be Conservative than Liberal.

Again, rents are low in small towns . . . £14 to £20 is paid in them by persons who in large towns pay £20 to £30. Hence the £14 to £20 occupiers in small towns are the equals in social position and Conservative feeling of those who pay £20 to £30 in large towns.

On these considerations I think we ought to agree to the £14 franchise for . . . we are likely to be more strengthened by the rural 2/3rds of the £14 to £20 franchise than weakened by the town 1/3rd. . . . East Sussex was carried against us last election solely by the Brighton freeholders. In every other polling district the Conservatives had a majority. By this Bill East Sussex will register 60% of 2700 £14 to £50 occupiers, of whom only 281 (those at Eastbourne) are in a town above 5,000 . . . and we shall carry any election to a certainty.' Baxter also forecast a Conservative victory in the South West Riding if the franchise were reduced and Dewsbury and the suburbs of Huddlesfield were excised.

[26] They were: Hon A. H. A. Anson; W. B. Beaumont; R. M. Biddulph; Lord E. Bruce; Maj. C. Bruce; Sir R. Bulkeley; Sir M. J. Cholmeley; Lord A. P. Clinton; Lord E. P. Clinton; Sir E. C. Dering; R. W. Duff; Lord Dunkellin; Lord Elcho; A. S. Finlay; Hon. C. W. W. Fitzwilliam; Earl Grosvenor; Lord R. Grosvenor; Hon. G. H. Heathcote; R. Lowe; J. Mackie; P. McLagan; M. H. Marsh; Col. G. M. Packe; R. B. Sheridan; G. Tomline; *Hansard* CLXXXIV, 405-7.

[27] *Hansard* CLXXXIV, 409-10.

[28] *Hansard* CLXXXIV, 418-21.

[29] *Hansard* CLXXXIV, 423, McLaren.

[30] *Hansard* CLXXXIV, 426.

[31] *Hansard* CLXXXIV, 445; see also *Illustrated London News*, 23 June 1866.

[32] Derby to Disraeli, 10 June 1866, Disraeli Papers, '14 Derby'.

[33] It was still very extensive in 1868; cf. A. F. Thompson, 'Gladstone's Whips and the General Election of 1868', *English Historical Review*, vol. LXXIII, 1948.

[34] *Hansard* CLXXXIV, 558-9, Gladstone.

[35] The gross estimated rental was 'the Rent at which the same [Hereditaments] might reasonably be expected to let from Year to Year, free of all usual Tenants Rates and Taxes, and Tithe Commutation Rent charge, if

any, and deducting therefrom the probable average Cost of the Repairs, Insurance, and other Expenses, if any, necessary to maintain them in a State to command such Rent . . .' 6 and 7 Will. c. 96, Section 1.

36 *Hansard* CLXXXIV, 553, Gladstone.

37 *Hansard* CLXXXIV, 576-7, Hibbert.

38 *Hansard* CLXXXIV, 578; cf. Powell, 582-5.

39 *Hansard* CLXXXIV, 629; 635-6.

40 *Hansard* CLXXXIV, 686, 26 June 1866.

41 H. C. E. Childers to Lord Clarence Paget, 2 July 1866, Spencer Childers, *Life and Correspondence of the Right Hon. Hugh C. E. Childers, 1827-96,* 2 vols, (London, 1901), vol. 1, p. 138.

42 Morley, *Gladstone,* vol. 2, p. 206.

43 Liberals who supported Dunkellin, but had not voted with Grosvenor: R. M. Biddulph—Denbighshire; Sir R. Blennerhasset—Galway; Lord J. T. Browne—Mayo (Dunkellin's cousin); Sir M. J. Cholmelely—North Lincolnshire; Lord E. P. Clinton—North Nottinghamshire; Sir E. C. Dering—East Kent; A. S. Finlay—Argyllshire; H. J. Foley and W. O. Foster—South Staffordshire; J. Goldsmid—Honiton; E. Heneage—Lincoln; E. McEvoy—Meath; Sir R. Peel—Tamworth; J. Pritchard—Bridgnorth; R. B. Sheridan—Dorchester; *Hansard* CLXXXIV, 639-41.

44 John, Earl Russell, *Recollections and Suggestions, 1813-1873* (London, 1875), p. 289.

IV   *The Resignation of the Government*

45 Russell to Clarendon, 31 May [1866], MS. Clar. Dep. C.93. MS. Film 468.

46 Brand to Russell, 3 June 1866, Hampden Papers.

47 Russell to Brand, 3 June [1866], Hampden Papers.

48 Gladstone to Russell, 4 June 1866, in Gooch (ed.), *Later Correspondence . . . of Russell,* vol. 2, p. 350.

49 Gladstone to Russell, 4 June 1866, Gladstone Papers, B.M. Add. MSS. 44293; Russell to Gladstone, 4 June 1866, Gladstone Papers, B.M. Add. MSS. 44293; Gladstone to Russell, 4 June 1866, Russell Papers, P.R.O. 30/22/16.

50 Granville to Gladstone, 11 June 1866, Fitzmaurice, *Granville,* vol. 1, pp. 506-7.

51 Gladstone to Russell, 11 June 1866, Russell Papers, P.R.O. 30/22/16.

52 Gladstone to Granville, and Russell to Granville, 13 June 1866. (Granville was the intermediary between Lansdowne and the Cabinet.) Fitzmaurice, *Granville,* vol. 1, p. 507.

53 Russell to Clarendon, 13 June 1866, MS. Clar. Dep. C.93 MS. Film 468.

54 Gladstone to Russell, 13 June 1866, Russell Papers, P.R.O. 30/22/16.

55 Queen Victoria to Earl Russell, 19 June 1866, *L.Q.V.* pp. 334-5.

56 Queen Victoria to Earl Russell, 20 June 1866, *L.Q.V.* pp. 335-6.

57 Gladstone to Russell, 20 June 1866, Russell Papers, P.R.O. 30/22/16.

58 Brand to Russell, 20 June 1866, Russell Papers, P.R.O. 30/22/16.

59 Russell to Lord Grey, 20 June 1866, Gladstone Papers, B.M. Add. MSS. 44293.

60 Gladstone to Russell, 20 June 1866, Russell Papers, P.R.O. 30/22/16.

61 Gladstone Papers, B.M. Add. MSS. 44411.

62 William Mackay, Chairman of the Haddington Parliamentary Reform Association, to Gladstone, 6 June 1866, B.M. Add. MSS. 44410.

63 Gladstone to Russell, 21 June 1866, Russell Papers, P.R.O. 30/22/16.

64 *Manchester Examiner,* 23 June 1866; see also J. F. Maguire to Gladstone, 21 June 1866, Gladstone Papers, B.M. Add. MSS. 44411.

65 Bright to Gladstone, 24 June 1866, Gladstone Papers, B.M. Add. MSS. 44112.

66 Charles Buxton to Gladstone, 22 June 1866, Gladstone Papers, B.M. Add. MSS. 44411.

67 H. H. Vivian to Gladstone, 25 June 1866, Gladstone Papers, B.M. Add. MSS. 44411.

68 T. D. Acland to Gladstone, n.d., [22? June 1866], Gladstone Papers, B.M. Add. MSS. 44092; Brand to Russell, 25 June 1866, Russell Papers, P.R.O. 30/22/16.

69 Brand to Russell, 23 June 1866, Russell Papers, P.R.O. 30/22/16.

70 Gladstone to Russell, 23 June 1866, in Gooch (ed.), *Later Correspondence . . . of Russell,* vol. 2, p. 352.

71 General Grey to Russell, 23 June 1866, Russell Papers, P.R.O. 30/22/16.

72 Drafts in Halifax Papers, 'Thursday', [21 June? 1866], B.M. Add. MSS. 49561.

73 Sir George Grey to Russell, 24 June 1866, Russell Papers, P.R.O. 30/22/16.

74 Russell to Brand, 23 June 1866, Hampden Papers; Brand to Russell, 24 June 1866, Russell Papers, P.R.O. 30/22/16.

75 Brand to Russell, 24 June 1866, Russell Papers, P.R.O. 30/22/16.

76 Sir George Grey to Russell, 24 June 1866, Russell Papers, P.R.O. 30/22/16.

77 Brand to Gladstone, 24 June 1866, Gladstone Papers, B.M. Add. MSS. 44193.

78 Brand to Russell, 25 June 1866, Russell Papers, P.R.O. 30/22/16.

79 Brand to Sir George Grey, 24 June 1866 [Draft] Hampden Papers. 'I think that we may settle . . . upon a Resolution in the terms of the enclosed —I have sent copies to Ld R. & Gladstone . . . & if they approve (as I cannot doubt) I shall place it in Crawford's hands'.

80 Earle to Disraeli n.d., [25 June? 1866], Disraeli Papers, 'Earle'.

81 Gladstone to Brand, 24 June 1866, Hampden Papers, Brand to Russell, 25 June 1866, Russell Papers, P.R.O. 30/22/16, Memorandum by Queen Victoria of conversation with Russell, 26 June 1866. *L.Q.V.* p. 339.

82 Russell to Sir G. Grey, (Draft) 'Evening', 25 June [1866], Halifax Papers, B.M. Add. MSS. 49561.

83 He apparently confused E. H. J. Craufurd, M.P. for Ayr, with R. W. Crawford, M.P. for London. The latter was to move the motion; another sympton of the aloofness of the Cabinet?

84 Clarendon to Russell, 25 June 1866, MS. Clar. Dep. C. 143.

85 Queen Victoria to Earl Russell, 26 June 1866, *L.Q.V.* p. 342.

5 THE REFORM BILL OF 1867

I *The Conservative Government and the Hyde Park Riots*

1 E.g. Lord A. P. Clinton to Disraeli, 9 September [1866], 28 October 1866, 'My ambition is to be in office, under the leadership of yourself & Lord Derby'. Derby had already ignored an earlier application from him. Clinton's endeavour to marry a Rothschild heiress also failed, after her father rejected him with a 'most paltry excuse' and refused to pay his debts. Clinton then applied for 'any Colonial Governorship that was vacant' and recalled his 'faithful service' as an Adullamite. He failed in this ambition too. Clinton to Disraeli, 15 September 1867; Clinton to Disraeli, 13 March 1868; see also Sir George Bowyer to Disraeli, 5 July 1866, Disraeli Papers, 'Clinton', 'Bowyer'.

2 Stafford Northcote, Diary, 3 February [1866], Lang, *Northcote,* pp. 138-9.

3 Northcote, Diary, 22 February [1866], Iddesleigh Papers, B.M. Add. MSS. 50063A.

4 Northcote, Diary, 3 February [1866], Lang, *Northcote,* p. 139.

5 Derby to Disraeli, 22 or 23 June 1866; quoting Grosvenor to Wilton, Monypenny and Buckle, *Disraeli,* vol. 2, p. 173.

6 Derby to Disraeli, reporting conversation with Elcho, n.d. [23 June? 1866], Disraeli Papers, '14 Derby', cf. Malmesbury, Diary, 27 June 1866, *Memoirs,* vol. 2, p. 357.

7 Earle to Disraeli, n.d. [24 or 25 June? 1866], Disraeli Papers, 'Earle'. M. and B., *Disraeli,* vol. 2, p. 175.

8 Disraeli to Derby, 25 June 1866. M. and B., *Disraeli,* vol. 2, p. 174.

9 Disraeli to Derby, 23 June 1866. M. and B., *Disraeli,* vol. 2, p. 174.

10 M. and B., *Disraeli,* vol. 2, p. 180; see also Gavin Burns Henderson, 'Ralph Anstruther Earle', *Crimean War Diplomacy and Other Historical Essays.*

11 Memorandum by the Earl of Derby, 28 June 1866, *L.Q.V.* p. 345.

12 Derby to Clarendon, 28 June 1866, Maxwell, *Clarendon,* vol. 2, p. 317. Stafford Northcote, Diary, 29 June 1866, Iddesleigh Papers, B.M. Add. MSS. 50063A.

13 Memorandum by Lord Derby, 29 June [1866], Disraeli Papers, '14 Derby'. Stafford Northcote, Diary, 29 June 1866, Iddesleigh Papers, B.M. Add. MSS. 50063A. Gregory, *Autobiography,* p. 245.

14 Derby to Disraeli, 30 June 1866, Disraeli Papers, '14 Derby'. The assertion (*Complete Peerage,* vol. 2, p. 79n.d.(5)), that Lansdowne's death had a determining influence on the course of events, is unlikely. The negotiations between Derby and Lansdowne had failed several days before the latter's sudden paralysis and death on 5 July.

15 Disraeli to Derby, 25 June 1866, M. and B., *Disraeli,* vol. 2, p. 174.

16 M. and B., *Disraeli,* vol. 2, p. 18.

17 Taylor to Disraeli, 'Wednesday night', [27 June? 1866], Disraeli Papers, 'Taylor'; see also M. and B., *Disraeli,* vol. 2, p. 175.

18 Northcote to Carnarvon, 25 June 1866, Hardinge, *Carnarvon,* vol. 1, p. 283.

19 M. and B., *Disraeli,* vol. 2, p. 177.

20 Stafford Northcote, Diary, 4 July [1866], Iddesleigh Papers, B.M. Add. MSS. 50063A.

21 Earle to Disraeli, n.d. [25 June? 1866], Disraeli Papers, 'Earle'.

22 *Annual Register,* 1866, pp. 182-3. *The Times,* 23, 27 July 1866.

23 M. Arnold, *Culture and Anarchy* (Cambridge, 1950). First published in the *Cornhill Magazine,* January, February, June, July, September 1868. The 'Introduction' and 'Sweetness and Light' were first given as 'Culture and its Enemies' in May 1867, as Arnold's concluding lecture as Professor of Poetry at Oxford.

24 Gillespie, *Labour and Politics,* pp. 238 ff. (Lancashire Reform Conference); E. R. Jones, *Life and Speeches of Joseph Cowen M.P.* (London, [1886]), pp. 23-30, (Northern Reform Union); W. Robertson, *Life . . . of . . . John Bright* (London, 1883), pp. 383-4, (Leeds Working Men's Parliamentary Reform Association); A. W. Humphrey, *Life of Robert Applegarth* (London, [1913]), pp. 57-8, (London Manhood Suffrage and Vote by Ballot Association).

25 *Annual Register,* 1864, pp. 49-50.

26 H. Evans, *Sir Randal Cremer, His Life and Work* (London, 1909), pp. 43-4; H. Broadhurst M.P., *The Story of His Life told by Himself* (London, 1901), pp. 35-7; also S. Coltham, 'George Potter, the Junta, and the Beehive', *International Review of Social History,* vol. 9, part 3, 1964, pp. 391-432.

27 G. J. Holyoake, *Sixty Years of an Agitator's Life,* 2 vols, (London, 1906), vol. 2, pp. 48-57. Somewhat the same trouble occurred then as in 1866 and 1867. The Government resigned before the meeting was held, whereupon the committee tried to call it off, but was forced to go on with it when the crowds continued to arrive.

28 Manners, Journal, 22 July [1866], C. Whibley, *Lord John Manners and His Friends,* 2 vols, (Edinburgh, 1925), vol. 2, p. 117.

29 'Opinions of Law Officers on Meetings in Hyde Park', [28 July? 1866], Disraeli Papers, B.XI.H.23a.

30 H. B. Bonner, *Charles Bradlaugh, a Record of His Life and Work,* 2 vols, (London, 1895), vol. 1, p. 223.

31 Bright to George Howell, 19 July 1866, Leech, *Public Letters of . . . John Bright,* pp. 90-1; see also A. Miall, *Life of Edward Miall* (London, 1884), p. 260.

32 Frost, *Forty Years Recollections,* pp. 309-10; Evans, *Cremer,* p. 44; L. Blanc, *Dix Ans de l'histoire D'Angle-terre,* 10 vols, (Paris, 1880), vol. 6, p. 265; *Hansard* CLXXXIV, 1408 ff.; *The Hyde Park Cases, 1866; Report of the Reform League Investigating Committee* (London, 1866).

33 Whibley, *Manners,* Journal [26? July 1866], pp. 117-18.

34 Broadhurst, *Autobiography,* p. 40; M. and B., *Disraeli,* vol. 2, p. 186.

35 Holyoake, *Sixty Years . . . ,* vol. 2, p. 186-90; Whibley, *Manners,* vol. 2, pp. 118-19. The story was revived in the celebrated *Punch* cartoon: 'Walpole is a Noodle—Beales is a Bully', after the League successfully challenged the Government over the right to meet in the Park in May 1867. See *Punch,* 18 May 1867.

36 Whibley, *Manners,* vol. 2, pp. 118-19; Holyoake, *Sixty Years . . . ,* vol. 2, pp. 186-7; *The Times,* 26 July 1866.

37 *The Times,* 25 July 1866.

38 Quoted by Derby, *Hansard* CLXXXIV, 1493.

39 *D.N.B.,* 'Walpole', vol. xx, 667.

40 J. S. Mill, *Autobiography* (London, 1873), pp. 290-1; *The Times,* 28 July 1866.

41 *Working Man,* 4 August 1866.

42 Evans, *Cremer,* p. 45.

43 *Working Man,* 4 August 1866.

44 Quoted by Asa Briggs, *Victorian People,* p. 206.

45 *English Leader,* 28 July 1866; see also Joseph McCabe, *Life and Letters of George Jacob Holyoake,* 2 vols, (London, 1908), vol. 2, p. 27.

46 Emily Eden to Lord Clarendon, July 1866, Maxwell, *Clarendon,* vol. 2, p. 321.

47 Disraeli to Derby, 29 July 1866, M. and B., *Disraeli,* vol. 2, pp. 186-7.

48 *Hansard* CLXXXIV, 1143-4; see also *Illustrated London News,* 28 July 1866.

II *The Resolutions*

49 Derby to Disraeli, 16 September 1866, Jones, *Lord Derby,* pp. 296-7.

50 *Hansard* CLXXXVIII, 1783.

51 Disraeli to Derby, 24 September 1866, M. and B., *Disraeli,* vol. 2, p. 188.

52 Cranborne to Disraeli, 25 September [1866], Salisbury Papers, 'Disraeli'.

53 Derby to Disraeli, 27 September 1866, Disraeli Papers, '14 Derby'.

54 Derby to Disraeli, 9 October 1866, Disraeli Papers, '14 Derby'.

55 Disraeli to Derby, 12 October 1866, M. and B., *Disraeli,* vol. 2, p. 188.

56 Ibid.

57 Carnarvon, Journal, 8 November 1866, Hardinge, *Carnarvon,* vol. 1, p. 336.

58 Lady Gwendolen Cecil, *Life of Robert, Marquis of Salisbury,* 4 vols, (London, 1921-32), vol. 1, p. 218; Hardinge, *Carnarvon,* vol. 1, pp. 340-1; Martin, *Sherbrooke,* vol. 2, p. 309.

59 Carnarvon, Memorandum of conversation, 27 October 1866, Hardinge, *Carnarvon,* vol. 1, p. 334.

60 Disraeli to Cranborne, 26 December 1866, Cecil, *Salisbury,* vol. 1, p. 214.

61 Derby to Disraeli, 30 October 1866, Disraeli Papers, '14 Derby'.

62 Queen Victoria to Lord Derby, 28 October 1866, M. and B., *Disraeli,* vol. 2, pp. 191-2; Stafford Northcote to Disraeli, 17 October 1866, M. and B., *Disraeli,* vol. 2, p. 190.

63 Derby to Disraeli, 19 October 1866, M. and B., *Disraeli,* vol. 2, p. 193.

64 Disraeli to Stafford Northcote, 22 October 1866, M. and B., *Disraeli,* vol. 2, p. 191; cf. Disraeli to Cranborne, 26 December 1866, Cecil, *Salisbury,* vol. 1, p. 214, 'the Whigs are very unanimous in wishing the question settled—but you and I are not Whigs'.

65 Carnarvon, Memorandum of conversation, 27 October 1866, Hardinge, *Carnarvon,* vol. 1, p. 334.

66 Disraeli to Derby, 18 November 1866, M. and B., *Disraeli,* vol. 2, p. 194.

67 Derby to Disraeli, [18 November?] 1866, Disraeli Papers, '14 Derby'.

68 'Resolutions Provisionally adopted, Nov. 8, 1866', Disraeli Papers, '14 Derby'.

69 Derby to Disraeli, 22 December [1866], Disraeli Papers, '14 Derby'.

70 Barnett Smith, *Bright,* vol. 2, p. 216.

71 Robertson, *Bright,* pp. 433-4.

72 Scottish Reform League, *Great Reform Demonstrations at Glasgow, 16th October 1866* (Glasgow, 1866).

73 Wemyss Reid, *Memoirs,* p. 113.

74 Thorold Rogers (ed.), *Speeches of the Right Hon. John Bright on Parliamentary Reform,* 2 vols, (London, 1869), p. 386.

75 J. Sullivan, 'The Banner of Victory's Car', adapted from the song translated from the French by M. F. Tupper, Howell Collection.

76 Speech at Albion Hotel, Manchester, 25 September 1866, *Speeches on Parliamentary Reform,* p. 20.

77 Gladstone to Brand, 30 October 1866, Morley, *Gladstone,* vol. 2, p. 222.

78 Quoted by Bright in speech at Manchester, 25 September 1866, *Speeches on Parliamentary Reform,* p. 18.

79 J. Arthur Partridge to J. S. Mill, 1 August 1866; Mill to Partridge, draft, n.d., Mill-Taylor Collection, vol. 1.

80 Secretary of the Manchester Branch of the Reform Union to Brand, 17 September 1866; Draft of Brand's reply, 3 October 1866, Hampden Papers.

81 Sir George Grey to Brand, 12 October 1866, Hampden Papers.

82 Russell to Amberley, 31 August 1866, Bertrand and Patricia Russell (eds), *The Amberley Papers,* 2 vols, (London, 1937), vol. 1, p. 540.

83 Brand to Russell, 28 August 1866, Hampden Papers.

84 Reported by Lord Houghton to his wife, 21 November 1866, Reid, *Houghton,* vol. 2, p. 158.

85 Kate's Journal, 28 November 1866, *The Amberley Papers,* vol. 1, p. 530.

86 *Globe,* 4 December 1866.

87 Lennox to Disraeli, '1.5 p.m.', 3 December 1866, Disraeli Papers, 'Lennox'.

88 *Morning Advertiser,* 4 December 1866, Cutting, Disraeli Papers, 'Reform'.

89 *Daily News,* 4 December 1866, Disraeli Papers, 'Newspaper Cuttings 1866'.

90 Pakington to Disraeli, 4 December 1866, Disraeli Papers, 'Pakington'.

91 Derby to Pakington, 4 December 1866, Pakington MSS. M/P/88.

92 W. N. Denison to G. S. Beecroft, 12 December 1866, G. S. Beecroft to Disraeli, 14 December 1866, Disraeli Papers, B.XI.J.60.

93 Stanley to Disraeli, 2 January 1867, M. and B., *Disraeli,* vol. 2, p. 220.

94 Corry to Disraeli, 2 January 1867, M. and B., *Disraeli,* vol. 2, p. 220.

95 Disraeli to Cranborne, 26 December 1866, Cecil, *Salisbury,* vol. 1, p. 214.

96 D. B.[axter], 'Memorandum on Plurality of Votes' n.d., [January?] 1867, Disraeli Papers, B.XI.G.47.

97 Lord John Manners, 'Memo on Resolutions', 16 January 1867, Disraeli Papers, 'Manners'.

98 Lord Cranborne, 'Memo on Resolutions', 15 January 1867, Disraeli Papers, 'Cranborne'; see also B.XI.J.203.

⁹⁹ Lord Naas, 'Memo' n.d. [16 January?] 1867, Disraeli Papers, B.XI.J.202.

¹ Sir Stafford Northcote, 'Memo on Reform', 16 January 1867, Disraeli Papers, 'Northcote'.

² Sir Stafford Northcote, 'Memo on Resolution', 3 January 1867, Disraeli Papers, 'Northcote'.

³ Cranborne to Disraeli, 1 February 1867, Salisbury Papers, 'Disraeli'.

⁴ Cranborne to Disraeli, 1 February 1867, Cecil, *Salisbury*, vol. 1, p. 224.

⁵ Carnarvon to Disraeli, 2 February 1867, Hardinge, *Carnarvon*, vol. 1, p. 341.

⁶ The system worked under four separate Acts: Sturges Bournes Act of 1818 allowed one vote for each £25 rating, up to six votes; the Poor Law Act of 1834 incorporated Sturges Bourne's provisions for owners, and allowed occupiers one vote for each £200 rating up to three votes: as each owner could vote in both capacities, the highest possible number of votes was nine; the Public Health Act of 1848 and the Local Government Act of 1858 each allowed one vote for each £50 rating up to six votes; and the same for occupiers, thus permitting a maximum of twelve votes.

⁷ D. B[axter], 'Memorandum on Plurality of Votes', n.d. [January?] 1867, Disraeli Papers, B.XI.G.47.

⁸ Ibid.

⁹ Derby to Disraeli, 2 February 1867, M. and B., *Disraeli*, vol. 2, p. 223.

¹⁰ Pakington to Disraeli, 1 February 1867, Disraeli Papers, 'Pakington'.

¹¹ Disraeli to Derby, 4 February 1867, M. and B., *Disraeli*, vol. 2, p. 224.

¹² Cranborne-Carnarvon Memorandum, Cecil, *Salisbury*, vol. 1, p. 222. 'Your attention will be again called to the State of the Representation of the People in Parliament; and I trust that your Deliberations, conducted in a Spirit of Moderation and mutual Forbearance, may lead to the Adoption of Measures which, without unduly disturbing the Balance of political Power, shall freely extend the Elective Franchise'. *Hansard* CLXXXV, 6; cf. M. and B., *Disraeli*, vol. 2, p. 225.

¹³ Hardinge, *Carnarvon*, vol. 1, p. 342.

¹⁴ Disraeli to Derby, 4 February 1867, M. and B., *Disraeli*, vol. 2, p. 224.

¹⁵ *Hansard* CLXXXV, 67-74.

¹⁶ Resolution in Derby's Hand; marked by [Corry?] 'Altered in Cabinet Wed. February 6', Disraeli Papers, B.XI.J.204a.

¹⁷ General Peel to Disraeli, 7 February 1867, Disraeli Papers, 'Peel'.

¹⁸ Disraeli to Derby, 7 February 1867, M. and B., *Disraeli*, vol. 2, pp. 225-6.

¹⁹ Disraeli to Derby, Thursday [7 February?] 1867, M. and B., *Disraeli*, vol. 2, p. 226.

²⁰ *Hansard* CLXXXV, 214 ff.

²¹ Malmesbury, *Memoirs*, vol. 2, p. 365.

²² *Hansard* CLXXXV, 243-9.

III *Lurching into Reform: the Household Suffrage and Ten Minute Bills*

²³ *Hansard* CLXXXV, 337.

²⁴ *Hansard* CLXXXV, 338-9.

²⁵ Cranborne-Carnarvon Memorandum, Cecil, *Salisbury*, vol. 1, p. 227.

[26] M. and B., *Disraeli*, vol. 2, p. 229.

[27] Disraeli, Draft of letter to Queen recording the conversation [16? February 1867], M. and B., *Disraeli*, vol. 2, p. 229.

[28] Elizabeth Longford, *Victoria R.I.* (London, 1964), p. 352.

[29] M. and B., *Disraeli*, vol. 2, pp. 229-30.

[30] Cecil, *Salisbury,* vol. 1, pp. 229-30.

[31] 'Journal', Saturday, 16 February 1867, Hardinge, *Carnarvon*, vol. 1, p. 344; cf. Malmesbury, *Memoirs*, vol. 2, p. 365.

[32] Hardinge, *Carnarvon*, vol. 1, p. 345.

[33] Diary, 20 February 1867, *Cranbrook*, vol. 1, p. 199.

[34] Carnarvon, 'Journal', 21 February 1867, Hardinge, *Carnarvon*, vol. 1, p. 345.

[35] Corry to Disraeli, 22 February 1867, Disraeli Papers, B.XI.J.4.

[36] [G. Ward Hunt?] to Disraeli, Friday, 22 February [1867], Disraeli Papers, B.XI.J.71.

[37] A. Millikin to Corry, 23 February 1867, Disraeli Papers, B.XI.G.8.; see also *P.P.*, 1867, vol. LVI, 'Number of Savings Bank Depositors in England and Wales'.

[38] 'Secret draft of Reform Bill', and Minutes, n.d., Disraeli Papers, B.XI.H.25.

[39] *P.P.*, 1861, vol. XXXIV, no. 509.

[40] 'Memorandum of No. of Males paying 20/- in direct Taxes', n.d., also 'Memo of Direct Taxation Clauses in 1852 and 1854 Bills', Disraeli Papers, B.XI.H.14,15 and B.XI.G.30,50.

[41] Baxter, 'Confidential Cabinet Memorandum on the Suffrage', n.d., Disraeli Papers, B.XI.E.13[i].

[42] Disraeli to Derby, 4 February 1867, M. and B., *Disraeli*, vol. 2, p. 224.

[43] A. J. Murray to Derby, Camberwell, 26 January 1867, Disraeli Papers, B.XI.J.65.

[44] Gibbs, *Parliamentary Reform* . . . [March] 1866; Disraeli Papers, B.XI.G.2.

[45] Gibbs, *Parliamentary Reform* . . . (3rd ed.), 5 March 1867.

[46] Hardinge, *Carnarvon*, vol. 1, pp. 345-6.

[47] M. and B., *Disraeli*, vol. 2, p. 232.

[48] Cranborne to Carnarvon, 22 February 1867, Hardinge, *Carnarvon*, vol. 1, p. 346.

[49] Carnarvon, 'Notes', 24 February 1867, Hardinge, *Carnarvon*, vol. 1, p. 347.

[50] Cranborne to Derby, 'Sunday evening', [24 February 1867], M. and B., *Disraeli*, vol. 2, p. 233.

[51] M. and B., *Disraeli*, vol. 2, p. 232; Disraeli to Derby, 25 February 1867, M. and B., *Disraeli*, vol. 2, p. 234.

[52] Baxter to Derby, 28 February 1867, Disraeli Papers, B.XI.J.74.

[53] Carnarvon, Journal, Monday, 25 February 1867, Hardinge, *Carnarvon*, vol. 1, pp. 348-9.

[54] Manners, Journal, 26 February [1867], Whibley, *Manners*, vol. 2, p. 123.

[55] T. E. Kebbel, *Life of Lord Beaconsfield* (London, 1888), p. 112; *Hansard* CLXXXV, 954-6.

56 *Hansard* CLXXXV, 970.

57 *Hansard* CLXXXV, 990-1.

58 Stanley to Disraeli, 26 February 1867, Disraeli Papers, '15 Derby'.

59 Derby to Disraeli, '10 p.m.', 26 February [1867], Disraeli Papers, '14 Derby'; Disraeli to Derby, 27 February 1867, M. and B., *Disraeli*, vol. 2, pp. 240-1.

60 Carnarvon, 'Journal', Hardinge, *Carnarvon*, p. 349.

61 *Hansard* CLXXXV, 1021-4.

62 E.g. *Hansard* CLXXXVIII, 1606, 15 July 1867; Speech at Edinburgh Banquet, 29 October 1867, in T. E. Kebbel, *Selected Speeches of the late the Right Honourable The Earl of Beaconsfield*, 2 vols, (London, 1882), vol. 1, p. 479.

63 T. E. Kebbel, *Lord Beaconsfield and other Tory Memories* (London, 1907), p. 87.

64 S. R. Graves, 'Memorandum', M. and B., *Disraeli*, vol. 2, p. 237.

65 R[ichard] P. L[ong] to Disraeli, n.d. [1 March? 1867], Disraeli Papers, B.XI.J.205.

66 M. and B., *Disraeli*, vol. 2, p. 242.

67 Banks Stanhope to Taylor (to be sent to Derby), 13 March 1867, Disraeli Papers, 'Banks Stanhope'.

68 T. Mainwaring to Lord John Manners, n.d. enclosure with Manners to Disraeli, 28 February 1867; also Baxter to Derby (reporting views of Grosvenor and Elcho), 28 February 1867, Disraeli Papers, B.XI.J.74.

69 Queen Victoria to Lord Derby, 28 February 1867, M. and B., *Disraeli*, vol. 2, p. 243; Queen Victoria, 'Journal', 27 February 1867, *L.Q.V.*, p. 402.

70 Baxter to Derby, 28 February 1867, Disraeli Papers, B.XI.J.74.

71 Derby to Cranborne, 1 March 1867, Cranborne to Derby, draft 1 March [1867], Salisbury Papers, 'Stanley'.

72 Sir Henry Edwards to Disraeli, 2 March [1867], Disraeli Papers, B.XI.J.77.

73 Lord John Manners to Disraeli, 27 February 1867, Whibley, *Manners*, vol. 2, pp. 123-6.

74 Manners, 'Journal', Saturday, 2 March [1867], Whibley, *Manners*, vol. 2, p. 126; Carnarvon, 'Notes', 2 March 1867, Hardinge, *Carnarvon*, vol. 1, p. 350.

75 Disraeli to Derby, 26 February 1867, M. and B., *Disraeli*, vol. 2, p. 238; Lord Lonsdale to Disraeli, 2 March 1867, Disraeli Papers, D.XI.J.75.

IV *The Transformation of the Suffrage Bill*

76 Baxter to Corry, 16 March 1867, Disraeli Papers, B.XI.J.93.

77 Disraeli to Corry, 7 March 1867, Disraeli Papers, B.XI.J.8.

78 Disraeli to [Baxter?] draft n.d., Disraeli Papers, B.XI.J.186.

79 See pp. 194-5.

80 Derby to Disraeli, 'Sunday', [10 March 1867?], Disraeli Papers, '14 Derby'.

81 Reform Bill draft, 16 March 1867, Disraeli Papers, B.XI.H.24; see also Disraeli to General Grey, 15 March 1867, *L.Q.V.*, p. 408.

82 M. and B., *Disraeli*, vol. 2, p. 234.

83 Pakington to Disraeli, 4 December 1866, Disraeli Papers, 'Pakington'.

84 *Morning Star*, 14, 18 March 1867, cf. Pakington to Disraeli, 15 March 1867. 'I am truly sorry for the view you take of what I said at Droitwich I cannot see it in the same light. It seems to me that the best excuse for the mistake to [which?] the Govt. had pleaded guilty by retracing their steps, was the hurried decision to which we were driven by the retirement of our colleagues at the last moment.' Disraeli Papers, 'Pakington'.

85 George Graham to Corry, 16 March 1867, Disraeli Papers, B.XI.J.95; B.XI.G.46a.

86 G. H[ardy], 'Memorandum on Assessed Taxes and The Franchise', 18 March 1867, Disraeli Papers, B.XI.J.97; cf. 'Armorial Bearings and the Assessed Taxes', *New Monthly Magazine*, vol. 135, 1865.

87 G. W. H[unt] to Disraeli, 'Memo. on Income Tax Franchise', 31 March [1867], Disraeli Papers, B.XI.J.213; see also Cranborne to Derby, 22 February 1867, M. and B., *Disraeli*, vol. 2, p. 232.

88 Baxter to Disraeli, 14 March 1867, Disraeli Papers, B.XI.J.89; Baxter to Corry, 16 March 1867, Disraeli Papers, B.XI.J.93.

89 M. and B., *Disraeli*, vol. 2, p. 252n.

90 W. Clive to Taylor, 6 March 1867, Disraeli Papers, B.XI.J.82.

91 W. T. Cox to Colonel Taylor, 5 March 1867, Disraeli Papers, B.XI.J. 81: Viscount Galway to Disraeli, 6 March 1867, Disraeli Papers, B.XI.J.83.

92 Russell to Brand, 18 July 1866, Hampden Papers.

93 Denison to Brand, 12 October 1866, Hampden Papers.

94 Sir George Grey to Brand, 19 October 1866, Hampden Papers.

95 Lord Granville to Viscount Halifax, 31 January 1867, Maxwell, *Clarendon*, vol. 2, p. 330.

96 Sir David Dundas to Viscount Halifax, 2 February 1867, ibid.

97 W. E. Baxter to Gladstone, 12 February 1867, Gladstone Papers, B.M. Add. MSS. 44412.

98 Stanley to Disraeli, 14 February [1867] 'information authentic and certain', Disraeli Papers, '15 Derby'.

99 Lambert to Gladstone, 17 February 1867, Gladstone Papers, B.M. Add. MSS. 44235.

1 *Hansard* CLXXXV, 979.

2 *Hansard* CLXXXV, 992, Warner; 1025 ff., Bright.

3 *Hansard* CLXXXV, 982 ff.

4 C. P. Villiers to J. T. Delane, 26 February 1867, in A. I. Dasent, *John Thadeus Delane, Editor of 'The Times'*, 2 vols, (London, 1908), vol. 2, pp. 189-90.

5 Diary, 26 February [1867], R. A. J. Walling (ed.), *The Diaries of John Bright* (New York, 1931), p. 295.

6 Bernal Osborne to Delane, 26 February 1867, Dasent, *Delane*, vol. 2, p. 191.

7 *Morning Star*, 27 February 1867.

8 Gladstone to Argyll, 9 March 1867, Gladstone Papers, B.M. Add. MSS. 44100.

9 Glyn to Brand, 16 March 1867; Brand to Gladstone, 16 March 1867, Gladstone Papers, B.M. Add. MSS. 44194.

10 Sir William Heathcote to Cranborne, 16 March 1867; also Horsman to Cranborne, 10 March 1867, Salisbury Papers.

11 Bright, Diary, 19 March 1867, Walling, *Diaries*, p. 299.

12 *Hansard* CLXXXVI, 11 ff.

13 *Hansard* CLXXXVI, 6-7.

14 *Hansard* CLXXXVI, 7-10.

15 *Hansard* CLXXXVI, 28.

16 *Hansard* CLXXXVI, 26-46, 475.

17 *Hansard* CLXXXVI, 67-8.

18 *Graham v. Tate, Maule and Selwyn Reports,* vol. 1, pp. 609-11; cf. Cox, *The Reform Bills of 1866 and 1867,* p. 182.

19 *Hansard* CLXXXVI, 491-8, Gladstone.

20 *Hansard* CLXXXVI, 512, Hardy; 586, Palmer.

21 *Hansard* CLXXXVI, 642-64.

22 Saunderson to his wife, 27 March [1867], Reginald Lucas, *Colonel Saunderson, M.P.* (London, 1908), p. 36.

23 Edward B. Russell, 'Sessio Mirabilis', *Belgravia,* vol. 3, September 1867, p. 366.

24 Bright, Diary, 21 March 1867, Walling, *Diaries,* p. 299. F. H. Berkeley told Acland that *abstractedly* [sic] the right thing would be to oppose the 2d reading but that the feeling of the party was so strong the other way that there was no choice open'. T. D. Acland to Gladstone, 22 March [1867], Gladstone Papers, B.M. Add. MSS. 44092.

25 *Hansard* CLXXXVI, 1292.

26 *Morning Star,* 6 April 1867.

27 Ibid.

28 Memo., n.d., Gladstone Papers, B.M. Add. MSS. 44755.

29 *Morning Star,* 6 April 1867; Clay to Disraeli, 24 March 1867, Disraeli Papers, 'Clay'; E. H. Coleridge, *Life and Correspondence of John Duke, Lord Coleridge, Chief Justice of England,* 2 vols, (London, 1904), vol. 2, p. 66.

30 T. D. Acland to Gladstone, 5 April 1867, Gladstone Papers, B.M. Add. MSS. 44092.

31 Clay to Disraeli, 'Very Confidential', 6 April [1867], Disraeli Papers, 'Clay'.

32 Taylor to Disraeli, 'Sunday 7 oc.' [7 April 1867], Disraeli Papers, 'Taylor'.

33 Denison to Disraeli, 7 April 1867, Disraeli Papers, 'Denison'.

34 The *Day,* 10, 18, 26 April 1867; Mackie, *McLaren,* vol. 2, p. 163.

35 Those who attended Monday's meeting included: Owen Stanley, Beaumaris, who presided; Col. Akroyd, Halifax; J. Candlish, Sunderland; J. Clay, Kingston-upon-Hull; F. Crossley, Yorkshire, North-West Riding; J. D. Dent, Scarborough; L. L. Dillwyn, Swansea; H. Fawcett, Brighton; Sir J. Hanmer, Flint; T. E. Headlam, Newcastle-on-Tyne; G. Hodgkinson, Newark; W. Jackson, Derbyshire North; H. Lewis, Marylebone; J. Locke, Southwark; W. Morrison, Plymouth; C. M. Norwood, Kingston-upon-Hull; J. Pim, Dublin; E. Potter, Rochdale; J. B. Smith, Stockport; J. Steel, Clitheroe; W. T. Torrens, Finsbury; D. J. Reardon, Athlone; Sir E. T. Colebrooke, Lanark Co.; H. E. Crum-Ewing, Paisley; R. Dalglish, Glasgow; M. Grant Duff, Elgin Burghs; A. Kinnaird, Perth; D. McLaren, Edinburgh; L. Oliphant, Stirling Burghs; Col. Sykes, Aberdeen; R. M. Biddulph, Denbighshire; G. Clive, Hereford; J. Goldsmid, Honiton; H. G. Gridley, Weymouth; Serj. Kinglake, Rochester; Sir H. Rawlinson, Frome; A. Russell, Tavistock; H. Russell, Bedfordshire; J. A. Samuda, Tavistock; B. Samuelson, Banbury;

C. Seely, Lincoln; A. Seymour, Totnes; H. D. Seymour, Poole; James Wyld, Bodmin; Col. French, Roscommon Co.; J. L. O'Beirne, Cashel. There were thought to be present about four other Irish members whose names I have been unable to trace: The *Day*, 10 April 1867. Goldsmid and Kinnaird subsequently denied taking part in the proceedings and declared that they had attended out of curiosity and ignorance of the purpose of the meeting: *Morning Star*, 10 April 1867.

36 *Hansard* CLXXXVI, 1629, 12 April 1867.

37 Pope Hennessy to Disraeli, 8 March 1867, Disraeli Papers, 'Pope Hennessy'.

38 D. J. Reardon to Gladstone, 8 June 1868, Gladstone Papers, B.M. Add. MSS. 44415; see also *Daily Telegraph*, 15 April 1867: a letter from 'An Old Liberal' claims that Corbally and McEvoy voted for the Bill as part of a bargain that the Goverment would carry their Irish Ecclesiastical Titles Bill. Bowyer may well have been interested in this, too.

39 *Hansard* CLXXXVIII, 1571; cf. Oliphant's views as quoted by P. Henderson, *The Life of Laurence Oliphant* (London, 1956), p. 134, and White's speech at the Brighton Reform Meeting, *Morning Star*, 10 April 1867.

40 *Hansard* CLXXXVI, 1268-70; Coleridge, *Life of J. D. Coleridge*, vol. 2, pp. 68-9; Gathorne-Hardy, Diary, 9 April [1867], *Cranbrook*, vol. 1, p. 205.

41 E.g. White at Brighton Reform Meeting, *Morning Star*, 10 April 1867.

42 Elcho to Corry, 1 April 1867, Disraeli Papers, B.XI.J.107.

43 Gathorne-Hardy, Diary, 11, 12 April [1867], *Cranbrook*, vol. 1, pp. 205-6.

44 Cf. Malmesbury, *Memoirs*, 13 April [1867], vol. 2, p. 369.

45 Corry to Disraeli, 10 April [1867], Disraeli Papers, B.XI.J.15; Taylor to Disraeli 10.45 [a.m.? 11 April 1867], Disraeli Papers, 'Taylor'.

46 *Hansard* CLXXXVI, 1487-98.

47 *Hansard* CLXXXVI, 1503-6.

48 *Hansard* CLXXXVI, 1508, Darby Griffith.

49 *Hansard* CLXXXVI, 1541; cf. Sir Henry Edwards at the Demonstration of the Wakefield Conservative Working Men's Association: 'They indeed were determined to pass that Bill, upon which they held their station as ministers (hear hear). They were pledged to reform, not to revolution, and this the country might rely upon as a truly Conservative measure. Let them see what that Bill was. It was the most liberal that had ever been placed on the table of the House of Commons. (cheers) . . . They had beaten Mr. Gladstone and his satellites, and carried . . . the main principle of the Bill. . . . But they must not hallo until they were out of the wood; they had a seditious press and an unscrupulous party to contend with . . .' *Halifax Standard*, 22 April 1867, Disraeli Papers, 'Edwards'.

50 Malmesbury, *Memoirs*, vol. 2, p. 369; Edward Taylor to Disraeli, 'Sunday night' [7 April? 1867], Disraeli Papers, 'Taylor'.

51 *The Times*, 9 April 1867.

52 *Hansard* CLXXXVI, 1942-3, Horsman, 3 May 1867.

53 Gathorne-Hardy, Diary, 13 April [1867], *Cranbrook*, vol. 1, p. 206; *Hansard* CLXXXVI, 1587-98; 1706-9.

54 M. and B., *Disraeli*, vol. 2, p. 265.

55 *Hansard* CLXXXVI, 504-18; 1646-61.

56 *Hansard* CLXXXVI, 1684-8.

57 T. D. Acland to his wife, 10 April 1867, in A. H. D. Acland, *Memoirs and Letters of the Right Honourable Sir Thomas Dyke Acland* (P.P., 1902), pp. 263-4.

58 Kebbel, *Lord Beaconsfield and Other Tory Memoirs,* p. 40.

59 M. and B., quoting Kebbel, *Disraeli,* vol. 2, p. 267.

60 Morley, *Gladstone,* vol. 2, p. 233.

61 Brand, memorandum, n.d., Gladstone Papers, B.M. Add. MSS. 44755; cf. *Hansard* CLXXXVI, 1699-1703.

62 P. A. Taylor, Letter to his constituents, *Morning Star,* 20 April 1867.

63 Gladstone to Russell, 19 April 1867, Gladstone Papers, B.M. Add. MSS. 44293.

64 Octavius Duncombe to Disraeli, 13 April 1867, Disraeli Papers, B.XI.J.118. Duncombe was member for the East Riding of Yorkshire.

65 The Earl of Ilchester to Henry Whitmore, 9 April [1867], Disraeli Papers, B.XI.J.113b.

V *The Transformation Completed*

66 Argyll to Gladstone, 23 April 1867, Argyll, *Autobiography and Memoirs,* vol. 2, p. 236; *Hansard* CLXXXVI, 882.

67 Section XVIII, see p. 36.

68 Taylor to Disraeli, 26 April [1867] reporting remarks of Sir Thomas Bateson, M.P. for Devizes, Disraeli Papers, 'Taylor'.

69 W. Earle Welby to Taylor, 30 April 1867, Disraeli Papers, 'Taylor'.

70 Noel to Taylor, 16 April [1867], and Noel to Taylor, 25 April [1867], Disraeli Papers, 'Taylor'.

71 Gathorne-Hardy to Disraeli, n.d. [2 May? 1867], Disraeli Papers, 'Cranbrook'.

72 *Hansard* CLXXXVI, 1879-82.

73 *Hansard* CLXXXVI, 1883.

74 They were: A. A. Bathurst; Sir W. P. Gallwey; G. Greenall; H. G. Liddell; F. S. Powell; G. S. Stucley; C. W. W. Wynn; *Hansard* CLXXXVI, 1908-11; see also *Hansard* CLXXXVII, 310, E. Greene.

75 *Hansard* CLXXXVI, 1939.

76 Smith, *Bright,* vol. 2, p. 248; Sir John Mowbray, *Seventy Years at Westminster* (Edinburgh, 1900), Diary, 12 February 1867, p. 232. Bright was in the Reform Club playing billiards, but refused to leave his game to come to the window. Kate's Journal, 11 February 1867, *Amberley Papers,* vol. 2, p. 17.

77 The *Day,* 19 March 1867. Report on Reform meeting in Trafalgar Square; see also Charles Bradlaugh, *Reform or Revolution.*

78 *Morning Star,* 16 April 1867.

79 The *Day,* 3 April 1867; see also *Full Reports of the Reform League Deputations to . . . W. E. Gladstone . . . and B. Disraeli April 6, 1867.*

80 The *Day,* 24 April 1867.

81 Reform League Minutes, 18 April 1866, Howell Collection, Bishopsgate Institute.

82 S. Walpole, 'Confidential Cabinet Memorandum', 1 May 1867, Disraeli Papers, B.XI.H.23b; cf. *The Times,* 1-7 May 1867; also Royden Harrison, 'The 10th April of Spencer Walpole: The Problem of Revolution in Relation

to Reform, 1865-1867', *International Review of Social History*, vol. 7, part 3, 1962.

[83] *Hansard* CLXXXVII, 225.

[84] The *Day*, 2 May 1867.

[85] *Hansard* CLXXXVI, 1978-9, Elcho; 1981, Selwyn.

[86] *Hansard* CLXXXVI, 1984.

[87] William Bateman to Disraeli, 'Sunday night, Carlton Club', [5 May 1867], Disraeli Papers, B.XI.J.129.

[88] *Hansard* CLXXXVI, 2024-6.

[89] The third and fourth sections of the clause were then to read: '3. Has, during the time of such occupation, been rated as an ordinary occupier in respect of the premises so occupied by him within the borough to all rates (if any) made for the relief of the poor in respect of such premises, and 4. Has, before the 20th day of July in the same year, paid an equal amount in the pound to that payable by other ordinary occupiers in respect of the said premises, up to the preceding 5th day of January.' *Hansard* CLXXXVI, 1941.

[90] Sir William Heathcote to Cranborne, 6 May 1867, Salisbury Papers, 'Heathcote'.

[91] *P.P.*, 1867, vol. LVI, nos. 305, 121; also G. Shaw Lefevre, *The Personal Payment of Rates*, pp. 18-19.

[92] Robert Upperton to Spofforth, 30 April 1867, Disraeli Papers, B.XI.G. 19a,c.

[93] *Cook v. Luckett, Lutwyches Registration Cases*, 1846, pp. 432-40; also Cox, *Reform Bills of 1866 and 1867*, p. 168 ff.

[94] *Hansard* CLXXXVII, 443; cf. *Grahame v. Tate, Maule and Selwyn Reports*, vol. 1, pp. 609-11; also Cox, *Reform Bills of 1866 and 1867*, pp. 182, 186-8.

[95] *Hansard* CLXXXVII, 268-71.

[96] The 'freebooters' who voted for the Government were:
E. Akroyd; A. Bass; M. T. Bass; T. Chambers; R. Dalglish; L. L. Dillwyn; T. E. Headlam; G. Hodgkinson; E. James; A. W. Kinglake; J Lamont; J. H. Lewis; L. B. Mackinnon; W. A. Mackinnon; W. Morrison; T. Parry; J. A. Roebuck; B. Samuelson; C. Seely; A. Seymour; H. D. Seymour; A. Smith; J. B. Smith; W. H. Sykes; G. H. Whalley; J. Wyld. The Adullamites: Visct. Andover; Hon. A. Anson; Sir G. Bowyer; Lords J. T. Browne, E. Bruce, C. Bruce, A. P. Clinton; F. Doulton; R. W. Duff; Lord Dunkellin; Lord Elcho; Hon. C. W. W. Fitzwilliam; Earl Grosvenor; Lord R. Grosvenor; Hon. G. H. Heathcote; S. Laing; E. McEvoy; J. N. McKenna; J. Mackie; P. McLagan; M. H. Marsh; A. Mitchell; O. Stock.

[97] T. Hughes to Earl de Grey, 10 May 1867, Ripon Papers, B.M. Add. MSS. 43548. The Liberal betrayal sickened Bright too: He told J. B. Smith that his 'was the most entirely wrong and the most disgraceful vote . . . given by any Liberal member within [his] . . . recollection'. He came home early the following night 'and closed with Milton, who seems to take me for the time being above the troubles of this world and the meanness of common men'. Diary, 10 May 1867, Walling, *Diaries*, p. 304.

[98] *Hansard* CLXXXVII, 28-32; 454-6.

[99] Disraeli to Stanley, 22 April 1867; Stanley to Disraeli, n.d., M. and B., *Disraeli*, vol. 2, pp. 269-70.

[1] Glyn to Gladstone, 17 May 1867, Gladstone Papers, B.M. Add. MSS. 44347.

2 *Hansard* CLXXXVII, 456-67.

3 *Hansard* CLXXXVII, 461; also 463, Schreiber; 466.

4 *Hansard* CLXXXVII, 469.

5 *Hansard* CLXXXVII, 469-71.

6 John Lambert, 'Memorandum on Lodger Franchise', 19 July 1867, Disraeli Papers, B.XI.L.14.

7 *P.P.*, 1874, vol. LIII, no. 57.

8 'The Journeyman Engineer' [Thomas Wright], *The Great Unwashed* (London, 1868), pp. 73-4.

9 Bright to Gladstone, 11 May 1867, Williams, *Gladstone*, pp. 152-5.

10 *Hansard* CLXXXVII, 712.

11 *Hansard* CLXXXVII, 708-12; cf. M. T. Bass, 719-20.

12 Trevelyan, *Bright*, p. 376.

13 The deputation included Bright, and M.P.s: Ayrton, Tower Hamlets; Baines, Leeds; Barnes, Bolton; Bazley, Manchester; Candlish, Sunderland; Cheetham, Salford; Cowen, Newcastle-on-Tyne; Edwards, Windsor; Fawcett, Brighton; Gilpin, Northampton; Gray, Kilkenny; Hadfield, Sheffield; Potter, Rochdale; J. B. Smith, Stockport; Stansfeld, Halifax; Watkin, Stockport. There were also George Wilson, the veteran Free Trader, Sir John Bowring, Sir Henry Hoare and over three hundred clergymen, iron-masters, mill-owners and manufacturers: Cox, *The Reform Bills of 1866 and 1867*, p. 199.

14 R. Montagu to Taylor, n.d., (reporting conversation with Dalglish), Disraeli Papers, B.XI.J.195.

15 *Hansard* CLXXXVII, 719-20, 743-6.

16 *Hansard* CLXXXVII, 1182.

17 W. White, *The Inner Life of the House of Commons*, 2 vols, (London, 1877), vol. 2, pp. 66-7.

18 *Hansard* CLXXXVII, 720-6.

19 *Hansard* CLXXXVII, 354.

20 *Hansard* CLXXXVII, 735-53.

21 *Hansard* CLXXXVII, 739-40, Sandford; 756, Cranborne.

22 *Hansard* CLXXXVII, 804, Knightley, 20 May 1867.

23 Disraeli to Gathorne-Hardy, 18 May 1867, Hardy, *Cranbrook*, vol. 1, pp. 207-10; Gathorne-Hardy to Disraeli, 18 May 1867, Disraeli Papers, 'Cranbrook'.

24 D[israeli] to Corry, 'Sunday', [12? May 1867], Corry to Disraeli, Monday, 13 May [1867], Disraeli Papers, B.XI.J.32, 25.

25 See below pp. 226-7.

26 *Hansard* CLXXXVII, 1177-80.

27 Cf. J. S. Mill, Speech at Reform Meeting at St James' Hall, *Daily News*, 27 May 1867, Cutting, Mill-Taylor Collection, Box V.

28 Russell to Gladstone, 24 May 1867, Gladstone Papers, B.M. Add. MSS. 44293.

29 *Hansard* CLXXXVII, 1189.

30 *Hansard* CLXXXVII, 1180-88.

31 J. Lambert, 'Analysis of replies from Vestry Clerks', 25 May 1867, Disraeli Papers, B.XI.L.7; *P.P.*, 1867, vol. VIII, no. 67.

32 A. S. Mitchell to Disraeli, 20 May 1867, Disraeli Papers, B.XI.J.145.

[33] Lefevre, *The Personal Payment of Rates,* pp. 32-3.

[34] Evidence of Robert Vagg, Vestry Clerk, St Matthews, Bethnal Green, Select Committee on Poor Rate Assessment, 1867-8. *P.P.*, 1867-8, vol. XIII, q. 2645.

[35] J. T. Bunce, *History of the Corporation of Birmingham* (Birmingham, 1885), vol. 2, pp. 41-2; cf. Select Committee on Poor Rate, *P.P.*, 1867-8, vol. XII, qq. 1475-8, 1618-27.

[36] J. Lambert, 'Memorandum' [1872], Disraeli Papers, B.XI.E.21. Lambert's calculations are based on *Accounts and Papers,* 1868-9, vol. L, no. 11.

[37] 33 and 34 Vict. c. 41; cf. B. Keith-Lucas, *The English Local Government Franchise* (Oxford, 1952).

[38] 'Select Committee on Registration of Voters', qq. 1268-71.

[39] 'The Parliamentary and Municipal Registration Act', 41 and 42 Vict. c. 26.

[40] *Hansard* CLXXXVIII, 1531-2, Cranborne.

[41] *P.P.*, 1867, vol. LVI, no. 136.

[42] Cox, *The Reform Bills of 1866 and 1867*, p. 201.

[43] *P.P.*, 1868-9, vol. L, no. 11.

[44] *P.P.*, 1867-8, vol. XIII, 'Report of Select Committee on Rates', qq. 3766, 3767; 1462-3, Birmingham; 3799-800, Bristol; 3096-100, Manchester; 4948-53, Norwich.

[45] Ibid., q. 514; *P.P.*, 1868-9, vol. VII, *Report from the Select Committee on Registration of Voters,* p. IV, q. 2810, Lambert.

[46] 'Select Committee on Rates', *Report*, p. XXXII; qq. 1472-3, 3241, 4840-44, 4871-2.

[47] *Daily News*, 3 December 1867; *Hansard* CLXXXVII, 817-45.

[48] *Hansard* CLXXXVII, 833-5, Denman.

[49] *Hansard* CLXXXVIII, 1453; *National Secular Society Almanack,* 1871, p. 5.

[50] *Hansard* CLXXXVII, 845-50.

[51] *Hansard* CLXXXVII, 991-9.

[52] Thring, 'Memo on copyhold franchise', 23 May 1867, Disraeli Papers, B.XI.J.214.

[53] Cf. Cox, *The Reform Bills of 1866 and 1867*, pp. 212-13.

[54] *Hansard* CLXXXVII, 999.

[55] Colebrooke dropped 'or other building' from the amendment.

[56] Thring [?] 'Memorandum on "Lands and Tenements"', n.d., Disraeli Papers, B.XI.G.39.

[57] They were: Hon. A. H. A. Anson; W. B. Beaumont; Lords E. Bruce, C. Bruce, and Elcho; Earl Fitzwilliam; R. Fort; W. H. Gregory; E. McEvoy; J. N. McKenna; J. Mackie; P. McLagan; and the freebooters: R. Dalglish; Sir G. Grey; E. James; D. J. Reardon; J. A. Roebuck; D. Salomons; A. Smith; J. B. Smith; *Hansard* CLXXXVII, 1153-5.

[58] *Hansard* CLXXXVII, 1157, Sir Thomas Lloyd.

[59] *Hansard* CLXXXVII, 1232-43.

[60] 6 Anne c. 41; *Hansard* CLXXXVIII, 612-16; CLXXXIX, 740-7.

[61] *Hansard* CLXXXVIII, 625-45.

[62] *Hansard* CLXXXVIII, 646-7.

[63] R. Harrison, 'The British Working Class and the General Election of 1868', *International Review of Social History,* vols 5, 6, 1960-1.

64 W. B. Gwyn, *Democracy and the Cost of Politics in Britain* (London, 1962), pp. 147-77.

65 *Hansard* CLXXXVIII, 1539.

66 *Hansard* CLXXXVIII, 1561-74, Beresford Hope; 1574, Barrow; 1587, Sandford; 1595, Cecil.

67 Bright, *Diary*, 15 July [1867], Walling, *Diaries*, p. 310.

VI   *The Bill in the House of Lords and the Cumulative Voting Clause*

68 Russell to Granville, 21 April 1867, Granville Papers, P.R.O. G.D. 29/18.

69 *Hansard* CLXXXVIII, 1804.

70 Derby to Disraeli, 18 July 1867, Disraeli Papers, '14 Derby'.

71 *Hansard* CLXXXVIII, 1917.

72 *Hansard* CLXXXVIII, 1850, Beauchamp, the adjective originally was Bright's—cf. ibid, 1854; 1975, Feversham.

73 *Hansard* CLXXXIX, 840-1; 705 ff.

74 *Hansard* CLXXXIX, 740 ff.

75 *Hansard* CLXXXIX, 738-40.

76 *Hansard* CLXXXIX, 288-9, De Grey; 1322-3, Harrowby; cf. Stanhope, 1320, and the 'Protest Against the Third Reading of the Representation of the People Bill' entered by Ellenborough and Selkirk, ibid; 952-3.

77 *Hansard* CLXXXIX, 751; 1106 ff.; cf. Baxter, 'Memo', n.d., Disraeli Papers, B.XI.E.15(i).

78 These were: Berkshire, Buckinghamshire, Cambridgeshire, Dorset, Herefordshire, Hertfordshire, Oxfordshire and the boroughs of Birmingham, Glasgow, Leeds, Liverpool, Manchester.

79 *Hansard* CLXXXIX, 468 ff.

80 Mill to J. E. Cairns, 2 March 1859, Mill-Taylor Collection, vol. 4, London School of Economics; T. Hare, *The Machinery of Representation* (London, 1857); H. Fawcett, *Mr. Hare's Reform Bill Simplified and Explained* (London, 1860); Mill to Fawcett, 5 February 1860, Mill-Taylor Collection, vol. 3; Mill to Max Kyllman, 30 May 1865, H. S. R. Elliot, *The Letters of J. S. Mill*, 2 vols, (London, 1910), vol. 2, p. 39.

81 *Hansard* CLXXXVII, 1343 ff.

82 *Hansard* CLXXXVIII, 1103, Mill; 1086, Fawcett. For Horsfall's motion, see p. 217.

83 *Hansard* CLXXXVIII, 1037-124.

84 *Hansard* CLXXXIX, 1171.

85 *Hansard* CLXXXIX, 1179-83.

86 Hanham, *Elections And Party Management*, p. 398.

87 Ibid., pp. 17-32.

VII   *The Redistribution Bill and the Reform Acts for Scotland and Ireland*

88 Cf. Baxter to Disraeli, 20 October 1866, and 28 February 1867, Disraeli Papers, B.XI.J.57, 73.

89 The reports of the Royal Commissions investigating elections in Great Yarmouth, Lancaster, Reigate and Totnes appeared very opportunely for the Government, especially when their impact was reinforced by the accounts

of the Waterford election. Gross corruption was proved in all four, and although disenfranchisement for corruption was not mentioned in the preamble to the Bill, Disraeli availed himself of the opportunity to seize their seven seats. The boroughs had only three representatives left in the House in 1867, and they had not a hope of making an effective protest amidst the general indignation. Cf. C. O'Leary, *The Elimination of Corrupt Practices in British Elections 1868-1911* (Oxford, 1962), pp. 28-33.

90 Hartlepool, Darlington, Middlesbrough, Dewsbury, Barnsley, St Helens, Burnley, Birkenhead, Staleybridge, Torquay, Croydon, Gravesend, and a new division of Tower Hamlets.

91 *Hansard* CLXXXV, 946 ff.

92 *Hansard* CLXXXVII, 1388 ff.

93 *Hansard* CLXXXVII, 1401 ff.

94 Sir Henry Edwards to Disraeli, 2 May [should be June? 1867], Disraeli Papers, B.XI.J.127.

95 *Hansard* CLXXXVII, 1400; see also 1405, Samuda-Tavistock.

96 *Hansard* CLXXXVII, 1403-13, Newdegate; 1427-8, Butler-Johnstone.

97 Lord Henry Lennox to Disraeli, 2 June [1867], Disraeli Papers, 'Lennox'.

98 Lowe to Lady Salisbury, 3 July 1867, quoted in Lady Burghclere (ed.), *A Great Lady's Friendships* (London, 1933), pp. 128-9.

99 *Hansard* CLXXXVII, 1500-23.

1 *Hansard* CLXXXVII, 1776 ff.

2 Sixteen Conservatives, including most of the Cranborne 'Cave', and the two members for Liverpool, voted for Laing's amendment, while eleven Adullamites and five Liberal freebooters voted with the Government against it. The Conservatives were: Lord E. Cecil; Lord Cranborne; R. A. Earle; S. R. Graves; E. W. T. Hamilton; Sir W. Heathcote; A. J. Beresford Hope; T. B. Horsfall; Sir R. Knightley; J. Laird; Sir T. D. Lloyd; C. N. Newdegate; G. M. W. Sandford; C. Schreiber; Lord H. F. Thynne; J. R. Yorke. The Adullamites: Hon. Maj. Anson; Sir G. Bowyer; Lord J. T. Browne; Lord E. Bruce; Lord Dunkellin; F. Doulton; Lord Elcho; Lord R. Grosvenor; G. H. Heathcote. The Freebooters: A. S. Ayrton; A. Bass; J. A. Roebuck; A. Smith; J. Wyld. *Hansard* CLXXXVII, 1969-72.

3 *Hansard* CLXXXVIII, 811 ff.; cf. White, *The Inner Life of the House of Commons*, vol. 2, pp. 71-2.

4 *Hansard* CLXXXVIII, 844; White, ibid.

5 *Hansard* CLXXXVIII, 1228 ff.

6 Sir John Walsh to Disraeli, 14 May [1867], Disraeli Papers, B. XI. J.140.

7 George Charles Gordon-Lennox to Disraeli, 28 March 1867; Whitmore, 6 April 1867; Disraeli, 8 April 1867, Disraeli Papers, B.XI.J.105; B.XI.J.111b; B.XI.J.112.

8 Arabella Darby Griffith to Disraeli, 21 and 24 May [1867], Disraeli Papers, B.XI.J.146, 149.

9 *Hansard* CLXXXVIII, 271 ff.; 522-8.

10 *P.P.*, 1831-2, vol. XXXVI, 'Report on Boundaries of Boroughs of England and Wales', *P.P.*, 1868, vol. XXXII.

11 Stafford Northcote to Walpole, 3 June 1867, Iddesleigh Papers, B.M. Add. MSS. 50047.

[12] Stafford Northcote to Corry, 11 June [1867], Disraeli Papers, 'Stafford Northcote'; A. C. Veley to Charles Du Cane, 26 June 1867, Disraeli Papers, B.XI.K.126.

[13] *Report*, pp. 214-16; J. Ludlow (Conservative agent for Manchester) to Spofforth, 19 April 1866, Disraeli Papers, B.XI.F.20b, c.

[14] *Report*, p. 29; S. S. Lloyd (Conservative agent for Birmingham) to Spofforth, 12 June 1867, Disraeli Papers, B.XI.G.25.

[15] *Report*, pp. 48-50; Messrs Vizard and Co. to Spofforth, n.d., Disraeli Papers, B.XI.H.4.

[16] *Report*, pp. 222-4, 27-8, 124-6.

[17] *Report*, pp. 246-8; 'The Chairman of the Conservative Working Men's Association' to Spofforth, n.d., Disraeli Papers, B.XI.H.6.

[18] Report, p. 341; Cuthbert V. Laws to Spofforth, n.d., Disraeli Papers, B.XI.H.4.

[19] *Report*, pp. 302-3; Messrs Maxwell and Moore to Spofforth, n.d., Disraeli Papers, B.XI.H.8.

[20] Report, pp. 370-2, 264-5; Stegant (Conservative agent for South Hants) to Spofforth, n.d., Disraeli Papers, B.XI.H.6.

[21] *P.P.*, 1867-8, vol. VIII, no. 311, 'Papers laid before the Select Committee on the Boundary of Boroughs', pp. 9, 30, 127.

[22] Baxter to Corry, 16 March 1867, Disraeli Papers, B.XI.J.94.

[23] *Report*, pp. 460-2; Banks Stanhope to Disraeli, 11 May 1867, Disraeli Papers, B.XI.J.137.

[24] S. T. Kekewich to Disraeli, 8 June 1867, Disraeli Papers, B.XI.J. 158a,b; *Report*, pp. 449-51.

[25] Baxter to Corry, 18 April 1867, Disraeli Papers, B.XI.K.11.

[26] W. Gore Langton to Disraeli, 28 April 1867, Disraeli Papers, B.XI. J.122; *Report*, pp. 92-4, 224-5.

[27] Henry Selwin to [Disraeli?], December 1866, Lord Eustace Cecil to Disraeli, 2 January 1867, Charles Du Cane to Disraeli, 27 June 1867, Disraeli Papers, 'Selwin' and B.XI.J.62, B.XI.K.a,b,c; *Hansard* CLXXXVIII, 1479-80, Sandford; *Report*, pp. 452-4.

[28] R. J. Harvey to Disraeli, 9 June 1867, Disraeli Papers, B.XI.J.160.

[29] Ed. Fernie to Spofforth, 3 July 1867, Disraeli Papers, B.XI.G.27a,b.

[30] T. Collins to Disraeli, 7 June 1867, Disraeli Papers, B.XI.J.154a,b; *Report*, pp. 174-6.

[31] Hon. E. W. Lascelles to Taylor, 18 June 1867, Disraeli Papers, B.XI. G.13a; Gash, *Politics in the Age of Peel*, pp. 219-20; *Report*, pp. 240-1.

[32] R. J. Harvey to Disraeli, 9 June 1867, Disraeli Papers, B.XI.J.160; *Report*, pp. 330-1.

[33] Sandford to Disraeli, 11 April [1867], Disraeli Papers, B.XI.J.116; *Report*, pp. 212-13.

[34] R. D. Baxter to Spofforth, 1 July 1867, Disraeli Papers, B.XI.K.23b.

[35] A. Montague (Melton Park, Doncaster) to Sir Henry Edwards, 27 June [1867], Disraeli Papers, B.XI.G.14; *Report*, pp. 472-6.

[36] *Hansard* CXCII, 250 ff.; 'Report of Select Committee into Boundaries of Boroughs', *P.P.*, 1867-8, vol. VIII, no. 311.

[37] Alsop (Secretary of Conservative Association of Birkenhead) to Spofforth, n.d., [3 June? 1868]; Trotter to Spofforth, n.d., [3 June? 1868], Disraeli Papers, B.XI.H.6,7.

[38] Baker and Brown (Conservative Agents for Warwick) to [Spofforth], n.d., [3 June? 1868]; Whittaker (Conservative Agent for Oldham) to [Spofforth], n.d., [3 June? 1868]; Fred. Langham (Conservative Agent for Hastings) to [Spofforth], n.d., [3 June? 1868]; Maude (Conservative Agent for Reading) to [Spofforth], n.d., [3 June? 1868]; Chevallier (Agent for East Surrey Conservative Registration Society), n.d., [3 June? 1868], Disraeli Papers, B.XI.H.5,6,9,

[39] *Hansard* CXCII, 250 ff., 430 ff., 1044 ff., 1406 ff.; 31 and 32 Vict. c. 46.

[40] Farries, *Electoral Equality* . . . ; see also C. Seymour, *Electoral Reform in England and Wales.*

[41] R. D. Baxter, *English Parties and Conservatism* (London, 1870), p. 56.

[42] A. Frisby, 'Voters *not* Votes: The Relative Strength of Political Parties as shown by the last two General Elections', *Contemporary Review,* vol. 38, 1880. A. Frisby 'Has Conservatism increased in England since the last Reform Bill?', *Fortnightly Review,* vol. 30, 1881; *Financial Reformer,* December 1868.

[43] *Hansard* CLXXXVII, 1936, Disraeli; CLXXXVIII, 706 ff., Fortescue; 713, the O'Donoghue.

[44] 2 and 3 Will. IV c. 65, sections XI; 31 and 32 Vict. c. 48, section 18.

[45] *Hansard* CLXXXVII, 416 [13 May 1867].

[46] *Hansard* CLXXXVII, 404.

[47] *Hansard* CLXXXVII, 424 ff., 440 ff.

[48] *Hansard* CLXXXVII, 428 ff., CLXXXIX, 331-3.

[49] Ardrossan, Coatbridge, Wishaw, Barrhead, Johnston, Helensburgh, Kirkintillock, Pollokshaws, Hawick and Galashiels were to be added to Haddington, and Alloa was to be coupled with Stirling; *Hansard* CXC, 811 ff.

[50] Except in 1874, when they lost one of the seats, it made little difference to the Liberal hold on the city; *Hansard* CXCII, 461-3.

[51] *Hansard* CXCII, 1893 ff.

6 CONCLUSION

[1] *Hansard* CLXXXII, 2155-9.

[2] C. H. Pearson, 'On The Working of Australian Institutions', *Essays on Reform,* pp. 198 ff.

[3] *Hansard* CLXXXIII, 1602; cf. G. Smith, 'The Experience of the American Commonwealth', *Essays on Reform,* pp. 217 ff.

[4] L. Stephen, 'Popular Constituencies', *Essays on Reform,* pp. 91 ff.

[5] C. B. Adderley, *Europe Incapable of American Democracy* (London, 1867), p. 38.

[6] *Hansard* CLXXXIX, 933.

[7] *Liverpool Mail,* 15 June 1867.

[8] *Hansard* CLXXXVIII, 1576.

[9] *Hansard* CLXXXIII, 103.

[10] *Hansard* CLXXXVIII, 1114.

[11] Speech at Merchant Taylors' Banquet, 11 June 1867, *Morning Post,* 12 June 1867.

[12] B. Cracroft, 'The Analysis of the House of Commons', *Essays on Reform,* pp. 182-3.

13 *Hansard* CLXXXVI, 6-7.

14 *Hansard* CLXXXIII, 60-5; CLXXXVIII, 1594.

15 *Hansard* CLXXXII, 1276-7; CLXXXVIII, 1599.

16 *Hansard* CLXXXVII, 311; CLXXXIV, 578.

17 Cf. [Anthony Trollope?], 'The Leap in the Dark', *Saint Paul's*, vol. 1, October 1867; see also [Lord Cranborne], 'The Conservative Surrender', *Quarterly Review*, vol. CXXIII, October 1867.

18 'Refusal of Invitation to the First Dinner of the London & Westminster Working Men's Conservative Association', Draft, October 1867, Disraeli Papers, B.XIII.96a,b.

19 *Representative Reform. Report of the Committee appointed by . . . The Reform League, and Others, on Mr. Hare's Scheme of Representation, 28th February, 7 and 21 March 1868* (London, 1868); also C. Bradlaugh, *The Real Representation of the People* (London, n.d.), see also R. Harrison, 'The British Working Class and the General Election of 1868', *International Review of Social History*, vol. 5, part 2, 1960; vol. 6, part 1, 1961.

20 Beales, *A Word to the New Electors, especially the Working Men, From the President of the Reform League*.

21 R. Harrison, 'The British Working Class and the General Election of 1868'.

22 *P.P.*, 1866, vol. LVII, 'Electoral Returns'; *Accounts and Papers*, 1874, vol. LIII.

23 Baxter, *Results of the General Election*, p. 17.

24 *Report of Select Committee into Registration of Voters, Accounts and Papers*, 1868-9, vol. VII, no. 301, evidence of William Cremer and S. J. Mitchell, qq. 1, 2207, 2216, 2221, 2225, 2783-4; also *Report of Select Committee into Registration of Voters in Counties (England and Wales)*, *P.P.*, 1870, vol. VI, no. 360, and W. M. Torrens to Disraeli, 4 August 1868 (setting out lodgers' registration difficulties), Disraeli Papers, B.XI.M.32a.

25 *Accounts and Papers*, 1874, vol. LIII, no. 57.

26 'Gain or Loss? The Statistics of the Campaign', *Blackwood's Magazine*, vol. CV, January 1869; Baxter, *Results of the General Election, passim*.

27 There is an important study of this trend by J. Cornford, 'The Transformation of Conservatism in the Late Nineteenth Century', *Victorian Studies*, vol. 7, no. 1, September 1963.

28 Charles Dickens to G. W. Rusden, 24 August 1868, Rusden Collection, Trinity College, Melbourne.

29 *P.P.*, 1866, vol. LVII, 'Electoral Returns'; 1877, vol. LXVIII, no. 432. *Dod's Parliamentary Companion*, 'New Parliament', 1868, 1874.

30 John Lambert, Memorandum, 26 March 1872, Disraeli Papers, B.XI. E.21; *Report of Select Committee into Registration of Voters*, *P.P.*, 1868-9, vol. VII, no. 301.

31 T. R. Tholfsen, 'The Origins of the Birmingham Caucus', *Historical Journal*, vol. 2, 1959; see also B. D. White, *A History of the Corporation of Liverpool, 1835-1914* (Liverpool, 1951), ch. 8 and W. V. Harcourt, Memorandum to Liberal agents in Oxford 'Private and Confidential', 10 August 1868. 'If the whole number of Electors were divided, so that an equal number might be apportioned amongst each of the 72 Members of the General Committee of the Liberal Association, and each of the 72 . . . made it their business to ascertain personally the views of such portion of the Electors, the work would be satisfactorily accomplished . . .

A small book containing a list of 75 Electors (taken consecutively from the street lists) should be supplied to each of the 72. . . . The books should be numbered and arranged with blank spaces opposite to the names, and ample space for remarks upon each name . . . ascertain:

(1) Whether he is a member of the Liberal Association, or if not, whether he will become so.

(2) Whether he has promised or will promise to support the Liberal candidates.

(3) If not, whether he has supported the Tory Candidate.

(4) If not, what is likely to be his course of conduct.

(5) In case of hostile persons, whether they can be objected to.

(6) In case of persons not on the Register, whether they are entitled to claim.

(7) Whether the voter has resided in Oxford for a twelve month ending June 1868.

. . . When this information is procured, the Agents of the Liberal Association will be able absolutely to make up the claims and objections on the Register, and to estimate accurately the real value of the canvass.' Cardwell Papers, P.R.O. G.D. 48/8/51.

[32] *P.P.*, 1865, vol. XLVII, no. 195; *P.P.*, 1866, vol. VII, 'Electoral Returns'; *P.P.*, 1877, vol. LXVIII, no. 432; Baxter, *Results of the General Election*.

[33] N. Gash, *Politics in the Age of Peel*, pp. 89-90; *Accounts and Papers*, 1874, vol. LIII, no. 57.

[34] A. Frisby, 'Has Conservatism increased in England since the last Reform Bill?', *Fortnightly Review*, pp. 718 ff.

[35] *Hansard* CLXXXVII, 1955-60.

[36] *Representative Reform*.

[37] [George Eliot], 'Address to the Working Men, by Felix Holt', *Blackwood's Magazine*, vol. CIII, January 1868; see also J. Roach, 'Liberalism and the Victorian Intelligentsia', *Cambridge Historical Journal*, vol. 13, 1957.

[38] Walter Bagehot, *Physics and Politics* (London, 1872), first part published in *Fortnightly Review*, vol. 8, November 1867.

[39] C. Patmore '1867'. Privately printed and circulated, 1868.

[40] T. Carlyle, 'Shooting Niagara: And After?', *Macmillan's Magazine*, August 1867; reprinted in *Critical and Miscellaneous Essays*, vol. 7, pp. 202-3.

[41] E.g. Speech at Merchant Taylors' Hall, reported in *Morning Post*, 12 June 1867, and Speech at Edinburgh on 'The Reform Bill', 29 October 1867, in Kebbel, *Selected Speeches*, vol. 2, pp. 479 ff.

BIBLIOGRAPHY

I MANUSCRIPTS

Bright Papers, British Museum
Cardwell Papers, Public Record Office
Carnarvon Papers, Public Record Office
Clarendon Papers, Bodleian Library
Disraeli Papers, Hughenden Manor, Buckinghamshire
Gladstone Papers, British Museum
Granville Papers, Public Record Office
Halifax Papers, British Museum
Hampden Papers, in the care of the Clerk of the House of
    Commons
Howell Collection, including the papers of the Reform League,
    Bishopsgate Institute
Iddesleigh Papers, British Museum
Layard Papers, British Museum
Mill-Taylor Collection, British Library of Political and Economic
    Science
Pakington Papers, in the possession of Cmdr the Lord Hampton;
    the Old Rectory, Holt, Worcestershire
Ripon Papers, British Museum
Russell Papers, Public Record Office
Salisbury Papers, Library of Christ Church, Oxford

II OFFICIAL PAPERS

Hansard's Parliamentary Debates, Third Series.
*Report of Select Committee on probable Increase of Electors in
    Counties and Boroughs from Reduction of Franchise, and what
    Change is likely to be made in Constituencies by such increase,*
    ... P.P., 1860, vol. XIII, p. 1.
*Return of Parliamentary Boroughs, population in 1831 and esti-
    mated population in 1866; number of Electors; working classes*

on Parliamentary register; Parliamentary and Municipal Electors; Boroughs in which Small Tenements and Local Rating Acts are in force . . . and, of the several Counties, population; male occupiers and electors; gross estimated rental and rateable value; Members returned, P.P., 1866, vol. LVII, p. 215.

Return of Number of Male Occupiers in each Parliamentary Borough or within seven miles, assessed at various gross estimated rentals, from under £4 to at £10 and over; . . . Electors on register in 1865-66; with estimate of number of electors, if franchises were extended in male occupiers assessed at gross estimated rentals of £9, £8, £7, and £6, P.P., 1866, vol. LVII, p. 555.

Return of Parliamentary Cities and Boroughs with Electors on registers; persons of working classes on register; proportion of latter to whole number of Electors . . ., P.P., 1866, vol. LVII, p. 747.

Reprint of Bills to Amend Laws as to Representation of the People in Parliament in years 1852, 1854, 1859, 1860, P.P., 1866, vol. LVII, p. 639.

Return of Occupants of Dwelling-houses under £10 rental in each Parish within any Parliamentary Burgh assessed to Poor Rates in 1865-66 . . . Parishes in which no assessment is levied on relief of the Poor in terms of Act 8 & 9 Vict. c. 83 . . . number, who, before 20th July 1866, paid such Poor Rates, etc.; Electors now on roll of each Burgh, etc.; P.P., 1867, vol. LVI, p. 557.

Boundary Commissioners: *Report for England and Wales, 1868*, P.P., 1867-8, vol. XXXII, p. 1.

Report of Select Committee on Laws affecting Registration of persons entitled to Vote in Election of Members for Boroughs, P.P., 1868-9, vol. VII, p. 301.

Report of Select Committee on Parliamentary and Municipal Elections, P.P., 1870, vol. VI, p. 1.

Return of number of Dwelling-houses on account of which landlord or owner pays Poor Rates by agreement with overseers or other authority in Cities and Boroughs returning Members to Parliament, Accounts and Papers, 1867-8, vol. LVI, p. 479.

Return of Number of Electors on register in each of the Parliamentary Cities and Boroughs; distinguishing those entitled to Vote as householders under 'The Representations of the People Act, 1867' from those entitled to Vote as £10 occupiers;

number who Voted at last General Election, Accounts and Papers, 1868-9, vol. L, p. 109.

Return for each Parliamentary City, Town and Borough in England, Wales, Scotland, and Ireland, Population in 1866; number of Electors on register in 1866, 1869, 1873; number entitled to vote as Occupiers, Lodgers, etc. . . ., Accounts and Papers, 1874, vol. LIII, p. 43.

Return of Population in 1871; number of Electors in 1868 and 1877; number of Members; amount of Property and Income Tax charged in each County and Parliamentary Division of a County in United Kingdom: Similar return for Cities and Boroughs, Accounts and Papers, 1877, vol. LXVIII, p. 309.

III CONTEMPORARY BOOKS, PAMPHLETS AND ARTICLES

Adams, W. P., *An Argument for Complete Suffrage.* London, 1860.

Anstey, T. C., *Plea of the Unrepresented Commons for Restitution of Franchise.* London, 1866.

——, *On Some Supposed Constitutional Restraints on the Parliamentary Franchise.* London, 1867.

Atkinson, W., *The Franchise and Vote by Ballot.* London, 1858.

Aytoun, J., *Parliamentary Reform, and The Way To Obtain It.* London, 1865.

Babbage, C., *Thoughts upon an Extension of the Franchise.* London, 1865.

Bagehot, W., *The English Constitution.* 2nd ed., [1872] London, 1891.

——, *Essays on Parliamentary Reform.* London, 1883.

Baxter, R. D., *The New Reform Bill.* 2nd ed., London, April 1866.

——, *The Redistribution of Seats and the Counties.* London, 1866.

——, *National Income.* London, 1868.

——, *The Results of the General Election.* London, 1869.

——, *The Taxation of the United Kingdom.* London, 1869.

Beales, E., *Speech . . . at the Meeting At St. Martin's Hall, in Support of The League. May 13, 1865.* London, 1865.

——, *A Word to the New Electors, especially the Working Men, from the President of the Reform League.* London, n.d. [1868?].

Beesly, E. S., *Letters to the Working Classes.* London, 1870.

Best, W. M., *The Elective Franchise in Ancient Times: or Universal Suffrage, Manhood Suffrage, or Residential Manhood Suffrage Never the Law of England.* London, 1867.

Blackie, J. S., *Democracy. A debate between Professor Blackie . . . and . . . Ernest Jones.* 2nd ed., London, 1885.

Bodichon, Mrs B., *Objections to the Enfranchisement of Women Considered.* London, 1866.

——, *Reasons for the Enfranchisement of Women.* London, 1866.

Bodington, G., *On Household Suffrage. Triennial Parliaments, and Reform of the House of Commons.* London, 1867.

Bond, J., *A Few Observations on the Justice of an Extension of the Suffrage.* Liverpool, 1867.

Bradlaugh, C., *Reform or Revolution.* London, 1867.

——, *The Real Representation of the People.* London, n.d.

[Brewster, D.], *The Radical Party.* London, 1867.

Bright, J., *Speeches on Parliamentary Reform, Etc.* Manchester, n.d.

[Bright, J.], *Mr. Bright's Reform Bill.* London, 1859.

Carlyle, T., 'Shooting Niagara: and after?' *Macmillan's Magazine*, vol. xvi, August 1867; reprinted with corrections and additions, London, 1867.

Cole, H. W., *The Middle Classes and the Borough Franchise.* London, 1866; 2nd ed., 1867.

Cox, E. W., *Representative Reform.* 3rd ed., London, 1867.

Cox, H., *A History of The Reform Bills of 1866 and 1867.* London, 1868.

——, *Whig and Tory Administrations during the Last Thirteen Years.* London, 1868.

Cracroft, B., *Essays, Political and Miscellaneous.* 2 vols. London, 1868.

[Cranborne, Lord], 'The Conservative Surrender', *Quarterly Review*, vol. cxxiii, October 1867.

[Eliot, George], 'Address to the Working Men, by Felix Holt', *Blackwood's Magazine*, vol. ciii, January 1868.

Farrand, B., *Parliamentary Reform. Comprehensive Reform of the Commons House of Parliament, The True Policy of Conservatism and The Hope of the Nation.* London, 1867.

Farries, R. S. E., *Electoral Equality. . . .* London, 1872.

'Fortunae Faber', *The Franchise: Freemen: Free Trade.* London, 1867.

Full Reports of the Reform League Deputations to . . . W. E. Gladstone . . . and . . . B. Disraeli, April 6 1867. London, 1867.

'The Future of Reform', *Westminster Review*, vol. 32, July 1867.

'Gain or Loss? The Statistics of the Campaign', *Blackwood's Magazine*, vol. cv, January 1869 .

Gibbs, E. J., *Parliamentary Reform, considered as a question of Principle and not of Party, dedicated by permission to the Right Hon. Earl Grey.* 1st ed., London and Wolverhampton, March 1866; 2nd ed., 15 February 1867; 3rd ed., 5 March 1867.

Gladstone, W. E., *Speech of the Chancellor of the Exchequer on the Bill For The Extension of the Suffrage in Towns.* London, 1864.

——, *Speeches on Parliamentary Reform in 1866.* London, 1866.

The Government and the People! The Great Reform League Demonstration in Hyde Park. n.d. [1866?].

Grey, Earl, *Parliamentary Government considered with reference to A Reform of Parliament.* London, 1858.

Hare, T., *The Machinery of Representation.* London, 1857.

Harrison, F., 'Our Venetian Constitution', *Fortnightly Review*, vol. 5, March 1867.

——, 'The Transit of Power', *Fortnightly Review*, vol. 3, April 1868.

[Harrison, ed.?], *Questions for a Reformed Parliament.* London, 1867.

——, *Essays on Reform.* London, 1867.

Hill, F., *Parliamentary Reform.* London, 1865.

The Hyde Park Cases, 1866. London, 1866.

'J. Brain—Workman', *A Few Words on Reform addressed to John Handy—Workman.* London, 1867.

'A Journeyman Engineer' [Thomas Wright], *Some Habits and Customs of the Working Classes.* London, 1867.

'J.S.', *The Reformer's Year-Book and Political Annual 1867.* London, 1867.

Kinnear, J. B., *Principles of Reform: Political and Legal.* London, 1865.

——, 'Representation of Minorities', *Fortnightly Review*, vol. 4, February 1866.

Lang, A., *Life, Letters, and Diaries of Sir Stafford Northcote, First Earl of Iddesleigh.* Edinburgh, 1891.

Leech, H. J. (ed.), *The Public Letters of the Right Hon. John Bright.* 2nd ed., London, 1895.

Lefevre, G. S., *The Personal Payment of Rates and The Reform Act of 1867.* London, 1868.

Levi, L., 'The Representation of the People', *Social Science Review*, vol. 4, October 1865.

——, *Wages and Earnings of the Working Classes*. London, 1867.

'Lord Macaulay's New Zealander', *The History of the English Revolution of 1867*. London, 'A.D. 3867'.

Lorimer, J., *Constitutionalism of the Future, or Parliament the Mirror of the Nation*. Edinburgh, 1865.

Lowe, R., *Speeches and Letters on Reform; with a Preface*. London, 1867.

Ludlow, J. M. and L. Jones, *Progress of the Working Classes 1832-1867*. London, 1867.

Macfie, R. B., *Speech Delivered at a Meeting of the Liverpool Reform League*. Liverpool, December 1866.

Marshall, J. G., *Parliamentary Reform, Address to the Working Men of Leeds*. London, 1861.

——, *The New Franchise: How to Use It*. London, 1867.

Maurice, F. D., *The Workman and the Franchise*. . . . London, 1866.

Milburn, A., *Reform Explained and Simplified*. . . . London, n.d. [1867].

Mill, J. S., *Thoughts on Parliamentary Reform*. London, 1859.

——, *Representative Government*. 1st ed., London, 1861; Everyman ed., London, 1948.

'One of Themselves', *The Borough Franchise, A Word to the Middle Class*. London, 1859.

Pearse, C., *An Essay on Legislative Representation*. London, 1865.

'The Progress of the Question', *Blackwood's Magazine*, vol. CIII, July 1867.

'Proportion of Electors to Population of various constituencies', *Journal of the Statistical Society of London*, vol. 28, 1865.

Reform Illusions, 1867.

Reform, Johnny Bull's Vision. London, 1866.

'Reform,' *Look before you leap*. London, 1859.

Reform Meetings, The Real Facts. London, 1866.

Rich, H., *Parliamentary Reform, What and Where*. London, 1858.

Rogers, J. E. Thorold (ed.), *Speeches on Questions of Public Policy, by the Right Hon. John Bright*. 2 vols. London, 1869.

Russell, John, Earl, *An Essay on the History of the English Government and Constitution*. 2nd ed., London, 1865; new ed., 1873.

Scrope, G. P., *No Vote No Rate or Household Suffrage made at once Safe and Popular*. London, 1867.

Seager, C., *The Suffrage As A Moral Right*. London, 22 March 1867.

———, *The Cumulative Vote*. 2nd ed., London, 11 June 1867.

Seymour, H. D., 'Public Affairs', *Fortnightly Review*, vol. 1, new series, January 1867.

Smith, A., *Constitutional Reflections on the Present Aspects of Parliamentary Government*. London, 1866.

Smith, J. R., *Personal Representation*. London, 1866.

[Trollope, Anthony?], 'The Leap in the Dark', *Saint Paul's*, vol. 1, October 1867.

Weston, J. *et al.*, *Reform Songs . . . Sung . . . at the Agriculture Hall by the Reform Minstrels*. n.d.

White, W., *The Inner Life of the House of Commons*, 2 vols. London, 1897.

White, W. H., *An Argument for an Extension of the Franchise*. London, 1866.

Wilson, E., 'Principles of Reform', *Fortnightly Review*, vol. 4, February 1866.

A Workingman's Dream of Reform. London, 1859.

IV   SECONDARY AUTHORITIES

Briggs, A., *Victorian People*. London, 1954.

Burns, J. H., 'J. S. Mill and Democracy', *Political Studies*, vol. 5, 1957.

Cannan, E., *The History of Local Rates in England*. 2nd ed., London, 1912.

Cowling, M., 'Derby, Disraeli and Fusion, October 1865 to July 1866', *Historical Journal*, vol. 8, no. 1, 1965.

Gillespie, F. E., *Labor and Politics in England 1850-1867*. Durham N.C., 1927.

Hanham, H. J., *Elections and Party Management*. London, 1959.

Harrison, R., 'The British Working Class and the General Election of 1868', *International Review of Social History*, vol. 5, 1960; vol. 6, 1961.

———, 'The 10th April of Spencer Walpole: The Problem of Revolution in Relation to Reform, 1865-1867', *International Review of Social History*, vol. 7, 1963.

Herrick, F. H., 'The Reform Bill of 1867 and the British Party System', *Pacific Historical Review*, vol. 3, 1934.

——, 'The Second Reform Movement in Britain 1850-65', *Journal of the History of Ideas*, vol. 9, 1948.

Hobsbawn, E. J., 'The Labour Aristocracy in Nineteenth Century Britain', in John Saville (ed.), *Democracy and the Labour Movement*. London, 1954.

Jones, W. D., *Lord Derby and Victorian Conservatism*. Oxford, 1956.

Park, J. H., *The English Reform Bill of 1867*. New York, 1920.

Seymour, C., *Electoral Reform in England and Wales*. New Haven, 1915.

Smith, F. B., ' "Democracy" in the Second Reform Debates', *Historical Studies, Australia and New Zealand*, no. 43, October 1964.

Tholfsen, T. R., 'The Origins of the Birmingham Caucus', *Historical Journal*, vol. 2, 1959.

——, 'The Transition to Democracy in Victorian England', *International Review of Social History*, vol. 6, 1961.

Thompson, A. F., 'Gladstone's Whips and the General Election of 1868', *English Historical Review*, vol. LXIII, 1948.

Williams, W. E., *The Rise of Gladstone to the Leadership of the Liberal Party 1859 to 1868*. Cambridge, 1934.

INDEX

Aberdeenshire, 226
Acland, T. D., 69, 117, 181
Adderley, C. B., 61, 105, 125, 217, 231
Adullamites: origins, 44, 49, 81-2; aims, 57, 63; tactics (in 1866) 89-90, 97, 100-1, 103-6 *passim*, 109-11, 121-2, 123-4, (in 1867) 160, 164-5 *passim*, 181-2, 192, 194, 206, 213-14, 230, 234
Agitations for Reform, *see* Reform
Akroyd, E., 182
Andover, Viscount, 182
Anson, A. H. A., 182
Applegarth, Robert, 187
Argyll, eighth Duke of, 56, 61, 64, 66, 93, 119
Arnold, Matthew, 126, 132, 241
Arundel, 16
Ashburton, 16
Australian colonies, 8, 76, 77-8, 81, 230-1
Aylesbury, 42, 171
Ayrshire, 226
Ayrton, A. S., 118, 201; his amendment of 1867, 184, 185-6

Bagehot, Walter, 2-3, 79, 241
Bailey, Sir J. R., 50
Baines, Edward, 20, 22, 30, 47, 49, 51, 56, 57, 141, 188, 217
Ballot, 32, 239
Baring, A. H., 183
Baring, Thomas, 164
Barnsley, 10, 217
Barrow, W. H., 205
Bass, M. A., 182
Bass, M. T., 29, 52, 61, 182, 197, 205
Bassetlaw, 42
Bath, fourth Marquis of, 124, 136
Baxter, R. D., 9, 67, 106, 134, 144, 146, 151-6 *passim*, 160, 161, 163, 164, 171, 204, 211, 214, 219-23 *passim*

Baxter, W. E., 57, 185, 231
Beales, Edmond, 13, 23, 26, 128-32 *passim*, 142, 143, 175, 187, 188
Beaumont, H. F., 222-3
Beaumont, W. B., 44, 98-100 *passim*, 119, 125
Beecroft, G. S., 144, 159
Beesly, E. S., 9
Bentinck, George, 124, 159, 161
Berkeley, F. H., 30, 32, 47
Beverley, 21
Bewdley, 95
Birkenhead, 220, 224
Birmingham, 16, 65, 94, 96, 172, 192, 195, 201, 202, 203, 220, 224
Booth, G. Sclater-, 97
Bouverie, E. P., 65, 99, 101
Bowyer, Sir George, 44, 83
Bradlaugh, Charles, 128, 131, 187, 188, 189
Brady, J., 183
Brand, Henry, 54-5, 58, 88, 91-5, 104, 111-14 *passim*, 117-18, 141, 142, 164, 167, 180, 182
Brett, William, 198
Bridgnorth, 95
Bridport, 95, 100
Briggs, Professor Asa, 132
Bright, John: purpose of Reform, 21-2, 25, 78, 81-2; attempted agitations in 1850s, 29, 32, 34, 38-41; relations with Russell Ministry, 60, 62, 65, 90, 115, 116; aids demonstrations in 1866-7, 128, 134, 141, 143, 190; attitude to Reform Bill of 1867, 157, 166, 177, 213, 218, 219; suggests way around compounder difficulty, 194-7
Brighton, 172, 191
Briscoe, J. I., 182

291